1001
Cupcakes, Cookies
& other tempting treats

1001
Cupcakes, Cookies
& other tempting treats

CONSULTANT EDITOR: **Susanna Tee**

First published in 2009
Love Food ® is an imprint of Parragon Books Ltd

Parragon
Queen Street House
4 Queen Street
Bath BA1 1HE, UK

ISBN: 978-1-4075-8335-8
Printed in Indonesia

Created and produced by Ivy Contract

Photography: Sian Irvine
Food styling by Jack Sargeson, Anna Irvine and Maud Eden
New recipes by Susanna Tee with Sarah Banbery and Jacqueline Bellefontaine

Notes for the Reader

This book uses both metric and imperial measurements. Follow the same
units of measurement throughout; do not mix metric and imperial. All spoon
measurements are level: teaspoons are assumed to be 5 ml, and tablespoons are
assumed to be 15 ml. Unless otherwise stated, milk is assumed to be full fat, eggs
and individual vegetables are medium, and pepper is freshly ground black pepper.

The times given are an approximate guide only. Preparation times differ according
to the techniques used by different people and the cooking times may also vary
from those given. Optional ingredients, variations or serving suggestions have not
been included in the calculations.

Recipes using raw or very lightly cooked eggs should be avoided by infants, the
elderly, pregnant women, convalescents and anyone suffering from an illness.
Pregnant and breastfeeding women are advised to avoid eating peanuts and peanut
products. Sufferers from nut allergies should be aware that some of the ready-
made ingredients used in the recipes in this book may contain nuts. Always check
the packaging before use.

Contents

Introduction

The cupcakes, cookies and other tempting treats included in this book are easy and enjoyable to make, fun to eat and great to share whatever the time of day. Every home should have a well-stocked jar of them waiting to be dipped into, and they are the perfect choice for a mid-morning coffee or afternoon tea, at a children's party or on a festive occasion. Whatever the reason, you are sure to find what you are looking for among the 1001 delicious goodies that have been gathered together in this comprehensive collection.

The making of cookies started in ancient Egypt with a mixture of flour and water that was baked on both sides on a griddle, resulting in a flat, hard cake. To this mixture, leaveners were added to make the cake rise, and then sugar to sweeten it. Wood-burning and coal-fired ovens were developed, and from these humble beginnings, cookies and other treats such as pastries, cupcakes, muffins, bars and brownies have evolved. Today every country has its own favourite recipe, be it chocolate chip cookies, biscotti or oatcakes – the list is endless!

The star ingredients

Sugar, fat, eggs, flour and a liquid are the basic ingredients that the majority of the recipes share.

Sugar

Caster sugar is usually recommended because it dissolves more easily than granulated sugar. Nevertheless, granulated sugar can be used if necessary.

Fat

Butter is the fat that is suggested in most of the recipes, as this adds richness and gives the best flavour. However, margarine can be used as an alternative, and is less expensive. It is important, though, to use a margarine containing not less that 60 per cent fat; choose a hard margarine that is described on the packet as suitable for baking. The exception is when a recipe calls for a soft margarine. In this instance all the ingredients are beaten together with an electric whisk until mixed.

Eggs

The size of eggs used in the recipes is medium unless otherwise stated. If possible, use eggs that are at room temperature because cold eggs can cause the mixture to curdle and will result in a less soft mixture.

Flour

The flour used in the recipes may be plain or self-raising. Should you need self-raising flour but only have plain, sift 2½ teaspoons of baking powder into every 225 g/ 8 oz plain flour.

Liquid

The liquid in the recipes is used to bind the ingredients together and is usually milk, eggs, butter, oil, water or fruit juice.

Equipment & helpful techniques

To make any of the recipes in this book requires very little special equipment and, in many cases, improvisation can be helpful! Nevertheless, here are some suggestions that you may find useful:

● Use your hands! Dampen them slightly when shaping cookies into a ball.

● A hand-held electric whisk is useful for whisking and beating mixtures together but, failing this, use a balloon whisk for whisking and a wooden spoon for creaming.

● If you don't have a tin of the size that is specified in the recipe, you can often improvise. A quantity of mixture designed for a square tin will fill a 2.5 cm/1 inch larger round tin and vice versa. When making bar cookies, recipes that specify a particular size of tin can equally be made in a tin with different dimensions but the same capacity.

● Use a food processor for rubbing fat into flour, but when the eggs or liquid are added make sure you blend them quickly, as overworked dough will be tough.

● When preparing a tin for baking brownies and bar cookies, especially one that is not shallow, line with baking paper, letting it hang over the edge of the tin. This makes it easier when lifting and removing the brownies or cookies later.

● If a recipe asks for toasted nuts and you do not have any, you can toast them yourself (see right).

To toast nuts

Preheat the oven to 180°C/350°F/Gas Mark 4. Spread the nuts in a single layer on a baking sheet and cook in the preheated oven for 5–10 minutes, turning and watching them carefully until golden brown.

To melt chocolate

In a bowl

Many of the recipes require you to melt chocolate in a heatproof bowl set over a saucepan of simmering water. This is the safest way to melt it because it will not overheat and become dry. Make sure the bowl does not touch the water.

In a microwave

Break the chocolate into a heatproof bowl and cook on Low until the chocolate is soft on top. As a guide, 100 g/3½ oz will take about 4 minutes. Check and stir every minute.

Assuring success

Almost all the recipes in the book are easy to make. Follow these useful suggestions and you will be guaranteed success every time you bake:

• Preheat the oven for 10–15 minutes before baking, even if the oven manufacturer's instructions suggest that this is not necessary. If you have a fan-assisted oven, reduce the temperature according to their instructions.

• It is important that ingredients are measured accurately, so it is worth investing in good-quality scales and standard measuring spoons.

• Get into the habit of preparing baking sheets, paper cases and tins before commencing preparation, as mixtures that contain self-raising flour start to activate once the liquid has been added to them and should therefore be baked as soon as possible after they have been prepared.

• When butter or hard margarine needs to be softened before blending with another ingredient, either remove it from the refrigerator and leave at room temperature for about 1 hour, or cut into cubes, place in a bowl and microwave on High for 10 seconds until softened slightly. Be careful not to allow it to melt.

• It is not necessary to sift flour unless you are combining several dry ingredients to facilitate even mixing.

• After adding the flour to a cupcake or muffin mixture, do not over-beat it as this will make the mixture tough.

• Where dough has to be refrigerated to make it firmer and easier to handle, you can speed this up by wrapping the dough in baking paper and placing in the freezer for a third of the time that you would normally refrigerate it.

• Do not over-beat brownie or bar cookie mixtures as this can make them rise too much and sink when they cool.

• Always place cookie dough on cold baking sheets to prevent the dough from spreading excessively and browning too much around the edges. When making a large quantity of cookies, leave the baking sheet to cool for a few minutes in between batches.

• Bake cookies on non-stick baking sheets or line them with baking paper but, unless specified in the recipe, do not grease the sheets as the cookies will spread excessively, become too thin and brown too quickly around the edges.

• Place cookies well apart on the baking sheet to allow room for them to spread during cooking. Unless they are particularly large, a gap of 5 cm/2 inches is usually enough.

• Position baking sheets of cupcakes, cookies, bars or muffins on the middle rack of the oven for even browning.

• Unless otherwise stated, transfer cookies to a wire rack as soon as they are firm enough to handle, and cupcakes and muffins directly after they are removed from the oven, and leave to cool. This will allow the steam to evaporate and prevent them from becoming soggy.

• When baking cupcakes and muffins, try to resist the temptation to open the oven door during the first half of the cooking time as cold air can cause the mixture to sink in the middle.

Bake & store

With a few exceptions, most of the cupcakes, cookies and other tempting treats in this book will keep well in a tin or airtight container and, in the case of brownies and bar cookies, even in the baking tin in which they were cooked, if it is kept tightly covered with foil. The following tips will also help, however:

● Ideally, store baked cupcakes, cookies and muffins undecorated. Any item that is decorated with cream, cream cheese or yogurt should be stored in the refrigerator.

● Store soft cookies separately from crisp varieties so that they don't all become soft, and don't store cookies and cakes together as the cookies will absorb moisture from the cakes and soften.

● Store different flavoured cookies separately so that their flavours do not mingle together.

● Only store cookies when they are completely cold because if stored while still warm they are liable to stick together.

● One or two sugar cubes added to a tin of cookies helps to keep them crisp.

● Most cupcakes, cookies, muffins and pastries can be frozen and thawed at short notice, but most are best when just baked.

The presentation

Finally, when serving your cupcakes, cookies or other tempting treats, presentation makes all the difference. Serve the delicate types on fine china or glass plates, or use cake stands and baskets lined with napkins, or even tins lined with baking paper can be used.

The beautifully photographed recipes in this book will capture your imagination – and with 1001 of them to choose from you are really spoilt for choice!

The finishing touches

Glacé icing

115 g/4 oz icing sugar
1 tbsp cold water

Sift the icing sugar into a bowl and gradually add the water, then beat together until the icing coats the back of a spoon. Use as required and leave to set.

Variations
Orange or lemon icing: replace the water with orange or lemon juice.
Chocolate icing: replace 2 tablespoons of the icing sugar with 2 tablespoons of cocoa powder.
Coffee icing: mix 1 teaspoon of instant coffee with 1 tablespoon of boiling water. Cool and mix with the icing sugar as before.
Liqueur icing: replace the water with 1 tablespoon of liqueur.
Orange flower or rose water icing: add ½ tablespoon of orange flower or rose water to ½ tablespoon of water and mix with the icing sugar.
Mocha icing: replace 2 tablespoons of the sugar with 2 tablespoons of cocoa and mix 1 teaspoon of instant coffee with 1 tablespoon of boiling water. Leave to cool and mix with the icing sugar and cocoa as before.

Buttercream icing

225 g/8 oz butter, softened
1 tbsp cream or milk
350 g/12 oz icing sugar

Place the butter and cream in a bowl and beat together. Gradually sift in the icing sugar and beat until smooth.

Variations
Orange or lemon buttercream: substitute fresh orange or lemon juice for the cream and add a little orange or yellow food colouring.
Chocolate buttercream: replace 55 g/ 2 oz of the sugar with 55 g/2 oz cocoa.
Coffee buttercream: replace the cream with 1 tablespoon of cold strong espresso coffee and ¼ teaspoon of coffee extract.
Mocha buttercream: replace 55 g/ 2 oz of the sugar with 55 g/2 oz cocoa and replace the cream with 1 tablespoon of cold espresso coffee.
Nut buttercream: Beat 175 g/6 oz butter with the sugar, then add ¼ teaspoon of vanilla extract, 55 g/ 2 oz smooth peanut or almond butter, and 100 g/3½ oz chopped pecan nuts or blanched almonds to the finished icing, and beat well.

Crème au beurre

2 egg yolks
175 g/6 oz butter, softened
75 g/6 oz caster sugar
4 tbsp water

Place the egg yolks in a bowl and whisk lightly. Place the butter in a separate bowl and beat until fluffy. Place the sugar and water into a saucepan and heat gently until the sugar has dissolved, then bring to the boil and boil for 2–3 minutes, or until the temperature reads 107°C/225°F on a sugar thermometer. Whisking all the time, pour the syrup into the egg yolks in a thin stream and continue to whisk the mixture until it is thick and cold. Gradually beat the egg mixture into the butter until combined.

Variations
Chocolate crème au beurre: add 1½ tablespoons of chocolate extract to the finished icing.
Coffee crème au beurre: add 1½ tablespoons of coffee extract to the finished icing.
Mocha crème au beurre: mix 1 tablespoon of chocolate extract with ½ tablespoon of coffee extract. Add to the finished icing and beat well to combine.
Orange or lemon crème au beurre: stir 2 tablespoons of juice and 1 teaspoon of finely grated rind of either lemon or orange into the icing and beat well to combine.
Strawberry or raspberry crème au beurre: add 2 tablespoons of strawberry or raspberry syrup to the icing and beat well to combine.

Royal icing

3 large egg whites
500 g/1 lb 2 oz icing sugar
1 tsp liquid glycerine

Place the egg whites in a large bowl and gradually sift in 200 g/7 oz icing sugar, stirring in between each addition until the mixture is thick. Whisk the mixture, gradually adding the remaining sugar. Whisk for 10 minutes, or until the icing is stiff. Stir in the glycerine until smooth.

Fondant icing

450 g/1 lb icing sugar
1 large egg white
30 g/1 oz liquid glycerine
1 tsp vanilla extract or almond extract

Sift the icing sugar into a large bowl and gradually beat in the egg white until the mixture is thick and smooth. Beat in the glycerine and vanilla extract.

Almond paste

175 g/6 oz icing sugar, plus extra for dusting
175 g/6 oz caster sugar
2 large eggs, plus 1 large egg yolk
½ tsp almond extract
1 tsp lemon juice
350 g/12 oz ground almonds

Sift the icing sugar into a heatproof bowl and stir in the caster sugar. Whisk the 2 eggs with the egg yolk and stir into the sugar. Place the bowl over a saucepan of simmering water and whisk for 10–12 minutes, or until thick and pale. Sit the base of the bowl in cold water. Whisk in the almond extract and lemon juice and whisk until cool. Stir in the almonds and beat to form a paste. Roll the almond paste to the desired size on a work surface dusted with icing sugar.

Apricot glaze

200 g/7 oz smooth apricot jam
100 g/3½ oz caster sugar
225 ml/8 fl oz water

Sift the apricot jam into a saucepan and stir in the sugar and water. Heat gently up to simmering point and stir until clear. Leave to cool before using.

Royal icing

10

Fudge icing

Fudge icing

100 g/3½ oz caster sugar
90 ml/3 fl oz evaporated milk
40 g/1½ oz butter
¼ tsp vanilla extract

Place the sugar and evaporated milk into a saucepan and stir, then heat gently until the sugar has dissolved. Bring to the boil, then reduce the heat and simmer for 5–6 minutes. Remove from the heat and add the butter and vanilla and whisk until smooth. Leave to cool, cover and chill for 2 hours until thick.

Variations
Coffee fudge icing: replace the vanilla extract with 1 tablespoon of coffee extract.
Chocolate fudge icing: add 115 g/ 4 oz chopped plain chocolate with the butter and stir until melted.
Coconut fudge icing: add 2 tablespoons of grated creamed coconut with the butter and stir.
Nut fudge icing: stir in 100 g/3½ oz chopped toasted pecans to the icing.

Butterscotch icing

55 g/2 oz butter
100 g/3½ oz soft light brown sugar
pinch of salt
90 ml/3 fl oz evaporated milk
225 g/8 oz icing sugar
½ tsp vanilla extract

Place the butter, brown sugar, salt and evaporated milk in a saucepan and heat until the sugar has dissolved, then stir until smooth. Remove from the heat and leave to cool slightly. Sift in the icing sugar and vanilla and beat well. Leave to cool completely.

Cream cheese icing

125 g/4½ oz butter, softened
225 g/8 oz full-fat cream cheese
450 g/1 lb icing sugar
1 tsp vanilla extract

Place the butter and cream cheese in a large bowl and beat together until light and fluffy. Gradually sift in the icing sugar and the vanilla and beat until smooth.

Vanilla frosting

25 g/1 oz butter, softened
1 vanilla pod
225 g/8 oz icing sugar
3-4 tbsp double cream

Place the butter in a bowl and beat until fluffy. Split the vanilla pod lengthways and add the seeds to the butter, then sift in the icing sugar and beat until smooth. Add the cream and beat again until creamy.

Chocolate frosting

100 g/3½ oz plain chocolate, chopped
140 g/5 oz butter, softened
140 g/5 oz icing sugar
½ tsp chocolate extract

Place the chocolate in a heatproof bowl, set the bowl over a saucepan of gently simmering water and heat until melted. Leave to cool. Place the butter in a bowl and beat until fluffy, then sift in the sugar and beat until smooth. Add the cooled chocolate and chocolate extract and beat until combined.

American frosting

225 g/8 oz caster sugar
4 tbsp water
¼ tsp cream of tartar
½ tsp vanilla extract
1 large egg white

Place the sugar, water and cream of tartar into a saucepan and heat gently until the sugar has dissolved. Add the vanilla and heat (without boiling), stirring, until the temperature reads 120°C/250°F on a sugar thermometer. Leave to cool slightly. Whisk the egg white in a large bowl until stiff, then continue whisking as you add the syrup in a thin stream and continue to whisk until smooth and thick.

Seven-minute frosting

1 large egg white
pinch of salt
300 g/10½ oz caster sugar
5 tbsp water
¼ tsp cream of tartar
1 tsp vanilla extract

Place the egg white in a heatproof bowl and add the salt, sugar, water and cream of tartar. Beat together then place the bowl in a double boiler over boiling water and whisk for 7 minutes until stiff peaks form. Remove from the heat, add the vanilla and beat until smooth.

Chocolate ganache

150 g/5½ oz plain chocolate, chopped
150 ml/5 fl oz double cream

Place the chocolate in a heatproof bowl. Pour the cream into a pan and bring gently up to simmering point. Pour the hot cream over the chocolate and mix until smooth.

Crème au beurre

Cute Cupcakes and Buns

115 g/4 oz butter, softened
115 g/4 oz caster sugar
2 eggs, lightly beaten
115 g/4 oz self-raising flour

TOPPING
200 g/7 oz icing sugar
about 2 tbsp warm water
a few drops of food colouring (optional)
sugar flowers, hundreds and thousands,
   glacé cherries and/or chocolate
   strands, to decorate

Preheat the oven to 190°C/375°F/Gas Mark 5. Line 2 x 12-hole bun tins with 16 paper cases. Place the butter and sugar in a large bowl and beat together until light and fluffy, then gradually beat in the eggs. Sift in the flour and fold into the mixture. Spoon the mixture into the paper cases.

Bake in the preheated oven for 15–20 minutes. Transfer to a wire rack to cool completely.

To make the icing, sift the icing sugar into a bowl and stir in just enough warm water to mix to a smooth paste that is thick enough to coat the back of a wooden spoon. Stir in a few drops of food colouring, if using, then spread the icing over the fairy cakes and decorate, as liked.

02   Orange fairy cakes

Add the grated rind of ½ orange to the cake mixture after beating in the eggs. Use orange juice instead of water when making the icing.

03   Lemon fairy cakes

Add the grated rind of ½ lemon to the cake mixture after beating in the eggs. Use lemon juice instead of water when making the icing.

04   Chocolate fairy cakes

Replace 25 g/1 oz of the flour with 2 tablespoons of cocoa powder and add 2 teaspoons of cocoa powder to the icing sugar when making the icing.

05   Coffee fairy cakes

Dissolve 2 tablespoons of instant coffee in 3 tablespoons of boiling water. Add about two thirds to the cake mixture after beating the eggs. Add the remainder to the icing sugar when making the icing.

06   Mocha fairy cakes

Dissolve 1 tablespoon of instant coffee in 2 tablespoons of boiling water and beat in after adding the eggs. Add 1 tablespoon of cocoa powder to the flour and fold in. For a mocha icing, add 1 teaspoon of cocoa powder to the icing sugar. Dissolve 1 teaspoon of instant coffee in 1 tablespoon of boiling water and stir into the icing sugar mixture with enough water until smooth.

07   Almond fairy cakes

Add 1 teaspoon of almond extract after beating in the eggs. Replace 25 g/ 1 oz of the flour with ground almonds.

08   Nutty fairy cakes

Add 40 g /1½ oz finely chopped walnuts, pecan nuts or toasted hazelnuts before folding in the flour.

Sweet shop vanilla cupcakes

140 g/5 oz butter, softened, or soft
  margarine
140 g/5 oz caster sugar
1½ tsp vanilla extract
2 large eggs, lightly beaten
200 g /7 oz self-raising flour

TOPPING
1 quantity buttercream icing (page 10)
a selection of classic small sweets, such
  as jelly beans, to decorate

Preheat the oven to 190°C/375°F/Gas Mark 5. Line 2 x 12-hole bun tins with 18 paper cases. Place the butter and sugar in a large bowl and beat together until light and fluffy, then beat in the vanilla extract. Gradually beat in the eggs, then sift in the flour and fold into the mixture. Spoon the mixture into the paper cases.

Bake in the preheated oven for 12–15 minutes, or until golden and springy to the touch. Transfer to a wire rack to cool completely.

Place the buttercream in a piping bag fitted with a small star nozzle and pipe the buttercream on top of each cake. Arrange the sweets on top to decorate.

10 *Sweet shop chocolate cupcakes*

Reduce the vanilla extract to ½ teaspoon. Melt 70 g/2½ oz plain chocolate, broken into pieces, and stir into the cake mixture after beating in the eggs. Decorate with chocolate buttercream icing (page 10) and small chocolate sweets, such as buttons.

11 *Birthday party cakes*

225 g/8 oz butter, softened, or soft
  margarine
225 g/8 oz caster sugar
4 eggs
225 g/8 oz self-raising flour

TOPPING
175 g/6 oz butter, softened
350 g/12 oz icing sugar

a variety of sweets and chocolates, sugar-
  coated chocolates, dried fruits, edible
  sugar flower shapes, cake decorating
  sprinkles, sugar strands, silver or gold
  dragées, hundreds and thousands,
  various tubes of coloured writing
  icing and candles and candleholders
  (optional), to decorate

Preheat the oven to 180°C/350°F/Gas Mark 4. Line 2 x 12-hole bun tins with 24 paper baking cases. Place the butter, sugar, eggs and flour in a large bowl and beat together until just smooth. Spoon the mixture into the paper cases.

Bake in the preheated oven for 15–20 minutes, or until well risen, golden brown and firm to the touch. Transfer to a wire rack to cool.

To make the icing, place the butter in a bowl and beat until fluffy. Sift in the icing sugar and beat together until smooth and creamy.

When the cakes are cold, spread the icing on top of each cake, then decorate as you like and place a candle in the top of each, if using.

12 *Citrus almond party cakes*

For more grown-up party cakes, replace 55 g/2 oz of the flour with ground almonds and fold in 25 g/1 oz finely chopped mixed peel. Decorate with sugared almonds.

25 g/1 oz plain chocolate, broken into
    pieces
125 g/4½ oz butter, softened
125 g/4½ oz caster sugar
150 g/5½ oz self-raising flour
2 large eggs
2 tbsp cocoa powder
icing sugar, for dusting

LEMON BUTTERCREAM ICING
100 g/3½ oz butter, softened
225 g/8 oz icing sugar
grated rind of ½ lemon
1 tbsp lemon juice

Preheat the oven to 180°C/350°F/Gas Mark 4. Line a 12-hole bun tin
with 12 paper cases. Place the chocolate in a heatproof bowl, set the
bowl over a saucepan of gently simmering water and heat until melted,
then leave to cool slightly.

Place the butter, sugar, flour, eggs and cocoa in a large bowl and beat
together until the mixture is just smooth. Beat in the melted chocolate.
Spoon the mixture into the paper cases.

Bake in the preheated oven for 15 minutes, or until springy to the
touch. Transfer to a wire rack to cool completely.

To make the icing, place the butter in a bowl and beat until fluffy,
then gradually sift in the icing sugar and beat to combine. Beat in the
lemon rind, then gradually beat in the lemon juice. Cut the top off each
cake, then cut the top in half. Pipe the buttercream over the cut surface
of each cake and push the 2 cut cake pieces into the icing to form wings.
Dust with sifted icing sugar.

14 *Chocolate orange butterfly cakes*

*Add the grated rind of ½ orange and 2 tablespoons of orange juice to the cake
mixture. For the icing, replace the lemon juice and rind with orange juice
and rind and decorate the completed cakes with very fine strips of orange
rind, if liked.*

15 *Chocolate nut butterfly cakes*

*Add 40 g/1½ oz finely chopped hazelnuts to the cake mixture. Sprinkle a few
chopped toasted hazelnuts on the top to decorate.*

16 *White chocolate butterfly cakes*

*Replace the melted plain chocolate with melted white chocolate. Decorate the
cakes with chocolate buttercream icing (page 10).*

140 g/5 oz butter
100 g/3½ oz soft light brown sugar
100 g/3½ oz honey
200 g/7 oz self-raising flour

1 tsp ground allspice
2 eggs, lightly beaten
24 whole blanched almonds

Preheat the oven to 180°C/350°F/Gas Mark 4. Line 2 x 12-hole bun tins with 24 paper cases. Place the butter, sugar and honey in a large saucepan and heat gently, stirring, until the butter is melted. Remove the pan from the heat. Sift together the flour and allspice and stir into the mixture in the saucepan, then beat in the eggs until smooth.

Spoon the mixture into the paper cases and place an almond on top of each one. Bake in the preheated oven for 20–25 minutes, or until well risen and golden brown. Transfer to a wire rack to cool completely.

18 *Pecan & maple spice cakes*

Replace the honey with maple syrup and the allspice with cinnamon. Decorate each cake with a pecan nut instead of an almond.

19 *Nutmeg & hazelnut cakes*

Add 25 g/1 oz finely chopped toasted hazelnuts to the honey and butter mixture. Replace the allspice with nutmeg and decorate each cake with a hazelnut instead of an almond.

20 Jumbo chocolate chip cupcakes

MAKES 8

100 g/3½ oz butter, softened, or soft margarine
100 g/3½ oz caster sugar
2 large eggs
100 g/3½ oz self-raising flour
100 g/3½ oz plain chocolate chips

Preheat the oven to 190°C/375°F/Gas Mark 5. Line a 12-hole muffin tin with 8 paper cases.

Place the butter, sugar, eggs and flour in a large bowl and beat together until just smooth. Fold in the chocolate chips. Spoon the mixture into the paper cases.

Bake in the preheated oven for 20–25 minutes, or until well risen and golden brown. Transfer to a wire rack to cool completely.

21 Choc & nut cupcakes

Replace the plain chocolate chips with 55 g/2 oz milk chocolate chips and 55 g/2 oz chopped hazelnuts.

22 Sugar-coated chocolates cupcakes

Replace the plain chocolate chips with sugar-coated chocolates.

115 g/4 oz butter, softened, or soft margarine
115 g/4 oz caster sugar
2 large eggs, lightly beaten

4 tsp lemon juice
175 g/6 oz self-raising flour
115 g/4 oz currants
2–4 tbsp milk, if necessary

Preheat the oven to 190°C/375°F/Gas Mark 5. Line 2 x 12-hole bun tins with 18 paper cases. Place the butter and sugar in a large bowl and beat together until light and fluffy. Gradually beat in the eggs, then beat in the lemon juice with 1 tablespoon of the flour. Fold in the remaining flour and the currants. If necessary, add a little milk to give a soft dropping consistency. Spoon the mixture into the paper cases.

Bake in the preheated oven for 15–20 minutes, or until well risen and golden brown. Transfer to a wire rack to cool completely.

24 *Sultana & orange queen cakes*

Replace the currants with sultanas. Replace the lemon juice with orange juice and add the grated rind of ½ orange with the juice.

25 *Iced queen cakes*

Sift 150 g/5½ oz icing sugar into a small bowl and stir in about 4 teaspoons of lemon juice. Mix to a smooth icing that will coat the back of a wooden spoon. Spread the icing over the cakes so that you can just see the edges of the cake.

26 *Rose petal cupcakes*

MAKES 12

115 g/4 oz butter, softened
115 g/4 oz caster sugar
2 eggs, lightly beaten
1 tbsp milk
few drops of essence of rose oil
¼ tsp vanilla extract
175 g/6 oz self-raising flour
silver dragées, to decorate

CRYSTALLIZED ROSE PETALS
12–24 rose petals
lightly beaten egg white, for brushing
caster sugar, for sprinkling

ICING
85 g/3 oz butter, softened
175 g/6 oz icing sugar
pink or purple food colouring
(optional)

To make the crystallized rose petals, gently rinse the petals and dry well with kitchen paper. Using a pastry brush, paint both sides of a rose petal with egg white, then coat well with caster sugar. Place on a tray and repeat with the remaining petals. Cover the tray with foil and leave overnight.

Preheat the oven to 200°C/ 400°F/Gas Mark 6. Line a 12-hole bun tin with 12 paper cases.

Place the butter and sugar in a large bowl and beat together until light and fluffy, then gradually beat in the eggs. Stir in the milk, rose essence and vanilla extract, then fold in the flour. Spoon the mixture into the paper cases.

Bake in the preheated oven for 12–15 minutes, or until well risen and golden brown. Transfer to a wire rack to cool completely.

To make the icing, place the butter in a large bowl and beat until fluffy. Sift in the icing sugar and mix well together. Add a few drops of pink or purple food colouring to match the rose petals, if liked.

When the cupcakes are cold, spread the icing on top of each cake. Top with 1–2 crystallized rose petals and sprinkle with silver dragées to decorate.

115 g/4 oz plain flour
2 tsp ground ginger
¾ tsp ground cinnamon
1 piece stem ginger, finely chopped
¾ tsp bicarbonate of soda
4 tbsp milk
85 g/3 oz butter, softened, or soft margarine
70 g/2½ oz soft dark brown sugar

2 tbsp black treacle
2 eggs, lightly beaten
1 piece stem ginger, sliced, to decorate

ICING
85 g/3 oz butter, softened
175 g/6 oz icing sugar
2 tbsp ginger syrup from the stem ginger jar

Preheat the oven to 160°C/325°F/Gas Mark 3. Line 2 x 12-hole bun tins with 16 paper cases. Sift the flour, ground ginger and cinnamon together into a bowl. Add the chopped ginger and toss in the flour mixture until it is well coated. Place the bicarbonate of soda and milk in a separate bowl and stir to dissolve.

Place the butter and sugar in a large bowl and beat together until light and fluffy.

Beat in the treacle, then gradually mix in the eggs. Beat in the flour mixture and then gradually add the milk. Spoon the mixture into the paper cases.

Bake in the preheated oven for 20 minutes, or until well risen and golden brown. Transfer to a wire rack to cool competely.

To make the icing, place the butter in a bowl and beat until fluffy. Sift in the icing sugar, add the ginger syrup and beat together until smooth and creamy.

When the cupcakes are cold, spread the icing on top of each cake, then decorate with pieces of the stem ginger to decorate.

28 *Sticky gingernut cupcakes*

Add 40 g/1½ oz finely chopped walnuts or pecan nuts with the chopped stem ginger. Decorate with chopped nuts.

200 ml/7 fl oz water
85 g/3 oz butter
85 g/3 oz caster sugar
1 tbsp golden syrup
3 tbsp milk
1 tsp vanilla extract
1 tsp bicarbonate of soda
225 g/8 oz plain flour
2 tbsp cocoa powder

TOPPING
50 g/1¾ oz plain chocolate, broken into pieces
4 tbsp water
50 g/1¾ oz butter
50 g/1¾ oz white chocolate, broken into pieces
350 g/12 oz icing sugar
100 g/3½ oz plain chocolate shavings and 100 g/3½ oz white chocolate shavings, to decorate

Preheat the oven to 180°C/350°F/Gas Mark 4. Line 2 x 12-hole bun tins with 20 paper cases. Place the water, butter, sugar and syrup in a saucepan and heat gently, stirring, until the sugar has dissolved. Bring to the boil, reduce the heat and cook gently for 5 minutes. Leave to cool.

Meanwhile, place the milk and vanilla extract in a bowl. Add the bicarbonate of soda and stir to dissolve. Sift the flour and cocoa into a separate bowl and add the syrup mixture. Stir in the milk and beat until smooth, then spoon the mixture into the paper cases.

Bake in the preheated oven for 20 minutes, or until well risen and firm to the touch. Transfer to a wire rack to cool completely.

To make the icing, place the plain chocolate in a small heatproof bowl, add half the water and half the butter, set the bowl over a saucepan of gently simmering water and heat until melted. Stir until smooth and then leave to stand over the water. Repeat with the white chocolate and remaining water and butter. Sift half the icing sugar into each bowl and beat until smooth and thick.

When the cupcakes are cold, top alternately with each icing, then leave to set. Decorate with chocolate shavings.

30 *Pecan fudge cupcakes*

Stir 40 g/1½ oz chopped pecan nuts into the flour and cocoa powder mixture before adding the syrup. Sprinkle chopped nuts instead of chocolate shavings on top of the icing.

55 g/2 oz butter, softened, or soft
margarine
225 g/8 oz soft light brown sugar
115 g/4 oz crunchy peanut butter
2 eggs, lightly beaten
1 tsp vanilla extract
225 g/8 oz plain flour
2 tsp baking powder
100 ml/3½ fl oz milk

FROSTING
200 g/7 oz full-fat soft cream cheese
25 g/1 oz butter, softened
225 g/8 oz icing sugar

Preheat the oven to 180°C/350°F/
Gas Mark 4. Line 2 x 12-hole
muffin tins with 16 paper cases.
Place the butter, sugar and peanut
butter in a bowl and beat together
for 1–2 minutes, or until well
mixed. Gradually beat in the eggs,
then add the vanilla extract. Sift
in the flour and baking powder,
then fold them into the mixture,
alternating with the milk. Spoon
the mixture into the paper cases.

Bake in the preheated oven for
25 minutes, or until well risen and
golden brown. Transfer to a wire
rack to cool completely.

To make the frosting, place
the cream cheese and butter in
a large bowl and beat together
until smooth. Sift the icing sugar
into the mixture, beat together
until well mixed, then spread the
frosting on top of each cupcake.

32 *Peanut butter & jam cupcakes*

*Spoon half the mixture into the paper cases then place about ½ teaspoon
of strawberry or raspberry jam into the centre of each. Carefully spoon the
remaining mixture into the paper cases so that it completely encloses the
jam. Sprinkle with a little demerara sugar and bake as before.*

33 *Chocolate peanut butter cupcakes*

*Spoon half the mixture into the paper cases then place about ½ teaspoon
of chocolate spread into the centre of each. Carefully spoon the remaining
mixture into the paper cases so that it completely encloses the chocolate
spread. Bake as before. Cool and spread with extra chocolate spread.*

34 *Moist walnut cupcakes*

85 g/3 oz walnuts
55 g/2 oz butter, softened, cut into
small pieces
100 g/3½ oz caster sugar
grated rind of ½ lemon
70 g/2½ oz self-raising flour
2 eggs
12 walnut halves, to decorate

ICING
55 g/2 oz butter, softened
85 g/3 oz icing sugar
grated rind of ½ lemon
1 tsp lemon juice

Preheat the oven to 190°C/375°F/ Gas Mark 5. Line a 12-hole bun tin with 12 paper cases. Place the walnuts in a food processor and pulse until finely ground. Be careful not to overgrind, as the nuts will turn to oil.

Add the butter, sugar, lemon rind, flour and eggs and blend until the mixture is evenly combined. Spoon the mixture into the paper cases.

Bake in the preheated oven for 20 minutes, or until well risen and golden brown. Transfer to a wire rack to cool completely.

To make the icing, place the butter in a bowl and beat until fluffy. Sift in the icing sugar, add the lemon rind and juice and mix well together. When the cupcakes are cold, spread the icing on top of each cupcake and top with a walnut half to decorate.

35 *Sticky orange & walnut cupcakes*

For the cupcakes, replace the lemon rind with orange rind. Instead of the icing, heat 6 tablespoons of orange juice with 2 tablespoons of caster sugar, stirring until the sugar dissolves, then boil until syrupy. Spoon the syrup over the hot cakes and leave to cool before serving.

36 *Moist pecan cupcakes*

Replace the walnuts with pecan nuts and the lemon rind and juice with orange rind and juice.

37 *Feathered-iced coffee cupcakes*

1 tbsp instant coffee granules
1 tbsp boiling water
115 g/4 oz butter, softened, or soft
margarine
115 g/4 oz soft light brown sugar
2 eggs
115 g/4 oz self-raising flour
½ tsp baking powder
2 tbsp soured cream

ICING
225 g/8 oz icing sugar
4 tsp warm water
1 tsp instant coffee granules
2 tsp boiling water

Preheat the oven to 190°C/375°F/ Gas Mark 5. Line 2 x 12-hole bun tins with 16 paper cases. Place the coffee granules in a cup or small bowl, add the boiling water and stir until dissolved. Leave to cool slightly. Place the butter, sugar and eggs in a large bowl. Sift in the flour and baking powder and beat until smooth. Add the dissolved coffee and soured cream and beat until mixed. Spoon the mixture into the paper cases.

Bake in the preheated oven for 20 minutes, or until well risen and golden. Cool on a wire rack.

To make the icing, sift 85 g/ 3 oz of the icing sugar into a bowl and add enough warm water to mix until thick enough to coat the back of a wooden spoon. Dissolve the coffee in the boiling water. Sift the remaining icing sugar into a bowl and stir in the dissolved coffee. Ice the cakes with the white icing, then pipe the coffee icing in parallel lines on top. Draw a skewer across the piped lines in both directions. Leave to set.

38 *Feathered-iced mocha cupcakes*

Replace the soured cream with 55 g/2 oz melted plain chocolate.

39 *Feathered-iced chocolate cupcakes*

Replace the coffee granules for the cake mixture with cocoa powder. To complete the cakes, melt 175 g/6 oz milk chocolate and 25 g/1 oz white chocolate in separate bowls and spoon the white chocolate into a piping bag fitted with a piping nozzle. Spread the milk chocolate over the top of the cakes, then quickly pipe the white chocolate in lines across the cakes. Drag a skewer across the piped lines in both directions to feather the chocolate.

115 g/4 oz butter, softened, or soft
margarine
115 g/4 oz caster sugar
2 tbsp milk
2 eggs, lightly beaten
85 g/3 oz self-raising flour
½ tsp baking powder
85 g/3 oz desiccated coconut
115 g/4 oz glacé cherries, quartered

TOPPING
1 quantity buttercream icing
(page 10)
12 whole glacé, maraschino or fresh
cherries, to decorate

Preheat the oven to 180°C/350°F/
Gas Mark 4. Line a 12-hole bun
tin with 12 paper cases.

Place the butter and sugar in a
large bowl and beat together until
light and fluffy. Stir in the milk and
then gradually beat in the eggs. Sift
in the flour and baking powder
and fold them in with the coconut.
Gently fold in most of the quartered
cherries.

Spoon the mixture into
the paper cases and scatter the
remaining quartered cherries evenly
on top.

Bake in the preheated oven for
20–25 minutes, or until well risen,
golden brown and firm to the
touch. Transfer to a wire rack to
cool completely.

When the cupcakes are cold,
place the buttercream in a piping
bag fitted with a large star nozzle
and pipe the buttercream on top
of each cupcake, then add a cherry
to decorate.

41 Iced coconut cherry cupcakes

*When cooled, cover with glacé icing (page 10). Cut 12 glacé cherries in half
and arrange two halves on each cake. Melt 50 g/2 oz plain chocolate and spoon
it into a piping bag fitted with a plain piping nozzle, then pipe cherry stems on
the icing to join the cherries in a bunch.*

42 Almond cherry cupcakes

Replace the coconut with ground almonds.

115 g/4 oz butter, softened, or soft
margarine
115 g/4 oz soft light brown sugar
juice and finely grated rind of 1 small
orange
2 large eggs, lightly beaten
175 g/6 oz carrots, grated
25 g/1 oz walnut pieces, roughly
chopped
125 g/4½ oz plain flour
1 tsp ground mixed spice
1½ tsp baking powder

ICING
280 g/10 oz mascarpone cheese
4 tbsp icing sugar
grated rind of 1 large orange

Preheat the oven to 180°C/350°F/
Gas Mark 4. Line a 12-hole muffin
tin with 12 paper cases.

Place the butter, sugar and
orange rind in a bowl and beat
together until light and fluffy,
then gradually beat in the eggs.
Squeeze any excess liquid from
the carrots and add to the mixture
with the walnuts and orange juice.
Stir until well mixed. Sift in the
flour, mixed spice and baking
powder and fold in. Spoon the
mixture into the paper cases.

Bake in the preheated oven
for 25 minutes, or until risen,
firm to the touch and golden
brown. Transfer to a wire rack to
cool completely.

To make the icing, place the
mascarpone cheese, icing sugar
and orange rind in a large bowl
and beat together until they are
well mixed.

When the cupcakes are cold,
spread the icing on top of each
cupcake, swirling it with a round-
bladed knife.

44 Carrot & lemon cupcakes

*Replace the orange rind and juice in the cakes with lemon rind and juice.
To make the icing, sift 175 g/6 oz icing sugar into a large bowl and beat in
enough lemon juice to make a smooth icing. Spread on top of the cakes and
leave plain or decorate with lemon jelly sweet slices.*

45 Chocolate carrot cupcakes

*Add 85 g/3 oz plain chocolate chips along with the carrot. Beat 55 g/2 oz
melted plain chocolate into the mascarpone icing before spreading on
the cupcakes.*

85 g/3 oz butter, softened, or soft
margarine
100 g/3½ oz caster sugar
2 eggs, lightly beaten
2 tbsp milk
55 g/2 oz plain chocolate chips
225 g/8 oz self-raising flour
25 g/1 oz cocoa powder

TOPPING
225 g/8 oz white chocolate, broken
into pieces
150 g/5½ oz low-fat cream cheese
chocolate curls, to decorate

Preheat the oven to 200°C/400°F/ Gas Mark 6. Line 2 x 12-hole bun tins with 18 paper cases. Place the butter and sugar in a large bowl and beat together until light and fluffy, then gradually beat in the eggs. Add the milk, then fold in the chocolate chips. Sift in the flour and cocoa powder, then fold into the mixture. Spoon the mixture into the paper cases and smooth the tops.

Bake in the preheated oven for 20 minutes, or until well risen and springy to the touch. Transfer to a wire rack to cool completely.

To make the icing, place the chocolate in a small heatproof bowl, set the bowl over a saucepan of gently simmering water and heat until melted. Leave to cool slightly. Place the cream cheese in a separate bowl and beat until softened, then beat in the slightly cooled chocolate.

When the cupcakes are cold, spread a little of the icing over the top of each cupcake, then leave to chill in the refrigerator for 1 hour before serving. Decorate with a few chocolate curls, if liked.

47 *White chocolate cupcakes*

Replace the plain chocolate chips with 85 g/3 oz white chocolate chips. Omit the cocoa powder and increase the flour to 250 g/9 oz. Decorate with white chocolate curls made with a potato peeler.

48 *With chocolate mascarpone icing*

For the icing, replace the cream cheese with mascarpone and decorate with milk chocolate curls.

115 g/4 oz self-raising flour
½ tsp baking powder
115 g/4 oz butter, softened, or soft
margarine
115 g/4 oz caster sugar
2 eggs
finely grated rind of ½ lemon
2 tbsp milk
icing sugar, for dusting

LEMON BUTTERCREAM ICING
85 g/3 oz butter, softened
175 g/6 oz icing sugar
1 tbsp lemon juice

Preheat the oven to 190°C/375°F/ Gas Mark 5. Line a 12-hole bun tin with 12 paper cases.

Sift the flour and baking powder into a large bowl, add the butter, sugar, eggs, lemon rind and milk and beat together until smooth. Spoon the mixture into the paper cases.

Bake in the preheated oven for 15–20 minutes, or until well risen and golden brown. Transfer to a wire rack to cool completely.

To make the icing, place the butter in a bowl and beat until fluffy. Sift in the icing sugar, add the lemon juice and beat together until smooth and creamy. When the cupcakes are cold, cut the top off each cake then cut the top in half.

Spread or pipe a little of the lemon icing over the cut surface of each cupcake, then gently press the 2 cut cake pieces into it at an angle to resemble butterfly wings. Dust with sifted icing sugar before serving.

50 *Orange butterfly cakes*

Replace the lemon rind and juice with orange rind and juice.

51 *Vanilla butterfly cakes*

Omit the lemon rind from the cake mixture and replace the lemon juice in the icing with 1 teaspoon of vanilla extract. Decorate with sugar sprinkles, if liked.

225 g/8 oz plain flour
1¼ tsp baking powder
¼ tsp bicarbonate of soda
2 ripe bananas
115 g/4 oz butter, softened, or soft margarine
115 g/4 oz caster sugar
½ tsp vanilla extract

2 eggs, lightly beaten
4 tbsp soured cream
55 g/2 oz pecan nuts, roughly chopped

TOPPING
115 g/4 oz butter, softened
115 g/4 oz icing sugar
25 g/1 oz pecan nuts, finely chopped

Preheat the oven to 190°C/375°F/Gas Mark 5. Line 2 x 12-hole bun tins with 24 paper cases. Sift together the flour, baking powder and bicarbonate of soda. Place the bananas in a separate bowl and mash with a fork.

Place the butter, sugar and vanilla extract in a large bowl and beat together until light and fluffy, then gradually beat in the eggs. Stir in the mashed bananas and soured cream. Fold in the flour mixture and chopped nuts. Spoon the mixture into the paper cases.

Bake in the preheated oven for 20 minutes, or until well risen and golden brown. Transfer to a wire rack to cool completely.

To make the topping, place the butter in a bowl and beat until fluffy. Sift in the icing sugar and mix together well. Spread the icing on top of each cupcake and sprinkle with the pecan nuts before serving.

53 *Banana & date cupcakes*

Omit the pecan nuts from the cakes and the topping and add 55 g/2 oz chopped dates, folding in with the flour.

54 *Banana & chocolate cupcakes*

Replace the pecan nuts with 85 g/3 oz plain or milk chocolate chips. Decorate the tops of the cakes with chocolate curls or chocolate sugar strands.

55 *Banana & butterscotch cupcakes*

Replace the pecan nuts with 85 g/3 oz butterscotch-flavoured chips. Decorate the tops with a few more butterscotch chips, if liked.

75 g/2¾ oz butter, softened, or soft
margarine
100 g/3½ oz caster sugar
1 large egg, lightly beaten
2 tbsp milk
100 g/3½ oz self-raising flour
1 tsp baking powder
75 g/2¾ oz cranberries, frozen

Preheat the oven to 180°C/350°F/ Gas Mark 4. Line 2 x 12-hole bun tins with 14 paper cases.

Place the butter and sugar in a large bowl and beat together until light and fluffy, then gradually beat in the egg and stir in the milk. Sift in the flour and baking powder and fold into the mixture. Gently fold in the frozen cranberries. Spoon the mixture into the paper cases.

Bake in the preheated oven for 15–20 minutes, or until well risen and golden brown. Transfer to a wire rack to cool completely.

57 *Frozen blueberry cupcakes*

Replace the frozen cranberries with frozen blueberries.

58 *Cherry cupcakes*

Replace the frozen cranberries with canned black cherries. Drain well and halve each cherry before adding to the mixture.

½ tsp bicarbonate of soda
280 g/10 oz jar Bramley apple sauce
55 g/2 oz butter, softened, or soft
margarine
85 g/3 oz demerara sugar
1 large egg, lightly beaten
175 g/6 oz self-raising flour
½ tsp ground cinnamon
½ tsp freshly ground nutmeg

TOPPING
50 g/1¾ oz plain white flour
50 g/1¾ oz demerara sugar
¼ tsp ground cinnamon
¼ tsp freshly grated nutmeg
35 g/1¼ oz butter, cut into
small pieces

Preheat the oven to 180°C/350°F/ Gas Mark 4. Line 2 x 12-hole bun tins with 14 paper cases.

First, make the topping. Place the flour, sugar, cinnamon and nutmeg in a large bowl. Add the butter and rub it in with your fingertips until the mixture resembles fine breadcrumbs. Reserve until required.

To make the cupcakes, add the bicarbonate of soda to the jar of apple sauce and stir until dissolved. Place the butter and sugar in a large bowl and beat together until light and fluffy, then gradually beat in the egg. Sift in the flour, cinnamon and nutmeg and fold into the mixture, alternating with the apple sauce. Spoon the mixture into the paper cases. Scatter the reserved topping over each cupcake to cover the tops and press down gently.

Bake in the preheated oven for 20 minutes, or until well risen and golden brown. Leave the cakes for 2–3 minutes in the tins before serving warm, or transfer to a wire rack to cool completely.

60 *Apricot streusel cupcakes*

Drain a 280 g/10 oz can of apricots, reserving the juice. Chop the apricots and mix a little of the juice with 1 teaspoon of cornflour. Place the apricots in a saucepan with the juice and bring to the boil. Add the cornflour mixture and cook over a low heat, stirring, until thickened. Leave to cool, then complete as before, replacing the apple sauce with the apricot mixture.

61 *Cranberry streusel cupcakes*

Replace the apple sauce with cranberry sauce.

62 *Cherry streusel cupcakes*

Replace the apple sauce with half a 400 g/14 oz can of cherry pie filling.

55 g/2 oz butter, softened, or soft
margarine
55 g/2 oz caster sugar
1 large egg
85 g/3 oz self-raising flour
1 tbsp cocoa powder
55 g/2 oz plain chocolate
icing sugar, for dusting

Preheat the oven to 190°C/375°F/ Gas Mark 5. Line a 12-hole bun tin with 8 paper cases.

Place the butter, sugar, egg, flour and cocoa powder in a large bowl and beat together until just smooth. Spoon half of the mixture into the paper cases. Using a teaspoon, make an indentation in the centre of each cake. Break the chocolate into 8 even squares and place a piece in each indentation, then spoon the remaining cake mixture on top.

Bake in the preheated oven for 20 minutes, or until well risen and springy to the touch.

Leave the cupcakes in the tin for 2–3 minutes before serving warm, dusted with sifted icing sugar.

64 *White chocolate-centred cupcakes*

Replace the plain chocolate with squares of white chocolate.

65 *Vanilla & chocolate cupcakes*

Increase the flour to 100 g/3½ oz and omit the cocoa powder. Add ½ teaspoon of vanilla extract to the butter and sugar, and use milk chocolate instead of the plain chocolate.

50 g/1¾ oz plain chocolate, broken
into pieces
60 g/2¼ oz butter
115 g/4 oz cherry jam
60 g/2¼ oz caster sugar
2 large eggs
100 g/3½ oz self-raising flour

TOPPING
4 tsp kirsch liqueur
150 ml/5 fl oz double cream
12 fresh, glacé or maraschino cherries
chocolate curls, to decorate

Bake in the preheated oven for 20 minutes, or until firm to the touch. Leave to cool in the tin for 10 minutes, then transfer to a wire rack to cool completely.

When the cupcakes are cold, sprinkle the kirsch over the tops of each and leave to soak for at least 15 minutes.

When ready to decorate, place the cream in a bowl and whip until soft peaks form. Spread the cream on top of the cupcakes with a knife to form the cream into peaks. Top each cupcake with a cherry and decorate with chocolate curls.

67 *Chocolate strawberry cupcakes*

Replace the cherry jam with strawberry jam and sprinkle the cold cupcakes with brandy instead of kirsch. Decorate each cupcake with a small whole strawberry.

Preheat the oven to 180°C/350°F/Gas Mark 4. Line a 12-hole muffin tin with 12 paper cases. Place the chocolate and butter in a saucepan and heat gently, stirring constantly, until melted. Pour into a large bowl, then stir until smooth and leave to cool slightly. Add the jam, sugar and eggs to the cooled chocolate and beat together. Add the flour and stir together until combined. Spoon the mixture into the paper cases.

115 g/4 oz butter, softened, plus extra
for greasing
4 tbsp strawberry jam
115 g/4 oz caster sugar
2 eggs, lightly beaten
1 tsp vanilla extract
115 g/4 oz self-raising flour
6 whole strawberries, to decorate
icing sugar, for dusting

in the centre, comes out clean. If overbrowning, cover the cupcakes with a sheet of foil. Leave the cupcakes to cool for 2–3 minutes, then carefully lift the cups from the tin and place them on saucers.

Top each cupcake with a strawberry, then dust them with sifted icing sugar. Serve warm with the remaining strawberries on the side.

69 *Warm raspberry cupcakes*

Replace the strawberry jam with raspberry jam and decorate with fresh raspberries.

70 *Warm peach cupcakes*

Replace the strawberry jam with a few well-drained canned peach slices and decorate with extra peach slices.

Preheat the oven to 180°C/350°F/Gas Mark 4. Grease 6 x 200-ml/7-fl oz heavy round teacups with butter. Spoon 2 teaspoons of the strawberry jam into the bottom of each teacup.

Place the butter and sugar in a large bowl and beat together until light and fluffy. Gradually add the eggs, beating well after each addition, then add the vanilla extract. Sift in the flour and fold into the mixture. Spoon the mixture into the teacups.

Stand the cups in a roasting tin, then pour in enough hot water to come one third up the sides of the cups. Bake in the preheated oven for 40 minutes, or until well risen and golden brown, and a skewer, inserted

2 slices canned pineapple in natural
juice
85 g/3 oz butter, softened, or soft
margarine
85 g/3 oz caster sugar
1 large egg, lightly beaten
85 g/3 oz self-raising flour

FROSTING
25 g/1 oz butter, softened
100 g/3½ oz soft cream cheese
grated rind of 1 lemon or lime
100 g/3½ oz icing sugar
1 tsp lemon juice or lime juice

Preheat the oven to 180°C/350°F/Gas Mark 4. Line a 12-hole bun tin with 12 paper cases. Drain the pineapple, reserving the juice.

Finely chop the pineapple slices. Place the butter and sugar in a large bowl and beat together until light and fluffy, then gradually beat in the egg. Add the flour and fold into the mixture. Fold in the chopped pineapple and 1 tablespoon of the reserved pineapple juice. Spoon the mixture into the paper cases.

Bake in the preheated oven for 20 minutes, or until well risen and golden brown. Transfer to a wire rack to cool completely.

To make the frosting, place the butter and cream cheese in a large bowl and beat together until smooth, then add the lemon or lime rind.

Sift the icing sugar into the mixture and beat together until well mixed. Gradually beat in the lemon or lime juice, adding enough to form a spreading consistency.

When the cupcakes are cold, spread the frosting on top of each cake, or fill a piping bag fitted with a large star nozzle and pipe the frosting on top.

72 *Pina colada cupcakes*

Add 25 g/1 oz desiccated coconut and an extra ½ tablespoon of pineapple juice to the cake mixture. For the frosting, beat 2 tablespoons of desiccated coconut into the frosting and replace the lemon or lime juice with rum.

73 *Shredded orange cupcakes*

85 g/3 oz butter, softened, or soft
margarine
85 g/3 oz caster sugar
1 large egg, lightly beaten
85 g/3 oz self-raising flour
25 g/1 oz ground almonds
grated rind and juice of 1 small
orange

TOPPING
1 orange
55 g/2 oz caster sugar
15 g/½ oz toasted flaked almonds

Preheat the oven to 180°C/350°F/
Gas Mark 4. Line a 12-hole bun
tin with 12 paper cases. Place
the butter and sugar in a large
bowl and beat together until light
and fluffy, then gradually beat in
the egg. Add the flour, ground
almonds and orange rind and fold
into the mixture, then fold in the
orange juice. Spoon the mixture
into the paper cases.

Bake in the preheated oven for
20–25 minutes, or until well risen
and golden brown.

Meanwhile, make the topping.
Using a citrus zester, pare the rind
from the orange, then squeeze
the juice. Place the rind, juice
and sugar in a saucepan and heat
gently, stirring, until the sugar has
dissolved, then leave to simmer
for 5 minutes.

When the cupcakes are cooked,
prick them all over with a skewer
and spoon the warm syrup and
rind over each cake.

Scatter the flaked almonds on
top and transfer to a wire rack to
cool completely.

74 *Shredded lemon cupcakes*

Replace the orange rind and juice with lemon rind and juice.

75 *Lime & coconut cupcakes*

Replace the orange rind and juice in the cake with the rind and juice of
1½ limes. Add 25 g/1 oz desiccated coconut to the mixture. For the topping
use the pared rind of 1 lime and the juice of 2 limes in place of the orange
rind and juice. Replace the flaked almonds with toasted desiccated coconut.

76 *Mocha cupcakes with whipped cream*

2 tbsp instant espresso coffee powder
85 g/3 oz butter
85 g/3 oz caster sugar
1 tbsp clear honey
200 ml/7 fl oz water
225 g/8 oz plain flour
2 tbsp cocoa powder
1 tsp bicarbonate of soda
3 tbsp milk
1 large egg, lightly beaten

TOPPING
225 ml/8 fl oz whipping cream
cocoa powder, for dusting

Preheat the oven to 180°C/350°F/
Gas Mark 4. Line 2 x 12-hole bun
tins with 20 paper cases. Place
the coffee powder, butter, sugar,
honey and water in a saucepan
and heat gently, stirring, until the
sugar has dissolved. Bring to the
boil, then reduce the heat and
leave to simmer for 5 minutes.
Pour into a large heatproof bowl
and leave to cool.

When the mixture has cooled,
sift in the flour and cocoa powder.
Place the bicarbonate of soda and
milk in a bowl and stir to dissolve,
then add to the mixture with
the egg and beat together until
smooth. Spoon the mixture into
the paper cases.

Bake in the preheated oven for
15–20 minutes, or until well risen
and firm to the touch. Transfer to
a wire rack to cool completely.

For the topping, place the
cream in a bowl and whip until
it holds its shape. Spoon heaped
teaspoonfuls of cream on top of
each cake, then dust lightly with
sifted cocoa powder.

77 *Mocha walnut cupcakes*

Add 40 g/1½ oz chopped walnuts to the mixture. For the topping, dissolve
2 teaspoons of coffee powder in 1 tablespoon of boiling water and leave
to cool. Lightly whip the cream until it begins to hold its shape, then add
the coffee and 2 tablespoons of icing sugar and whip until soft peaks form.
Spread on the cakes and decorate with walnut halves.

400 g/14 oz canned peach slices
in fruit juice
115 g/4 oz butter, softened
115 g/4 oz caster sugar
2 eggs, lightly beaten
115 g/4 oz self-raising flour
150 ml/5 fl oz double cream

Preheat the oven to 180°C/350°F/ Gas Mark 4. Line a 12-hole muffin tin with 12 paper cases. Drain the peaches, reserving the juice. Reserve 12 small slices and finely chop the remaining slices.

Place the butter and sugar in a large bowl and beat together until light and fluffy. Gradually beat in the eggs. Sift in the flour and fold into the mixture. Fold in the chopped peaches and 1 tablespoon of the reserved juice. Spoon the mixture into the paper cases.

Bake in the oven for 25 minutes, or until golden brown. Leave the cupcakes to cool in the tin for 10 minutes, then transfer to a wire rack to cool completely.

When ready to decorate, place the cream in a bowl and whip until soft peaks form. Spread the cream on top of the cupcakes, using a knife to form the cream into peaks. Place the reserved peach slices on top to decorate.

79 *Apricot cream cupcakes*

Use 8 apricot halves in fruit juice instead of the peach slices. Slice 4 halves into 3 slices each and reserve for decoration. Finely chop the 4 remaining apricot halves and add to the mix with 1 tablespoon of juice from the can.

80 *Dried apricot cupcakes*

Replace the can of peach slices with 85 g/3 oz finely chopped ready-to-eat dried apricots and add 1 tablespoon of orange juice to replace the fruit juice from the can. To decorate, dust lightly with sifted icing sugar.

24-carrot gold cupcakes

175 g/6 oz butter, softened, or soft
  margarine
115 g/4 oz golden caster sugar
2 eggs, lightly beaten
300 g/10 oz carrots, peeled and grated
55 g/2 oz walnuts, finely chopped
2 tbsp orange juice
grated rind of ½ orange

175 g/6 oz self-raising flour
1 tsp ground cinnamon
12 walnut halves, to decorate

FROSTING
115 g/4 oz full-fat cream cheese
225 g/8 oz icing sugar
1 tbsp orange juice

Preheat the oven to 180°C/350°F/Gas Mark 4. Line a 12-hole muffin tin with 12 paper cases. Place the butter and sugar in a large bowl and beat together until light and fluffy, then gradually beat in the eggs. Fold in the grated carrots, walnuts, and orange juice and rind. Sift in the flour and cinnamon and fold into the mixture until just combined. Spoon the mixture into the paper cases.

Bake in the preheated oven for 15–20 minutes, or until golden and springy to the touch. Transfer to a wire rack to cool completely.

To make the frosting, place the cream cheese, icing sugar and orange juice in a bowl and beat together. Spread over the top of the cakes, then decorate with walnut halves.

82 *9-carrot gold cupcakes*

Use 85 g/3 oz grated carrot and 85 g/3 oz grated courgettes, and replace the walnuts with 55 g/2 oz sultanas. Decorate the top of each cake with a pecan nut.

Pure indulgence almond cupcakes

100 g/3½ oz butter, softened
100 g/3½ oz caster sugar
2 eggs, lightly beaten
¼ tsp almond extract
4 tbsp single cream
175 g/6 oz plain flour
1½ tsp baking powder
70 g/2½ oz ground almonds

TOPPING
115 g/4 oz butter, softened
225 g/8 oz icing sugar
few drops of almond extract
25 g/1 oz toasted flaked almonds

Preheat the oven to 180°C/350°F/Gas Mark 4. Line a 12-hole muffin tin with 12 paper cases. Place the butter and sugar in a large bowl and beat together until light and fluffy. Gradually beat in the eggs, then add the almond extract and cream. Sift in the flour and baking powder and fold into the mixture, then fold in the ground almonds. Spoon the mixture into the paper cases.

Bake in the preheated oven for 25 minutes, or until golden brown and firm to the touch. Leave the cupcakes to cool in the tin for 10 minutes, then transfer to a wire rack to cool completely.

To make the icing, place the butter in a large bowl and beat until creamy. Sift in the icing sugar. Add the almond extract and beat together until smooth. Spread the icing on top of each cake, using a knife to form the icing into swirls. Sprinkle the flaked almonds over the top.

84 *'99' cupcakes*

175 g/6 oz butter, softened, or soft
   margarine
175 g/6 oz caster sugar
1 tsp vanilla extract
3 eggs, lightly beaten
55 g/2 oz ground almonds
150 g/5 oz self-raising flour

TOPPING
1 quantity buttercream icing (page 10)
8 mini chocolate flakes
sugar sprinkles
seedless raspberry jam (optional)

Preheat the oven to 180°C/350°F/Gas Mark 4. Line a 12-hole muffin tin with 8 paper cases. Place the butter and sugar in a large bowl amd beat together until light and fluffy, then beat in the vanilla extract. Gradually beat in the eggs, then fold in the almonds and flour. Spoon the mixture into the paper cases, peaking the mixture slightly in the middle.

Bake in the preheated oven for 20–25 minutes, or until golden and springy to the touch. Transfer to a wire rack to cool completely.

Spoon the buttercream into a piping bag fitted with a large star nozzle and pipe the icing over the cakes to peak like an ice-cream cone. Press a flake into each cake and scatter a few sprinkles on top. Warm the raspberry jam and drizzle a little over each cake, if liked.

85 *Chocolate '99' cupcakes*

Replace 25 g/1 oz flour with cocoa powder. Decorate with chocolate buttercream icing (page 10), chocolate sugar strands and a drizzle of chocolate sauce.

86 *Buttermilk & orange cupcakes*

140 g/5 oz soft dark brown sugar
240 g/8½ oz butter, softened
2 eggs, lightly beaten
200 g/7 oz plain flour
¾ tsp baking powder
½ tsp bicarbonate of soda

125 ml/4 fl oz buttermilk

ICING
225 g/8 oz icing sugar
finely grated rind of 2 oranges, plus
   1 tbsp juice

Preheat the oven to 180°C/350°F/Gas Mark 4. Line a 12-hole muffin tin with 12 paper cases. Place the brown sugar and 125 g/4½ oz of the butter in a large bowl and beat together until light and fluffy, then gradually beat in the eggs. Sift in the flour, baking powder and bicarbonate of soda and fold into the mixture, then fold in the buttermilk and grated orange rind of 1 orange. Spoon the mixture into the paper cases.

Bake in the preheated oven for 30 minutes, or until firm to the touch. Leave the cupcakes to cool in the tin for 10 minutes, then transfer to a wire rack to cool completely.

To make the icing, place the remaining butter in a large bowl and beat until fluffy. Sift in the icing sugar. Add the remaining orange rind and the juice and beat together until smooth.

When the cupcakes are cold, spread the icing on top, using a knife to form the icing into swirls.

100 g/3½ oz butter, softened, or soft margarine
100 g/3½ oz caster sugar
2 large eggs
100 g/3½ oz self-raising flour
100 g/3½ oz plain chocolate chips

Preheat the oven to 190°C/375°F/ Gas Mark 5. Line a 12-hole bun tin with 12 paper cases. Place the butter, sugar, eggs and flour in a large bowl and beat together until just smooth. Fold in the chocolate chips. Spoon the mixture into the paper cases.

Bake in the preheated oven for 15–20 minutes, or until well risen and golden brown. Transfer to a wire rack to cool completely.

88 *Triple chocolate cupcakes*

Reduce the flour to 85 g/3 oz and add 2 tablespoons of cocoa powder. Use a mixture of milk, white and plain chocolate chips.

89 *Butterscotch & peanut cupcakes*

Replace the chocolate chips with butterscotch-flavoured chips and add 40 g/1½ oz chopped peanuts to the mixture.

90 *With fudge frosting*

To make the frosting, place 40 g/1½ oz butter and 2 tablespoons of milk in a saucepan and heat, stirring, until the butter melts. Add 185 g/6½ oz icing sugar and 1½ tablespoons of cocoa powder and beat until smooth. Leave to cool slightly, then use to cover the cakes.

91 Fresh raspberry cupcakes

275 g/9½ oz fresh raspberries
150 ml/5 fl oz sunflower oil
2 eggs
140 g/5 oz caster sugar
½ tsp vanilla extract
275 g/9½ oz plain flour
¾ tsp bicarbonate of soda

TOPPING
150 ml/5 fl oz double cream
12 fresh raspberries
small mint leaves, to decorate

Preheat the oven to 180°C/350°F/Gas Mark 4. Line a 12-hole muffin tin with 12 paper cases. Place the raspberries in a large bowl and crush lightly with a fork.

Place the oil, eggs, sugar and vanilla extract in a large bowl and whisk together until well combined. Sift in the flour and bicarbonate of soda and fold into the mixture, then fold in the crushed raspberries. Spoon the mixture into the paper cases.

Bake in the preheated oven for 30 minutes, or until golden brown and firm to the touch. Leave the cupcakes to cool in the tin for 10 minutes, then transfer to a wire rack to cool completely.

When ready to decorate, place the cream in a bowl and whip until soft peaks form. Spread the cream on top of the cupcakes, using a knife to smooth the cream. Top each cupcake with a raspberry and decorate with mint leaves.

92 Fresh strawberry cupcakes

Replace the raspberries with the same quantity of strawberries and add the grated rind of 1 small orange to the mixture. If preferred, place the whipped cream into a piping bag fitted with a large star nozzle, and pipe the cream on top of the cupcakes to decorate.

93 Blueberry cupcakes

125 g/4½ oz butter, softened
140 g/5 oz caster sugar
2 eggs, lightly beaten
140 g/5 oz plain flour
½ tsp baking powder

125 g/4½ oz ready-to-eat dried
  blueberries
2 tbsp milk
icing sugar, for dusting

Preheat the oven to 180°C/350°F/Gas Mark 4. Line a 12-hole muffin tin with 12 paper cases. Place the butter and sugar in a large bowl and beat together until light and fluffy, then gradually beat in the eggs. Sift in the flour and baking powder and fold into the mixture, then fold in the blueberries and milk. Spoon the mixture into the paper cases.

Bake in the preheated oven for 25 minutes, or until golden brown and firm to the touch. Leave the cupcakes to cool in the tin for 10 minutes, then transfer to a wire rack to cool completely.

When the cupcakes are cold, dust with sifted icing sugar.

150 g/5½ oz butter, softened, or soft
   margarine
150 g/5½ oz caster sugar
1 tsp vanilla extract
2 large eggs, lightly beaten
140 g/5 oz self-raising flour
40 g/1½ oz cornflour

TO DECORATE
115 g/4 oz ready-to-roll fondant icing
yellow and green food colourings
300 g/10½ oz icing sugar
about 3 tbsp cold water
coloured sugar strands

Preheat the oven to 190°C/375°F/Gas Mark 5. Line 2 x 12-hole bun tins with 24 paper cases. Place the butter and sugar in a large bowl and beat together until light and fluffy, then beat in the vanilla extract. Gradually beat in the eggs. Sift in the flour and cornflour and fold into the mixture. Spoon the mixture into the paper cases.

Bake in the preheated oven for 12–15 minutes, or until golden and springy to the touch. Transfer to a wire rack to cool completely.

To decorate, divide the fondant in half and colour one half pale yellow. Roll out both halves, then use the sides of a round pastry cutter to cut out white and yellow petal shapes. Set aside.

Sift the icing sugar into a bowl and mix with the water until smooth. Place half of the icing in a small piping bag fitted with a small plain nozzle. Divide the remaining icing in half and colour one portion yellow and the other green.

Cover 12 cakes with yellow icing and 12 with green icing. Arrange white petals on top of the yellow icing to form flowers. Pipe a little blob of white icing into the centre of each flower, then sprinkle a few coloured sugar strands on top of the white icing to form the centre of the flower. Arrange the yellow petals on the green icing and decorate in the same way. Leave to set.

175 g/6 oz self-raising flour
1 tsp baking powder
175 g/6 oz caster sugar
175 g/6 oz very soft butter, cut into
   small pieces
3 eggs
1 tsp vanilla extract
2 tbsp milk

TO DECORATE
200 g/7 oz icing sugar
1 tbsp lemon juice
1–2 tbsp water
few drops of blue and green food
   colouring
white chocolate buttons
white chocolate rainbow buttons
jelly bug sweets

Preheat the oven to 180°C/350°F/Gas Mark 4. Line a 12-hole bun tin with 12 paper cases. Sift the flour, baking powder and sugar into a bowl. Add the butter, eggs, vanilla extract and milk and beat together until creamy. Spoon the mixture into the paper cases. Bake in the preheated oven for 15–20 minutes, or until risen and golden. Transfer to a wire rack to cool.

Place the icing sugar, lemon juice and water in a bowl and mix together until smooth. Colour half of the icing blue and half of the icing green. Spread the icing over the cakes. For flower cakes, place a white chocolate button in the centre and the rainbow ones around it. For bug cakes, pipe a leaf with green icing on each cake and top with a jelly bug.

175 g/6 oz butter, softened, or soft
    margarine
175 g/6 oz caster sugar
1 tsp vanilla extract
3 eggs, lightly beaten
55 g/2 oz desiccated coconut
150 g/5½ oz self-raising flour

TO DECORATE
1½ tsp cocoa powder
55 g/2 oz icing sugar
about 300 g/10½ oz ready-to-roll
    fondant icing
food colouring, such as pink, yellow,
    brown and black

Preheat the oven to 180°C/350°F/ Gas Mark 4. Line a 12-hole muffin tin with 9 paper cases. Place the butter and sugar in a large bowl and beat together until light and fluffy, then beat in the vanilla extract. Gradually beat in the eggs, then fold in the coconut and flour. Spoon the mixture into the paper cases. Bake in the preheated oven for 20–25 minutes, or until golden and springy to the touch. Transfer to a wire rack to cool completely.

To decorate, sift the cocoa powder and icing sugar into a small bowl and add enough cold water to mix to a smooth, thick icing. Spoon into a small piping bag fitted with a writing nozzle. Leave a small piece of fondant icing white and colour a small piece pink. Divide the remainder into 2 large pieces and one smaller piece. Colour one large piece grey, using a small amount of black food colouring, and the other yellow, and the small piece brown.

To make the elephants, roll out the grey icing and cut out 3 circles to fit the tops of the cake. To make the ears, cut out 6 circles and cut away one third of each circle. Roll out the pink icing and cut out 6 smaller circles, then cut away one third of each circle. Place on top of the grey circles, pinch in the centre and sides and fix to the cakes with a little water. Roll a little grey icing into a sausage shape to make the trunks and secure on the cakes with a little water. With a little white icing, make the eyes and tusks and secure to the cake. Pipe the eyes and eyebrows with the cocoa icing.

To make the monkeys, roll and cut out 3 circles of brown icing to fit the tops of the cake. Cut out the ears from brown icing and make the centres of the ears with pink icing. Secure to the cake by dampening with a little water. Cut out a circle of yellow icing and cut out a small nick at the top, shape into the monkey's face and secure to the cake. Make the eyes with a little white icing and pipe on the remaining features.

To make the lions, cut out 3 circles of yellow icing to fit the tops of the cake. Make the ears with brown and pink icing and secure to the cakes. Make the nose with brown icing and pipe on the features and the curly mane.

55 g/2 oz sultanas
grated rind and juice of ½ orange
115 g/4 oz butter, softened, or soft
    margarine
115 g/4 oz caster sugar
½ tsp vanilla extract
2 eggs, lightly beaten
175 g/6 oz self-raising flour
¼ quantity buttercream
    icing (page 10)

TO DECORATE
250 g/9 oz icing sugar, sifted
2–3 tbsp orange juice
sugar animal cake decorations

Preheat the oven to 180°C/350°F/Gas Mark 4. Line 2 x 12-hole bun tins with 15 paper cases. Place the sultanas in a saucepan with the orange rind and juice and gently heat until almost boiling. Remove from the heat and leave to cool.

Place the butter and sugar in a large bowl and beat together until light and fluffy, then beat in the vanilla extract. Gradually beat in the eggs, then fold in the sultanas and the juice. Sift in the flour and fold into the mixture. Spoon the mixture into the paper cases.

Bake in the preheated oven for 15–20 minutes, or until golden and springy to the touch. Transfer to a wire rack to cool completely.

To make the glacé icing, sift the icing sugar in a bowl and add enough orange juice to mix to a smooth coating consistency. Cover the cakes with the icing and leave to set.

To decorate, pipe a rosette of buttercream on the cakes and top with a sugar animal decoration.

175 g/6 oz butter, softened, or soft
  margarine
175 g/6 oz caster sugar
1 tsp vanilla extract
3 eggs, lightly beaten
150 g/5 oz raspberries
225 g/8 oz self-raising flour

TO DECORATE
1 quantity buttercream icing (page 10)
pink, black, red and yellow food
  colouring
2–3 oz ready-to-roll fondant icing
silver dragées
jelly sweets

Preheat the oven to 180°C/350°F/
Gas Mark 4. Line a 12-hole muffin
tin with 10 paper cases. Place the
butter and sugar in a large bowl
and beat together until light and
fluffy, then beat in the vanilla
extract.

Gradually beat in the eggs,
then fold the raspberries and
flour into the mixture. Spoon the
mixture into the paper cases.

Bake in the preheated oven for
20–25 minutes, or until golden
and springy to the touch. Transfer
to a wire rack to cool completely.

To decorate, colour the
buttercream pale pink, then
place in a piping bag fitted with
a large star nozzle and pipe the
buttercream on top of the cakes.

Colour the fondant and then
mould into different shapes, such
as handbags, high-heeled shoes or
rings. Arrange the shapes on the
cupcakes, then press silver dragées
into the icing to form the handle
of the bag and to decorate the
shoes. Use jelly sweets to make
the gems on the rings.

99 *Easy bling cupcakes*

To save time you can decorate the cakes with non-edible cake decorations:
look out for shoes, champagne bottles or plastic rings and jewellery.
Remember to remind people to remove them before eating. These would
not be suitable to serve to young children.

175 g/6 oz plain flour
20 g/¾ oz cocoa powder
¾ tsp bicarbonate of soda
200 g/7 oz caster sugar
50 ml/2 fl oz sunflower oil
175 ml/6 fl oz water

2 tsp white vinegar
½ tsp vanilla extract
150 g/5½ oz full-fat soft cream cheese
1 egg, lightly beaten
100 g/3½ oz plain chocolate chips

Preheat the oven to 180°C/350°F/Gas Mark 4. Line a 12-hole muffin
tin with 12 paper cases. Sift together the flour, cocoa powder and
bicarbonate of soda into a large bowl. Stir 150 g/5½ oz of the sugar into
the flour. Add the oil, water, vinegar and vanilla extract and stir well
together until combined.

Place the remaining sugar, cream cheese and egg in a large bowl and
beat together until well mixed. Stir in the chocolate chips.

Spoon the chocolate mixture into the paper cases and top each with
a spoonful of the cream cheese mixture.

Bake in the preheated oven for 25 minutes, or until firm to the
touch. Leave the cupcakes to cool in the tin for 10 minutes, then
transfer to a wire rack to cool completely.

101 *Lemon cheesecake cupcakes*

MAKES 12

60 g/2¼ oz butter
125 g/4½ oz digestive biscuits, crushed
85 g/3 oz caster sugar
275 g/9¾ oz full-fat soft cream cheese
2 large eggs

finely grated rind of 1 large lemon
2 tsp lemon juice
125 ml/4 fl oz soured cream
35 g/1¼ oz plain flour
2 small lemons, thinly sliced, to decorate

Preheat the oven to 160°C/325°F/Gas Mark 3. Line a 12-hole muffin tin with 12 paper cases. Place the butter in a saucepan and heat gently until melted. Remove from the heat, then add the crushed biscuits and 1 tablespoon of the sugar and mix well. Divide the biscuit mixture among the paper cases and press down firmly with the back of a teaspoon. Chill in the refrigerator.

Meanwhile, place the remaining sugar, cream cheese and eggs in a large bowl and beat together until smooth. Add the lemon rind and juice, and the soured cream and beat together until combined. Add the flour and beat well. Spoon the mixture into the paper cases.

Bake in the preheated oven for 30 minutes, or until set but not browned. Leave the cupcakes to cool for 20 minutes, then transfer to a wire rack to cool completely.

When the cupcakes are cold, chill in the refrigerator for at least 3 hours. Decorate each cupcake with a twisted lemon slice.

102 *Orange cheesecake cupcakes*

Replace the lemon rind and juice with orange rind and juice, and decorate each cupcake with a twisted orange slice.

103 *Easter cupcakes*

MAKES 12

115 g/4 oz butter, softened, or soft margarine
115 g/4 oz caster sugar
2 eggs, lightly beaten
85 g/3 oz self-raising flour
25 g/1 oz cocoa powder

TOPPING
85 g/3 oz butter, softened
175 g/6 oz icing sugar
1 tbsp milk
2–3 drops vanilla extract
2 x 130-g/4¾-oz packets mini sugar-coated chocolate eggs

Preheat the oven to 180°C/350°F/Gas Mark 4. Line a 12-hole bun tin with 12 paper cases.

Place the butter and sugar in a large bowl and beat together until light and fluffy, then gradually beat in the eggs. Sift in the flour and cocoa powder and fold into the mixture. Spoon the mixture into the paper cases.

Bake in the preheated oven for 15–20 minutes, or until well risen and firm to the touch. Transfer to a wire rack to cool.

To make the buttercream topping, place the butter in a bowl and beat until fluffy. Sift in the icing sugar and beat together until well mixed, adding the milk and vanilla extract.

When the cupcakes are cold, place the icing in a piping bag, fitted with a large star nozzle and pipe a circle around the edge of each cupcake to form a nest. Place chocolate eggs in the centre of each nest to decorate.

104 *Flaky Easter cupcakes*

Lightly crumble chocolate flakes and gently press into the buttercream topping around the edge of the cakes.

105 *Really chocolatey Easter cupcakes*

Add 85 g/3 oz chocolate chips to the cake mixture. Top the cupcakes with chocolate buttercream icing (page 10) and press a crumbled flake into the icing.

125 g/4½ oz butter, softened
200 g/7 oz caster sugar
4–6 drops almond extract
4 eggs, lightly beaten
150 g/5½ oz self-raising flour
175 g/6 oz ground almonds

TOPPING
450 g/1 lb white ready-to-roll fondant icing
55 g/2 oz green ready-to-roll coloured fondant icing
25 g/1 oz red ready-to-roll coloured fondant icing
icing sugar, for dusting

Preheat the oven to 180°C/350°F/Gas Mark 4. Line a 12-hole muffin tin with 12 paper cases. Place the butter, sugar and almond extract in a large bowl and beat together until light and fluffy, then gradually beat in the eggs. Sift in the flour and fold into the mixture, then fold in the ground almonds. Spoon the mixture into the paper cases.

Bake in the preheated oven for 20 minutes, or until well risen, golden brown and firm to the touch. Transfer to a wire rack to cool completely.

When the cupcakes are cold, knead the white icing until pliable, then roll out on a surface lightly dusted with icing sugar. Cut out 12 circles with a 7-cm/2¾-inch plain round cutter, re-rolling the icing as necessary. Place a circle on top of each cupcake.

Roll out the green icing on a surface lightly dusted with icing sugar. Using the palm of your hand, rub icing sugar into the icing to prevent it from spotting. Cut out 24 leaves with a holly leaf-shaped cutter, re-rolling the icing as necessary. Brush each leaf with a little cooled boiled water and place 2 leaves on top of each cupcake. Roll the red icing between the palms of your hands to form 36 berries and place 3 in the centre of the leaves on each cake, to decorate.

107 *Spicy Christmas cupcakes*

Add 1 teaspoon of mixed spice to the cake mixture. To decorate, cover the cakes with the white ready-to-roll icing. Use green fondant icing to cut out Christmas tree shapes and use yellow fondant icing to make a star for the top of the trees.

108 *Marzipan & fruit cupcakes*

Add 55 g/2 oz mixed dried fruit to the cake mixture. To decorate, roll out some marzipan and cut out star shapes. Brush the tops of the cakes with a little warmed apricot jam and arrange marzipan stars on top.

115 g/4 oz butter, softened, or soft margarine
115 g/4 oz caster sugar
2 eggs
115 g/4 oz self-raising flour

TOPPING
200 g/7 oz orange ready-to-roll coloured fondant icing
icing sugar, for dusting
55 g/2 oz black ready-to-roll coloured fondant icing
black writing icing
white writing icing

Preheat the oven to 180°C/350°F/ Gas Mark 4. Line a 12-hole bun tin with 12 paper baking cases. Place the butter, sugar, eggs and flour in a large bowl and beat together until smooth. Spoon the mixture into the paper cases.

Bake in the preheated oven for 15–20 minutes, or until well risen, golden brown and firm to the touch. Transfer to a wire rack to cool completely.

When the cupcakes are cold, knead the orange icing until pliable, then roll out on a surface dusted with icing sugar. Rub icing sugar into the icing to prevent it from spotting.

Cut out 12 circles with a 5.5-cm/2¼-inch round cutter, re-rolling the icing as necessary. Place a circle on top of each cake.

Roll out the black icing on a surface dusted with icing sugar. Rub icing sugar into the icing to prevent spotting. Cut out 12 circles with a 3-cm/1¼-inch round cutter and place them in the centre of the cakes. Using lack writing icing, pipe 8 legs onto each spider and draw eyes and a mouth with white writing icing.

110 *Pumpkin-decorated cupcakes*

Cover the cakes with white fondant icing. Use orange fondant icing to cut out and make pumpkin shapes. Pipe on the stems of the pumpkins with green writing icing and pipe a jagged mouth and eyes on the pumpkin with black writing icing.

111 *Spider web cupcakes*

Melt 55 g/2 oz plain chocolate and spoon into a piping bag fitted with a writing nozzle. Cover the cakes with glacé icing (page 10). Pipe circles of chocolate onto the cakes and, using a skewer, quickly drag the icing from the centre to the outside of the cakes several times to feather the chocolate into a spider web design.

112 *Valentine heart cupcakes*

MAKES 6

85 g/3 oz butter, softened, or soft margarine
85 g/3 oz caster sugar
½ tsp vanilla extract
2 eggs, lightly beaten
70 g/2½ oz plain flour
1 tbsp cocoa powder
1 tsp baking powder

MARZIPAN HEARTS
icing sugar, for dusting
35 g/1¼ oz marzipan
red food colouring (liquid or paste)

TOPPING
55 g/2 oz butter, softened
115 g/4 oz icing sugar
25 g/1 oz plain chocolate, melted
6 chocolate flower decorations

To make the hearts, line a baking sheet with baking paper and lightly dust with icing sugar. Knead the marzipan until pliable, then add a few drops of red colouring and knead until evenly coloured. Roll out the marzipan to a thickness of 5 mm/¼ inch on a surface dusted with icing sugar. Cut out 6 hearts with a small heart-shaped cutter and place on the sheet. Leave for 3–4 hours.

To make the cupcakes, preheat the oven to 180°C/350°F/Gas Mark 4. Line a 12-hole muffin tin with 6 paper cases. Place the butter, sugar and vanilla extract in a large bowl and beat together until light and fluffy, then gradually beat in the eggs. Sift in the flour, cocoa and baking powder and fold into the mixture. Spoon the mixture into the paper cases.

Bake in the preheated oven for 20–25 minutes, or until well risen and firm to the touch. Transfer to a wire rack to cool completely.

To make the topping, place the butter in a bowl and beat until fluffy. Sift in the icing sugar and beat until smooth. Add the melted chocolate and beat until mixed. Spread the icing on top of each cake and decorate with a chocolate flower.

113 *Cherry & vanilla heart cupcakes*

Increase the vanilla extract to 1 teaspoon and the flour to 85 g/3 oz. Omit the cocoa powder and add 40 g/1½ oz quartered glacé cherries. Decorate with vanilla buttercream icing instead of chocolate buttercream icing.

225 g/8 oz butter, softened
225 g/8 oz caster sugar
1 tsp vanilla extract
4 large eggs, lightly beaten
225 g/8 oz self-raising flour
5 tbsp milk

TOPPING
175 g/6 oz butter
350 g/12 oz icing sugar
25 g/1 oz silver or gold dragées

Preheat the oven to 180°C/350°F/Gas Mark 4. Line 2 x 12-hole bun tins with 24 silver or gold foil cake cases. Place the butter, sugar and vanilla extract in a large bowl and beat together until light and fluffy, then gradually beat in the eggs. Sift in the flour and fold into the mixture with the milk. Spoon the mixture into the foil cases.

Bake in the preheated oven for 15–20 minutes, or until well risen and firm to the touch. Transfer to a wire rack to cool completely.

To make the topping, place the butter in a large bowl and beat until fluffy. Sift in the icing sugar and beat together until well mixed. Place the topping in a piping bag fitted with a medium star-shaped nozzle.

When the cupcakes are cold, pipe circles of icing on top of each cake to cover the tops and sprinkle over the silver or gold dragées.

115 *Ruby wedding cupcakes*

Add 55 g/2 oz quartered glacé cherries to the cake mixture and decorate as before using red dragées

140 g/5 oz butter, softened, or soft
    margarine
140 g/5 oz caster sugar
1 tsp vanilla extract
3 eggs, lightly beaten
150 g/5½ oz self-raising flour
55 g/2 oz cocoa powder

TOPPING
1 quantity chocolate buttercream icing
    (page 10)
85 g/3 oz mini marshmallows
40 g/1½ oz walnuts, roughly chopped
55 g/2 oz milk chocolate or plain
    chocolate, broken into pieces

Preheat the oven to 180°C/350°F/Gas Mark 4. Line a 12-hole muffin tin with 10 paper cases. Place the butter and sugar in a large bowl and beat together until light and fluffy, then beat in the vanilla extract. Gradually beat in the eggs. Sift the flour and cocoa powder together and fold into the mixture. Spoon the mixture into the paper cases.

Bake in the preheated oven for 20–25 minutes, or until golden and springy to the touch. Transfer to a wire rack to cool completely.

To decorate, pipe the buttercream icing on top of each cake to form a peak in the centre. Mix the marshmallows and walnuts together and divide among the cakes, then press down lightly. Place the chocolate in a heatproof bowl, set the bowl over a saucepan of gently simmering water and heat until melted. Drizzle over the tops of the cakes and leave to set.

Baby shower cupcakes with sugared almonds

400 g/14 oz butter, softened
400 g/14 oz caster sugar
finely grated rind of 2 lemons
8 eggs, lightly beaten
400 g/14 oz self-raising flour

TOPPING
350 g/12 oz icing sugar
6–8 tsp hot water
red or blue food colouring (liquid
   or paste)
24 sugared almonds

Preheat the oven to 180°C/350°F/Gas Mark 4. Line 2 x 12-hole bun tins with 24 paper cases. Place the butter, sugar and lemon rind in a large bowl and beat together until light and fluffy, then gradually beat in the eggs. Sift in the flour and fold into the mixture. Spoon the mixture into the paper cases.

Bake in the preheated oven for 20–25 minutes, or until well risen, golden brown and firm to the touch. Transfer to a wire rack to cool.

When the cakes are cold, make the topping. Sift the icing sugar into a bowl, add the hot water and stir until smooth and thick enough to coat the back of a wooden spoon. Dip a skewer into the red or blue food colouring and stir it into the icing until it is evenly coloured pink or pale blue. Spoon the icing on top of each cake. Top each with a sugared almond and leave to set for about 30 minutes.

118 ### Scented baby shower cupcakes

Omit the lemon rind and add 1 tablespoon of chopped lavender or rosemary to the cake mixture after beating in the eggs. Decorate as before or with confetti-type sugar sprinkles.

119 ## Chocolate brownie cupcakes

225 g/8 oz plain chocolate, broken into
   pieces
85 g/3 oz butter
2 large eggs
200 g/7 oz soft dark brown sugar

1 tsp vanilla extract
140 g/5 oz plain flour
75g/2¾ oz walnuts, chopped into
   small pieces

Preheat the oven to 180°C/350°F/Gas Mark 4. Line a 12-hole muffin tin with 12 paper cases. Place the chocolate and butter in a saucepan and heat gently, stirring constantly, until melted. Remove from the heat and stir until smooth. Leave to cool slightly.

Place the eggs and sugar in a large bowl and whisk together, then add the vanilla extract. Stir in the flour until mixed together, then stir the melted chocolate into the mixture until combined. Stir in the chopped walnuts. Spoon the mixture into the paper cases.

Bake in the preheated oven for 30 minutes, or until firm to the touch but still slightly moist in the centre. Leave the cupcakes to cool for 10 minutes, then transfer to a wire rack to cool completely.

70 g/2½ oz plain chocolate, broken into
    pieces, plus extra to decorate
140 g/5 oz butter
140 g/5 oz caster sugar
2 large eggs, lightly beaten
2 tbsp brandy
175 g/6 oz self-raising flour
1 tbsp cocoa powder

TOPPING
200 ml/7 fl oz double cream
1 tbsp icing sugar
1 tbsp brandy
9 large ripe strawberries

Preheat the oven to 180°C/350°F/Gas Mark 4. Line a 12-hole muffin tin with 9 paper cases. Place the chocolate in a heatproof bowl, set the bowl over a saucepan of gently simmering water and heat until melted. Remove from the heat and leave to cool. Place the butter and sugar in a large bowl and beat together until light and fluffy, then gradually beat in the eggs. Stir in the brandy, followed by the melted chocolate, then carefully fold in the flour. Spoon the mixture into the paper cases.

Bake in the preheated oven for 20–25 minutes, or until golden and springy to the touch. Transfer to a wire rack to cool completely.

To decorate, place the cream, sugar and brandy in a bowl and whip together until just stiff. Spoon the cream into a piping bag fitted with a star nozzle and pipe a generous swirl of cream on top of each cake, then place a strawberry on top and sprinkle with grated chocolate.

121 *Nice & naughty*

Add 115 g/4 oz raspberries to the cake mixture and decorate with extra raspberries instead of the strawberries.

122 *Warm spiced apple pie cupcakes*

MAKES 12

50 g/1¾ oz butter, softened
70 g/2½ oz demerara sugar
1 egg, lightly beaten
150 g/5½ oz plain flour
1½ tsp baking powder
½ tsp ground mixed spice
1 large cooking apple, peeled, cored
    and finely chopped
1 tbsp orange juice

TOPPING
40 g/1½ oz plain flour
½ tsp ground mixed spice
25 g/1 oz butter
40 g/1½ oz caster sugar

Preheat the oven to 180°C/350°F/Gas Mark 4. Line a 12-hole muffin tin with 12 paper cases.

To make the topping, place the flour, mixed spice, butter and sugar in a large bowl and rub in with your fingertips until the mixture resembles fine breadcrumbs. Set aside.

To make the cupcakes, place the butter and sugar in a large bowl and beat together until light and fluffy, then gradually beat in the egg. Sift in the flour, baking powder and mixed spice and fold into the mixture, then fold in the chopped apple and orange juice.

Spoon the mixture into the paper cases. Add the topping to cover the top of each cupcake and press down gently.

Bake in the preheated oven for 30 minutes, or until golden brown. Leave the cupcakes to cool in the tin for 2–3 minutes and serve warm, or leave to cool for 10 minutes and then transfer to a wire rack to cool completely.

115 g/4 oz firm courgettes
85 g/3 oz plain chocolate, broken into pieces
2 large eggs
50 g/1¾ oz soft light brown sugar
90 ml/3 fl oz sunflower oil

115 g/4 oz plain flour
½ tsp baking powder
¼ tsp bicarbonate of soda
25 g/1 oz pecan nuts, finely chopped
icing sugar, for dusting

Preheat the oven to 180°C/350°F/Gas Mark 4. Line a 12-hole muffin tin with 12 paper cases. Peel and grate the courgettes, discarding any liquid. Reserve.

Place the chocolate in a heatproof bowl, set the bowl over a saucepan of gently simmering water and heat until melted. Remove from the heat and stir until smooth. Leave to cool slightly.

Place the eggs, sugar and oil in a large bowl and whisk together. Sift in the flour, baking powder and bicarbonate of soda and stir together until mixed. Stir in the courgettes, pecan nuts and melted chocolate until combined. Spoon the mixture into the paper cases.

Bake in the preheated oven for 25 minutes, or until firm to the touch. Leave the cupcakes to cool in the tin for 10 minutes, then transfer to a wire rack to cool completely. When the cupcakes are cold, dust with sifted icing sugar.

124 *Marbled chocolate cupcakes*

MAKES 21

175 g/6 oz soft margarine
175 g/6 oz caster sugar
3 eggs
175 g/6 oz self-raising flour
2 tbsp milk
55 g/2 oz plain chocolate, melted

Preheat the oven to 180°C/350°F/ Gas Mark 4. Line 2 x 12-hole bun tins with 21 paper cases. Place the margarine, sugar, eggs, flour and milk in a large bowl and beat together until just smooth. Divide the mixture between 2 bowls. Add the melted chocolate to one and stir until mixed. Using a teaspoon, and alternating the chocolate mixture with the plain, put 4 half-teaspoons into each case.

Bake in the preheated oven for 20 minutes, or until well risen. Transfer to a wire rack to cool.

125 *Chocolate orange marbled cupcakes*

Add the grated rind and juice of ½ small orange and a few drops of orange food colouring to the plain cake mixture.

126 *Iced marbled cupcakes*

Make the cakes as usual. Sift 250 g/9 oz icing sugar into a bowl and stir in 2–3 tablespoons of water until smooth. Divide the icing in half and add 1 tablespoon of cocoa powder to one portion, adding a little extra water if required. Spoon small amounts of each icing on top of the cakes and marble together to cover the cakes with the tip of a knife.

115 g/4 oz butter, softened
115 g/4 oz caster sugar
2 eggs, lightly beaten
115 g/4 oz self-raising flour
finely grated rind of 1 lemon
1 tbsp lemon curd
100 g/3½ oz fresh raspberries

TOPPING
25 g/1 oz butter
1 tbsp soft light brown sugar
1 tbsp ground almonds
1 tbsp plain flour

Preheat the oven to 200°C/400°F/Gas Mark 6. Line a 12-hole bun tin with 12 paper cases. To make the topping, place the butter in a saucepan and heat gently until melted. Pour into a bowl and add the sugar, ground almonds and flour and stir together until combined.

To make the cupcakes, place the butter and sugar in a large bowl and beat together until light and fluffy, then gradually add the eggs. Sift in the flour and fold into the mixture. Fold in the lemon rind, lemon curd and raspberries. Spoon the mixture into the paper cases. Add the topping to cover the top of each cupcake and press down gently.

Bake in the preheated oven for 15–20 minutes, or until golden brown and firm to the touch. Leave the cupcakes to cool for 10 minutes, then transfer to a wire rack to cool completely.

300 g/10½ oz plain chocolate, broken
  into pieces
150 g/5½ oz butter, cut into cubes
250 g/9 oz golden syrup
100 g/3½ oz Brazil nuts, roughly
  chopped

100 g/3½ oz ready-to-eat dried raisins
200 g/7 oz cornflakes
18 glacé cherries, to decorate

Place 18 paper cases on a baking sheet. Place the chocolate, butter and golden syrup into a large saucepan and heat gently until the butter has melted and the ingredients are runny but not hot. Remove from the heat and stir until well mixed.

Add the chopped nuts and raisins to the pan and stir together until the fruit and nuts are covered in chocolate. Add the cornflakes and stir until combined.

Spoon the mixture evenly into the paper cases and top each with a glacé cherry. Leave to set in a cool place for 2–4 hours before serving.

Devil's food cake with chocolate frosting   MAKES 18

50 g/1¾ oz butter, softened, or soft margarine	FROSTING
115 g/4 oz soft dark brown sugar	125 g/4½ oz plain chocolate, broken into pieces
2 large eggs	2 tbsp caster sugar
115 g/4 oz plain white flour	150 ml/5 fl oz soured cream
½ tsp bicarbonate of soda	
25 g/1 oz cocoa powder	CHOCOLATE STICKS (optional)
125 ml/4 fl oz soured cream	100 g/3½ oz plain chocolate

Preheat the oven to 180°C/350°F/Gas Mark 4. Line 2 x 12-hole bun tins with 18 paper baking cases. Place the butter, sugar, eggs, flour, bicarbonate of soda and cocoa powder in a large bowl and beat together until just smooth. Fold in the soured cream. Spoon the mixture into the paper cases.

Bake in the preheated oven for 20 minutes, or until well risen and firm to the touch. Transfer to a wire rack to cool completely.

To make the frosting, place the chocolate in a heatproof bowl, set the bowl over a saucepan of gently simmering water and heat until melted. Leave to cool slightly, then whisk in the sugar and soured cream until combined. Spread the frosting over the tops of the cakes and chill in the refrigerator before serving.

Decorate with chocolate sticks made by shaving plain chocolate with a potato peeler, if liked.

Strawberry shortcakes   MAKES 6

85 g/3 oz butter, plus extra for greasing
225 g/8 oz self-raising flour, plus extra for dusting
½ tsp baking powder
100 g/3½ oz caster sugar
1 egg, lightly beaten
2–3 tbsp milk, plus extra for brushing
FILLING
1 tsp vanilla extract
250 g/9 oz mascarpone cheese
3 tbsp icing sugar, plus extra for dusting
400 g/14 oz strawberries

Preheat the oven to 180°C/350°F/Gas Mark 4. Lightly grease a large baking sheet. Sift the flour, baking powder and sugar into a bowl. Add the butter and rub it in with your fingertips until the mixture resembles breadcrumbs.

Place the egg and 2 tablespoons of the milk in a bowl and beat together, then stir in the dry ingredients with a fork to form a soft, but not sticky, dough, adding more milk if necessary. Turn the dough out onto a lightly floured work surface and roll out to about 2 cm/¾ inch thick. Cut out rounds with a 7-cm/2¾-inch biscuit cutter. Press the trimmings together and cut out more rounds. Place the rounds on the baking sheet and brush with milk.

Bake in the preheated oven for 12–15 minutes, until firm and golden brown. Transfer to a wire rack to cool.

To make the filling, stir the vanilla extract into the mascarpone cheese with 2 tablespoons of the icing sugar. Reserve a few whole strawberries, then slice the rest. Sprinkle with the remaining tablespoon of icing sugar. Split the shortcakes in half horizontally.

Spoon half the mascarpone mixture onto the bases and top with sliced strawberries. Spoon over the remaining mascarpone mixture and replace the shortcake tops. Dust with icing sugar and top with the whole strawberries.

Raspberry shortcakes

Replace the strawberries with whole raspberries and sandwich with the mascarpone filling.

85 g/3 oz butter, plus extra
for greasing
175 g/6 oz pitted dates, chopped
175 ml/6 fl oz boiling water
½ tsp bicarbonate of soda
140 g/5 oz caster sugar
1 large egg, lightly beaten
½ tsp vanilla extract
175 g/6 oz self-raising flour

TOFFEE SAUCE
85 g/3 oz soft light brown sugar
40 g/1½ oz butter
2 tbsp single cream or milk

Preheat the oven to 180°C/350°F/
Gas Mark 4. Grease and line a
20-cm/8-inch square cake
tin. Place the dates in a small
saucepan with the boiling water
and bicarbonate of soda. Heat
gently for 5 minutes, without
boiling, until the dates are soft.

Place the butter and sugar in a
large bowl and beat together until
light and fluffy. Beat in the egg,
vanilla extract and date mixture.
Sift in the flour and fold into the
mixture. Pour the mixture into
the cake tin.

Bake in the preheated oven for
40–45 minutes, or until firm to
the touch and starting to shrink
away from the sides of the tin.

To make the toffee sauce, place
the brown sugar, butter and cream
in a saucepan and heat gently
until dissolved, then simmer
gently, stirring, for 2 minutes.

Prick all over the surface of
the cake with a skewer or fork and
pour the hot toffee sauce evenly
over the top. Leave it to cool in the
tin, then cut into squares.

133 *Sticky toffee & walnut squares*

*Reduce the amount of dates to 140 g/5 oz and add 55 g/2 oz chopped walnuts
to the cake mixture with the cooked dates. A further 25 g/1 oz finely chopped
walnuts can also be added to the toffee sauce.*

134 *Sticky toffee apple squares*

*Reduce the amount of dates to 140 g/5 oz and add 1 peeled, cored and
chopped dessert apple to the cake mixture with the cooked dates.*

135 *Sticky toffee & banana squares*

Add 1 ripe mashed banana to the cake mixture after adding the dates.

136 Toffee apple cakes

55 g/2 oz butter, plus extra for greasing
2 dessert apples
1 tbsp lemon juice
250 g/9 oz plain flour
2 tsp baking powder
1½ tsp ground cinnamon
70 g/2½ oz soft light brown sugar
100 ml/3½ fl oz milk
100 ml/3½ fl oz apple juice
1 egg, lightly beaten

TOFFEE TOPPING
2 tbsp single cream
40 g/1½ oz soft light brown sugar
15 g/½ oz butter

Preheat the oven to 200°C/400°F/Gas Mark 6. Grease a 12-hole muffin tin. Core and coarsely grate one of the apples and set aside. Slice the remaining apple into 5 mm/¼ inch thick wedges and toss in the lemon juice. Sift together the flour, baking powder and cinnamon, then stir in the sugar and grated apple.

Place the butter in a saucepan and heat gently until melted, then mix with the milk, apple juice and egg. Stir the liquid mixture into the dry ingredients, mixing lightly until just combined.

Spoon the mixture into the muffin tin and arrange 2 apple slices on top of each. Bake in the preheated oven for 20–25 minutes or until risen, firm and golden brown. Run a knife round the edge of each cake to loosen, then transfer to a wire rack to cool completely.

For the topping, place all the ingredients in a small pan and heat, stirring, until the sugar is dissolved. Increase the heat and boil for 2 minutes, or until syrupy. Cool slightly, then drizzle over the cakes and leave to set.

137 Toffee pear cakes

Replace the apples with pears and the cinnamon with allspice.

138 Cinnamon rolls

100 g/3½ oz butter, melted, plus extra for greasing
350 g/12 oz self-raising flour, plus extra for dusting
pinch of salt
2 tbsp caster sugar
1 tsp ground cinnamon
2 egg yolks
200 ml/7 fl oz milk, plus extra for glazing

FILLING
1 tsp ground cinnamon
55 g/2 oz soft light brown sugar
2 tbsp caster sugar
15 g/½ oz butter, melted

ICING
125 g/4½ oz icing sugar
2 tbsp cream cheese, softened
15 g/½ oz butter, softened
about 2 tbsp boiling water
1 tsp vanilla extract

Preheat the oven to 180°C/350°F/Gas Mark 4. Grease a 20-cm/8-inch round cake tin and line the base with baking paper. Place the flour, salt, sugar and cinnamon in a large bowl and mix together. Place the butter, egg yolks and milk in a separate bowl and whisk together, then combine with the dry ingredients to form a soft dough. Turn out onto a large piece of baking paper lightly sprinkled with flour and roll out to a rectangle measuring 30 x 25 cm/12 x 10 inches.

To make the filling, mix the ingredients together, then spread over the dough and roll up like a Swiss roll, to form a log. Cut the dough into 8 even-sized slices with a sharp knife and pack into the tin. Brush gently with extra milk. Bake in the preheated oven for 30–35 minutes, or until golden brown. Leave to cool for 5 minutes before removing from the tin.

Sift the icing sugar into a large bowl and make a well in the centre. Place the cream cheese and butter in the centre, pour over the water and stir to mix. Add extra boiling water, a few drops at a time, until the icing coats the back of a spoon. Stir in the vanilla extract and drizzle over the rolls. Serve warm or cold.

139 Sultana & walnut rolls

Sprinkle 40 g/1½ oz sultanas and 25 g/1 oz chopped walnuts over the filling before rolling up.

55 g/2 oz butter, cut into pieces, plus extra for greasing
450 g/1 lb plain flour, plus extra for dusting
½ tsp salt
2 tsp baking powder
2 tbsp caster sugar
250 ml/9 fl oz milk, plus extra for brushing
strawberry jam and clotted cream, to serve

Preheat the oven to 220°C/425°F/Gas Mark 7. Grease a baking sheet. Sift the flour, salt and baking powder into a large bowl. Add the butter and rub it in with your fingertips until the mixture resembles breadcrumbs. Stir in the sugar. Stir in enough of the milk to bring the mixture together into a soft dough.

Gently roll the dough out on a lightly floured work surface until it is about 1 cm/½ inch thick. Cut out the scones with a 6-cm/2½-inch biscuit cutter and place on the baking sheet. Brush with a little milk.

Bake in the preheated oven for 10–12 minutes, or until golden and well risen. Cool on a wire rack and serve with strawberry jam and clotted cream.

141 *Fruit scones*

Stir 55 g/2 oz sultanas into the scone mixture with the sugar and serve with butter.

142 *Citrus scones*

Stir 55 g/2 oz mixed peel into the scone mixture with the sugar and serve with marmalade and cream.

143 *Lemon scones*

Stir the grated rind of 1 lemon into the scone mixture with the sugar and serve with lemon curd.

144 *Sweet walnut scones*

Add 55 g/2 oz chopped walnuts and use soft light brown sugar instead of caster sugar. Serve with butter.

145 *Chocolate scones*

70 g/2½ oz butter, cut into pieces, plus
    extra for greasing
280 g/10 oz self-raising flour
1 tbsp caster sugar

55 g/2 oz chocolate chips
150 ml/5 fl oz milk, plus extra
    for brushing
plain flour, for dusting

Preheat the oven to 220°C/425°F/Gas Mark 7. Lightly grease a baking sheet. Sift the flour into a large bowl. Add the butter and rub it in with your fingertips until the mixture resembles fine breadcrumbs. Stir in the sugar and chocolate chips, then stir in enough of the milk to bring the mixture together into a soft dough.

Roll the dough out on a lightly floured work surface to form a 10 x 15-cm/4 x 6-inch rectangle, about 2.5 cm/1 inch thick. Cut the dough into 9 rectangles and place the scones, spaced well apart, on the baking sheet. Brush the tops with a little milk.

Bake in the preheated oven for 10–12 minutes, or until risen and golden. Transfer to a wire rack to cool.

146 *Chocolate & peanut scones*

Replace 25 g/1 oz flour with cocoa powder and replace the chocolate chips with peanut-flavoured chips.

147 *London buns*

MAKES 10

oil, for greasing
500 g/1 lb 2 oz strong white bread flour
85 g/3 oz butter, cut into pieces
55 g/2 oz caster sugar
½ tsp salt
1 tsp easy-blend dried yeast
1 tsp caraway seeds (optional)

2 eggs, lightly beaten
about 150 ml/5 fl oz tepid milk
115 g/4 oz sultanas
55 g/2 oz mixed peel
beaten egg, to glaze
demerara sugar or crushed sugar cubes,
    to decorate

Lightly grease a large bowl and 2 baking sheets. Place the flour in a large bowl, add the butter and rub it in until the mixture resembles breadcrumbs. Stir in the sugar, salt, yeast and caraway seeds, if using. Add the eggs and enough milk to mix to form a soft pliable dough. Knead well for 10 minutes, then place in the lightly oiled bowl and cover loosely. Leave in a warm place to rise for about 1 hour.

Tip the dough out onto a lightly floured work surface and knead in the sultanas and mixed peel. Divide the dough into 10 pieces. Shape each piece into a ball and place on the baking sheets. Cover loosely and leave in a warm place to rise for about 45 minutes.

Preheat the oven to 200°C/400°F/Gas Mark 6. Brush the bread with the egg and sprinkle a little demerara sugar on top. Bake in the preheated oven for 12–15 minutes, or until the buns sound hollow when tapped on the bottom. Transfer to a wire rack to cool.

148 Australian lamingtons

55 g/2 oz butter, plus extra for greasing
6 eggs
150 g/5½ oz caster sugar
175 g/6 oz plain flour
250 g/9 oz desiccated coconut

ICING
500 g/1 lb 2 oz icing sugar
40 g/1½ oz cocoa powder
85 ml/3 fl oz boiling water
75 g/2¾ oz butter, melted

Preheat the oven to 180°C/350°F/Gas Mark 4. Grease a 20-cm/8-inch square cake tin and line the base with baking paper. Place the butter in a saucepan and heat gently until melted, then leave to cool slightly.

Place the eggs and sugar in a heatproof bowl, set the bowl over a pan of gently simmering water and whisk until pale and thick enough to leave a trail when the whisk is lifted. Remove from the heat, sift in the flour and fold in. Fold in the melted butter. Pour into the tin.

Bake in the preheated oven for 35–40 minutes, or until risen, golden and springy to the touch. Leave in the tin for 2–3 minutes, then turn out onto a wire rack to cool. When cold, cut the cake into 16 squares.

For the icing, sift together the icing sugar and cocoa into a bowl and stir in the water and butter until smooth. Spread out the coconut on a plate. Dip each piece of cake into the icing and coat evenly, then place in the coconut and turn to coat. Leave the cakes on baking paper to set.

149 Raspberry lamingtons

Replace the chocolate covering with raspberry jam. Gently heat 185 g/6½ oz raspberry jam in a small saucepan until runny. Brush the jam over the squares then dip in the desiccated coconut to coat evenly.

150 Cinnamon squares

225 g/8 oz butter, softened, plus extra for greasing
225 g/8 oz caster sugar
3 eggs, lightly beaten
225 g/8 oz self-raising flour

½ tsp bicarbonate of soda
1 tbsp ground cinnamon
150 ml/5 fl oz soured cream
55 g/2 oz sunflower seeds

Preheat the oven to 180°C/350°F/Gas Mark 4. Grease a 23-cm/9-inch square cake tin and line the base with baking paper.

Place the butter and sugar in a large bowl and beat together until light and fluffy, then beat in the eggs.

Sift together the flour, bicarbonate of soda and cinnamon into the mixture and fold in. Spoon in the soured cream and sunflower seeds and mix gently until well combined.

Spoon the mixture into the tin and smooth the surface with the back of a spoon or a knife.

Bake in the preheated oven for 45 minutes, or until the mixture is firm to the touch. Loosen the edges with a round-bladed knife, then transfer to a wire rack to cool completely. Slice into squares before serving.

151 Apple & cinnamon squares

Add 1 dessert apple, peeled, cored and chopped, to the mixture after beating in the eggs.

152 Seedy ginger squares

Replace the cinnamon with ground ginger and add 40 g/1½ oz chopped stem ginger after beating in the eggs.

140 g/5 oz butter, plus extra for greasing
3 eggs
1 egg yolk
1 tsp vanilla extract

140 g/5 oz caster sugar
140 g/5 oz plain flour
1 tsp baking powder

Preheat the oven to 190°C/375°F/Gas Mark 5. Lightly grease 30 holes in 3 standard-sized madeleine tins. Place the butter in a saucepan and heat until melted, then leave to cool.

Place the eggs, egg yolk, vanilla extract and sugar in a large bowl and whisk until very pale and thick. Sift in the flour and baking powder and fold in, then fold in the melted butter. Spoon the mixture into the tins.

Bake in the preheated oven for 8–10 minutes, or until risen and golden brown. Remove the cakes carefully from the tins and leave to cool on a wire rack. They are best served the day they are made.

154 *Almond madeleines*

Replace the vanilla extract with almond extract. Reduce the flour to 115 g/4 oz and fold in 25 g/1 oz ground almonds with the flour.

155 *Chocolate-dipped madeleines*

Place 225 g/8 oz plain or milk chocolate in a heatproof bowl, set the bowl over a saucepan of gently simmering water and heat until melted. Remove from the heat. Line a couple of baking sheets with baking paper. Dip the plain or almond madeleines in the chocolate to half cover, letting the excess chocolate drip back into the bowl, and place on the baking paper to set.

oil, for greasing
200 ml/7 fl oz milk
1 tsp saffron threads
500 g/1 lb 2 oz strong white bread flour
55 g/2 oz butter, cut into pieces
55 g/2 oz icing sugar

½ tsp salt
1 tsp easy-blend dried yeast
1 egg
40 raisins
beaten egg, to glaze

Lightly grease a bowl and 2 baking sheets. Heat the milk in a small saucepan until almost boiling. Add the saffron and stir, then remove from the heat and leave for 20 minutes.

Place the flour in a large bowl. Add the butter and rub it in until the mixture resembles breadcrumbs, then stir in the sugar, salt and yeast.

Add the saffron milk and egg and mix to form a soft pliable dough. Knead well for 10 minutes, then place in the lightly greased bowl and loosely cover. Leave in a warm place to rise for about 1 hour.

Knead the dough on a lightly floured work surface. Divide the dough into 10 pieces. Shape each piece into a smooth ball, then roll into a rope about 25 cm/10 inches long. Pinch the ends of each rope together, then twist into a figure-of-eight and place on the baking sheet so that the ends are in the centre and underneath. Press a couple of raisins onto each loop of the dough. Cover and leave in a warm place to rise for 45 minutes.

Preheat the oven to 200°C/400°F/Gas Mark 6. Brush the bread with an egg glaze, then bake in the preheated oven for 12–15 minutes, or until the buns sound hollow when tapped on the bottom. Transfer to a wire rack to cool completely.

157 *Saffron loaf*

After leaving to rise, knock back the dough and lightly knead. Shape into a sausage shape and place in a greased 900 g/2 lb loaf tin. Cover loosely and leave to rise until doubled in size. Bake in the preheated oven for 40–45 minutes, or until golden and the loaf sounds hollow when tapped underneath. While still warm, brush the top of the loaf with a little golden syrup, then leave to cool. Serve sliced with butter.

158 *Spanish churros*   MAKES 28

85 g/3 oz butter, cut into pieces
225 ml/8 fl oz water
6 tbsp caster sugar

150 g/5½ oz plain flour
3 eggs, lightly beaten
sunflower oil, for deep-frying

Place the butter in a saucepan with the water and 2 tablespoons of the sugar and heat gently until the butter melts. Increase the heat and bring to a rapid boil, then remove from the heat and add the flour all in one go. Beat until the mixture forms a ball. Leave to cool slightly, then gradually beat in the eggs until smooth and glossy.

Spoon the mixture into a piping bag fitted with a large star nozzle and pipe 10-cm/4-inch strips on a sheet of baking paper, then chill for 30 minutes, or until just firm.

Heat the oil in a suitable pan to 180°C/350°F. Cooking in batches, remove the churros from the baking paper and place in the hot oil. Deep-fry for 3–4 minutes, turning once until crisp and golden. Remove with a slotted spoon and drain on kitchen paper. Repeat until all the mixture has been used. Dust with the remaining sugar and leave to cool.

159 *Cinnamon churros*

Add 1 teaspoon of ground cinnamon to the sugar before dusting. If liked, 1 teaspoon of ground cinnamon can also be added to the mixture itself.

French galettes

25 g/1 oz butter, plus extra for greasing
350 g/12 oz puff pastry
plain flour, for dusting
2 eating apples, peeled, cored and thinly sliced
1 tbsp demerara sugar
½ tsp fennel seeds

Preheat the oven to 200°C/400°F/Gas Mark 6. Grease a baking sheet. Place the butter in a saucepan and heat gently until melted, then leave to cool slightly.

Roll the pastry out on a floured work surface and cut out 4 x 13-cm/5-inch rounds using a small saucer as a guide. Place on the baking sheet. Lightly score a 1-cm/½-inch border in the pastry and prick the centre of the pastry all over with a fork. Brush the pastry with the melted butter, then arrange the apple slices in a spiral in the centre of the pastry, taking care not to overlap the border. Sprinkle with sugar and fennel and brush with melted butter. Bake in the preheated oven for 25–30 minutes, or until the pastry is crisp and golden.

161 *Brandied peach galettes*

Prepare the pastry as before. Slice 3 peaches and arrange in a spiral in the centre of the pastries. Sprinkle with a little brandy and 2 tablespoons of soft light brown sugar. Dot with a little butter and bake for 20–25 minutes.

162 *Pear galettes*

Replace the apples with pears and sprinkle with a few chopped pecan nuts.

163 *Lemon & polenta berry squares*

175 g/6 oz butter, softened, plus extra for greasing
175 g/6 oz caster sugar
3 large eggs, lightly beaten
100 g/3½ oz ground almonds
150 g/5½ oz polenta
2 tsp baking powder
finely grated rind of 1 lemon
2 tbsp lemon juice
300 g/10½ oz frozen small berry fruits, such as cranberries, raspberries, blueberries, blackcurrants and redcurrants
icing sugar, to decorate

Preheat the oven to 180°C/350°F/Gas Mark 4. Grease a 23-cm/9-inch shallow square cake tin and line the base with baking paper. Place the butter and sugar in a large bowl and beat together until light and fluffy, then gradually beat the eggs into the mixture until smooth. Add the ground almonds, polenta, baking powder, lemon rind and juice and stir together until well mixed. Stir in the fruit of your choice. Spoon the mixture into the tin and spread out evenly.

Bake in the preheated oven for 45 minutes, or until golden brown and firm to the touch. Transfer to a wire rack to cool completely.

Sift icing sugar lightly over to decorate and cut into squares.

600 g/1 lb 5 oz strong white flour, plus extra for dusting
7 g/¼ oz easy-blend dried yeast
115 g/4 oz caster sugar
½ tsp salt
1 tsp ground cinnamon
85 g/3 oz butter
2 large eggs

300 ml/10 fl oz milk
oil, for greasing
1 small egg, for glazing

FILLING
6 tbsp chocolate hazelnut spread
200 g/7 oz milk chocolate, chopped

Place the flour, yeast, sugar, salt and cinnamon in a large bowl and mix together.

Place the butter in a saucepan and heat gently until melted, then leave to cool slightly. Whisk in the eggs and milk, then pour into the flour mixture and mix well to form a soft dough.

Knead the dough on a floured work surface for 10 minutes, until smooth, then place in a large floured bowl, cover with clingfilm and leave to rise in a warm place for 1½–2 hours.

When you are ready to make the buns, preheat the oven to 220°C/ 425°F/Gas Mark 7. Lightly grease 2 baking sheets. Remove the dough from the bowl and punch down. Divide the dough into 4 pieces and roll each piece into a rectangle about 2.5 cm/1 inch thick. Spread each rectangle with the chocolate hazelnut spread and scatter with the chopped chocolate. Roll up each piece from one of the long edges, then cut into 6 pieces.

Place each swirl, cut-side down, on the baking sheets and brush well with the beaten egg.

Bake in the preheated oven for 12–15 minutes or until cooked through and serve warm.

- -

165 *Extra nutty chocolate swirls*

When the dough is rolled out, spread with 9 tablespoons of chocolate hazelnut spread, then sprinkle with 140 g/5 oz chopped toasted hazelnuts.

166 *Spanish buñuelos*

MAKES 12

3 tbsp sunflower oil, plus extra for deep-frying
2 large eggs
90 ml/3¼ fl oz milk
325 g/11½ oz plain flour, plus extra for dusting

1 tsp baking powder
2 tsp soft light brown sugar
4 tbsp caster sugar
1 tsp ground cinnamon

Place the oil, eggs and milk in a large bowl and whisk together. Place the flour, baking powder and sugar in a separate bowl and mix well, then pour in the egg mixture and mix well to form a dough. Knead the dough on a lightly floured surface until very smooth.

Divide the dough into 12 and roll into balls. Flatten each into 8–10-cm/3–4-inch rounds and leave to rest for 20 minutes. Place the caster sugar and cinnamon in a bowl and mix together. Reserve.

Heat the oil in a suitable saucepan to 190°C/375°F and deep-fry

the buñuelos in batches for 2–3 minutes, or until puffed and golden on both sides, turning once. Remove with a slotted spoon and drain on kitchen paper. Repeat until all the buns are cooked. Sprinkle with the cinnamon sugar and serve warm.

sunflower oil, for greasing and cooking
450 g/1 lb strong white flour
55 g/2 oz butter, cut into pieces
25 g/1 oz caster sugar, plus extra
to dust
½ tsp salt
7 g/¼ oz sachet easy-blend dried yeast
1 egg, lightly beaten
175 ml/6 fl oz lukewarm milk
150 g/5½ oz seedless raspberry jam

Lightly grease a large bowl and 2 baking sheets. Place the flour in a large bowl, add the butter and rub it in until the mixture resembles breadcrumbs. Stir in the sugar, salt and yeast. Make a well in the centre and add the egg and milk, then mix to form a soft pliable dough. Knead well for 10 minutes, then place in the greased bowl and cover. Leave in a warm place to rise for about 1 hour.

Knead the dough on a floured work surface, then divide into 10 pieces. Shape each piece into a ball and place on the baking sheets. Cover and leave in a warm place to double in size for 45 minutes.

Heat the oil in a suitable saucepan to 180°C/350°F and deep-fry the doughnuts in 2–3 batches for 2–3 minutes on each side. Drain and dust with sugar.

Place the jam in a piping bag fitted with a plain nozzle. Insert a sharp knife into each doughnut and twist to make a hole. Push the point of the nozzle into the hole and pipe in some jam.

168 *Ring doughnuts*

After the first rise, knock back the dough and knead again. Roll out until it is 1 cm/½ inch thick. Cut 8-cm/3¼-inch circles with a round cookie cutter, then use a 2.5-cm/1-inch cutter to cut out the centre. Place on baking sheets to rise. Re-roll the dough trimmings as necessary. Deep-fry as before and dust with caster sugar mixed with ground cinnamon or spread the tops with a little glacé icing (page 10) and sprinkle with coloured sugar strands.

169 *Custard doughnuts*

Fill with ready-made custard and flavour the custard with a little melted chocolate, if liked.

170 Gingerbread

175 g/6 oz butter, plus extra for greasing
150 g/5½ oz soft dark brown sugar
175 g/6 oz golden syrup
finely grated rind and juice of 1 small orange
2 large eggs, lightly beaten
225 g/8 oz self-raising flour
100 g/3½ oz wholemeal flour
2 tsp ground ginger
40 g/1½ oz chopped glacé ginger or stem ginger
pieces of glacé ginger or stem ginger, to decorate

Preheat the oven to 180°C/350°F/Gas Mark 4. Grease a deep 23-cm/9-inch square cake tin and line the base with baking paper. Place the butter, sugar and golden syrup in a saucepan and heat gently, stirring until melted.

Remove from the heat. Beat in the orange rind and juice, eggs, flours and ground ginger, then beat thoroughly to mix evenly. Stir in the glacé ginger. Spoon the batter into the tin.

Bake in the preheated oven for 40–45 minutes, or until risen and firm to the touch. Leave to cool in the tin for 10 minutes, then turn out and leave to cool completely on a wire rack. Cut into squares and decorate with some glacé ginger.

171 Nutty gingerbread

Replace the ginger pieces with 85 g/3 oz chopped walnuts or pecan nuts.

172 Apple gingerbread

150 g/5½ oz butter, plus extra for greasing
175 g/6 oz soft brown sugar
2 tbsp black treacle
225 g/8 oz plain flour
1 tsp baking powder
2 tsp bicarbonate of soda
2 tsp ground ginger
150 ml/5 fl oz milk
1 egg, lightly beaten
2 dessert apples, peeled, chopped and coated with 1 tbsp lemon juice

Preheat the oven to 160°C/325°F/Gas Mark 3. Grease a 23-cm/9-inch square cake tin and line with baking paper. Place the butter, sugar and treacle in a saucepan and heat gently until the butter is melted, then leave to cool.

Sift the plain flour, baking powder, bicarbonate of soda and ground ginger into a large bowl. Stir in the milk, egg and cooled buttery liquid, followed by the chopped apples coated with the lemon juice and mix together gently. Pour the mixture into the tin and smooth the surface.

Bake in the preheated oven for 30–35 minutes, or until the cake has risen and a fine skewer inserted into the centre comes out clean. Leave the cake to cool in the tin before turning out and cutting into 12 bars.

173 Pear gingerbread

Replace the apples with dessert pears. Add 25 g/1 oz chopped stem ginger to the mixture with the ground ginger, for an extra ginger flavour.

174 Lemon drizzle squares

150 g/5½ oz butter, softened, or soft
margarine, plus extra for greasing
175 g/6 oz caster sugar
2 eggs
finely grated rind of 1 lemon
175 g/6 oz self-raising flour

125 ml/4 fl oz milk
icing sugar, for dusting

SYRUP
140 g/5 oz icing sugar
50 ml/2 fl oz fresh lemon juice

Preheat the oven to 180°C/350°F/Gas Mark 4. Grease an 18-cm/7-inch square cake tin and line with baking paper.

Place the butter, sugar and eggs in a large bowl and beat together until light and fluffy. Stir in the lemon rind, then sift in the flour and fold into the mixture. Stir in the milk. Spoon the mixture into the cake tin, smoothing the top.

Bake in the preheated oven for 45–50 minutes, or until golden brown and firm to the touch. Leave the tin on a wire rack.

To make the syrup, place the icing sugar and lemon juice in a small saucepan and heat gently, stirring, until the sugar dissolves. Do not boil.

Prick the warm cake all over with a fork, and spoon the hot syrup evenly over the top, allowing it to be absorbed.

Leave to cool completely in the tin, then turn out the cake, cut into 12 pieces and dust with sifted icing sugar.

175 Citrus drizzle slices

Replace the lemon rind with the grated rind of ½ orange and 1 lime in the cake mixture. For the syrup, squeeze the lime and add enough orange juice to make up to 50 ml/2 fl oz, and add the grated rind of ½ orange.

176 Rock cakes

115 g/4 oz butter, plus extra for greasing
225 g/8 oz plain flour
2 tsp baking powder
85 g/3 oz soft light brown sugar
85 g/3 oz mixed dried fruit

finely grated rind of 1 lemon
1 egg
1–2 tbsp milk
2 tsp demerara sugar

Preheat the oven to 200°C/400°F/Gas Mark 6. Lightly grease 2 baking sheets. Sift the flour and baking powder into a large bowl. Add the butter and rub it in with your fingertips until the mixture resembles breadcrumbs. Stir in the brown sugar, mixed dried fruit and lemon rind.

Place the egg and a tablespoon of the milk in a bowl and beat lightly, then stir into the flour mixture, adding a little more milk if necessary, until it starts to bind together to form a moist but firm dough. Spoon small heaps of the mixture onto the baking sheets. Sprinkle with the demerara sugar.

Bake in the preheated oven for 15–20 minutes, or until golden brown and firm. Use a palette knife to transfer the cakes to a wire rack to cool.

177 Citrus rock cakes

Replace the dried fruit with chopped mixed peel and add orange juice instead of the milk.

85 g/3 oz butter, diced, plus extra
for greasing
450 g/1 lb self-raising flour, plus extra
for dusting
pinch of salt
50 g/1¾ oz caster sugar
50 g/1¾ oz pecorino cheese
100 g/3½ oz walnut pieces
about 300 ml/10 fl oz milk

Preheat the oven to 200°C/400°F/
Gas Mark 6. Grease a baking
sheet. Sift the flour and salt into
a large bowl. Add the butter and
rub it in with your fingertips
until the mixture resembles fine
breadcrumbs. Stir in the sugar,
cheese and walnuts. Stir in enough
of the milk to bring the mixture
together into a soft dough.

Gently roll the dough out on a
lightly floured work surface until
it is about 2.5–3 cm/1–1¼ inch
thick. Cut out rounds with a
6-cm/2½-inch round biscuit
cutter (make the scones smaller
or larger if you prefer). Place the
rounds on a baking sheet.

Bake in the preheated oven for
15 minutes, or until golden brown
and firm to the touch. Transfer to
a wire rack to cool.

179 *Olive & walnut scones*

Replace the pecorino with 55 g/2 oz pitted green olives, chopped.

180 *Sun-dried tomato & pecorino scones*

Replace the walnuts with 4 pieces of sun-dried tomato in oil, chopped.

vegetable oil, for greasing and cooking
450 g/1 lb strong white bread flour,
plus extra for dusting
½ tsp salt
1 tsp caster sugar
1½ tsp easy-blend dried yeast
250 ml/9 fl oz lukewarm water
125 ml/4 fl oz natural yogurt
40 g/1½ oz semolina

Grease a bowl and dust a baking sheet with flour. Sift the flour and salt together into a bowl and stir in the sugar and yeast. Make a well in the centre and add the water and yogurt. Stir until the dough begins to come together, then knead until it comes away from the side of the bowl. Knead the dough on a floured surface for 5–10 minutes, or until smooth and elastic.

Shape the dough into a ball, place it in the greased bowl and cover with a damp tea towel. Leave to rise in a warm place for 30–40 minutes.

Knead the dough on a floured surface, then roll out until it is about 2 cm/¾ inch thick. Cut out 10–12 rounds with a 7.5-cm/3-inch biscuit cutter and sprinkle each round with semolina. Transfer the rounds to the baking sheet, cover and leave in a warm place for 30 minutes.

Heat a griddle or large frying pan over a medium–high heat and brush with oil. Add half the muffins and cook for 7–8 minutes on each side until golden brown. Cook the remaining muffins in the same way.

182 *Cheese muffins*

Stir in 85 g/3 oz finely grated Cheddar cheese with the sugar and yeast.

183 *Black pepper muffins*

Stir in 1 teaspoon of coarsely ground black pepper with the sugar and yeast.

Cheese & mustard scones

50 g/1¾ oz butter, cut into pieces, plus extra for greasing
225 g/8 oz self-raising flour, plus extra for dusting
1 tsp baking powder
pinch of salt

125 g/4½ oz mature Cheddar cheese, grated
1 tsp mustard powder
150 ml/5 fl oz milk, plus extra for brushing
pepper

Preheat the oven to 220°C/425°F/Gas Mark 7. Lightly grease a baking sheet. Sift the flour, baking powder and salt into a large bowl. Add the butter and rub it in with your fingertips until the mixture resembles breadcrumbs. Stir in the cheese, mustard and enough milk to form a soft dough.

Knead the dough very lightly on a floured work surface, then flatten it out into a round with the palm of your hand to a thickness of about 2.5 cm/1 inch.

Cut the dough into 8 wedges with a knife. Brush each one with a little milk and sprinkle with pepper to taste.

Bake in the preheated oven for 10–15 minutes, or until golden brown. Transfer to a wire rack to cool slightly before serving.

185 *Cheese & herb scones*

Replace the mustard with 1 tablespoon of chopped fresh herbs, such as chives, parsley, sage, rosemary or thyme.

186 *Cheddar & caraway scones*

Replace the mustard with 1½ teaspoons of caraway seeds.

187 *Cornbread squares*

vegetable oil, for greasing
175 g/6 oz plain flour
1 tsp salt
4 tsp baking powder
1 tsp caster sugar
280 g/10 oz polenta

115 g/4 oz butter, softened, cut into pieces
4 eggs
250 ml/8 fl oz milk
3 tbsp double cream

Preheat the oven to 200°C/400°F/Gas Mark 6. Grease a 20-cm/8-inch square cake tin. Sift together the flour, salt and baking powder into a bowl. Add the sugar and polenta and stir to mix. Add the butter and rub it in with your fingertips until the mixture resembles breadcrumbs.

Place the eggs, milk and cream in a bowl and lightly beat together, then stir into the polenta mixture until thoroughly combined. Spoon the mixture into the tin and smooth the surface.

Bake in the preheated oven for 30–35 minutes, or until a skewer inserted into the centre of the loaf comes out clean. Leave to cool for 5–10 minutes, then cut into squares and serve warm.

188 *Chilli cornbread*

Stir in 1–2 teaspoons of dried red chilli flakes into the mixture with the sugar and polenta.

189 *Pepper & sweetcorn cornbread*

Sauté 1 deseeded and chopped red pepper in 1 tablespoon of oil until just tender. Leave to cool, then stir in 115 g/4 oz sweetcorn kernels and add to the mixture with the milk and cream.

vegetable oil, for greasing
350 g/12 oz strong white flour, plus
extra for dusting
2 tsp salt
7 g/¼ oz easy-blend dried yeast
1 tbsp lightly beaten egg
200 ml/7 fl oz lukewarm water
1 egg white
2 tsp water
2 tbsp caraway seeds

Grease a bowl and 2 baking sheets. Dust another baking sheet with flour. Sift the flour and salt together into a bowl and stir in the yeast. Make a well in the centre, pour in the egg and the water and mix to form a dough. Knead the dough on a lightly floured work surface for 10 minutes, until smooth.

Shape the dough into a ball, place it in the greased bowl and cover with a damp tea towel. Leave to rise in a warm place for 1 hour.

Turn the dough onto a lightly floured work surface and knock back with your fist. Knead for 2 minutes, then divide into 10 pieces. Shape each piece into a ball and leave to rest for 5 minutes. Gently flatten each ball with a lightly floured hand and make a hole in the centre with the handle of a wooden spoon. Put the bagels on the floured sheet, cover with a damp tea towel and leave to rise in a warm place for 20 minutes.

Preheat the oven to 220°C/ 425°F/Gas Mark 7 and bring a large saucepan of water to the boil. Reduce the heat until the water is barely simmering, then add 2 bagels. Poach for 1 minute, then turn over and poach for a further 30 seconds. Remove with a slotted spoon and drain on a tea towel. Poach the remaining bagels in the same way. Transfer the bagels to the greased baking sheets. Place the egg white and water in a bowl and beat together, then brush it over the bagels. Sprinkle with the caraway seeds.

Bake in the preheated oven for 25–30 minutes, or until golden brown. Transfer to a wire rack to cool completely.

191 *Cinnamon & raisin bagels*

Add 1 teaspoon of ground cinnamon to the flour and make the dough as described. Leave to rise. After knocking back the dough, knead in 55 g/2 oz raisins then shape and complete as described, omitting the caraway seeds.

Crowd-pleasing Cookies and Biscuits

115 g/4 oz butter, softened, plus extra
    for greasing
115 g/4 oz light muscovado sugar
1 egg
100 g/3½ oz porridge oats
1 tbsp milk
1 tsp vanilla extract

125 g/4½ oz plain flour
1 tbsp cocoa powder
½ tsp baking powder
175 g/6 oz plain chocolate, broken
    into pieces
175 g/6 oz milk chocolate, broken
    into pieces

Preheat the oven to 180°C/350°F/Gas Mark 4. Grease 2 large baking sheets. Place the butter and sugar in a large bowl and beat together until light and fluffy. Beat in the egg, then add the oats, milk and vanilla extract and beat together until well blended. Sift the flour, cocoa and baking powder into the mixture and stir. Stir in the chocolate pieces.

Place dessertspoonfuls of the mixture on the baking sheets and flatten slightly with a fork. Bake in the preheated oven for 15 minutes, or until slightly risen and firm.

Leave to cool on the baking sheets for 2 minutes, then transfer the cookies to wire racks to cool completely.

193 *White chocolate chip cookies*

Replace the plain and milk chocolate with 275 g/9¾ oz chopped white chocolate.

194 *Almond cookies with a cherry on top*

MAKES 25

200 g/7 oz butter, cut into cubes, plus
    extra for greasing
90 g/3¼ oz caster sugar
½ tsp almond extract

280 g/10 oz self-raising flour
25 g/1 oz ground almonds
25 glacé cherries (total weight about
    125 g/4½ oz)

Preheat the oven to 180°C/350°F/Gas Mark 4. Grease several large baking sheets.

Place the butter in a large saucepan and heat gently until melted. Remove from the heat. Add the sugar and almond extract to the pan and stir together. Add the flour and ground almonds and mix to form a smooth dough.

Roll small pieces of the dough between your hands into smooth balls to make 25 in total. Place on the baking sheets, spaced well apart, and flatten slightly with your hands, then press a cherry gently into the centre of each cookie. Bake in the preheated oven for 10–15 minutes, or until golden brown.

Leave to cool for 2–3 minutes on the baking sheets, then transfer the cookies to a wire rack to cool completely.

195 *Cookies & cream sandwiches*

MAKES ABOUT 15

125 g/4½ oz butter, softened
75 g/2¾ oz icing sugar
115 g/4 oz plain flour
40 g/1½ oz cocoa powder
½ tsp ground cinnamon

FILLING
125 g/4½ oz plain chocolate, broken
 into pieces
50 ml/2 fl oz double cream

Preheat the oven to 160°C/325°F/Gas Mark 3. Line 2 large baking sheets with baking paper. Place the butter and sugar in a large bowl and beat together until light and fluffy. Sift the flour, cocoa and cinnamon into the mixture and mix to form a dough.

Place the dough between 2 sheets of baking paper and roll out until the dough is 3 mm/⅛ inch thick. Cut out 6-cm/2½-inch rounds and place on the baking sheets. Bake in the preheated oven for 15 minutes, or until firm to the touch. Leave to cool for 2 minutes on the baking paper, then transfer the cookies to wire racks to cool completely.

Meanwhile, make the filling. Place the chocolate and cream in a saucepan and heat gently until the chocolate has melted. Stir until smooth. Leave to cool, then chill in the refrigerator for 2 hours, or until firm. Sandwich the biscuits together in pairs with a spoonful of the chocolate cream and serve.

196 *With strawberry filling*

Replace the plain chocolate with white chocolate, chop 85 g/3 oz dried strawberries into small pieces and fold into the chilled filling.

197 *Classic oatmeal biscuits*

MAKES 30

175 g/6 oz butter or margarine, plus
 extra for greasing
275 g/9¾ oz demerara sugar
1 egg
4 tbsp water

1 tsp vanilla extract
375 g/13 oz rolled oats
140 g/5 oz plain flour
1 tsp salt
½ tsp bicarbonate of soda

Preheat the oven to 350°F/180°C/Gas Mark 4. Grease 2 large baking sheets. Place the butter and sugar in a large bowl and beat together until light and fluffy. Beat in the egg, water and vanilla extract until the mixture is smooth. Mix the oats, flour, salt and bicarbonate of soda together in a separate bowl, then gradually stir the oat mixture into the creamed mixture until thoroughly combined.

Place tablespoonfuls of the mixture onto the baking sheets, spaced well apart. Bake in the preheated oven for 15 minutes, or until golden brown. Transfer to a wire rack to cool completely.

198 *Oatmeal & vine fruit biscuits*

Add 85 g/3 oz chopped sultanas and raisins to the dough mix.

199 *Peanut sitting pretties*

MAKES 18

115 g/4 oz unsalted butter, softened
50 g/1¾ oz demerara sugar
1 large egg, separated
½ tsp vanilla extract
140 g/5 oz plain flour
pinch of salt

150 g/5½ oz chopped mixed nuts
36 chocolate- or sugar-coated peanuts,
 to decorate

ICING
1 quantity buttercream icing (page 10)

Place the butter and sugar in a large bowl and beat together until light and fluffy. Stir in the egg yolk and vanilla extract and beat together, then add the flour and salt and beat to combine. Wrap the dough in clingfilm and chill in the refrigerator for 3 hours.

Preheat the oven to 180°C/350°F/Gas Mark 4. Line a large baking sheet with baking paper.

Lightly whisk the egg white in a clean bowl and spread the chopped nuts out on a plate. Roll walnut-sized pieces of the dough into balls. Dip each ball in the egg white then roll in the nuts to coat and place on the baking sheet. Bake in the preheated oven for 5 minutes, then remove and make an indentation with your thumb in the middle of each cookie. Bake for a further 5 minutes, then leave the cookies to cool completely on the baking sheet.

To make the buttercream icing, place the butter in a large bowl and beat until soft. Sift in the icing sugar and beat together until smooth. Spoon a little filling into the indentation of each cookie and top each one with 2 chocolate- or sugar-coated peanuts.

200 *With hazelnut & chocolate topping*

Replace the buttercream icing with 140 g/5 oz hazelnut chocolate spread.

201 *Fluttering butterfly cookies*

MAKES 25

175 g/6 oz unsalted butter, softened,
 plus extra for greasing
200 g/7 oz caster sugar
1 large egg, lightly beaten
1 tsp vanilla extract or almond extract
300 g/10½ oz plain flour, plus extra
 for dusting
pinch of salt

TOPPING
150 g/5½ oz icing sugar
about 1 tbsp cold water
yellow, pink and blue food colouring
silver dragées
coloured writing icing

Place the butter and sugar in a large bowl and beat together until light and fluffy. Whisk the egg and vanilla together in a separate bowl, then beat into the butter mixture. Sift in the flour and salt and mix to form a dough. Wrap in clingfilm and chill for 30 minutes.

Preheat the oven to 180°C/350°F/Gas Mark 4. Grease a large baking sheet. Roll the dough out on a floured work surface to 5 mm/¼ inch thick. Cut out shapes with a flour-dipped butterfly-shaped cookie cutter and place on the baking sheet. Bake in the preheated oven for 12–15 minutes, or until they are golden brown. Leave to cool on wire racks.

To make the icing, sift the icing sugar into a bowl, add the water and mix until smooth. Divide the icing into portions and tint to pastel shades with food colouring. Spread the icing over the cookies and decorate with silver dragées. Leave to set, then finish decorating with writing icing.

175 g/6 oz unsalted butter, softened
100 g/3½ oz soft light brown sugar
1 large egg, lightly beaten
1 tbsp clear honey
280 g/10 oz plain flour, plus extra
   for dusting
½ tsp ground cinnamon

TO DECORATE
115 g/4 oz icing sugar
about ½ tsp cold water
3 tbsp chocolate sprinkles
20 gum drops
coloured writing icing

Place the butter and sugar in a large bowl and beat together until light and fluffy. Add the egg and honey and stir to combine. Sift in the flour and cinnamon and mix to form a soft dough. Wrap the dough in clingfilm and chill in the refrigerator for 30 minutes.

Preheat the oven to 190°C/375°F/Gas Mark 5. Line a large baking sheet with baking paper. Cut the dough in half and roll in the remaining flour, then roll out each piece between 2 sheets of clingfilm. Using a 7-cm/2¾-inch cookie cutter, cut out 10 discs from each piece and place on the baking sheet. Bake in the preheated oven for 10–12 minutes, or until golden brown. Leave to cool for 5 minutes, then transfer the cookies to a wire rack to cool completely.

Sift the icing sugar into a bowl, add the water and mix until smooth. Spread the cookies with a thin layer of icing, then use the chocolate sprinkles for hair and a gum drop for the nose. Leave to set, then draw in the eyes and mouth with the writing icing.

203 *Fairy faces*

For fairy faces, ice the biscuits according to the recipe but use 3 tablespoons of pink sprinkles for the hair and use pink writing icing for the face.

125 g/4½ oz unsalted butter, softened
125 g/4½ oz caster sugar
1 large egg yolk

100 g/3½ oz plain flour
1 tsp ground cinnamon

Preheat the oven to 200°C/400°F/Gas Mark 6. Line a large baking sheet with baking paper.

Place the butter and 25 g/1 oz of the sugar in a large bowl and beat together until light and fluffy. Add the egg yolk and mix together, then sift in the flour and mix to form a soft dough.

Mix the remaining sugar with the cinnamon. Take a teaspoon of dough and roll it in the sugar mixture. Place on the baking sheet and use a fork to press down until the cookie is 1 cm/½ inch thick. Repeat until all the dough is used up. Bake in the preheated oven for 10 minutes, or until golden brown. Leave to cool on a wire rack.

205 *Coconut buttery fork cookies*

Add 100 g/3½ oz shredded coconut to the dough and roll the cookies in the remaining caster sugar, but omit the cinnamon.

225 g/8 oz butter, softened
140 g/5 oz caster sugar
1 egg yolk, lightly beaten
2 tsp vanilla extract
225 g/8 oz plain flour
55 g/2 oz cocoa powder

pinch of salt
about 90 white mini marshmallows,
 halved horizontally
4 tbsp peach jam
4 tbsp yellow sugar sprinkles

Place the butter and sugar in a large bowl and beat together until light and fluffy, then beat in the egg yolk and vanilla extract.

Sift together the flour, cocoa and salt into the mixture and stir until thoroughly combined. Halve the dough, roll each piece into a ball, wrap in clingfilm and chill in the refrigerator for 30–60 minutes.

Preheat the oven to 190°C/ 375°F/Gas Mark 5. Line 2 large baking sheets with baking paper.

Unwrap the dough and roll out between 2 sheets of baking paper to about 1 cm/½ inch thick. Cut out 30 cookies with a 5-cm/2-inch flower cookie cutter and put them on the baking sheets, making sure they are spaced well apart.

Bake in the preheated oven for 10–12 minutes, or until firm. Remove from the oven but do not turn off the heat. Arrange the pieces of marshmallow over the petals of the flowers, cutting them to fit if necessary. Return to the oven for 30–60 seconds, or until the marshmallow has softened.

Leave to cool on the baking sheets for 5–10 minutes, then transfer the cookies to wire racks to cool completely. Meanwhile, heat the jam in a small saucepan, strain into a bowl and leave to cool. Pipe a small circle of jam in the centre of each flower and top with the sugar sprinkles.

207 *Chocolate button daisies*

Omit the cocoa powder from the dough mixture and use chocolate buttons instead of the marshmallows.

50 g/1¾ oz unsalted butter
50 g/1¾ oz caster sugar
50 g/1¾ oz golden syrup
50 g/1¾ oz plain flour

25 g/1 oz glacé cherries, chopped
50 g/1¾ oz flaked almonds
50 g/1¾ oz candied peel, chopped
175 g/6 oz plain chocolate, chopped

Preheat the oven to 180°C/350°F/Gas Mark 4. Line 2 large baking sheets with baking paper. Heat the butter, sugar and golden syrup together in a saucepan over a low heat until the butter is melted and the sugar is dissolved. Stir in the flour, cherries, almonds and candied peel.

Make the florentines in batches: place heaped teaspoons of the mixture on the baking sheets, spaced well apart, and flatten slightly with the back of a spoon. Bake in the preheated oven for 8–10 minutes, or until golden brown. Leave to cool on the baking sheets for 2–3 minutes, then transfer to a wire rack and leave until cold. Repeat until you have 20 florentines.

Place the chocolate in a heatproof bowl, set the bowl over a saucepan of gently simmering water and heat until melted. Using a pastry brush, spread the chocolate over the base of each florentine and place chocolate side up on a wire rack to cool and set.

209 *Ginger florentines*

Replace the glacé cherries and candied peel with 85 g/3 oz chopped crystallized ginger.

210 *Whirly pinwheel cookies*

100 g/3½ oz unsalted butter, softened
50 g/1¾ oz caster sugar
50 g/1¾ oz cornflour
100 g/3½ oz plain flour, plus 1 tbsp
    for dusting
1 large egg yolk
1 tbsp milk
2 tbsp cocoa powder

Place the butter and sugar in a large bowl and beat together until light and fluffy. Sift in the cornflour and the flour and mix well to combine, then add the egg yolk and a little milk to form a stiff dough.

Divide the dough mixture in half, add the cocoa powder to one half and mix well together. Wrap both doughs in clingfilm and chill in the refrigerator for 30 minutes.

Roll each piece of dough into a rectangle 3 mm/⅛ inch thick. Lay the chocolate dough on top of the white dough, then press together and trim the edges. Roll up lengthways, wrap tightly in clingfilm and chill in the refrigerator for 30 minutes.

Preheat the oven to 180°C/350°F/Gas Mark 4. Unwrap the dough and cut across the roll into 20 slices, then place the cookies on a non-stick baking sheet. Bake in the preheated oven for 15–20 minutes. Leave to cool on a wire rack.

211 *Hazelnut whirly pinwheel cookies*

Add 3 tablespoons of finely chopped hazelnuts to the chocolate dough and knead in before chilling the dough.

212 *Good-for-you wholemeal biscuits*

300 g/10½ oz plain wholemeal flour,
    plus extra for dusting
2 tbsp wheatgerm
¼ tsp bicarbonate of soda
½ tsp salt
50 g/1¾ oz caster sugar
125 g/4½ oz unsalted butter, cubed
1 large egg, lightly beaten
1 tsp vanilla extract

Preheat the oven to 170°C/325°F/Gas Mark 3. Place the flour, wheatgerm, bicarbonate of soda, salt and sugar in a large bowl and stir together until combined. Add the butter and rub it in until the mixture resembles breadcrumbs.

Whisk the egg and vanilla extract in a separate bowl and add to the mixture, adding a little cold water if needed to bring the dough together. Roll the dough out on a floured board. Use a 7-cm/2¾-inch floured cookie cutter to cut out the biscuits and place them on non-stick baking sheets, re-rolling the dough when necessary.

Bake in batches in the preheated oven for 20–25 minutes, or until dry but not brown. Leave to cool on a wire rack.

213 *Fruit wholemeal biscuits*

Knead 2 tablespoons of chopped currants or chopped mixed peel and ½ teaspoon of mixed ground spice into the dough before rolling out.

214 German lebkuchen

3 eggs
200 g/7 oz caster sugar
55 g/2 oz plain flour
2 tsp cocoa powder
1 tsp ground cinnamon
½ tsp ground cardamom
¼ tsp ground cloves
¼ tsp ground nutmeg

175 g/6 oz ground almonds
55 g/2 oz mixed peel, finely chopped

TO DECORATE
115 g/4 oz plain chocolate
115 g/4 oz white chocolate
sugar crystals

Preheat the oven to 180°C/350°F/Gas Mark 4. Line several large baking sheets with baking paper. Place the eggs and sugar in a heatproof bowl set over a saucepan of gently simmering water and whisk until thick and foamy. Remove the bowl from the pan and continue to whisk for 2 minutes.

Sift the flour, cocoa, cinnamon, cardamom, cloves and nutmeg into the bowl and stir in with the ground almonds and mixed peel. Drop heaped teaspoonfuls of the mixture onto the baking sheets, spreading them gently into smooth mounds.

Bake in the preheated oven for 15–20 minutes, or until light brown and slightly soft to the touch. Leave to cool on the baking sheets for 10 minutes, then transfer the cookies to wire racks to cool completely.

Place the plain and white chocolate in 2 separate heatproof bowls, set the bowls over 2 pans of gently simmering water and heat until melted. Dip half the biscuits in the melted plain chocolate and half in the white chocolate. Sprinkle with sugar crystals and leave to set.

215 With violets & ginger topping

Omit the sugar crystals and top each cookie with either a crystallized violet or a piece of crystallized ginger.

216 Pistachio & almond tuiles

1 egg white
55 g/2 oz caster sugar
25 g/1 oz plain flour
25 g/1 oz pistachio nuts, finely chopped

25 g/1 oz ground almonds
½ tsp almond extract
40 g/1½ oz butter, melted and cooled

Preheat the oven to 160°C/325°F/Gas Mark 3. Line 2 large baking sheets with baking paper. Place the egg white and sugar in a large bowl and whisk together lightly, then stir in the flour, pistachio nuts, ground almonds, almond extract and butter to form a soft paste.

Place walnut-sized spoonfuls of the mixture on the baking sheets and use the back of the spoon to spread as thinly as possible. Bake in the preheated oven for 10–15 minutes, or until pale golden.

Quickly lift each biscuit with a palette knife and place over the side of a rolling pin to shape into a curve. When set, transfer to a wire rack to cool completely.

217 Hazelnut & almond tuiles

Replace the pistachio nuts with 25 g/1 oz finely chopped toasted hazelnuts.

Spanish almond cookies

75 g/2¾ oz unsalted butter, softened,
    plus extra for greasing
55 g/2 oz blanched almonds
75 g/2¾ oz caster sugar

¼ tsp almond extract
55 g/2 oz plain flour
2 large egg whites

Preheat the oven to 180°C/350°F/Gas Mark 4. Grease several large baking sheets with butter.

Finely chop the almonds. Place the butter and sugar in a large bowl and beat together until light and fluffy. Add the almond extract, flour and chopped almonds and stir together until incorporated.

Place the egg whites in a large bowl and whisk until soft peaks form and they hold their shape but are not dry. Fold the egg whites into the almond mixture, then place 15 teaspoonfuls of the mixture onto the baking sheets, spaced well apart.

Bake in the preheated oven for 15–20 minutes, or until lightly golden brown around the edges. Leave to cool slightly on the baking sheets for 2–3 minutes, then transfer the cookies to a wire rack to cool completely.

Dutch macaroons

2 large egg whites
pinch of salt
225 g/8 oz caster sugar
175 g/6 oz ground almonds
225 g/8 oz plain chocolate, chopped

Preheat the oven to 180°C/350°F/Gas Mark 4. Line 2 large baking sheets with rice paper. Whisk the egg whites in a large bowl until soft peaks form.

Add the salt and half the sugar and whisk again until stiff and glossy, then fold in the remaining sugar and the almonds.

Spoon the mixture into a piping bag fitted with a 1-cm/½-inch nozzle and pipe 6 x 7.5-cm/3-inch long fingers of the mixture onto each baking sheet. Bake in the preheated oven for 15–20 minutes, until golden. Cool on a wire rack, then tear off excess rice paper around the cookies.

Line a baking sheet with baking paper. Place the chocolate in a heatproof bowl, set the bowl over a saucepan of gently simmering water and heat until melted. Dip the base of each cookie into the chocolate, then place upside down on the baking sheet to set.

With white chocolate coating

Replace the plain chocolate with 225 g/8 oz white chocolate.

221 Tangy lemon jumbles

1 tsp groundnut oil, for greasing
100 g/3½ oz unsalted butter, softened
125 g/4½ oz caster sugar
juice and finely grated rind of 1 lemon
1 large egg, lightly beaten
350 g/12 oz plain flour, plus extra for
    dusting

1 tsp baking powder
1 tbsp milk
25 g/1 oz icing sugar, for dusting

Preheat the oven to 170°C/375°F/Gas Mark 3. Grease 2 large baking sheets with the oil. Place the butter, sugar and lemon rind in a large bowl and beat together until light and fluffy. Alternately add the egg and 4 tablespoons of lemon juice to the mixture, beating well between each addition. Sift in the flour and baking powder and mix well, then add the milk to form a smooth dough.

Turn the dough onto a floured work surface and divide into 40 pieces. Roll each piece into a sausage, then form into an S-shape and place on the baking sheets. Bake in the preheated oven for 15–20 minutes. Leave to cool on a wire rack, then dust with sifted icing sugar.

222 Orange jumbles

Replace the lemon juice and rind with orange juice and rind.

223 Jewish oznei haman

115 g/4 oz unsalted butter, softened
100 g/3½ oz caster sugar
½ tsp vanilla extract
3 large egg yolks
300 g/10½ oz plain flour, plus extra for
    dusting
1 large egg, lightly beaten, for brushing

FILLING
50 g/1¾ oz poppy seeds
1 tbsp clear honey
25 g/1 oz caster sugar
finely grated rind of 1 lemon
1 tbsp lemon juice
4 tbsp water
40 g/1½ oz ground almonds
1 large egg, lightly beaten
40 g/1½ oz raisins

For the filling, place the poppy seeds, honey, sugar, lemon rind and juice and the water in a saucepan and stir over a medium heat until just boiling. Remove from the heat and beat in the almonds, egg and raisins. Leave to cool.

Preheat the oven to 180°C/350°F/Gas Mark 4. Line 2 large baking sheets with baking paper. Roll the dough out on a floured work surface to 5 mm/¼ inch thick. Using an 8-cm/3¼-inch

floured cookie cutter, cut out 20 cookies. Re-roll any trimmings. Spoon the filling into the middle of each dough piece and brush the edges with the egg. Bring them to the centre to form a tricorn shape, then press the edges together. Place 10 cookies on each baking sheet, spaced well apart and brush with more egg. Bake in the preheated oven for 25–30 minutes, or until golden. Leave to cool on a wire rack.

Place the butter and sugar in a large bowl and beat together until light and fluffy. Whisk the vanilla extract and egg yolks together in a separate bowl, then add to the butter mixture and mix well.

Sift in the flour and mix to a smooth dough. Wrap in clingfilm and chill in the refrigerator for 30 minutes.

224 With fruit filling

Replace the poppy seed filling with 200 g/7 oz fruit jam or apple sauce.

Hearts & diamonds

225 g/8 oz butter, softened
140 g/5 oz caster sugar
1 egg yolk, lightly beaten
2 tsp vanilla extract
280 g/10 oz plain flour
pinch of salt
100 g/3½ oz white chocolate chips

FILLING
5–6 tbsp redcurrant or cranberry jam
½ tsp lemon juice
85 g/3 oz curd cheese
2 tbsp double cream
2 tsp icing sugar
few drops of vanilla extract

Place the butter and sugar in a bowl and beat together until light and fluffy, then beat in the egg yolk and vanilla extract.

Sift together the flour and salt into the mixture, add the chocolate chips and stir until combined. Halve the dough, shape into balls, wrap in clingfilm and chill for 30–60 minutes.

Preheat the oven to 190°C/375°F/Gas Mark 5. Line 2 large baking sheets with baking paper. Unwrap the dough and roll out between 2 sheets of baking paper. Cut out cookies with a 6-cm/2½-inch square fluted cutter and place half of them on a baking sheet, spaced well apart.

Using small heart- and diamond-shaped cutters, cut out the centres of the remaining cookies and remove them. Place the cookies on the other baking sheet, spaced well apart. Bake in the preheated oven for 10–15 minutes.

Leave to cool for 5–10 minutes, then transfer the cookies to wire racks to cool completely.

To make the jam filling, place the jam and lemon juice into a small saucepan and heat gently until the mixture is runny, then bring to the boil and boil for 3 minutes. Leave to cool.

Beat the curd cheese, cream, sifted icing sugar and vanilla extract together in a bowl until combined. Spread the cream mixture over the whole cookies, add a little of the jam and top with the cut-out cookies.

226 *Lemon hearts & diamonds*

Replace the jam in the filling with 1 teaspoon of finely grated lemon rind and ½ teaspoon of lemon oil.

227 *Clubs & spades*

225 g/8 oz butter, softened
140 g/5 oz caster sugar
1 egg yolk, lightly beaten
2 tsp vanilla extract
280 g/10 oz plain flour
pinch of salt
100 g/3½ oz plain chocolate chips

FILLING
55 g/2 oz butter, softened
1 tsp golden syrup
85 g/3 oz icing sugar
1 tbsp cocoa powder

Preheat the oven to 190°C/375°F/Gas Mark 5. Line 2 large baking sheets with baking paper. Unwrap the dough and roll out between 2 sheets of baking paper. Cut out cookies with a 6-cm/2½-inch square fluted cutter and put half of them on a baking sheet, spaced well apart. Using small club- and spade-shaped cutters, cut out the centres of the remaining cookies and remove them. Place the cookies on the other baking sheet, spaced well apart.

Bake in the preheated oven for 10–15 minutes, or until light golden brown. Leave to cool on the baking sheets for 5–10 minutes, then transfer the cookies to wire racks to cool completely.

For the filling, place the butter and golden syrup in a bowl and sift in the icing sugar and cocoa. Beat well until smooth. Spread the chocolate cream over the whole cookies and top with the cut-out cookies.

Place the butter and sugar in a large bowl and beat together until light and fluffy, then beat in the egg yolk and vanilla extract. Sift together the flour and salt into the mixture, add the chocolate chips and stir until thoroughly combined. Halve the dough, shape into balls, wrap in clingfilm and chill in the refrigerator for 30–60 minutes.

228 *With jam filling*

Replace the filling with 150 g/5½ oz seedless raspberry jam.

125 g/4½ oz unsalted butter, softened
125 g/4½ oz soft light brown sugar
1 large egg, lightly beaten
pinch of salt
250 g/9 oz plain flour, plus extra for
   dusting
1 tsp ground cinnamon

½ tsp ground nutmeg
¼ tsp ground cloves
¼ tsp ground cardamom
¼ tsp ground ginger
1 tsp baking powder
85 g/3 oz flaked almonds

Place the butter and sugar in a large bowl and beat together until light and fluffy, then add the egg and salt and mix to combine. Sift in the flour, spices and baking powder and mix to form a dough. Wrap the dough in clingfilm and chill in the refrigerator for 6 hours, or overnight.

Preheat the oven to 160°C/325°F/Gas Mark 3. Remove the dough from the refrigerator and allow to come to room temperature, then roll out on a floured work surface. Use a floured cookie cutter to cut out the speculaas (or use a speculaas mould), then scatter over the almonds and press into the biscuits. Place on 2 large non-stick baking sheets.

Bake in the preheated oven for 18–20 minutes or until golden brown. Leave to cool on the baking sheet.

230 *Iced speculaas*

Bake the cookies without the flaked almonds and when cool spread the cookies with icing made by sifting 150 g/5½ oz icing sugar and 1 teaspoon of mixed ground spice into a bowl, then adding 1 tablespoon of warm water and mixing until smooth. Leave to set.

350 g/12 oz unsalted butter, softened
85 g/3 oz icing sugar
½ tsp vanilla extract

300 g/10½ oz plain flour
50 g/1¾ oz cornflour

Preheat the oven to 180°C/350°F/Gas Mark 4. Line 2 large baking sheets with baking paper. Place the butter and sugar in a large bowl and beat together until light and fluffy, then beat in the vanilla extract. Sift over the flour and cornflour and mix thoroughly.

Spoon the mixture into a piping bag fitted with a large star nozzle and pipe 32 cookies onto each baking sheet, spaced well apart.

Bake in the preheated oven for 15–20 minutes, or until golden brown. Leave to cool on the baking sheet.

232 *With mascarpone cheese filling*

Make a double quantity of cookies and use 200 g/7 oz of mascarpone cheese beaten with 2 tablespoons of icing sugar to sandwich the cookies together. Makes 32.

233 Bourbon balls

225 g/8 oz vanilla wafers
150 g/5½ oz pecan nuts, chopped
25 g/1 oz cocoa powder
150 g/5½ oz icing sugar
50 ml/2 fl oz light corn (or use golden) syrup
50 ml/2 fl oz bourbon

Place the vanilla wafers in a food processor and pulse to form rough crumbs, then add the nuts and pulse again until they are finely chopped. Tip into a large bowl and sift in half the cocoa and 100 g/3½ oz icing sugar, then stir together. Gradually add the corn syrup and bourbon and mix together thoroughly.

Sift the remaining sugar and cocoa onto a large plate. Shape the mixture into 2-cm/¾-inch balls and roll in the sugar and cocoa mixture to coat. Place the balls in layers between baking paper in a sealed container and chill in the refrigerator for up to 3 days before serving.

234 Chocolate liqueur balls

Replace the bourbon with chocolate cream liqueur.

235 Thumbprint cookies

115 g/4 oz unsalted butter, softened
125 g/4½ oz caster sugar
1 large egg, separated
1 tsp vanilla extract
175 g/6 oz plain flour
pinch of salt
25 g/1 oz ground almonds
100 g/3½ oz seedless raspberry jam

Preheat the oven to 180°C/350°F/Gas Mark 4. Line 2 large baking sheets with baking paper. Place the butter and 100 g/3½ oz of the sugar in a large bowl and beat together until light and fluffy. Add the egg yolk and vanilla extract and beat well to combine. Sift in the flour and salt and mix well.

Mix the remaining sugar and the ground almonds together and spread out on a plate. Lightly whisk the egg white in a separate bowl. Roll walnut-sized pieces of dough into balls, then dip each ball into the egg white and roll in the almond sugar. Place the balls on the baking sheets and make a deep indentation in each cookie.

Bake in the preheated oven for 10 minutes. Remove from the oven, press down again on each indentation and fill it with jam. Bake for a further 10–12 minutes or until the cookies are golden brown, turning the baking sheets once. Leave to cool on a wire rack.

236 With lemon curd filling

Replace the raspberry jam with lemon curd.

237 Chocolate buttons

2 sachets instant chocolate or fudge
  chocolate drink
1 tbsp hot water
225 g/8 oz butter, softened

140 g/5 oz caster sugar, plus extra
  for sprinkling
1 egg yolk, lightly beaten
280 g/10 oz plain flour
pinch of salt

Empty the chocolate drink sachets into a bowl and stir in the hot water to make a paste. Place the butter and sugar in a large bowl and beat together until light and fluffy, then beat in the egg yolk and chocolate paste. Sift the flour and salt into the mixture and stir until thoroughly combined. Halve the dough, shape into rounds, wrap in clingfilm and chill in the refrigerator for 30–60 minutes.

Preheat the oven to 190°C/375°F/Gas Mark 5. Line 2 large baking sheets with baking paper. Unwrap the dough and roll out between 2 sheets of baking paper to 3 mm/⅛ inch thick. Cut out rounds with a plain 5-cm/2-inch cutter. Using a 3-cm/1¼-inch cap from a soft drink or mineral water bottle, make an indentation in the centre of each button. Using a wooden toothpick, make 4 holes in the centre of each button, then put them on the baking sheets, spaced well apart, and sprinkle with caster sugar. Bake in the preheated oven for 10–15 minutes, or until firm. Leave to cool on the baking sheets for 5–10 minutes, then transfer to wire racks to cool completely.

238 Spanish panellets

1 small potato, peeled
500 g/1 lb 2 oz granulated sugar
225 ml/8 fl oz water
¼ tsp lemon juice
finely grated rind of 1 lemon
450 g/1 lb ground almonds
1 tsp groundnut oil, for oiling
150 g/5½ oz pine kernels
50 g/1¾ oz candied fruit, chopped

Cut the potato in half. Place in a saucepan of boiling water and cook until tender. Drain and mash well with a fork, then cool.

Place the sugar and water in a medium pan and heat gently, stirring until the sugar has dissolved. Increase the heat and bring to the boil, then add the lemon juice and simmer until thick. Remove the pan from the heat and beat in the potato, lemon rind and ground almonds until the mixture is thick. Leave to cool, then cover with clingfilm and chill in the refrigerator overnight.

Preheat the oven to 190°C/ 375°F/Gas Mark 5. Grease 2 large baking sheets with the oil. Roll teaspoons of dough into balls, then roll two thirds of the balls in the pine kernels and top the remaining ones with candied fruit pieces. Bake in the preheated oven for 4 minutes, or until just golden brown. Leave to cool on a wire rack.

239 Cocoa, coffee & coconut panellets

Omit the pine kernels and candied fruit pieces. Divide the dough into 3 portions: knead in 1 teaspoon of cocoa powder to one portion and form into balls, use 1 teaspoon of espresso powder for a coffee flavour and roll the last portion in desiccated coconut before baking.

125 g/4½ oz blanched almonds
15 g/½ oz candied orange peel
15 g/½ oz plain flour
60 g/2¼ oz caster sugar
4½ tsp water

100 g/3½ oz icing sugar, plus extra
  for dusting
50 g/1¾ oz cornflour
1 large egg white
¾ tsp baking powder

Place the almonds, candied orange peel and flour in a food processor and pulse to form a paste.

Place the caster sugar and water in a saucepan and bring to a boil, then reduce the heat and simmer for 2–3 minutes, or until reduced to a thick syrup. Remove from the heat, add the almond paste and mix together. Transfer to a bowl and leave to cool for about 1 hour.

Preheat the oven to 140°C/275°F/Gas Mark 1. Line a large baking sheet with rice paper. Reserve 1 teaspoon of the icing sugar and sift the remaining icing sugar and cornflour onto a work surface.

Place the egg white and reserved icing sugar in a large bowl and whisk until stiff. Add the baking powder to the almond paste, then fold in the whisked egg white until combined. Turn the mixture onto the work surface and roll into a log shape about 6 cm/2½ inches thick, then flatten until it is 4 cm/1½ inches thick. Cut into 1-cm/½-inch slices, place on the baking sheet and form into a diamond shape.

Bake in the preheated oven for about 30 minutes or until risen but still soft in the centre. Leave to cool on the baking sheet for 2–3 minutes, then transfer to a wire rack and to cool completely. Serve dusted with sifted icing sugar.

241 *Langues de chat*

MAKES 28

55 g/2 oz butter, plus extra for greasing
55 g/2 oz caster sugar
1 egg, lightly beaten
55 g/2 oz self-raising flour

Preheat the oven to 220°C/425°F/Gas Mark 7. Lightly grease 2 large baking sheets.

Beat the butter and sugar together until pale and fluffy. Gradually beat in the egg. Fold in the flour.

Spoon the mixture into a piping bag fitted with a 1-cm/½-inch plain nozzle. Pipe 5-cm/2-inch biscuits on the baking sheet, spacing them well apart. Bake for 5 minutes, or until just golden around the edges.

Leave to stand for 1 minute to firm slightly, then transfer to a wire rack to cool completely.

242 *Mocha-filled langues de chat*

Make a double quantity of cookies. Beat together 55 g/2 oz butter and 55 g/2 oz icing sugar until pale and fluffy, then beat in 1 tablespoon of strong black coffee to make a coffee cream. Use to sandwich the biscuits together. Melt 85 g/3 oz chocolate in bowl over a pan of gently simmering water, then leave to cool slightly. Dip half of each biscuit sandwich in the chocolate to coat. Place on baking trays lined with baking paper and leave to set.

243 *Chocolate orange langues de chat*

Add the grated rind of 1 orange to the biscuit mixture. Line 2 large baking sheets with baking paper. Melt 115 g/4 oz plain chocolate in a bowl over a pan of gently simmering water, then allow to cool slightly. Dip each biscuit into the chocolate so that half the biscuit is covered, allowing the excess to run back into the bowl. Place on the baking trays and leave to set.

244 Chocolate-tipped finger rolls

250 g/9 oz icing sugar
125 g/4½ oz plain flour
pinch of salt
6 large egg whites
1 tbsp double cream

1 tsp vanilla extract
125 g/4½ oz unsalted butter, melted
    and cooled
125 g/4½ oz plain chocolate, chopped

Sift the icing sugar, flour and salt into a large bowl, then stir and make a well in the middle. Lightly whisk the egg whites in a separate bowl, add the cream, vanilla extract and butter and mix, then pour into the flour and mix until smooth. Cover and chill overnight in the refrigerator.

Preheat the oven to 200°C/400°F/Gas Mark 6. Have a wooden spoon and wire rack ready. Spoon 4 tablespoons of the batter onto a large, non-stick baking sheet. Using the back of a spoon, spread thinly into ovals 13 cm/5 inches long, spaced well apart. Bake in the preheated oven for 5–6 minutes, or until just browning at the edges. Prepare the second baking sheet while the first batch is cooking.

Using a palette knife, take a cookie and roll around the handle of the wooden spoon to make a cigarette shape. Transfer to the wire rack to cool and repeat with the remaining cookies. Repeat baking and rolling the cookies until all the batter is used.

When the finger rolls are cold, place the chocolate in a heatproof bowl, set the bowl over a saucepan of gently simmering water and heat until melted. Dip one end of each roll into the chocolate, then place on a wire rack to set, leaving the chocolate section standing off the edge.

245 With white chocolate coating

Once the plain chocolate is set, put 125 g/4½ oz white chocolate in a heatproof bowl, set the bowl over a pan of simmering water and heat until melted. Dip the other end of the cookies in the white chocolate and leave to set.

246 Chinese fortune cookies

1-2 tbsp groundnut oil, for greasing
2 large egg whites
½ tsp vanilla extract
3 tbsp vegetable oil
100 g/3½ oz plain flour
1½ tsp cornflour
pinch of salt
150 g/5½ oz caster sugar
3 tsp water

Write fortune messages on thin strips of paper. Preheat the oven to 180°C/350°F/Gas Mark 4 and grease 2 large baking sheets with a little groundnut oil (do not preheat). Place the egg whites, vanilla extract and vegetable oil in a large bowl then, using an electric whisk, beat together for 1 minute until frothy but not stiff.

Sift the flour, cornflour, salt and sugar into a large bowl, stir in the water and mix. Add the egg white mixture and whisk until smooth. Make the cookies in batches of two by spooning 1 scant tablespoon of batter onto each half of the baking sheet and tilting the baking sheet until the batter circles measure 8 cm/3 inches. Bake for 7-8 minutes, until the edges are beginning to brown.

Work quickly to shape the cookies while still hot. Remove a cookie from the baking sheet with a spatula and fold the cookie in half to form a semi-circle. Pinch together at the top and fold the cookie over the rim of a cup. Then insert an index finger into each open end: bring your thumbs together to press into the middle to form the shape of the fortune cookie. Thread through the strip of paper and place on kitchen paper to cool. Repeat the process until all the batter is used.

Neapolitan cookies

225 g/8 oz butter, softened
140 g/5 oz caster sugar
1 egg yolk, lightly beaten
1 tsp vanilla extract
300 g/10½ oz plain flour
1 tbsp cocoa powder

½ tsp almond extract
few drops of green food colouring
1 egg white, lightly beaten
salt

Place the butter and sugar in a large bowl and beat together until light and fluffy, then beat in the egg yolk. Divide the mixture among 3 bowls.

Beat the vanilla extract into the first bowl. Sift together 100 g/3½ oz of the flour and a pinch of salt into the mixture and stir until combined. Shape into a ball, wrap in clingfilm and chill in the refrigerator for 30–60 minutes. Sift together 100 g/3½ oz of the flour, the cocoa and a pinch of salt into the second bowl and stir until combined. Shape into a ball, wrap in clingfilm and chill in the refrigerator.

Beat the almond extract into the third bowl. Sift together the remaining flour and a pinch of salt into the bowl and stir until combined. Mix in a few drops of green food colouring, then form into a ball, wrap in clingfilm and chill in the refrigerator.

Preheat the oven to 190°C/375°F/Gas Mark 5. Line 2 large baking sheets with baking paper. Roll out each piece of dough between 2 sheets of baking paper to rectangles. Brush the top of the vanilla dough with a little beaten egg white and place the chocolate rectangle on top. Brush this with a little beaten egg white and place the almond rectangle on

top. Using a sharp knife, cut into 5-mm/¼-inch thick slices, then cut each slice in half. Place on the baking sheets and bake in the preheated oven for 10–12 minutes. Leave to cool for 5–10 minutes, then transfer the cookies to wire racks to cool completely.

248 *Chocolate-coated Neapolitan cookies*

Put 150 g/5½ oz plain chocolate in a heatproof bowl, set the bowl over a saucepan of gently simmering water and heat until melted. Dip each end of the cooled cookies in the chocolate and leave to set on baking paper.

249 *White chocolate cookies*

115 g/4 oz butter, softened, plus extra
    for greasing
115 g/4 oz soft light brown sugar
1 egg, lightly beaten
250 g/9 oz self-raising flour

pinch of salt
125 g/4½ oz white chocolate, chopped
50 g/1¾ oz chopped Brazil nuts

Preheat the oven to 190°C/375°F/Gas Mark 5. Lightly grease several large baking sheets. Place the butter and sugar in a large bowl and beat together until light and fluffy. Gradually add the egg, beating well after each addition. Sift the flour and salt into the creamed mixture and blend well. Stir in the chocolate chunks and chopped nuts.

Place heaped teaspoonfuls of the mixture on the baking sheets, putting no more than 6 on each sheet because the cookies will spread during cooking. Bake in the preheated oven for 10–12 minutes, or until just golden brown. Transfer the cookies to wire racks to cool completely.

250 *Cardamom & white chocolate cookies*

Omit the nuts and add 1 teaspoon of ground cardamom to the cookie dough.

125 g/4½ oz butter, softened
175 g/6 oz caster sugar
1 egg, lightly beaten
½ tsp vanilla extract
125 g/4½ oz plain flour
35 g/1¼ oz cocoa powder
½ tsp bicarbonate of soda

Preheat the oven to 180°C/350°F/
Gas Mark 4. Line several large
baking sheets with baking paper.

Place the butter and sugar in
a large bowl and beat together
until light and fluffy. Add the egg
and vanilla extract and mix until
smooth. Sift in the flour, cocoa
and bicarbonate of soda and beat
until well mixed.

With dampened hands, roll
walnut-sized pieces of the dough
into smooth balls. Place on the
baking sheets, spaced well apart.

Bake in the preheated oven for
10–12 minutes, or until set. Leave
to cool on the baking sheets for
5 minutes, then transfer the
cookies to wire racks to cool
completely before serving.

252 *With chocolate topping*

As the cookies cool, put 75 g/2¾ oz plain chocolate in a heatproof bowl, set
the bowl over a saucepan of gently simmering water and heat until melted.
Remove from the heat and stir until smooth. Spoon the chocolate into a
piping bag fitted with a writing nozzle and drizzle the chocolate over the
cookies in a decorative zigzag pattern, then leave to set.

253 *Sugar-coated midnight cookies*

Sprinkle 50 g/1¾ oz granulated sugar on a large plate. Roll each ball
of dough in the sugar to coat before placing on the baking sheets.

450 g/1 lb plain flour, plus extra for
    dusting
2 tsp baking powder
225 g/8 oz butter, cut into cubes, plus
    extra for greasing

350 g/12 oz caster sugar
2 large eggs, lightly beaten
2 tsp vanilla extract

Sift the flour and baking powder into a large bowl. Add the butter
and rub it in with your fingertips until the mixture resembles fine
breadcrumbs. Stir the sugar into the mixture, add the eggs and vanilla
extract and mix together to form a soft dough.

Turn the mixture onto a lightly floured work surface and divide
the dough in half. Shape each piece of dough into a log shape about
6 cm/2½ inches thick. Wrap each log in baking paper and then in foil
and chill in the refrigerator for at least 8 hours, or until required.

Preheat the oven to 190°C/375°F/Gas Mark 5. Grease several large
baking sheets.

Slice the dough into as many 8-mm/⅜-inch slices as required and
place on the baking sheets, spaced well apart. Return any remaining
dough to the refrigerator for up to 1 week, or to the freezer until
required. Bake in the preheated oven for 10–15 minutes, or until golden
brown. Leave on the baking sheet to cool slightly for 2–3 minutes, then
transfer the cookies to a wire rack to cool completely.

255 *Cherry refrigerator cookies*

Finely chop 100 g/3½ oz glacé cherries and add to the mixture with
the caster sugar.

256 *Chocolate refrigerator cookies*

Finely grate 100 g/3½ oz plain chocolate and add to the mixture with
the caster sugar.

257 *Coconut refrigerator cookies*

Add 100 g/3½ oz desiccated coconut to the mixture with the caster sugar.

258 *Dried fruit refrigerator cookies*

Finely chop 100 g/3½ oz sultanas, raisins or cranberries and add to
the mixture with the caster sugar.

259 *Ginger refrigerator cookies*

Omit the vanilla extract and sift 3 teaspoons of ground ginger into
the mixture with the flour.

260 *Lemon refrigerator cookies*

Omit the vanilla extract and finely grate the rind of 2 lemons into
the mixture with the caster sugar.

261 *Orange refrigerator cookies*

Omit the vanilla extract and finely grate the rind of 2 oranges into
the mixture with the caster sugar.

262 *Spicy refrigerator cookies*

Omit the vanilla extract and sift 4 teaspoons of ground mixed spice into
the mixture with the flour.

263 *Walnut refrigerator cookies*

Chop 100 g/3½ oz walnut halves and add to the mixture with
the caster sugar.

225 g/8 oz butter, softened
140 g/5 oz caster sugar
1 egg yolk, lightly beaten
2 tsp vanilla extract
250 g/9 oz plain flour

25 g/1 oz cocoa powder
pinch of salt
350 g/12 oz plain chocolate, chopped
55 g/2 oz dried cherries

Preheat the oven to 190°C/375°F/Gas Mark 5. Line 2 large baking sheets with baking paper. Place the butter and sugar in a large bowl and beat together until light and fluffy, then beat in the egg yolk and vanilla extract. Sift together the flour, cocoa and salt into the mixture, add the chopped chocolate and dried cherries and stir until combined.

Scoop up tablespoons of the mixture and shape into balls. Place them on the baking sheets, spaced well apart, and flatten slightly.

Bake in the preheated oven for 12–15 minutes. Leave to cool on the baking sheets for 5–10 minutes, then transfer the cookies to wire racks to cool completely.

265 *Triple chocolate cookies*

Replace the dried cherries with 70 g/2½ oz white chocolate chips.

266 *Simple biscuits*

MAKES 25

175 g/6 oz plain flour, plus extra
for dusting
¼ tsp ground nutmeg
115 g/4 oz unsalted butter, softened
50 g/1¾ oz caster sugar

Preheat the oven to 180°C/350°F/ Gas Mark 4. Sift the flour and nutmeg into a large bowl. Add the butter and rub it into the mixture until it resembles breadcrumbs. Add the sugar and knead together to form a stiff dough. Roll the dough out on a lightly floured work surface to about 5 mm/ ¼ inch thick. Using a 7-cm/ 2¾-inch round cookie cutter dipped in flour, cut out 25 cookies. Re-roll any trimmings. Place the cookies on 2 large non-stick baking sheets.

Bake in the preheated oven for 8–10 minutes, or until pale golden. Transfer to a wire rack and leave to cool completely.

267 *Spiced biscuits*

Add ¼ teaspoon of ground cinnamon, ¼ teaspoon of mixed ground spice and ¼ teaspoon of ground cardamom to the flour and nutmeg.

225 g/8 oz butter, softened
140 g/5 oz caster sugar
1 egg yolk, lightly beaten
2 tsp vanilla extract
225 g/8 oz plain flour
55 g/2 oz cocoa powder
pinch of salt

TOPPING
8 chocolate-coated fudge fingers, broken
   into pieces
4 tbsp double cream

Place the butter and sugar in a large bowl and beat together until light and fluffy, then beat in the egg yolk and vanilla.

Sift the flour, cocoa and salt into the mixture and stir until combined. Halve the dough, shape into balls, wrap in clingfilm and chill in the refrigerator for 30–60 minutes.

Preheat the oven to 190°C/375°F/Gas Mark 5. Line 2 large baking sheets with baking paper.

Unwrap the dough and roll out between 2 sheets of baking paper to about 3 mm/⅛ inch thick. Cut out cookies with a 6-cm/2½-inch square cutter and place them on the baking sheets, spaced well apart. Bake in the preheated oven for 10–15 minutes or until golden brown. Leave to cool on the baking sheets for 5–10 minutes, then transfer them to wire racks to cool completely.

To make the chocolate fudge topping, place the fudge fingers into a heatproof bowl, set the bowl over a saucepan of gently simmering water and heat until melted. Remove the bowl from the heat and gradually whisk in the cream. Leave to cool, then chill until spreadable. Spread the cold fudge topping over the cookies before serving.

269 *Fudge fingers*

Cut the dough into long fingers rather than squares and spread with the fudge topping.

225 g/8 oz butter, softened
140 g/5 oz caster sugar
1 egg yolk, lightly beaten
2 tsp apple juice
280 g/10 oz plain flour
½ tsp ground cinnamon
½ tsp mixed spice
pinch of salt
100 g/3½ oz ready-to-eat dried apple,
   finely chopped

FILLING
1 tbsp caster sugar
1 tbsp custard powder
125 ml/4 fl oz milk
5 tbsp apple sauce

Place the butter and sugar in a large bowl and beat together until light and fluffy, then beat in the egg yolk and apple juice. Sift together the flour, cinnamon, mixed spice and salt into the mixture, add the apple and stir until combined. Halve the dough, shape into balls, wrap in clingfilm and chill for 30–60 minutes.

Preheat the oven to 190°C/375°F/Gas Mark 5. Line 2 large baking sheets with baking paper. Unwrap the dough and roll out between 2 sheets of baking paper. Cut out cookies with a 5-cm/2-inch square cutter and place them on the baking sheets, spaced well apart. Bake in the preheated oven for 10–15 minutes or until light golden brown. Leave to cool for 5–10 minutes, then transfer to wire racks to cool completely.

To make the apple filling, mix the sugar, custard powder and milk together in a saucepan. Bring to the boil, stirring constantly and cook until thickened. Remove the pan from the heat and stir in the apple sauce. Cover the surface with clingfilm and leave to cool.

Spread the filling over half the cookies and top with the remainder.

271 *Chocolate-dipped apple spice cookies*

Omit the apple filling and place 150 g/5½ oz white chocolate in a heatproof bowl, set the bowl over a saucepan of gently simmering water and heat until melted. Dip half of each cookie and leave to set on baking paper. Makes about 30.

272 *Blueberry & cranberry cinnamon cookies*

225 g/8 oz butter, softened
140 g/5 oz caster sugar
1 egg yolk, lightly beaten
2 tsp vanilla extract
280 g/10 oz plain flour

1 tsp ground cinnamon
pinch of salt
55 g/2 oz dried blueberries
55 g/2 oz dried cranberries
55 g/2 oz pine kernels, chopped

Preheat the oven to 190°C/375°F/Gas Mark 5. Line 2 large baking sheets with baking paper. Place the butter and sugar in a large bowl and beat together until light and fluffy, then beat in the egg yolk and vanilla extract. Sift together the flour, cinnamon and salt into the mixture. Add the blueberries and cranberries and stir until thoroughly combined.

Spread out the pine kernels in a shallow dish. Scoop up tablespoons of the mixture and roll them into balls. Roll the balls in the pine kernels to coat, then place on the baking sheets, spaced well apart, and flatten slightly. Bake in the preheated oven for 10–15 minutes.

Leave to cool on the baking sheets for 5–10 minutes, then transfer the cookies to wire racks to cool completely.

273 *Macadamia nut cinnamon cookies*

Replace the pine kernels with 85 g/3 oz chopped macadamia nuts.

274 *Blueberry orange cookies*

225 g/8 oz butter, softened
140 g/5 oz caster sugar
1 egg yolk, lightly beaten
1 tsp orange extract
280 g/10 oz plain flour
pinch of salt
100 g/3½ oz dried blueberries

TOPPING
100 g/3½ oz cream cheese
grated rind of 1 orange
40 g/1½ oz macadamia nuts, finely
    chopped

Place the butter and sugar in a large bowl and beat together until light and fluffy, then beat in the egg yolk and orange extract. Sift together the flour and salt into the mixture, add the blueberries and stir until thoroughly combined. Shape the dough into a log, wrap in clingfilm and chill in the refrigerator for 30–60 minutes.

Preheat the oven to 190°C/375°F/Gas Mark 5. Line 2 large baking sheets with baking paper. Unwrap the log, then cut into 5-mm/¼-inch slices with a sharp serrated knife and place them on the baking sheets, spaced well apart. Bake in the preheated oven for 10–15 minutes, or until golden brown. Leave to cool on the baking sheets for 5–10 minutes, then transfer the cookies to wire racks to cool completely.

Just before serving, beat the cream cheese in a bowl and stir in the orange rind. Spread the mixture over the cookies and sprinkle with the nuts.

275 Caribbean cookies

225 g/8 oz butter, softened
140 g/5 oz caster sugar
1 egg yolk, lightly beaten
2 tsp rum or rum flavouring

280 g/10 oz plain flour
pinch of salt
100 g/3½ oz desiccated coconut
4 tbsp lime marmalade

Preheat the oven to 190°C/375°F/Gas Mark 5. Line 2 large baking sheets with baking paper. Place the butter and sugar in a large bowl and beat together until light and fluffy, then beat in the egg yolk and rum. Sift together the flour and salt into the mixture, add the coconut and stir until combined.

Scoop up tablespoons of the dough and place them on the baking sheets, spaced well apart. Make a hollow in the centre of each with the dampened handle of a spoon and fill the hollows with the marmalade.

Bake in the preheated oven for 10–15 minutes, or until light golden brown. Leave to cool on the baking sheets for 5–10 minutes, then transfer the cookies to wire racks to cool completely.

276 Rainbow cookies

Use a variety of fillings for the cookies – try lime, lemon or passion fruit curd, and seedless strawberry or blackcurrant jam.

277 Chewy candied fruit cookies

225 g/8 oz butter, softened
140 g/5 oz caster sugar
1 egg yolk, lightly beaten
2 tsp vanilla extract
280 g/10 oz plain flour
pinch of salt

TOPPING
4 tbsp maple syrup
55 g/2 oz butter
55 g/2 oz caster sugar
115 g/4 oz ready-to-eat dried peaches, chopped
55 g/2 oz glacé cherries, chopped
55 g/2 oz chopped mixed peel
85 g/3 oz macadamia nuts, chopped
25 g/1 oz plain flour

Place the butter and sugar in a large bowl and beat together until light and fluffy, then beat in the egg yolk and vanilla extract. Sift together the flour and salt into the mixture and stir until thoroughly combined. Halve the dough, shape into balls, wrap in clingfilm and chill in the refrigerator for 30–60 minutes.

Preheat the oven to 190°C/375°F/Gas Mark 5. Line 2 large baking sheets with baking paper. Unwrap the dough and roll out between 2 sheets of baking paper. Cut out rounds with a 6-cm/2½-inch plain round cutter and place them on the baking sheets, spaced well apart.

To make the topping, place the maple syrup, butter and sugar into a saucepan and melt over a low heat, stirring occasionally. Meanwhile, place the fruit, mixed peel, nuts and flour into a bowl and mix well. When the syrup mixture is combined, stir it into the fruit mixture and divide the topping among the cookies, gently spreading it out to the edges.

Bake in the preheated oven for 10–15 minutes, until firm. Leave to cool for 5–10 minutes, then transfer to wire racks to cool completely.

278 With hazelnut topping

Replace the macadamia nuts in the topping with hazelnuts.

225 g/8 oz butter, softened
140 g/5 oz caster sugar
1 egg yolk, lightly beaten
2 tsp vanilla extract

280 g/10 oz plain flour
pinch of salt
40 g/1½ oz desiccated coconut
60 g/2¼ oz dried cranberries

Preheat the oven to 190°C/375°F/Gas Mark 5. Line 2 large baking sheets with baking paper. Place the butter and sugar in a large bowl and beat together until light and fluffy, then beat in the egg yolk and vanilla extract. Sift together the flour and salt into the mixture, add the coconut and cranberries and stir until combined. Scoop up tablespoons of the dough and place in mounds on the baking sheets, spaced well apart.

Bake in the preheated oven for 12–15 minutes, or until golden brown. Leave to cool on the baking sheets for 5–10 minutes, then transfer the cookies to wire racks to cool completely.

280 *Coconut & papaya cookies*

Replace the cranberries with chopped dried papaya.

281 *Chocolate, date & pecan nut pinwheels*

225 g/8 oz butter, softened
200 g/7 oz caster sugar
1 egg yolk, lightly beaten
225 g/8 oz plain flour
55 g/2 oz cocoa powder
pinch of salt

100 g/3½ oz pecan nuts, finely ground
280 g/10 oz dried dates, coarsely chopped
finely grated rind of 1 orange
175 ml/6 fl oz orange flower water

Place the butter and 140 g/5 oz of the sugar in a large bowl and beat together until light and fluffy, then beat in the egg yolk. Sift together the flour, cocoa and salt into the mixture, add the nuts and stir until combined. Halve the dough, shape into balls, wrap in clingfilm and chill in the refrigerator for 30–60 minutes.

Meanwhile, place the dates, orange rind, orange flower water and remaining sugar into a saucepan and cook over a low heat, stirring, until the sugar has dissolved. Bring to the boil, then reduce the heat and simmer, for 5 minutes. Pour the mixture into a bowl, cool, then chill.

Unwrap the dough and roll out between 2 pieces of baking paper to rectangles 5 mm/¼ inch thick. Spread the filling over the rectangles and roll up like a Swiss roll. Wrap in the paper and chill in a refrigerator for 30 minutes.

Preheat the oven to 190°C/ 375°F/ Gas Mark 5. Line 2 large baking sheets with baking paper. Unwrap the rolls, cut into 1-cm/½-inch slices and place them on the baking sheets.

Bake in the preheated oven for 15–20 minutes, or until golden brown. Leave to cool on the baking sheets for 5–10 minutes, then transfer the cookies to wire racks to cool completely.

282 *Fig & walnut pinwheels*

Replace the dates and nuts with 280 g/10 oz chopped dried figs and 100 g/ 3½ oz chopped walnuts. Replace the orange flower water and orange rind with 30 ml/1 oz brandy and 1 teaspoon of vanilla extract.

283 Date & lemon spirals

225 g/8 oz butter, softened
175 g/6 oz caster sugar
1 egg yolk, lightly beaten
1 tsp lemon extract
280 g/10 oz plain flour
pinch of salt

280 g/10 oz dried dates, pitted and
    finely chopped
2 tbsp clear lemon blossom honey
5 tbsp lemon juice
1 tbsp finely grated lemon rind
125 ml/4 fl oz water
1 tsp ground cinnamon

Place the butter and 140 g/5 oz of the sugar in a large bowl and beat together until light and fluffy, then beat in the egg yolk and lemon extract. Sift together the flour and salt into the mixture and stir until combined. Shape the dough into a ball, wrap in clingfilm and chill in the refrigerator for 30–60 minutes.

Meanwhile, place the dates, honey, lemon juice and lemon rind in a saucepan and stir in the water. Bring to the boil, stirring constantly, then reduce the heat and simmer gently for 5 minutes. Leave to cool, then chill in the refrigerator for 15 minutes. Mix the cinnamon and remaining sugar together in a small bowl.

Unwrap the dough and roll out between 2 sheets of baking paper into a 30-cm/12-inch square. Sprinkle the cinnamon and sugar mixture over the dough and roll lightly with the rolling pin.

Spread the date mixture over the dough, then roll up like a Swiss roll. Wrap in clingfilm and chill for 30 minutes.

Preheat the oven to 190°C/375°F/Gas Mark 5. Line 2 large baking sheets with baking paper. Unwrap the roll and cut into thin slices with a sharp serrated knife. Put them on the baking sheets spaced well apart. Bake in the preheated oven for 12–15 minutes, or until golden brown. Leave to cool for 5–10 minutes, then carefully transfer to wire racks to cool completely.

284 Fig & rose water spirals

Replace the dates and lemon extract, juice and rind with 280 g/10 oz dried chopped figs and add 1 teaspoon of rose water to the fig mixture.

285 Chocolate & hazelnut drops

225 g/8 oz butter, softened
140 g/5 oz caster sugar
1 egg yolk, lightly beaten
2 tsp vanilla extract
225 g/8 oz plain flour
55 g/2 oz cocoa powder

pinch of salt
55 g/2 oz ground hazelnuts
55 g/2 oz plain chocolate chips
4 tbsp chocolate and hazelnut spread

Preheat the oven to 190°C/375°F/Gas Mark 5. Line 2 baking sheets with baking paper. Place the butter and sugar in a large bowl and beat together until light and fluffy, then beat in the egg yolk and vanilla extract. Sift together the flour, cocoa and salt into the mixture, add the ground hazelnuts and chocolate chips and stir until combined.

Scoop out tablespoons of the mixture and shape into balls, then place them on the baking sheets, spaced well apart. Use the dampened handle of a wooden spoon to make a hollow in the centre of each cookie. Bake in the preheated oven for 12–15 minutes.

Leave to cool on the baking sheets for 5–10 minutes, then transfer the cookies to wire racks to cool completely. When cold, fill the hollows with the chocolate and hazelnut spread.

Grapefruit & apple mint cookies

225 g/8 oz butter, softened
140 g/5 oz caster sugar, plus extra for
    sprinkling
1 egg yolk, lightly beaten
2 tsp grapefruit juice

280 g/10 oz plain flour
pinch of salt
grated rind of 1 grapefruit
2 tsp finely chopped fresh apple mint

Place the butter and sugar in a large bowl and beat together until light and fluffy, then beat in the egg yolk and grapefruit juice. Sift together the flour and salt into the mixture, add the grapefruit rind and mint and stir until thoroughly combined. Halve the dough, shape into balls, wrap in clingfilm and chill in the refrigerator for 30–60 minutes.

Preheat the oven to 190°C/375°F/Gas Mark 5. Line 2 large baking sheets with baking paper. Unwrap the dough and roll out between 2 sheets of baking paper to 3 mm/⅛ inch thick. Cut out cookies with a 5-cm/2-inch flower cutter and place them on the baking sheets, spaced well apart. Sprinkle with caster sugar.

Bake in the preheated oven for 10–15 minutes, or until golden brown. Leave to cool on the baking sheets for 5–10 minutes, then transfer the cookies to wire racks to cool completely.

287 Lemon & thyme cookies

Replace the grapefruit juice with lemon juice and replace the mint with 1 teaspoon of chopped fresh thyme leaves.

288 Chocolate mint cookie sandwiches

225 g/8 oz butter, softened
140 g/5 oz caster sugar
1 egg yolk, lightly beaten
2 tsp vanilla extract
250 g/9 oz plain flour
25 g/1 oz cocoa powder
pinch of salt

55 g/2 oz glacé cherries, finely chopped
15 after-dinner mint thins
115 g/4 oz plain chocolate, broken
    into pieces
55 g/2 oz white chocolate, broken
    into pieces

Place the butter and sugar in a large bowl and beat together until light and fluffy, then beat in the egg yolk and vanilla extract. Sift together the flour, cocoa and salt into the mixture, add the cherries and stir until thoroughly combined. Halve the dough, shape into balls, wrap in clingfilm and chill in the refrigerator for 30–60 minutes.

Preheat the oven to 190°C/375°F/Gas Mark 5. Line 2 large baking sheets with baking paper. Unwrap the dough and roll out between 2 sheets of baking paper. Cut out cookies with a 6-cm/2½-inch plain square cutter and place them on the baking sheets, spaced well apart.

Bake in the preheated oven for 10–15 minutes, or until firm. Remove from the oven and place an after-dinner mint on top of half of the cookies, then cover with the remaining cookies. Press down gently and leave to cool on the baking sheets.

Place the plain chocolate in a heatproof bowl, set the bowl over a saucepan of gently simmering water and heat until melted. Leave to cool. Place the cookies on a wire rack over a sheet of baking paper. Spoon the plain chocolate over them, then tap the rack to level the surface and leave to set.

Place the white chocolate in a heatproof bowl, set the bowl over a pan of gently simmering water and heat until melted. Leave to cool, then pipe or drizzle it over the cookies and leave to set.

289 Jam rings

225 g/8 oz butter, softened
140 g/5 oz caster sugar, plus extra
for sprinkling
1 egg yolk, lightly beaten
2 tsp vanilla extract
280 g/10 oz plain flour
pinch of salt
1 egg white, lightly beaten

FILLING
55 g/2 oz butter, softened
100 g/3½ oz icing sugar
5 tbsp strawberry or raspberry
jam, warmed

Place the butter and sugar in a large bowl and beat together until light and fluffy, then beat in the egg yolk and vanilla extract. Sift together the flour and salt into the mixture and stir until combined. Halve the dough, shape into balls, wrap in clingfilm and chill in the refrigerator for 30–60 minutes.

Preheat the oven to 190°C/375°F/Gas Mark 5. Line 2 large baking sheets with baking paper. Unwrap the dough and roll out between 2 sheets of baking paper. Cut out biscuits with a 7-cm/2¾-inch fluted round cutter and place half of them on a baking sheet, spaced well apart. Using a 4-cm/1½-inch plain round cutter, cut out the centres of the remaining biscuits and remove, then place the rings on the other baking sheet, spaced well apart.

Bake in the preheated oven for 7 minutes, then brush the biscuit rings with beaten egg white and sprinkle with caster sugar. Bake for a further 5–8 minutes, or until light golden brown. Leave to cool on the baking sheets for 5–10 minutes, then transfer the cookies to wire racks to cool completely.

To make the jam filling, place the butter and icing sugar in a large bowl and beat together until smooth and combined. Spread the filling over the whole biscuits and top with a little jam. Place the rings on top and press gently together.

290 Lemon rings

Add finely grated lemon rind to the butter filling and replace the jam with lemon curd.

291 Jam sandwich biscuits

225 g/8 oz unsalted butter, softened
100 g/3½ oz caster sugar
200 g/7 oz plain flour, plus extra
for dusting
pinch of salt
100 g/3½ oz ground almonds
55 g/2 oz seedless raspberry jam
55 g/2 oz apricot jam
2 tbsp icing sugar

Place the butter and sugar in a large bowl and beat together until light and fluffy. Add the flour, salt and ground almonds and bring together to form a soft dough. Wrap the dough in clingfilm and chill in the refrigerator for 2 hours.

Preheat the oven to 150°C/300°F/Gas Mark 2. Roll the dough out on a floured work surface to about 5 mm/¼ inch thick. Using a 7-cm/2¾-inch cookie cutter dipped in flour, cut out 48 shapes. Re-roll any trimmings and cut out more cookies. Use a small round cookie cutter to cut out the centre from 24 of the shapes and place the cookies on 2 large, non-stick baking sheets. Bake in the preheated oven for 25–30 minutes, or until golden. Leave to cool completely on a wire rack.

Spoon the raspberry jam onto 12 of the complete cookies. Spoon the apricot jam onto the remaining 12. Sift the icing sugar over the cut-out cookies and use these to cover the jam-topped halves, pressing down gently.

292 Chocolate sandwich biscuits

Divide the dough in half, add 2 teaspoons of cocoa powder to one piece of dough and knead in before chilling. Make the cookies, cutting out the centres from the chocolate dough. Sandwich together with 125 g/4½ oz chocolate spread.

85 g/3 oz unsalted butter, softened
100 g/3½ oz caster sugar
2 large eggs
½ tsp vanilla extract
200 g/7 oz plain flour, plus extra
    for dusting

1 tsp baking powder
pinch of salt

ICING
150 g/5½ oz icing sugar
about 1 tbsp cold water
few drops of food colouring

Place the butter and sugar in a large bowl and beat together until light and fluffy. Whisk the eggs and vanilla extract in another bowl, then add to the butter and sugar mixture. Sift in the flour, baking powder and salt and beat together to form a dough. Wrap in clingfilm and chill in the refrigerator for 1 hour.

Preheat the oven to 180°C/350°F/Gas Mark 4. Line 2 large baking sheets with baking paper. Roll the dough out on a floured work surface to about 5 mm/¼ inch thick. Cut out cookies with a variety of cookie cutter shapes dipped in flour and place them on the baking sheets. Bake in the preheated oven for 10–12 minutes, or until golden brown. Leave to cool on wire racks.

When the cookies are cold, sift the icing sugar into a bowl and mix with the water until smooth. Colour the icing as desired and spread over the cookies, then leave to set.

294 *Xmas alphabet cut-outs*

Use alphabet cookie cutters to cut out letters, ice as before with red tinted icing and decorate with silver dragées.

295 *Chocolate orange cookies*

MAKES 30

90 g/3¼ oz butter, softened
60 g/2¼ oz caster sugar
1 egg
1 tbsp milk
280 g/10 oz plain flour, plus extra for
    dusting
2 tbsp cocoa powder

ICING
175 g/6 oz icing sugar
3 tbsp orange juice
a little plain chocolate, broken into pieces

Preheat the oven to 180°C/350°F/Gas Mark 4. Line 2 large baking sheets with sheets of greaseproof paper. Place the butter and sugar in a large bowl and beat together until light and fluffy. Beat in the egg and milk until thoroughly combined. Sift the flour and cocoa into the bowl and gradually mix together to form a soft dough.

Roll out the dough on a lightly floured work surface until about 5 mm/¼ inch thick. Cut out rounds with a 5-cm/2-inch fluted round biscuit cutter and place them on the baking sheets. Bake in the preheated oven for 10–12 minutes, or until golden. Leave to cool on the baking sheet for a few minutes, then transfer the cookies to a wire rack to cool completely and become crisp.

To make the icing, sift the icing sugar in a bowl and stir in enough orange juice to form a thin icing that will coat the back of the spoon. Place a spoonful of icing in the centre of each biscuit and leave to set.

Place the plain chocolate in a heatproof bowl, set the bowl over a saucepan of gently simmering water and heat until melted. Drizzle thin lines of melted chocolate over the biscuits and leave to set before serving.

296 *With coffee icing*

Replace the orange juice in the icing with 2–3 tablespoons of cold, strong espresso coffee.

140 g/5 oz plain chocolate, broken into
  pieces, to decorate
30 thinly pared strips of lime rind, to
  decorate
225 g/8 oz butter, softened
140 g/5 oz caster sugar
1 egg yolk, lightly beaten
2 tsp lime juice

280 g/10 oz plain flour
pinch of salt
finely grated rind of 1 lemon

ICING
1 tbsp lightly beaten egg white
1 tbsp lime juice
115 g/4 oz icing sugar

To make the decoration, place the chocolate in a heatproof bowl, set the bowl over a saucepan of gently simmering water and heat until melted. Leave to cool slightly. Line a baking sheet with baking paper. Dip the strips of lime rind into the chocolate until coated, then put on the baking sheet to set.

Place the butter and sugar in a large bowl and beat together until light and fluffy, then beat in the egg yolk and lime juice. Sift together the flour and salt into the mixture, add the lemon rind and stir until combined. Halve the dough, shape into balls, wrap in clingfilm and chill in the refrigerator for 30–60 minutes.

Preheat the oven to 190°C/375°F/Gas Mark 5. Line 2 large baking sheets with baking paper. Unwrap the dough and roll out between 2 sheets of baking paper to about 3 mm/⅛ inch thick. Cut out rounds with a 6-cm/2½-inch plain cutter and place them on the baking sheets. Bake in the preheated oven for 10–15 minutes, or until golden brown. Leave to cool on the baking sheets for 5–10 minutes, then transfer to wire racks to cool completely.

To make the icing, place the egg white and lime juice in a bowl and mix together, then gradually beat in the icing sugar until smooth. Ice the cookies and top with the chocolate-coated lime rind. Leave to set.

298 *With plain chocolate topping*

Omit the lime rind and simply drizzle the melted plain chocolate over the icing and leave to set.

---

299 *Lemon & sesame seed cookies*

2 tbsp sesame seeds
225 g/8 oz butter, softened
140 g/5 oz caster sugar
1 tbsp finely grated lemon rind
1 egg yolk, lightly beaten
280 g/10 oz plain flour
pinch of salt

ICING
115 g/4 oz icing sugar
few drops of lemon extract
1 tbsp hot water

Dry-fry the sesame seeds in a heavy-based frying pan over a low heat, stirring frequently, for 2–3 minutes, or until they give off their aroma. Leave to cool.

Place the butter, sugar, lemon rind and toasted seeds in a large bowl and beat together until light and fluffy, then beat in the egg yolk. Sift together the flour and salt into the mixture and stir until combined. Halve the dough, form it into balls, wrap in clingfilm and chill in the refrigerator for 30–60 minutes.

Preheat the oven to 190°C/375°F/Gas Mark 5. Line 2 large baking sheets with baking paper. Unwrap the dough and roll out between 2 sheets of baking paper. Cut out rounds with a 6-cm/2½-inch cutter and place them on the baking sheets, spaced well apart. Bake in the preheated oven for 10–12 minutes, or until light golden brown. Leave to cool on the baking sheets for 5–10 minutes, then transfer the cookies to wire racks to cool completely.

To make the icing, sift the icing sugar into a bowl, add the lemon extract and gradually stir in the hot water until the icing is smooth and has the consistency of thick cream. Leave the cooled cookies on the racks and spread the icing over them. Leave to set.

300 *Lime & sesame seed cookies*

Omit the lemon in this recipe and replace with lime, then top the icing with finely grated lime rind.

301 Mango, coconut & ginger cookies

MAKES ABOUT 30

225 g/8 oz butter, softened
140 g/5 oz caster sugar
1 egg yolk, lightly beaten
55 g/2 oz stem ginger, chopped, plus 2 tsp syrup from the jar
280 g/10 oz plain flour
pinch of salt
55 g/2 oz ready-to-eat dried mango, chopped
100 g/3½ oz desiccated coconut

Place the butter and sugar in a large bowl and beat together until light and fluffy, then beat in the egg yolk and ginger syrup. Sift together the flour and salt into the mixture, add the stem ginger and mango and stir until combined.

Spread out the coconut in a shallow dish. Shape the dough into a log and roll it in the coconut to coat. Wrap in clingfilm and chill in the refrigerator for 30–60 minutes.

Preheat the oven to 190°C/375°F/Gas Mark 5. Line 2 large baking sheets with baking paper. Unwrap the log and cut it into 5-mm/¼-inch slices with a sharp serrated knife and place them on the baking sheets, spaced well apart.

Bake in the preheated oven for 12–15 minutes, or until light golden brown. Leave to cool on the baking sheets for 5–10 minutes, then transfer the cookies to wire racks to cool completely.

302 Pineapple, coconut & ginger cookies

Replace the mango with chopped dried pineapple and make an icing by sifting 115 g/4 oz icing sugar into a bowl then add 1½ tablespoons of pineapple juice. Beat until smooth and use to ice the cooled cookies.

303 Pineapple & ginger creams

MAKES ABOUT 15

225 g/8 oz butter, softened
140 g/5 oz caster sugar
1 egg yolk, lightly beaten
2 tsp vanilla extract
280 g/10 oz plain flour
pinch of salt
100 g/3½ oz ready-to-eat dried pineapple, finely chopped
cocoa powder, for dusting
icing sugar, for dusting

GINGER CREAM
150 ml/5 fl oz Greek-style yogurt
1 tbsp golden syrup
1 tbsp ground ginger

Place the butter and sugar in a large bowl and beat together until light and fluffy, then beat in the egg yolk and vanilla extract. Sift together the flour and salt into the mixture, add the pineapple and stir until thoroughly combined. Halve the dough, shape into balls, wrap in clingfilm and chill in the refrigerator for 30–60 minutes.

Preheat the oven to 190°C/375°F/Gas Mark 5. Line 2 large baking sheets with baking paper.

Unwrap the dough and roll out between 2 sheets of baking paper. Cut out cookies with a 6-cm/2½-inch fluted round cutter and place them on the baking sheets, spaced well apart. Bake in the preheated oven for 10–15 minutes, or until light golden brown. Leave to cool on the baking sheets for 5–10 minutes, then transfer the cookies to wire racks to cool completely.

To make the ginger cream, place the yogurt, golden syrup and ground ginger in a bowl and beat together until thoroughly combined. Sandwich the cookies together with the ginger cream. Cover half of each cookie with a piece of paper and dust the exposed half with sifted cocoa. Cover the cocoa-dusted half of each cookie with a piece of paper and dust the exposed half with sifted icing sugar.

304 With pineapple icing

Instead of dusting the cookies with cocoa and icing sugar, make a pineapple icing by mixing 100 g/3½ oz sifted icing sugar and 1 tablespoon of pineapple juice together until smooth, then spread over the cookies and leave to set.

225 g/8 oz butter, softened
140 g/5 oz caster sugar
1 egg yolk, lightly beaten
2 tsp vanilla extract

280 g/10 oz plain flour
pinch of salt
55 g/2 oz glacé cherries, finely chopped
55 g/2 oz milk chocolate chips

Place the butter and sugar in a large bowl and beat together until light and fluffy, then beat in the egg yolk and vanilla extract. Sift together the flour and salt into the mixture, add the glacé cherries and chocolate chips and stir until thoroughly combined. Halve the dough, shape into balls, wrap in clingfilm and chill in the refrigerator for 30–60 minutes.

Preheat the oven to 190°C/375°F/Gas Mark 5. Line 2 large baking sheets with baking paper. Unwrap the dough and roll out between 2 sheets of baking paper to about 3 mm/⅛ inch thick. Cut out cookies with a diamond-shaped cutter and place them on the baking sheets.

Bake in the preheated oven for 10–15 minutes, or until light golden brown. Leave to cool on the baking sheets for 5–10 minutes, then transfer the cookies to wire racks to cool completely.

306 *Ginger & chocolate diamonds*

Replace the cherries and milk chocolate chips with crystallized ginger and white chocolate chips.

307 *Tropical fruit cookie sandwiches*

MAKES ABOUT 15

225 g/8 oz butter, softened
140 g/5 oz caster sugar
1 egg yolk, lightly beaten
2 tsp passion fruit pulp
280 g/10 oz plain flour
pinch of salt
40 g/1½ oz ready-to-eat dried mango, chopped
40 g/1½ oz ready-to-eat dried papaya, chopped

25 g/1 oz dried dates, pitted and chopped
3–4 tbsp shredded coconut, toasted

MASCARPONE CREAM
85 g/3 oz mascarpone cheese
3 tbsp Greek-style yogurt
7 tbsp ready-made custard
½ tsp ground ginger

Place the butter and sugar in a large bowl and beat together until light and fluffy, then beat in the egg yolk and passion fruit pulp. Sift together the flour and salt into the mixture, add the mango, papaya and dates and stir until combined. Shape the dough into a log, wrap in clingfilm and chill for 30–60 minutes.

Meanwhile, to make the mascarpone cream, place all the ingredients in a bowl and beat until smooth. Cover and chill in the refrigerator.

Preheat the oven to 190°C/375°F/Gas Mark 5. Line 2 large baking sheets with baking paper. Unwrap the dough, cut into slices with a sharp serrated knife and place them on the baking sheets, spaced well apart.

Bake in the preheated oven for 10–15 minutes, or until light golden brown. Leave to cool on the baking sheets for 5–10 minutes, then transfer the cookies to wire racks to cool completely.

When the cookies are cold, spread the chilled mascarpone cream over half of them, sprinkle with the toasted coconut and top with the remaining cookies.

308 *With coconut cream filling*

Omit the mascarpone cream and fill the cookies with 85 g/3 oz butter beaten with 3 tablespoons of creamed coconut, 100 g/3½ oz icing sugar and 3 tablespoons of desiccated coconut.

309 Apricot & pecan cookies

225 g/8 oz butter, softened
140 g/5 oz caster sugar
1 egg yolk, lightly beaten
2 tsp vanilla extract
280 g/10 oz plain flour

pinch of salt
finely grated rind of 1 orange
55 g/2 oz ready-to-eat dried apricots,
    chopped
100 g/3½ oz pecan nuts, finely chopped

Place the butter and sugar in a large bowl and beat together until light and fluffy, then beat in the egg yolk and vanilla extract. Sift together the flour and salt into the mixture, add the orange rind and apricots and stir until combined. Shape the dough into a log. Spread out the pecan nuts in a shallow dish. Roll the log in the nuts until well coated, then wrap in clingfilm and chill in the refrigerator for 30–60 minutes.

Preheat the oven to 190°C/375°F/Gas Mark 5. Line 2 large baking sheets with baking paper. Unwrap the dough, cut into 5-mm/¼-inch slices with a sharp serrated knife and place the slices on the baking sheets, spaced well apart.

Bake in the preheated oven for 10–12 minutes, or until golden brown. Leave to cool on the baking sheets for 5–10 minutes, then transfer the cookies to wire racks to cool completely.

310 Cherry or cranberries & pecan cookies

Replace the apricots with 70 g/2½ oz dried cherries or dried cranberries.

311 Chocolate & apricot cookies

225 g/8 oz butter, softened
140 g/5 oz caster sugar
1 egg yolk, lightly beaten
2 tsp amaretto liqueur
280 g/10 oz plain flour

pinch of salt
55 g/2 oz plain chocolate chips
55 g/2 oz ready-to-eat dried apricots,
    chopped
100 g/3½ oz blanched almonds, chopped

Place the butter and sugar in a large bowl and beat together until light and fluffy, then beat in the egg yolk and amaretto liqueur. Sift together the flour and salt into the mixture, add the chocolate chips and apricots and stir until thoroughly combined. Shape the mixture into a log. Spread out the almonds in a shallow dish and roll the log in them to coat. Wrap in clingfilm and chill in the refrigerator for 30–60 minutes.

Preheat the oven to 190°C/375°F/Gas Mark 5. Line 2 large baking sheets with baking paper. Unwrap the dough, cut into 5-mm/¼-inch slices with a sharp serrated knife and place them on the baking sheets, spaced well apart.

Bake in the preheated oven for 12–15 minutes, or until golden brown. Leave to cool for 5–10 minutes, then transfer the cookies to wire racks to cool completely.

312 *Margarita cookies*

225 g/8 oz butter, softened
140 g/5 oz caster sugar
finely grated rind of 1 lime
1 egg yolk, lightly beaten
2 tsp orange liqueur or 1 tsp orange
    extract

280 g/10 oz plain flour
pinch of salt

ICING
140 g/5 oz icing sugar
2 tbsp white tequila

Preheat the oven to 190°C/375°F/Gas Mark 5. Line 2 large baking sheets with baking paper. Place the butter, sugar and lime rind in a large bowl and beat together until light and fluffy, then beat in the egg yolk and orange liqueur. Sift together the flour and salt into the mixture and stir until combined. Scoop up tablespoons of the dough, place them on the baking sheets, and flatten gently.

Bake in the preheated oven for 10–15 minutes, or until light golden brown. Leave to cool on the baking sheets for 5–10 minutes, then carefully transfer the cookies to wire racks to cool completely.

Sift the icing sugar into a bowl and stir in enough tequila to give the mixture the consistency of thick cream. Leave the cookies on the wire racks and drizzle the icing over them with a teaspoon. Leave to set.

313 *With lime icing*

Replace the tequila in the icing with 2 tablespoons of fresh lime juice and scatter over finely grated lime zest.

314 *Mixed fruit cookies*

225 g/8 oz butter, softened
140 g/5 oz caster sugar
1 egg yolk, lightly beaten
280 g/10 oz plain flour
½ tsp mixed spice
pinch of salt

25 g/1 oz ready-to-eat dried apple,
    chopped
25 g/1 oz ready-to-eat dried pears,
    chopped
25 g/1 oz ready-to-eat prunes, chopped
finely grated rind of 1 orange

Place the butter and sugar in a large bowl and beat together until light and fluffy, then beat in the egg yolk. Sift together the flour, mixed spice and salt into the mixture, then add the apple, pear, prunes and orange rind and stir until combined. Shape the dough into a log, wrap in clingfilm and chill for 30–60 minutes.

Preheat the oven to 190°C/375°F/Gas Mark 5. Line 2 large baking sheets with baking paper.

Unwrap the log, cut it into 5-mm/¼-inch thick slices with a sharp serrated knife and place the slices on the baking sheets, spaced well apart. Bake in the preheated oven for 10–15 minutes, or until golden brown. Leave to cool on the baking sheets for 5–10 minutes, then transfer the cookies to wire racks to cool completely.

315 *Tropical fruit cookies*

Replace the apples, pears and prunes with chopped dried mango, pineapple and papaya.

Oaty raisin & hazelnut cookies

55 g/2 oz raisins, chopped
125 ml/4 fl oz orange juice
225 g/8 oz butter, softened
140 g/5 oz caster sugar
1 egg yolk, lightly beaten
2 tsp vanilla extract

225 g/8 oz plain flour
pinch of salt
55 g/2 oz rolled oats
55 g/2 oz hazelnuts, chopped
about 30 whole hazelnut

Preheat the oven to 190°C/375°F/Gas Mark 5. Line 2 large baking sheets with baking paper. Place the raisins in a bowl, add the orange juice and leave to soak for 10 minutes.

Place the butter and sugar in a large bowl and beat together until light and fluffy, then beat in the egg yolk and vanilla extract. Sift together the flour and salt into the mixture and add the oats and hazelnuts. Drain the raisins, add them to the mixture and stir until combined. Scoop up tablespoons of the mixture and place them in mounds on the baking sheets, spaced well apart. Flatten slightly and place a whole hazelnut in the centre of each cookie.

Bake in the preheated oven for 12–15 minutes, or until golden brown. Leave to cool on the baking sheets for 5–10 minutes, then transfer to wire racks to cool completely.

317 *Oaty sultana & walnut cookies*

Replace the raisins and hazelnuts with 55 g/2 oz chopped sultanas and 100 g/3½ oz chopped walnuts.

318 *Lemon polenta cookies*

100 g/3½ oz butter, softened
70 g/2½ oz caster sugar
2 large eggs, lightly beaten
finely grated rind of 1 lemon
1 tbsp lemon juice

150 g/5½ oz plain flour
70 g/2½ oz polenta
12 whole blanched almonds

Preheat the oven to 190°C/375°F/Gas Mark 5. Line several large baking sheets with baking paper. Place the butter and sugar in a large bowl and whisk until pale and creamy. Whisk the beaten eggs, lemon rind and juice into the mixture until smooth, then add the flour and polenta and beat together until mixed.

Place the mixture in a piping bag fitted with a plain 2-cm/¾-inch nozzle. Pipe swirls, measuring about 6 cm/2½ inches in diameter, onto the baking sheets, spaced well apart, and top each cookie with a blanched almond.

Bake in the preheated oven for 10–15 minutes, or until lightly golden brown. Leave to cool on the baking sheets for 5 minutes, then transfer the cookies to a wire rack to cool completely.

Orange & chocolate fingers

225 g/8 oz butter, softened
140 g/5 oz caster sugar
finely grated rind of 1 orange
1 egg yolk, lightly beaten
2 tsp orange juice

280 g/10 oz plain flour
1 tsp ground ginger
pinch of salt
115 g/4 oz plain chocolate, broken into
    pieces

Place the butter, sugar and orange rind in a large bowl and beat together until light and fluffy, then beat in the egg yolk and orange juice. Sift together the flour, ginger and salt into the mixture and stir until combined. Shape the dough into a ball, wrap in clingfilm and chill in the refrigerator for 30–60 minutes.

Preheat the oven to 190°C/375°F/Gas Mark 5. Line 2 large baking sheets with baking paper. Unwrap the dough and roll out between 2 sheets of baking paper to a rectangle. Using a sharp knife, cut it into 10 x 2-cm/4 x ¾-inch strips and place them on the baking sheets, spaced well apart.

Bake in the preheated oven for 10–12 minutes, or until light golden brown. Leave to cool for 5–10 minutes, then transfer to wire racks to cool completely.

Place the chocolate in a heatproof bowl, set the bowl over a saucepan of gently simmering water and heat until melted, then leave to cool. When the chocolate is cool but not set, dip the cookies diagonally into it to half coat, then place on the wire racks to set. You may find it easier to do this with tongs.

320 Lemon & white chocolate fingers

Replace the orange rind and juice with lemon and use melted white chocolate to half-coat the cookies.

Orange & lemon cookies

225 g/8 oz butter, softened
140 g/5 oz caster sugar
1 egg yolk, lightly beaten
280 g/10 oz plain flour
pinch of salt
finely grated rind of 1 orange
finely grated rind of 1 lemon

TO DECORATE
1 tbsp lightly beaten egg white
1 tbsp lemon juice
115 g/4 oz icing sugar
few drops of yellow food colouring
few drops of orange food colouring
about 15 lemon jelly slices
about 15 orange jelly slices

Place the butter and sugar in a large bowl and beat together until light and fluffy, then beat in the egg yolk. Sift together the flour and salt into the mixture and stir until combined. Halve the dough and knead the orange rind into one half and the lemon rind into the other. Shape into balls, wrap and chill for 30–60 minutes.

Preheat the oven to 190°C/375°F/Gas Mark 5. Line 2 large baking sheets with baking paper. Unwrap the orange-flavoured dough and roll out between 2 sheets of baking paper. Cut out rounds with a 6-cm/2½-inch plain cutter and place them on a baking sheet, spaced well apart. Repeat with the lemon-flavoured dough and cut-out crescents. Place them on the other baking sheet, spaced well apart.

Bake in the preheated oven for 10–15 minutes, or until golden brown. Leave to cool for 5–10 minutes, then transfer to wire racks to cool completely.

To decorate, mix the egg white and lemon juice together. Gradually beat in the icing sugar until smooth. Spoon half the icing into another bowl. Stir yellow food colouring into one bowl and orange into the other. Leave the cookies on the racks. Spread the icing over the cookies and decorate with jelly slices. Leave to set.

322 Raspberry cookies

Omit the citrus rind from the dough and replace the orange and yellow food colouring with red food colouring. Top the cookies with raspberry jellies.

323 Chocolate chip & cinnamon cookies

225 g/8 oz butter, softened
140 g/5 oz caster sugar
1 egg yolk, lightly beaten
2 tsp orange extract
280 g/10 oz plain flour
pinch of salt

100 g/3½ oz plain chocolate chips

CINNAMON COATING
1½ tbsp caster sugar
1½ tbsp ground cinnamon

Preheat the oven to 190°C/375°F/Gas Mark 5. Line 2 large baking sheets with baking paper. Place the butter and sugar in a large bowl and beat together until light and fluffy, then beat in the egg yolk and orange extract. Sift together the flour and salt into the mixture, add the chocolate chips and stir until thoroughly combined.

To make the cinnamon coating, mix the sugar and cinnamon together in a shallow dish. Scoop out tablespoons of the cookie dough, roll them into balls, then roll them in the cinnamon mixture to coat. Place them on the baking sheets, spaced well apart.

Bake in the preheated oven for 12–15 minutes, or until golden brown. Leave to cool on the baking sheets for 5–10 minutes, then transfer the cookies to wire racks to cool completely.

324 White chocolate & spice cookies

Replace the plain chocolate chips with 100 g/3½ oz white chocolate chips and replace the cinnamon with 1 tablespoon of ground mixed spice and ½ teaspoon of ground nutmeg.

325 Papaya & cashew nut cookies

225 g/8 oz butter, softened
140 g/5 oz caster sugar
1 egg yolk, lightly beaten
2 tsp lime juice
280 g/10 oz plain flour

pinch of salt
100 g/3½ oz ready-to-eat dried papaya, chopped
100 g/3 oz cashew nuts, finely chopped

Place the butter and sugar in a large bowl and beat together until light and fluffy, then beat in the egg yolk and lime juice.

Sift together the flour and salt into the mixture, add the papaya and stir until thoroughly combined.

Spread out the cashew nuts in a shallow dish. Shape the dough into a log and roll in the nuts to coat. Wrap the dough in clingfilm and chill in the refrigerator for 30–60 minutes.

Preheat the oven to 190°C/375°F/Gas Mark 5. Line 2 large baking sheets with baking paper.

Unwrap the dough, cut into slices with a sharp serrated knife and place them on the baking sheets, spaced well apart.

Bake in the preheated oven for 12–15 minutes, or until light golden. Leave to cool on the baking sheets for 5–10 minutes, then transfer the cookies to wire racks to cool completely.

326 With cashew icing

Beat 85 g/3 oz unsalted butter, 100 g/3½ oz icing sugar and 100 g/3½ oz cashew nut butter together until smooth and spread over the cooled cookies.

327 *Peach daiquiri cookies*

225 g/8 oz butter, softened
140 g/5 oz caster sugar
finely grated rind of 1 lime
1 egg yolk, lightly beaten
2 tsp white rum
280 g/10 oz plain flour
pinch of salt

100 g/3½ oz ready-to-eat dried peaches,
  chopped

ICING
140 g/5 oz icing sugar
2 tbsp white rum

Preheat the oven to 190°C/375°F/ Gas Mark 5. Line 2 baking sheets with baking paper.

Place the butter, sugar and lime rind in a large bowl and beat together until light and fluffy, then beat in the egg yolk and rum. Sift together the flour and salt into the mixture, add the peaches and stir until thoroughly combined. Scoop up tablespoons of the dough and place them on the baking sheets, then flatten gently. Bake in the preheated oven for 10–15 minutes, or until light golden brown. Leave to cool on the baking sheets for 5–10 minutes, then transfer the cookies to wire racks to cool completely.

Sift the icing sugar into a bowl and stir in enough rum until the mixture is the consistency of thick cream. Leave the cookies on the wire racks and drizzle the icing over them with a teaspoon. Leave to set.

328 *With peach icing*

Omit the dried peaches from the cookie dough and instead stir them into a double quantity of icing. Spoon the icing onto the cooled cookies, then spread to cover and leave to set.

329 *Peach, pear & plum cookies*

225 g/8 oz butter, softened
140 g/5 oz caster sugar
1 egg yolk, lightly beaten
2 tsp almond extract
280 g/10 oz plain flour
pinch of salt

55 g/2 oz ready-to-eat dried peaches,
  finely chopped
55 g/2 oz ready-to-eat dried pears, finely
  chopped
4 tbsp plum jam

Preheat the oven to 190°C/375°F/Gas Mark 5. Line 2 large baking sheets with baking paper. Place the butter and sugar in a large bowl and beat together until light and fluffy, then beat in the egg yolk and almond extract. Sift together the flour and salt into the mixture, add the dried fruit and stir until thoroughly combined.

Scoop up tablespoons of the mixture, roll them into balls and place on the baking sheets, spaced well apart. Make a hollow in the centre of each with the dampened handle of a wooden spoon and fill the hollows with the jam. Bake in the preheated oven for 12–15 minutes, or until light golden brown.

Leave to cool on the baking sheets for 5–10 minutes, then transfer the cookies to wire racks to cool completely.

330 *Extra peachy cookies*

Replace the plum jam with peach preserve and serve topped with chopped fresh peach.

331 Pear & mint cookies

225 g/8 oz butter, softened
140 g/5 oz caster sugar
1 egg yolk, lightly beaten
2 tsp vanilla extract
280 g/10 oz plain flour
pinch of salt
100 g/3½ oz ready-to-eat dried pears,
    finely chopped

ICING
115 g/4 oz icing sugar
few drops of peppermint extract
1 tbsp hot water

Place the butter and sugar in a large bowl and beat together until light and fluffy, then beat in the egg yolk and vanilla extract. Sift together the flour and salt into the mixture, add the pears and stir until thoroughly combined. Shape the dough into a log, wrap in clingfilm and chill in the refrigerator for 30–60 minutes.

Preheat the oven to 190°C/ 375°F/Gas Mark 5. Line 2 large baking sheets with baking paper.

Unwrap the log, cut it into 5-mm/¼-inch slices with a sharp serrated knife and place them on the baking sheets, spaced well apart. Bake in the preheated oven for 10–15 minutes, or until golden brown. Leave to cool on the baking sheets for 5–10 minutes, then transfer the cookies to wire racks to cool completely.

To decorate, sift the icing sugar into a bowl and stir in the peppermint extract. Gradually stir in the hot water until the icing has the consistency of double cream. Leave the cooled cookies on the wire racks and drizzle lines of icing over them with a teaspoon. Leave to set.

332 With pear liqueur icing

Replace the peppermint extract in the icing with a few drops of Poire William eau de vie.

333 Pear & pistachio cookies

225 g/8 oz butter, softened
140 g/5 oz caster sugar
1 egg yolk, lightly beaten
2 tsp vanilla extract
280 g/10 oz plain flour

pinch of salt
55 g/2 oz ready-to-eat dried pears,
    finely chopped
55 g/2 oz pistachio nuts, chopped
whole pistachio nuts, to decorate

Preheat the oven to 190°C/375°F/Gas Mark 5. Line 2 large baking sheets with baking paper. Place the butter and sugar in a large bowl and beat together until light and fluffy, then beat in the egg yolk and vanilla extract. Sift together the flour and salt into the mixture, add the pears and pistachios and stir until thoroughly combined.

Scoop up tablespoons of the mixture and roll into balls. Place them on the baking sheets, spaced well apart, and flatten slightly. Gently press a whole pistachio nut into the centre of each cookie.

Bake in the preheated oven for 10–15 minutes, or until golden brown. Leave to cool on the baking sheets for 5–10 minutes, then transfer the cookies to wire racks to cool completely.

334 Mango & macadamia nut cookies

Replace the dried pears and pistachio nuts with 55 g/2 oz chopped dried mangoes and 70 g/2½ oz chopped macadamia nuts.

335 Chocolate wholemeals

75 g/2¾ oz butter, plus extra for greasing
125 g/4½ oz demerara sugar
1 egg
1 tbsp wheatgerm

150 g/5½ oz wholewheat self-raising flour
70 g/2½ oz self-raising flour
125 g/4½ oz plain chocolate, broken into pieces

Preheat the oven to 180°C/350°F/Gas Mark 4. Lightly grease 2 large baking sheets. Place the butter and sugar in a large bowl and beat together until light and fluffy. Add the egg and beat well. Stir in the wheatgerm and flours, then bring the mixture together with your hands. Roll rounded teaspoonfuls of the mixture into balls and place them on the baking sheets, spaced well apart, then flatten slightly with the tines of a fork.

Bake in the preheated oven for 15–20 minutes, or until golden brown. Leave to cool for a few minutes, then transfer the cookies to a wire rack to cool completely.

Place the chocolate in a heatproof bowl, set the bowl over a saucepan of gently simmering water and heat until melted. Dip each biscuit in the chocolate to cover the flat side and a little way around the edges. Let the excess drip back into the bowl. Place the biscuits on a sheet of baking paper in a cool place and leave to set before serving.

336 Nutty chocolate wholemeals

Add 85 g/3 oz chopped almonds to the mixture before rolling into balls.

337 Iced cherry rings

115 g/4 oz butter, plus extra for greasing
85 g/3 oz caster sugar
1 egg yolk
finely grated rind of ½ lemon
200 g/7 oz plain flour, plus extra for dusting
55 g/2 oz glacé cherries, finely chopped

ICING
85 g/3 oz icing sugar
1½ tbsp lemon juice

Preheat the oven to 200°C/400°F/Gas Mark 6. Lightly grease 2 large baking sheets. Place the butter and sugar in a large bowl and beat together until light and fluffy. Beat in the egg yolk and lemon rind. Sift in the flour, stir, then add the glacé cherries and mix to form a soft dough.

Roll the dough out on a lightly floured work surface to 5 mm/¼ inch thick. Cut out 8-cm/3¼-inch rounds with a biscuit cutter, then cut out the centre of each with a 2.5-cm/1-inch cutter. Place the rings on the baking sheets. Re-roll any trimmings and cut out more cookies.

Bake in the preheated oven for 12–15 minutes, or until golden. Leave to cool for 2 minutes, then transfer to a wire rack to cool completely.

To make the icing, mix the icing sugar and lemon juice together until smooth. Drizzle the icing over the biscuits and leave until set.

338 Fruity rings

Replace the glacé cherries with chopped mixed peel. Tint the icing with a little yellow food colouring.

Plum & white chocolate cookies

225 g/8 oz butter, softened
140 g/5 oz caster sugar
1 egg yolk, lightly beaten
2 tsp vanilla extract
225 g/8 oz plain flour
55 g/2 oz cocoa powder
pinch of salt

100 g/3½ oz white chocolate, chopped

TOPPING
55 g/2 oz white chocolate, broken into
   pieces
15 ready-to-eat dried plums, halved

Place the butter and sugar in a large bowl and beat together until light and fluffy, then beat in the egg yolk and vanilla extract. Sift together the flour, cocoa and salt into the mixture and stir until combined. Halve the dough, shape into balls, wrap in clingfilm and chill for 30–60 minutes.

Preheat the oven to 190°C/375°F/Gas Mark 5. Line 2 large baking sheets with baking paper.

Unwrap a ball of dough and roll out between 2 sheets of baking paper to about 3 mm/⅛ inch thick. Cut out 15 rounds with a plain 5-cm/2-inch cutter and place them on the baking sheets, spaced well apart. Divide the chopped chocolate among the cookies.

Roll out the remaining dough between 2 sheets of baking paper and cut out rounds with a 6–7-cm/2½–2¾-inch cutter. Place them on top of the first cookies and press the edges together to seal. Bake in the preheated oven for 10–15 minutes, or until firm.

Leave to cool for 5–10 minutes, then transfer the cookies to wire racks to cool completely.

To decorate, place the chocolate in a heatproof bowl, set the bowl over a saucepan of gently simmering water and heat until melted. Leave to cool slightly. Dip the cut sides of the plums into the melted chocolate and stick them in the middle of the cookies. Spoon the remaining chocolate over them and leave to set.

340 *Walnut & apricot cookies*

Replace the dried plums with 15 walnut halves and 15 ready-to-eat dried apricots.

341 *Plum & custard cookies*

225 g/8 oz butter, softened
140 g/5 oz caster sugar
1 egg yolk, lightly beaten
2 tsp vanilla extract
175 g/6 oz plain flour
115 g/4 oz custard powder
pinch of salt
100 g/3½ oz ready-to-eat dried plums,
   finely chopped

CUSTARD CREAM
25 g/1 oz butter
225 g/8 oz icing sugar
2 tbsp milk
few drops of vanilla extract

Place the butter and sugar in a large bowl and beat together until light and fluffy, then beat in the egg yolk and vanilla extract. Sift together the flour, custard powder and salt into the mixture, add the plums and stir until combined. Halve the dough, shape into balls, wrap in clingfilm and chill in the refrigerator for 30–60 minutes.

Preheat the oven to 190°C/375°F/Gas Mark 5. Line 2 large baking sheets with baking paper. Unwrap the dough and roll out between 2 sheets of baking paper. Cut out cookies with a 6-cm/2½-inch fluted round cutter and place them on the baking sheets, spaced well apart. Using a small diamond-shaped cutter, stamp out the centres of half the cookies and remove.

Bake in the preheated oven for 10–15 minutes, or until light golden. Leave to cool on the baking sheets for 5–10 minutes,

then transfer the cookies to wire racks to cool completely.

To make the custard cream, place the butter in a small saucepan and heat gently until melted, then remove from the heat. Sift the icing sugar into the pan, add the milk and vanilla and beat until smooth and thoroughly combined. Spread the custard cream over the whole cookies and top with the cut-out cookies.

342 *Banana & custard cookies*

Replace the plums with finely chopped soft dried bananas.

343 Redcurrant & pastry cream cookies

225 g/8 oz butter, softened
140 g/5 oz caster sugar
1 egg yolk, lightly beaten
2 tsp vanilla extract
280 g/10 oz plain flour
pinch of salt

PASTRY CREAM
2 egg yolks, lightly beaten
4 tbsp caster sugar
1 tbsp cornflour
1 heaped tbsp plain flour
300 ml/10 fl oz milk
few drops of vanilla extract
1 egg white

TO DECORATE
15 small bunches of redcurrants
1 egg white, lightly beaten
2–3 tbsp caster sugar
225 g/8 oz icing sugar, sifted
¼ tsp lemon extract
2 tbsp warm water

Place the butter and sugar in a large bowl and beat together, then beat in the egg yolk and vanilla extract. Sift in the flour and salt and stir until thoroughly combined. Halve the dough, wrap in clingfilm and chill in the refrigerator for 45 minutes.

Preheat the oven to 190°C/375°F/Gas Mark 5. Line 2 large baking sheets with baking paper. Roll out the dough between sheets of baking paper. Cut out rounds with a 6-cm/2½-inch cookie cutter and place them on the baking sheets. Bake in the preheated oven for 12 minutes, or until golden brown. Leave to cool for 5 minutes, then transfer to wire racks to cool.

To make the pastry cream, beat the egg yolks and sugar together. Sift in the flours and beat well. Stir in 3 tablespoons of the milk and the vanilla extract. Bring the remaining milk to the boil, then whisk it into the mixture. Return to the pan and bring to the boil, stirring, then beat until cool.

Whisk the egg white until stiff. Spoon a little pastry cream into a bowl, fold in the egg white, then fold into the rest of the cream. Heat for 2 minutes, then leave to cool. Sandwich the cookies together with the pastry cream.

Dip the redcurrants into the beaten egg white and roll in caster sugar. Mix the icing sugar, lemon extract and water until smooth. Spread the icing over the cookies and decorate with the redcurrants.

344 All white pastry cream cookies

Replace the redcurrants with white currants.

345 Strawberry pinks

225 g/8 oz butter, softened
140 g/5 oz caster sugar
1 egg yolk, lightly beaten
1 tsp strawberry flavouring
280 g/10 oz plain flour
pinch of salt
100 g/3½ oz desiccated coconut
4 tbsp strawberry jam

Preheat the oven to 190°C/375°F/Gas Mark 5. Line 2 large baking sheets with baking paper. Place the butter and sugar in a large bowl and beat together until light and fluffy, then beat in the egg yolk and strawberry flavouring. Sift together the flour and salt into the mixture, add the coconut and stir until thoroughly combined.

Scoop up tablespoons of the mixture and roll them into balls, then place them on the baking sheets, spaced well apart. Use the dampened handle of a wooden spoon to make a hollow in the centre of each and fill the hollows with strawberry jam.

Bake in the preheated oven for 12–15 minutes, or until golden brown. Leave to cool on the baking sheets for 5–10 minutes, then transfer the cookies to wire racks to cool completely.

346 With marmalade filling

Replace the coconut with 50 g/1¾ oz chopped candied fruit and ½ teaspoon of finely grated orange rind. Fill the hollows with marmalade.

347 Banana & caramel cookies

225 g/8 oz butter, softened
140 g/5 oz caster sugar
1 egg yolk, lightly beaten
25 g/1 oz stem ginger, finely chopped,
    plus 2 tsp syrup from the jar

280 g/10 oz plain flour
pinch of salt
85 g/3 oz dried bananas, finely chopped
15 chocolate caramels

Place the butter and sugar in a large bowl and beat together until light and fluffy, then beat in the egg yolk, ginger and ginger syrup. Sift together the flour and salt into the mixture, add the bananas and stir until thoroughly combined. Halve the dough, shape into balls, wrap in clingfilm and chill in the refrigerator for 30–60 minutes.

Preheat the oven to 190°C/375°F/Gas Mark 5. Line 2 large baking sheets with baking paper. Unwrap the dough and roll out between 2 sheets of baking paper. Cut out cookies with a 6-cm/2½-inch fluted round cutter and place half of them on the baking sheets, spaced well apart. Place a chocolate caramel in the centre of each cookie, then top with the remaining cookies and pinch the edges of the rounds together.

Bake in the preheated oven for 10–15 minutes, or until light golden. Cool for 5–10 minutes, then transfer to wire racks to cool completely.

348 Banana & raisin cookies

25 g/1 oz raisins
125 ml/4 fl oz orange juice or rum
225 g/8 oz butter, softened
140 g/5 oz caster sugar
1 egg yolk, lightly beaten

280 g/10 oz plain flour
pinch of salt
85 g/3 oz dried bananas, finely chopped

Place the raisins in a bowl, pour in the orange juice or rum and leave to soak for 30 minutes. Drain the raisins, reserving any remaining liquid.

Preheat the oven to 190°C/375°F/Gas Mark 5. Line 2 large baking sheets with baking paper. Place the butter and sugar in a large bowl and beat together until light and fluffy, then beat in the egg yolk and 2 teaspoons of the reserved orange juice. Sift together the flour and salt into the mixture, add the raisins and dried bananas and stir until combined.

Place tablespoons of the mixture into heaps on the baking sheets, spaced well apart, then flatten them gently.

Bake in the preheated oven for 12–15 minutes, or until golden. Leave to cool on the baking sheets for 5–10 minutes, then transfer the cookies to wire racks to cool completely.

349 Banana & coconut cookies

Replace the raisins with 50 g/1¾ oz desiccated coconut.

225 g/8 oz butter, softened
140 g/5 oz caster sugar
2 tsp finely grated orange rind
1 egg yolk, lightly beaten
2 tsp vanilla extract
250 g/9 oz plain flour
25 g/1 oz cocoa powder
pinch of salt
100 g/3½ oz plain chocolate,
finely chopped

CHOCOLATE FILLING
125 ml/4 fl oz double cream
200 g/7 oz white chocolate,
broken into pieces
1 tsp orange extract

Preheat the oven to 190°C/375°F/ Gas Mark 5. Line 2 large baking sheets with baking paper.

Place the butter, sugar and orange rind in a large bowl and beat together until light and fluffy. Beat in the egg yolk and vanilla. Sift together the flour, cocoa and salt into the mixture, then add the chocolate and stir well. Scoop up tablespoons of the dough, roll into balls and place on the baking sheets, spaced well apart. Gently flatten and smooth the tops with the back of a spoon.

Bake in the preheated oven for 10–15 minutes, or until light golden. Leave to cool on the baking sheets for 5–10 minutes, then transfer to wire racks to cool completely.

To make the filling, bring the cream to the boil in a small saucepan, then remove the pan from the heat. Stir in the chocolate until the mixture is smooth, then stir in the orange extract. When the mixture is completely cool, sandwich the cookies together in pairs.

351 *With plain chocolate*

For the chocolate filling, replace the white chocolate with plain chocolate and sift over cocoa powder to finish.

352 *With plain & white chocolate*

Replace half the white chocolate with melted plain chocolate to make 2 fillings. Fill half the sandwiches with white filling and sift over icing sugar. Fill the remaining cookies with plain chocolate filling and sift over cocoa powder.

353 *Apple suns & pear stars*

225 g/8 oz butter, softened
140 g/5 oz caster sugar
1 egg yolk, lightly beaten
280 g/10 oz plain flour
pinch of salt
½ tsp mixed spice
55 g/2 oz ready-to-eat dried apple,
  finely chopped
½ tsp ground ginger
55 g/2 oz ready-to-eat dried pears,
  finely chopped
25 g/1 oz flaked almonds
1 egg white, lightly beaten
demerara sugar, for sprinkling

Place the butter and sugar in a large bowl and beat together until light and fluffy, then beat in the egg yolk. Sift together the flour and salt into the mixture and stir until combined. Transfer half the dough to another bowl. Add the mixed spice and dried apple to one bowl and mix well. Shape into a ball, wrap in clingfilm and chill for 30–60 minutes.

Add the ginger and dried pear to the other bowl and mix well. Shape into a ball, wrap in clingfilm and chill in the refrigerator for 30–60 minutes.

Preheat the oven to 190°C/375°F/Gas Mark 5. Line 2 large baking sheets with baking paper.

Unwrap the apple-flavoured dough and roll out between 2 sheets of baking paper to about 3 mm/⅛ inch thick. Cut out cookies with a sun-shaped cutter and place them on the baking sheet.

Repeat with the pear-flavoured dough. Cut out cookies with a star-shaped cutter and place them on the other baking sheet.

Bake in the preheated oven for 5 minutes, then remove the star-shaped cookies from the oven and sprinkle with the flaked almonds. Bake for a further 5–10 minutes. Remove the cookies from the oven but do not turn off the heat. Brush the apple suns with a little egg white and sprinkle with demerara sugar, then bake for a further 2–3 minutes. Leave all the cookies to cool for 5–10 minutes, then transfer them onto wire racks to cool completely.

354 *With apple icing*

Replace the flaked almonds, egg white and sugar topping with an apple glacé icing made by sifting 115 g/4 oz icing sugar into a bowl and beating in 1½ tablespoons of apple juice with a drop of green food colouring. Spread onto the cooled cookies.

355 *Orangines*

25 g/1 oz butter, softened, plus extra
  for greasing
15 g/½ oz candied orange peel
25 g/1 oz caster sugar
20 g/¾ oz plain flour
25 g/1 oz ground almonds
finely grated rind of 1 small orange
1 tsp orange juice

Preheat the oven to 180°C/350°F/Gas Mark 4. Grease several large baking sheets. Very finely chop the candied orange peel.

Place the butter and sugar in a large bowl and whisk together until pale and creamy. Add the flour, ground almonds, grated orange rind and juice and mix well together.

Place teaspoonfuls of the mixture onto the baking sheets, spacing them well apart. Bake in the preheated oven for 7–8 minutes, or until lightly golden brown around the edges. Leave on the baking sheets for 2–3 minutes, then transfer the cookies to wire racks to cool completely.

Citrus crescents

100 g/3½ oz butter, softened, plus extra
   for greasing
75 g/2¾ oz caster sugar
1 egg, separated
200 g/7 oz plain flour, plus extra for
   dusting

finely grated rind of 1 orange
finely grated rind of 1 lemon
finely grated rind of 1 lime
2–3 tbsp orange juice

Preheat the oven to 200°C/400°F/Gas Mark 6. Lightly grease 2 large baking sheets. Place the butter and sugar in a large bowl and beat together until light and fluffy, then gradually beat in the egg yolk. Sift the flour into the creamed mixture and mix until thoroughly combined. Add the orange, lemon and lime rinds with enough of the orange juice to form a soft dough.

Roll the dough out on a lightly floured work surface and cut out rounds with a 7.5-cm/3-inch biscuit cutter. Make crescent shapes by cutting away a quarter of each round. Re-roll the trimmings to make about 25 crescents. Place the crescents on the baking sheets and prick the surface of each crescent with a fork. Lightly whisk the egg white in a small bowl and brush it over the biscuits.

Bake in the preheated oven for 12–15 minutes, or until golden brown. Leave the cookies to cool on a wire rack before serving.

357 *With lemon cream*

Make a double quantity of the cookies. Prepare the lemon cream by beating 125 g/4½ oz softened butter with 175 g/6 oz icing sugar and 1 teaspoon of finely grated lemon rind, 1 tablespoon of lemon juice and ½ teaspoon of lemon oil, then use to sandwich the cookies together.

358 *Chocolate temptations*

90 g/3¼ oz butter, plus extra
   for greasing
365 g/12½ oz plain chocolate
1 tsp strong coffee
2 eggs
140 g/5 oz soft light brown sugar
185 g/6½ oz plain flour

¼ tsp baking powder
pinch of salt
2 tsp almond extract
85 g/3 oz Brazil nuts, chopped
85 g/3 oz hazelnuts, chopped
40 g/1½ oz white chocolate

Preheat the oven to 180°C/350°F/Gas Mark 4. Grease 2 large baking sheets. Place 225 g/8 oz of the plain chocolate with the butter and coffee into a heatproof bowl, set the bowl over a saucepan of simmering water and heat until the chocolate is almost melted. Remove and stir until smooth.

Beat the eggs in a bowl until fluffy, then gradually whisk in the sugar until thick. Add the chocolate to the egg mixture and stir to combine. Sift the flour, baking powder and salt into a separate bowl and stir into the chocolate. Chop 85 g/3 oz of the plain chocolate into pieces and stir into the mixture. Stir in the almond extract and nuts. Place 24 tablespoonfuls of the mixture onto the baking sheets. Bake in the preheated oven for 16 minutes. Transfer the biscuits to a wire rack to cool. To decorate, melt the remaining plain chocolate and white chocolate, in turn, then spoon into piping bags and pipe lines on the cookies. Leave to set.

Marshmallow s'mores

225 g/8 oz butter, softened
140 g/5 oz caster sugar
2 tsp finely grated orange rind
1 egg yolk, lightly beaten
250 g/9 oz plain flour
25 g/1 oz cocoa powder
½ tsp ground cinnamon

pinch of salt
30 yellow marshmallows, halved
    horizontally
300 g/10½ oz plain chocolate, broken
    into pieces
4 tbsp orange marmalade
15 walnut halves, to decorate

Place the butter, sugar and orange rind in a large bowl and beat together until light and fluffy, then beat in the egg yolk. Sift together the flour, cocoa, cinnamon and salt into the mixture and stir until combined. Halve the dough, shape into balls, wrap in clingfilm and chill for 30–60 minutes.

Preheat the oven to 190°C/375°F/Gas Mark 5. Line 2 large baking sheets with baking paper. Unwrap the dough and roll out between 2 sheets of baking paper. Cut out cookies with a 6-cm/2½-inch fluted round cutter and place them on the baking sheets, spaced well apart. Bake in the preheated oven for 10–15 minutes. Leave to cool for 5 minutes. Turn half the cookies upside down and put 4 marshmallow halves on each. Bake for a further 1–2 minutes. Leave the cookies to stand on wire racks for 30 minutes.

Place the chocolate in a heatproof bowl, set the bowl over a saucepan of gently simmering water and heat until melted. Leave to cool.

Line a baking sheet with baking paper. Spread the marmalade over the undersides of the uncovered cookies and place them on top of the marshmallow-covered cookies. Dip the cookies in the melted chocolate to coat, letting the excess drip back into the bowl, then place them on the baking sheet. Place a walnut half in the centre of each cookie and leave to set.

360 *White s'mores*

Replace the plain chocolate with white chocolate. Scatter over 100 g/3½ oz shelled, chopped pistachio nuts to replace the walnuts.

361 *Thanksgiving cookies*

225 g/8 oz butter, softened
140 g/5 oz caster sugar
1 egg yolk, lightly beaten
2 tsp orange juice
280 g/10 oz plain flour

pinch of salt
55 g/2 oz fresh or dried blueberries
55 g/2 oz fresh or dried cranberries
25 g/1 oz white chocolate chips

Preheat the oven to 190°C/375°F/Gas Mark 5. Line 2 large baking sheets with baking paper. Place the butter and sugar in a large bowl and beat together until light and fluffy, then beat in the egg yolk and orange juice. Sift together the flour and salt into the mixture, then add the blueberries, cranberries and chocolate chips and stir until combined.

Scoop up tablespoons of the dough and place them on the baking sheets, spaced well apart. Bake in the preheated oven for 10–15 minutes, or until light golden brown.

Leave to cool on the baking sheets for 5–10 minutes, then transfer the cookies to wire racks to cool completely.

362 *Cherry Thanksgiving cookies*

Replace the blueberries and cranberries with 100 g/3½ oz chopped dried cherries. Replace the white chocolate chips with plain chocolate chips.

363 Dinosaur cookies

MAKES 30

225 g/8 oz unsalted butter, softened
225 g/8 oz smooth peanut butter
200 g/7 oz granulated sugar
200 g/7 oz soft light brown sugar
2 tsp baking powder
¼ tsp salt

2 large eggs
1 tsp vanilla extract
275 g/9¾ oz plain flour, plus extra
    for dusting
silver dragées and green writing icing,
    to decorate

Place the butter and peanut butter in a large bowl and beat together until smooth. Add the sugars, baking powder and salt and beat well to combine. Whisk the eggs and vanilla extract together in a separate bowl, then add to the mixture and mix well. Sift in the flour and mix to form a smooth dough. Wrap in clingfilm and chill for 30 minutes.

Preheat the oven to 180°C/350°F/Gas Mark 4. Roll the dough out on a floured work surface and cut out shapes with dinosaur cookie cutters dipped in flour. Re-roll any trimmings and cut out more cookies. Press silver dragées into the dough for eyes and place on 2 large non-stick baking sheets. Bake in the preheated oven for 10–12 minutes.

Leave to cool for 2 minutes, then transfer to a wire rack to cool completely. When cold, decorate the dinosaurs with green writing icing.

364 Chocolate dinosaur cookies

Add 3 teaspoons of cocoa powder to the dough and knead in before chilling.

365 Bedtime bears

MAKES 25

115 g/4 oz unsalted butter, softened
90 g/3¼ oz caster sugar
1 tsp baking powder
pinch of salt
1 large egg, lightly beaten
1 tsp milk

1 tsp vanilla extract
25 g/1 oz cocoa powder, plus extra
    for dusting
140 g/5 oz plain flour
25 x 7-cm/2¾-inch biscuit bears
3 tbsp smooth peanut butter

Place the butter and sugar in a large bowl and beat together until light and fluffy. Add the baking powder, salt, egg, milk and vanilla extract and beat well. Sift in the cocoa and flour and mix to form a smooth dough. Wrap in clingfilm and chill in the refrigerator for 3 hours.

Preheat the oven to 180°C/350°F/Gas Mark 4. Roll the dough out on a work surface dusted with cocoa, then cut into 25 x 5-cm/2-inch squares. Place a biscuit bear diagonally on the square and secure with peanut butter. Fold up the bottom and sides of the dough to form a blanket around the bear, leaving the top third of the bear exposed. Press to secure and place on a large non-stick baking sheet. Bake in the preheated oven for 10 minutes. Cool on a wire rack.

366 With coloured blankets

Omit the cocoa powder and divide the dough into portions. Tint each portion with a few drops of different food colouring. Roll out and cut as usual, and wrap the biscuit bears in the coloured dough blankets.

111

250 g/9 oz unsalted butter, softened
275 g/9¾ oz caster sugar
2 large eggs, lightly beaten
450 g/1 lb plain flour, plus extra
for dusting
2 tsp baking powder
pinch of salt
few drops of food colouring
writing icing

Place the butter and sugar in a large bowl and beat together until light and fluffy. Gradually add the eggs and beat to combine, then sift in the flour, baking powder and salt and mix to form a dough. Wrap the dough in clingfilm and chill in the refrigerator for 2 hours.

Preheat the oven to 160°C/ 325°F/Gas Mark 3. Line 2 large baking sheets with baking paper.

Reserve one third of the dough and leave uncoloured. Divide the remaining dough into portions and knead in different food colourings. Shape the dough into animal shapes (see right) and

place the cookies on the baking sheets. Bake for 20–25 minutes. Leave to cool on a wire rack. Add eyes and other features with the writing icing.

Cow Cookie: shape an oval piece of coloured dough to 6 cm/ 2½ inches across for the body. Roll another piece of dough into a log 6 cm/2½ inches long and 1 cm/½ inch wide, then cut into 3 equal pieces – use 2 for the legs and 1 for the head. Roll uncoloured dough into small circles and use as the udder, nose and markings. Make a thin tail. Press the pieces well together.

Pig Cookie: shape an oval piece of coloured dough to 6 cm/ 2½ inches across for the body; flatten. Shape a smaller oval piece to 3 cm/1¼ inches for the head; flatten. Use uncoloured dough for the snout, ears and tail.

Fluffy Sheep Cookie: for the body, roll small balls of uncoloured dough and lay them on the baking sheet, touching each other in an oval shape. Use coloured dough to shape the head and feet.

368 *Party cookies*

100 g/3½ oz butter
100 g/3½ oz soft light brown sugar
1 tbsp golden syrup

150 g/5½ oz self-raising flour
85 g/3 oz sugar-coated chocolates

Preheat the oven to 180°C/350°F/Gas Mark 4. Line several large baking sheets with baking paper. Place the butter and sugar in a large bowl and whisk together until pale and creamy, then whisk the golden syrup into the mixture until smooth. Add 75 g/2¾ oz flour and whisk together until mixed. Stir in the sugar-coated chocolates and remaining flour then, with your hands, knead the mixture until smooth.

Roll small pieces of the dough between your hands into smooth balls to make 15 cookies in total and place them on the baking sheets, spacing them well apart. Bake in the preheated oven for 10–15 minutes, or until golden brown.

Leave on the baking sheets for 2–3 minutes, then transfer the cookies to a wire rack and leave to cool completely.

369 *Chocolate button cookies*

Replace the sugar-coated chocolates with chocolate buttons.

370 *Choco mint stars*

225 g/8 oz butter, softened
140 g/5 oz caster sugar
1 egg yolk, lightly beaten
1 tsp peppermint extract
280 g/10 oz plain flour
pinch of salt
100 g/3½ oz desiccated coconut

TO DECORATE
100 g/3½ oz white chocolate, broken
    into pieces
100 g/3½ oz milk chocolate, broken
    into pieces

Place the butter and sugar in a large bowl and beat together until light and fluffy, then beat in the egg yolk and peppermint extract. Sift together the flour and salt into the mixture, add the coconut and stir until combined. Divide the mixture in half, shape into balls, wrap in clingfilm and chill in the refrigerator for 30–60 minutes.

Preheat the oven to 190°C/ 375°F/Gas Mark 5. Line 2 large baking sheets with baking paper. Unwrap the dough and roll out between 2 sheets of baking paper to about 3 mm/⅛ inch thick.

Cut out stars with a 6–7-cm/ 2½–2¾-inch cutter and place them on the baking sheets, spaced well apart.

Bake in the preheated oven for 10–12 minutes, or until light golden. Leave to cool on the baking sheets for 5–10 minutes, then transfer the cookies to wire racks to cool completely.

Place the white chocolate and the milk chocolate in separate heatproof bowls, set the bowls over 2 saucepans of gently simmering water and heat until melted. Leave the cooled cookies on the racks and drizzle first with melted white chocolate and then with melted milk chocolate, using a teaspoon. Leave to set.

371 *White mint stars*

Omit the milk chocolate and melt 200 g/7 oz white chocolate in a heatproof bowl set over a pan of gently simmering water. Spread to cover each cookie and sprinkle over chocolate vermicelli.

372 Snickerdoodles

225 g/8 oz butter, softened
140 g/5 oz caster sugar
2 large eggs, lightly beaten
1 tsp vanilla extract
400 g/14 oz plain flour
1 tsp bicarbonate of soda
½ tsp freshly grated nutmeg

pinch of salt
55 g/2 oz pecan nuts, finely chopped

CINNAMON COATING
1 tbsp caster sugar
2 tbsp ground cinnamon

Place the butter and sugar in a large bowl and beat together until light and fluffy, then beat in the eggs and vanilla extract. Sift together the flour, bicarbonate of soda, nutmeg and salt into the mixture, add the pecan nuts and stir until thoroughly combined. Shape the dough into a ball, wrap in clingfilm and chill in the refrigerator for 30–60 minutes.

Preheat the oven to 190°C/375°F/Gas Mark 5. Line 2 large baking sheets with baking paper.

For the coating, mix the sugar and cinnamon in a shallow dish. Scoop up tablespoons of the dough and roll into balls. Roll each ball in the cinnamon mixture and place on the baking sheets, spaced well apart. Bake in the preheated oven for 10–12 minutes, or until golden brown. Cool for 5–10 minutes, then transfer to wire racks to cool completely.

373 Chocodoodles

Add 2 tablespoons of cocoa powder to the dough and roll the cookies in 2 tablespoons of caster sugar mixed with 1 tablespoon of cocoa before baking.

374 Melt-in-the-middles

85 g/3 oz plain chocolate, broken into
    pieces
115 g/4 oz butter, softened
140 g/5 oz caster sugar
1 egg yolk, lightly beaten
2 tsp vanilla extract
280 g/10 oz plain flour
1 tbsp cocoa powder
pinch of salt

FILLING
1 egg white
55 g/2 oz caster sugar
85 g/3 oz desiccated coconut
1 tsp plain flour
2 tbsp finely chopped ready-to-eat
    dried papaya

Preheat the oven to 190°C/375°F/Gas Mark 5. Line 2 large baking sheets with baking paper.

To make the middle filling, whisk the egg white in a large bowl until soft peaks form, then gradually whisk in the sugar. Gently fold in the coconut, flour and papaya and reserve.

Place the chocolate in a heatproof bowl, set the bowl over a saucepan of gently simmering water and heat until melted, then remove from the heat. Place the butter and sugar in a large bowl and beat together until light and fluffy, then beat in the egg yolk and vanilla extract. Sift together the flour, cocoa and salt into the mixture and stir until thoroughly combined. Stir in the melted chocolate and knead lightly.

Roll out the dough between 2 sheets of baking paper to 5–8 mm/ ¼–⅜ inch thick. Cut out rounds with a 7-cm/2¾-inch fluted round cutter and place them on the baking sheets. Using a 3-cm/1¼-inch plain round cutter, cut out the centres and remove them. Bake for 8 minutes, then remove from the oven and lower the temperature to 160°C/325°F/ Gas Mark 3. Spoon the filling mixture into the centre of the cookies. Place a sheet of foil over each baking sheet, crumpled so that it doesn't touch the cookies, to stop the filling mixture from browning.

Bake for a further 15–20 minutes, or until the middles are firm. Leave to cool on the baking sheets for 5–10 minutes, then transfer the cookies to wire racks to cool completely.

375 Crunchy muesli cookies

115 g/4 oz unsalted butter, softened, plus extra for greasing
85 g/3 oz demerara sugar
1 tbsp clear honey
115 g/4 oz self-raising flour
pinch of salt
60 g/2¼ oz ready-to-eat dried apricots, chopped
50 g/1¾ oz dried figs, chopped
115 g/4 oz porridge oats
1 tsp milk (optional)
40 g/1½ oz sultanas or cranberries
40 g/1½ oz walnut halves, chopped

Preheat the oven to 160°C/325°F/Gas Mark 3. Grease 2 large baking sheets. Place the butter, sugar and honey in a saucepan and heat over a low heat until melted. Mix to combine. Sift together the flour and salt into a large bowl and stir in the apricots, figs and oats. Pour in the butter and sugar mixture and mix to form a dough. If it is too stiff, add a little milk.

Divide the dough into 24 pieces and roll each piece into a ball. Place 12 balls on each baking sheet and press flat to a diameter of 6 cm/2½ inches. Mix the sultanas and walnuts together and press into the cookies. Bake in the preheated oven for 15 minutes, swapping the sheets halfway through. Leave to cool on the baking sheets.

376 With nutty topping

Chop 100 g/3½ oz mixed raw nuts and use to top the cookies before baking.

377 Rather large coconut macaroons

2 large egg whites
115 g/4 oz caster sugar
150 g/5½ oz desiccated coconut
8 glacé cherries

Preheat the oven to 180°C/350°F/Gas Mark 4. Line 2–3 large baking sheets with rice paper.

Place the egg whites in a large bowl and whisk until soft peaks form and they hold their shape but are not dry. Add the sugar to the egg whites and, using a large metal spoon, fold in until incorporated. Add the coconut and fold into the mixture. Place 8 heaped tablespoons of the mixture onto the baking sheets and place a cherry on top of each macaroon.

Bake in the preheated oven for 15–20 minutes, or until lightly golden brown around the edges. Leave on the baking sheets for 2–3 minutes, then transfer the macaroons to a wire rack to cool completely.

378 Nutty macaroons

Finely chop 50 g/1¾ oz almonds, hazelnuts, macadamia nuts, pecan nuts or walnuts and add to the mixture with the coconut.

Round & round the garden cherry garlands

150 g/5½ oz unsalted butter, softened
50 g/1¾ oz icing sugar
½ tsp vanilla extract

150 g/5½ oz plain flour
pinch of salt
70 g/2½ oz glacé cherries, finely chopped

Preheat the oven to 190°C/375°F/Gas Mark 5. Place the butter and sugar in a large bowl and beat together until light and fluffy. Add the vanilla extract and beat until combined. Sift in the flour and salt in batches, mixing well between each addition. Add the cherries and mix well.

Spoon the mixture into a piping bag fitted with a 2.5-cm/1-inch star nozzle and pipe rings onto 2 large non-stick baking sheets. Bake in the preheated oven for 8–10 minutes, or until light golden. Leave to cool on a wire rack.

380 With cherry icing

Make a butter icing with 85 g/3oz unsalted butter beaten with 150 g/5½ oz icing sugar and adding 50 g/1¾ oz chopped glacé cherries. Pipe the icing onto the cookies and decorate with small pieces of angelica.

381 Pistachio & almond cookies

225 g/8 oz butter, softened
140 g/5 oz caster sugar
1 egg yolk, lightly beaten
2 tsp almond extract

225 g/8 oz plain flour
pinch of salt
55 g/2 oz ground almonds
55 g/2 oz pistachio nuts, finely chopped

Place the butter and sugar in a large bowl and beat together until light and fluffy, then beat in the egg yolk and almond extract. Sift together the flour and salt into the mixture, add the ground almonds and stir until thoroughly combined. Halve the dough, shape into balls, wrap in clingfilm and chill in the refrigerator for 30–60 minutes.

Preheat the oven to 190°C/375°F/Gas Mark 5. Line 2 large baking sheets with baking paper. Unwrap the dough and roll out between 2 sheets of baking paper to about 3 mm/⅛ inch thick. Sprinkle half the pistachio nuts over each piece of dough and roll lightly with the rolling pin. Cut out cookies with a heart-shaped cutter and place them on the baking sheets, spaced well apart.

Bake in the preheated oven for 10–12 minutes. Leave to cool for 5–10 minutes, then transfer the cookies to wire racks to cool completely.

382 With pistachio cream

Whisk 200 ml/7 fl oz double cream to soft peaks with 2 tablespoons of icing sugar and ½ teaspoon of green food colouring. Fold in 85 g/3 oz chopped shelled pistachios and spoon into a bowl, then use as a dip for the cookies.

115 g/4 oz butter, softened
125 g/4½ oz caster sugar
125 g/4½ oz soft light brown sugar
2 large eggs, lightly beaten
1 tsp vanilla extract
280 g/10 oz plain flour
1 tsp bicarbonate of soda
300 g/10½ oz chocolate chunks

Preheat the oven to 180°C/350°F/ Gas Mark 4. Line several large baking sheets with baking paper.

Place the butter and sugars in a large bowl and whisk together until pale and creamy. Whisk the eggs and vanilla extract into the mixture until smooth. Sift in the flour and bicarbonate of soda and beat together until well mixed. Stir in the chocolate chunks.

Drop 12 large spoonfuls of the mixture onto the baking sheets, spacing them well apart.

Bake in the preheated oven for 15–20 minutes, or until set and golden brown. Leave to cool on the baking sheets for 2–3 minutes, then transfer the cookies to a wire rack and leave to cool completely.

384 *Giant chocolate chip cookies*

Replace the chocolate chunks with chocolate chips. These can be plain, milk or white chocolate, or use some of each.

385 *Indulgent chocolate chunk cookies*

Scatter 100 g/3½ oz chocolate chunks over the top of the cookies before baking in the oven.

386 Crunchy nut & honey sandwiches

300 g/10½ oz butter, softened
140 g/5 oz caster sugar
1 egg yolk, lightly beaten
2 tsp vanilla extract
280 g/10 oz plain flour

pinch of salt
40 g/1½ oz macadamia nuts, cashew
    nuts or pine kernels, chopped
85 g/3 oz icing sugar
85 g/3 oz clover or other set honey

Preheat the oven to 190°C/375°F/Gas Mark 5. Line 2 large baking sheets with baking paper. Place 225 g/8 oz of the butter and the caster sugar in a large bowl and beat together until light and fluffy, then beat in the egg yolk and vanilla. Sift together the flour and salt into the mixture and stir until combined. Scoop up tablespoons of the dough and roll into balls. Place half of them on a baking sheet, spaced well apart, and flatten gently. Spread out the nuts in a shallow dish and dip one side of the remaining dough balls into them, then place on the other baking sheet, nut side uppermost, and flatten gently.

Bake in the preheated oven for 10–15 minutes, or until light golden brown. Leave to cool on the baking sheets for 5–10 minutes, then transfer the cookies to wire racks to cool completely.

Place the remaining butter, the icing sugar and honey in a bowl and beat together until creamy. Spread the honey mixture over the plain cookies and top with the nut-coated cookies.

387 Nut & maple syrup sandwiches

Replace the macadamia nuts with chopped pecan nuts in the dough and replace the honey with maple syrup.

388 Golden hazelnut cookies

225 g/8 oz butter, softened
140 g/5 oz caster sugar
1 egg yolk, lightly beaten
225 g/8 oz plain flour
pinch of salt
55 g/2 oz ground hazelnuts

TOPPING
225 g/8 oz plain chocolate, broken
    into pieces
about 30 hazelnuts

Place the butter and sugar in a large bowl and beat together until light and fluffy, then beat in the egg yolk. Sift together the flour and salt into the mixture, add the ground hazelnuts and stir until thoroughly combined. Halve the dough, form into balls, wrap in clingfilm and chill in the refrigerator for 30–60 minutes.

Preheat the oven to 190°C/375°F/Gas Mark 5. Line 2 large baking sheets with baking paper.

Unwrap the dough and roll out between 2 sheets of baking paper. Cut out rounds with a plain 6-cm/2½-inch cutter and place them on the baking sheet, spaced well apart. Bake in the preheated oven for 10–12 minutes, or until golden brown. Leave to cool for 5–10 minutes, then transfer the cookies to wire racks to cool.

When the cookies are cool, place the wire racks over a sheet of baking paper. Place the chocolate in a heatproof bowl, set the bowl over a saucepan of gently simmering water and heat until melted. Leave to cool, then spoon the chocolate over the cookies. Gently tap the wire racks to level the surface and leave to set for a few minutes. Add a hazelnut to the centre of each cookie and leave to set.

389 With white chocolate coating

Replace the plain chocolate with white chocolate and chop the hazelnuts before scattering over the chocolate.

390 *Mega chip cookies*

225 g/8 oz butter, softened
140 g/5 oz caster sugar
1 egg yolk, lightly beaten
2 tsp vanilla extract
225 g/8 oz plain flour
55 g/2 oz cocoa powder

pinch of salt
85 g/3 oz milk chocolate chips
85 g/3 oz white chocolate chips
115 g/4 oz plain chocolate, roughly
    chopped

Preheat the oven to 190°C/375°F/Gas Mark 5. Line 2–3 baking sheets with baking paper. Place the butter and sugar in a large bowl and beat together until light and fluffy, then beat in the egg yolk and vanilla extract. Sift together the flour, cocoa and salt into the mixture, add both kinds of chocolate chips and stir until thoroughly combined.

Make 12 balls of the mixture, place them on the baking sheets, spaced well apart, and flatten slightly. Press the pieces of plain chocolate into the cookies.

Bake in the preheated oven for 12–15 minutes. Leave to cool on the baking sheets for 5–10 minutes, then transfer the cookies to wire racks to cool completely.

391 *Caramel chip cookies*

Replace the chocolate chips with 280 g/10 oz chopped caramel chocolate.

392 *Peanut partners*

225 g/8 oz butter, softened
140 g/5 oz caster sugar
1 egg yolk, lightly beaten
280 g/10 oz plain flour
1 tsp ground ginger
pinch of salt
2 tsp finely grated lemon rind

TOPPING
3 tbsp smooth peanut butter
3 tbsp icing sugar
whole or chopped roasted peanuts,
    to decorate

Place the butter and sugar in a large bowl and beat together until light and fluffy, then beat in the egg yolk. Sift together the flour, ginger and salt into the mixture, add the lemon rind and stir until thoroughly combined. Halve the dough, shape into balls, wrap in clingfilm and chill in the refrigerator for 30–60 minutes.

Preheat the oven to 190°C/375°F/Gas Mark 5. Line 2 large baking sheets with baking paper. Unwrap the dough and roll out between 2 sheets of baking paper to 3 mm/⅛ inch thick. Cut out rounds with a 6-cm/2½-inch fluted cutter and place them on the baking sheets, spaced well apart. Bake in the preheated oven for 10–15 minutes, until golden. Cool for 5–10 minutes, then transfer to wire racks to cool completely. To make the topping, beat the peanut butter and icing sugar together in a bowl, adding a little water if necessary. Spread the cookies with the mixture and decorate with peanuts.

393 *With peanut brittle topping*

For an alternative topping, spread the cookies with unsweetened smooth peanut butter and scatter over 150 g/5½ oz crushed peanut brittle.

394 Rich peanut & cream cookies sandwiches

6 tbsp salted peanuts
225 g/8 oz butter, softened
140 g/5 oz caster sugar
1 egg yolk, lightly beaten
280 g/10 oz plain flour

pinch of salt
½ tsp ground allspice
3 tbsp double cream
85 g/3 oz cream cheese
115 g/4 oz crystallized pineapple, chopped

Reserve half the peanuts and finely chop the remainder. Place the butter and sugar in a large bowl and beat together until light and fluffy, then beat in the egg yolk. Sift together the flour, allspice and salt into the mixture and stir until combined. Halve the dough, shape into balls, wrap in clingfilm and chill in the refrigerator for 30–60 minutes.

Preheat the oven to 190°C/375°F/Gas Mark 5. Line 2 large baking sheets with baking paper. Unwrap the dough and roll out between 2 sheets of baking paper. Sprinkle evenly with the reserved peanuts and lightly roll with the rolling pin. Cut out cookies with a 5–6-cm/2–2½-inch fluted round cutter and place them on the baking sheets, spaced well apart.

Bake in the preheated oven for 10–15 minutes, or until light golden. Leave to cool on the baking sheets for 5–10 minutes, then transfer the cookies to wire racks to cool completely.

Place the cream and cream cheese in a bowl and beat together until thick and smooth. Fold in the crystallized pineapple. Spread the mixture over the undersides of half the cookies and top with the remaining cookies, peanut-side uppermost.

395 With coconut peanut cream

For the filling, sift 55 g/2 oz icing sugar into a bowl and beat with 1 tablespoon of coconut rum and 85 g/3 oz crunchy peanut butter, then use this to sandwich the cookies together.

396 Pistachio nut biscuits

250 g/9 oz blanched pistachio nuts
125 g/4½ oz unsalted butter
finely grated rind of 1 lemon
100 g/3½ oz soft light brown sugar

1 egg
150 g/5½ oz self-raising flour
good pinch of salt

Place the pistachio nuts in a clean tea towel and rub vigorously to remove any papery skin. Place the butter, lemon rind and sugar in a large bowl and beat together until smooth. Add the egg and beat well. Sift together the flour and salt into the mixture. Crush the nuts and stir into the mixture until combined. Pour the mixture onto a large sheet of clingfilm and roll it up into a sausage shape. Twist the 2 ends of the clingfilm like a cracker and chill in the refrigerator for 20 minutes.

Preheat the oven to 180°C/350°F/Gas Mark 4. Line 2 large baking sheets with baking paper.

Unwrap the clingfilm, cut the filling into 5-mm/¼-inch thick rounds and place them on the baking sheets, evenly spaced apart. Bake in the preheated oven for 10–15 minutes, or until golden brown. Leave to cool on a wire rack.

397 Walnut & fig pinwheels

225 g/8 oz butter, softened
200 g/7 oz caster sugar
1 egg yolk, lightly beaten
225 g/8 oz plain flour
pinch of salt

55 g/2 oz ground walnuts
125 ml/4 fl oz water
280 g/10 oz dried figs, finely chopped
5 tbsp freshly brewed mint tea
2 tsp finely chopped fresh mint

Place the butter and 140 g/5 oz of the sugar in a large bowl and beat together until light and fluffy, then beat in the egg yolk. Sift together the flour and salt into the mixture, add the walnuts and stir until combined. Shape the dough into a ball, wrap in clingfilm and chill for 30–60 minutes.

Meanwhile, place the remaining sugar in a saucepan and stir in the water, then add the figs, mint tea and chopped mint. Bring to the boil, stirring constantly, until the sugar has dissolved, then reduce the heat and simmer gently, stirring occasionally, for 5 minutes. Leave to cool.

Unwrap the dough and roll out between 2 sheets of baking paper into a 30-cm/12-inch square. Spread the fig filling evenly over the dough, then roll up from a short side like a Swiss roll. Wrap in clingfilm and chill in the refrigerator for 30 minutes.

Preheat the oven to 190°C/ 375°F/Gas Mark 5. Line 2 large baking sheets with baking paper. Unwrap the roll and cut into thin slices with a sharp serrated knife. Place the slices on the baking sheets, making sure they are spaced well apart.

Bake in the preheated oven for 10–15 minutes, or until golden brown. Leave to cool on the baking sheets for 5–10 minutes, then transfer to wire racks to cool completely.

398 Date & pecan pinwheels

Replace the walnuts and figs with finely chopped pecan nuts and finely chopped, stoned dried dates.

399 Almond cookies with green tea cream

25 g/8 oz butter, softened
140 g/5 oz caster sugar, plus extra
    for sprinkling
1 egg yolk, lightly beaten
2 tsp vanilla extract
280 g/10 oz plain flour
pinch of salt
25 g/1 oz flaked almonds
1 egg white, lightly beaten

GREEN TEA CREAM
125 ml/4 fl oz milk
2 green tea teabags or 2 tsp green
    tea leaves
1 tbsp caster sugar
1 tbsp custard powder
125 g/4½ oz cream cheese

Place the butter and sugar in a large bowl and beat together until light and fluffy, then beat in the egg yolk and vanilla. Sift in the flour and salt and stir well. Halve the dough, wrap in clingfilm and chill for 30–60 minutes.

Preheat the oven to 190°C/ 375°F/Gas Mark 5. Line 2 large baking sheets with baking paper.

Roll out a dough ball between 2 sheets of baking paper. Cut out cookies with a 6-cm/2½-inch cutter and place on a baking sheet. Roll out the other dough ball until it is 1 cm/½ inch thick. Sprinkle with the almonds, cover with baking paper and roll out to 5 mm/¼ inch thick. Cut out 6-cm/2½-inch rounds and place on the other baking sheet. Brush with egg white and sprinkle with sugar. Bake in the preheated oven for 10–15 minutes, or until golden. Cool for 5–10 minutes, then transfer to wire racks.

Bring the milk to the boil, then remove from the heat. Add the tea, cover with clingfilm and infuse for 15 minutes. Strain into a clean pan. Stir in the sugar and custard powder and bring to the boil, stirring until thick. Cover and cool.

Beat the cream cheese until smooth. Beat in the green tea custard. Spread the cream over the plain cookies and top with the almond cookies.

400 With almond cream

Replace the green tea cream with almond cream made by beating 1 tablespoon of icing sugar and 1 teaspoon of almond extract into 125 g/ 4½ oz cream cheese.

401 Almond crunchies

225 g/8 oz butter, softened
140 g/5 oz caster sugar
1 egg yolk, lightly beaten
½ tsp almond extract

225 g/8 oz plain flour
pinch of salt
225 g/8 oz blanched almonds, chopped

Place the butter and sugar in a large bowl and beat together until light and fluffy, then beat in the egg yolk and almond extract. Sift together the flour and salt into the mixture, add the almonds and stir until thoroughly combined. Halve the dough, shape it into balls, wrap in clingfilm and chill in the refrigerator for 30–60 minutes.

Preheat the oven to 190°C/375°F/Gas Mark 5. Line 2–3 baking sheets with baking paper.

Shape the dough into about 50 small balls, flatten them slightly between the palms of your hands and place them on the baking sheets, spaced well apart. Bake in the preheated oven for 15–20 minutes, or until golden brown. Leave to cool on the baking sheets for 5–10 minutes, then transfer to wire racks to cool completely.

402 With marzipan filling

Cut 100 g/3½ oz marzipan into small cubes and press one piece into the middle of each cookie. Form the dough around the marzipan to completely enclose and bake as before.

403 Almond & raspberry jam drops

225 g/8 oz butter, softened
140 g/5 oz caster sugar
1 egg yolk, lightly beaten
2 tsp almond extract
280 g/10 oz plain flour

pinch of salt
55 g/2 oz almonds, toasted and chopped
55 g/2 oz chopped mixed peel
4 tbsp raspberry jam

Preheat the oven to 190°C/375°F/Gas Mark 5. Line 2 baking sheets with baking paper. Place the butter and sugar in a large bowl and beat together until light and fluffy, then beat in the egg yolk and almond extract. Sift together the flour and salt into the mixture, add the almonds and mixed peel and stir until thoroughly combined.

Scoop out tablespoons of the mixture and shape into balls with your hands, then place them on the baking sheets, spaced well apart. Use the dampened handle of a wooden spoon to make a hollow in the centre of each cookie and fill with raspberry jam. Bake in the preheated oven for 12–15 minutes, or until golden brown. Leave to cool for 5–10 minutes, then transfer to wire racks to cool completely.

404 Almond & strawberry jam drops

Replace the mixed peel with 55 g/2 oz chopped dried strawberries and replace the raspberry jam with strawberry jam.

405 *Nutty drizzles*

200 g/7 oz butter, plus extra for greasing
275 g/9¾ oz demerara sugar
1 egg
140 g/5 oz plain flour
1 tsp baking powder
1 tsp bicarbonate of soda
125 g/4½ oz rolled oats
1 tbsp bran

1 tbsp wheatgerm
115 g/4 oz mixed nuts, toasted and
   roughly chopped
200 g/7 oz plain chocolate chips
115 g/4 oz mixed raisins and sultanas
175 g/6 oz plain chocolate, roughly
   chopped

Preheat the oven to 180°C/350°F/Gas Mark 4. Grease 2 large baking sheets. Place the butter, sugar and egg in a large bowl and beat together until light and fluffy. Sift in the flour, baking powder and bicarbonate of soda. Add the oats, bran and wheatgerm and mix together until well combined. Stir in the nuts, chocolate chips and dried fruit. Place 24 rounded tablespoons of the mixture on the baking sheets.

Bake in the preheated oven for 12 minutes, or until golden brown. Leave to cool on wire racks.

Meanwhile, place the chocolate pieces in a heatproof bowl, set the bowl over a saucepan of gently simmering water and heat until melted. Stir the chocolate, then leave to cool slightly. Use a spoon to drizzle the chocolate in waves over the cookies, or spoon it into a piping bag and pipe zigzag lines over the biscuits.

406 *With nut chocolate topping*

Add 115 g/4 oz chopped mixed nuts to the melted chocolate and spread over the cookies.

407 *Cashew & poppy seed cookies*

225 g/8 oz butter, softened
140 g/5 oz caster sugar
1 egg yolk, lightly beaten
280 g/10 oz plain flour

1 tsp ground cinnamon
pinch of salt
115 g/4 oz cashew nuts, chopped
2–3 tbsp poppy seeds

Place the butter and sugar in a large bowl and beat together until light and fluffy, then beat in the egg yolk. Sift together the flour, cinnamon and salt into the mixture, add the nuts and stir until combined. Shape the dough into a log. Spread out the poppy seeds in a dish and roll the log in them until coated. Wrap in clingfilm and chill for 30–60 minutes.

Preheat the oven to 190°C/375°F/Gas Mark 5. Line 2 large baking sheets with baking paper.

Unwrap the dough, cut into 1-cm/½-inch slices with a sharp serrated knife and place them on the baking sheets. Bake in the preheated oven for 12 minutes, or until golden brown. Leave to cool on the baking sheets for 5–10 minutes, then transfer to wire racks to cool completely.

408 *Cashew cookies*

Omit the poppy seeds and roll the dough in 225 g/8 oz finely chopped cashew nuts.

175 g/6 oz butter, plus extra for greasing
200 g/7 oz soft light brown sugar
1 egg
70 g/2½ oz plain flour, plus extra for
    dusting (optional)
1 tsp bicarbonate of soda
pinch of salt
70 g/2½ oz wholemeal flour

1 tbsp bran
225 g/8 oz plain chocolate chips
185 g/6½ oz rolled oats
1 tbsp strong coffee
100 g/3½ oz hazelnuts, toasted
    and roughly chopped

Preheat the oven to 190°C/375°F/Gas Mark 5. Grease 2 large baking sheets. Place the butter and sugar in a large bowl and beat together until light and fluffy. Add the egg and beat well. Sift together the plain flour, bicarbonate of soda and salt into another bowl, then add in the wholemeal flour and bran. Mix in the egg mixture, then stir in the chocolate chips, oats, coffee and hazelnuts and mix well.

Place 24 rounded tablespoons of the mixture on the baking sheets, spaced well apart. Alternatively, with lightly floured hands, break off pieces of the mixture and roll into balls (about 25 g/1 oz each), place on the baking sheets and flatten.

Bake in the preheated oven for 16–18 minutes, or until golden brown. Leave to cool for 5 minutes, then transfer to a wire rack to cool completely.

410 *With ice cream filling*

Remove a tub of plain chocolate ice cream from the freezer and leave to soften at room temperature. Tip into a bowl and add 2 tablespoons of Kahlúa coffee liqueur and beat together. Use to sandwich the baked cookies together, then freeze the cookies for 10 minutes until firm. Makes 12.

411 *Jumbo oat & raisin chippers*

MAKES 15

85 g/3 oz rolled oats
100 g/3½ oz plain flour
½ tsp bicarbonate of soda
pinch of salt
60 g/2¼ oz unsalted butter, softened

100 g/3½ oz soft light brown sugar
50 g/1¾ oz granulated sugar
1 large egg
½ tsp vanilla extract
175 g/6 oz raisins

Preheat the oven to 190°C/375°F/Gas Mark 5. Place the oats in a food processor and pulse briefly, then tip into a bowl and sift in the flour, bicarbonate of soda and salt and stir together.

Place the butter and sugars in a large bowl and beat together until light and fluffy. Place the egg and vanilla extract in a separate bowl and whisk together, then add to the butter and mix well. Add the flour mixture, mix together, then add the raisins and mix thoroughly.

Divide the mixture into 15 balls and place on 2 large non-stick baking sheets, spaced well apart. Press the cookies into rough rounds. Bake in the preheated oven for 12 minutes, or until golden brown. Leave to cool for 5 minutes, then transfer to a wire rack to cool completely.

412 *Jumbo oat, apricot & prune chippers*

Replace the raisins with 100 g/3½ oz chopped dried apricots and 100 g/ 3½ oz chopped pitted prunes.

413 *Mocha walnut cookies*

115 g/4 oz butter, softened, plus extra
    for greasing
115 g/4 oz light muscovado sugar
85 g/3 oz caster sugar
1 tsp vanilla extract
1 tbsp instant coffee granules, dissolved in
    1 tbsp hot water

1 egg
175 g/6 oz plain flour
½ tsp baking powder
¼ tsp bicarbonate of soda
55 g/2 oz milk chocolate chips
55 g/2 oz walnut halves, roughly chopped

Preheat the oven to 180°C/350°F/Gas Mark 4. Grease 2 large baking sheets. Place the butter and sugars in a large bowl and beat together until light and fluffy. Place the vanilla extract, coffee and egg in a separate bowl and whisk together. Gradually add the coffee mixture to the butter and sugar, beating until fluffy. Sift the flour, baking powder and bicarbonate of soda into the mixture and fold in carefully. Fold in the chocolate chips and walnuts.

Spoon heaped teaspoons of the mixture onto the baking sheets, spaced well apart. Bake in the preheated oven for 10–15 minutes, or until crisp on the outside but soft inside. Leave to cool on the baking sheets for 2 minutes, then transfer to wire racks to cool completely

414 *With mocha icing*

Sift 100 g/3½ oz icing sugar into a bowl. Stir ½ teaspoon of instant espresso powder, ½ teaspoon of cocoa powder and 1 tablespoon of boiling water together until smooth. Add to the icing sugar and mix to a smooth icing, spread over the cookies and leave to set on a wire rack.

415 *Almond tuilles*

1 tsp groundnut oil, for greasing
85 g/3 oz unsalted butter, softened
70 g/2½ oz caster sugar

50 g/1¾ oz plain flour
pinch of salt
70 g/2½ oz flaked almonds

Preheat the oven to 200°C/400°F/Gas Mark 6 and grease 2 large baking sheets with the oil. Place the butter and sugar in a large bowl and beat together until light and fluffy. Sift together the flour and salt and fold into the mixture, then add the almonds and mix together.

Drop 12 teaspoons of batter on each baking sheet, spaced well apart, and spread into flat ovals with the back of a spoon.

Bake in the preheated oven for 5 minutes, or until golden. While the cookies are still warm, lift each one in turn and drape over a wooden rolling pin to make a curved shape. Leave for 1 minute to harden, then transfer to a wire rack to cool completely.

416 *With chocolate coating*

Place 150 g/5½ oz plain chocolate in a heatproof bowl, set the bowl over a saucepan of gently simmering water and heat until melted. Dip each tuile into the melted chocolate and leave to set on baking paper.

417 Camomile cookies

225 g/8 oz butter, softened
140 g/5 oz caster sugar, plus extra for
  coating
1 tbsp (3–4 tea bags) camomile or
  camomile and lime flower infusion tea
1 egg yolk, lightly beaten

1 tsp vanilla extract
280 g/10 oz plain flour
pinch of salt

Place the butter and sugar in a large bowl and beat together until light and fluffy. If using tea bags, remove the tea leaves from the bags. Stir the tea into the butter mixture, then beat in the egg yolk and vanilla extract. Sift together the flour and salt into the mixture and stir until thoroughly combined. Shape the dough into a log. Spread out the extra sugar in a shallow dish and roll the log in the sugar to coat. Wrap in clingfilm and chill in the refrigerator for 30–60 minutes.

Preheat the oven to 190°C/375°F/Gas Mark 5. Line 2 large baking sheets with baking paper.

Unwrap the log, cut into 5-mm/¼-inch slices with a sharp serrated knife and place them on the baking sheets, spaced well apart. Bake in the preheated oven for 10 minutes, or until golden. Leave to cool on the baking sheets for 5–10 minutes, then transfer the cookies to wire racks to cool completely.

418 Lemon verbena cookies

Replace the camomile tea with lemon verbena tea and add ½ teaspoon of finely grated lemon rind to the dough.

419 Nutty pecan cookies

150 g/5½ oz unsalted butter, softened
150 g/5½ oz caster sugar
225 g/8 oz self-raising flour

1–2 tbsp milk
½ tsp vanilla extract
280 g/10 oz pecan nuts

Preheat the oven to 190°C/375°F/Gas Mark 5. Line 2 large baking sheets with baking paper. Place the butter and sugar in a large bowl and beat together until light and fluffy. Sift in the flour and beat to combine. Add 1 tablespoon of milk and the vanilla extract and mix to form a dough, adding more milk if the dough is too stiff.

Reserve 20 pecan halves. Chop the remaining pecan nuts and knead in to the dough. Divide the dough into 20 and roll each piece into a ball. Place 10 balls on each baking sheet, spaced well apart. Press down to a thickness of 1 cm/½ inch, then press a pecan half into the centre of each cookie. Bake in the preheated oven for 10–15 minutes. Leave the cookies to cool on the baking sheets.

420 *Cappuccino cookies*

2 sachets instant cappuccino
1 tbsp hot water
225 g/8 oz butter, softened
140 g/5 oz caster sugar
1 egg yolk, lightly beaten
280 g/10 oz plain flour

pinch of salt

TOPPING
175 g/6 oz white chocolate, broken
   into pieces
cocoa powder, for dusting

Empty the cappuccino sachets into a small bowl and stir in the hot, but not boiling, water to make a paste. Place the butter and sugar in a large bowl and beat together until light and fluffy, then beat in the egg yolk and cappuccino paste. Sift together the flour and salt into the mixture and stir until combined. Halve the dough, shape into balls, wrap in clingfilm and chill for 30–60 minutes.

Preheat the oven to 190°C/375°F/Gas Mark 5. Line 2 large baking sheets with baking paper. Unwrap the dough and roll out between 2 sheets of baking paper. Cut out cookies with a 6-cm/2½-inch round cutter and place them on the baking sheets, spaced well apart. Bake in the preheated oven for 10–12 minutes, or until golden brown. Leave to cool for 5–10 minutes, then transfer to wire racks to cool completely.

Place the wire racks over a sheet of baking paper. Place the chocolate into a heatproof bowl, set the bowl over a saucepan of gently simmering water and heat until melted. Leave to cool, then spoon the chocolate over the cookies. Leave to set, then dust lightly with cocoa powder.

421 *With coffee bean topping*

Replace the cocoa powder with 100 g/3½ oz crushed chocolate-covered coffee beans, scatter them over the melted white chocolate topping and leave to set.

422 *Cinnamon & caramel cookies*

225 g/8 oz butter, softened
140 g/5 oz caster sugar
1 egg yolk, lightly beaten
1 tsp vanilla extract
280 g/10 oz plain flour

1 tsp ground cinnamon
½ tsp allspice
pinch of salt
25–30 caramels

Preheat the oven to 190°C/375°F/Gas Mark 5. Line 2 large baking sheets with baking paper. Place the butter and sugar in a large bowl and beat together until light and fluffy, then beat in the egg yolk and vanilla extract. Sift together the flour, cinnamon, allspice and salt into the mixture and stir until thoroughly combined.

Scoop up tablespoons of the mixture, shape into balls and place on the baking sheets, spaced well apart. Bake in the preheated oven for 8 minutes. Place a caramel on top of each cookie and bake for a further 6–7 minutes. Leave to cool on the baking sheets for 5–10 minutes, then transfer to wire racks to cool completely.

423 *Lemon & sweetie cookies*

Replace the cinnamon and allspice with 1 teaspoon of finely grated lemon rind. Replace the caramels with 25 lemon boiled sweets.

424 Fennel & angelica cookies

225 g/8 oz butter, softened
140 g/5 oz caster sugar
1 egg yolk, lightly beaten
1 tbsp finely chopped angelica

280 g/10 oz plain flour
pinch of salt
1 tbsp fennel seeds

Place the butter and sugar in a large bowl and beat together until light and fluffy, then beat in the egg yolk and angelica. Sift together the flour and salt into the mixture, add the fennel seeds and stir until thoroughly combined. Shape the dough into a log, wrap in clingfilm and chill in the refrigerator for 30–60 minutes.

Preheat the oven to 190°C/375°F/Gas Mark 5. Line 2 large baking sheets with baking paper. Unwrap the dough, cut into 1-cm/½-inch slices with a sharp serrated knife and place them on the baking sheets, spaced well apart. Bake in the preheated oven for 12–15 minutes, or until golden.

Leave to cool on the baking sheets for 5–10 minutes, then transfer the cookies to wire racks to cool completely.

425 Fennel, lemon & angelica cookies

Add 1 teaspoon of finely grated lemon rind and ½ teaspoon of lemon oil to the dough.

426 Sticky ginger cookies

225 g/8 oz butter, softened
140 g/5 oz caster sugar
1 egg yolk, lightly beaten
55 g/2 oz stem ginger, coarsely chopped,
   plus 1 tbsp syrup from the jar

280 g/10 oz plain flour
pinch of salt
55 g/2 oz plain chocolate chips

Place the butter and sugar in a large bowl and beat together until light and fluffy, then beat in the egg yolk and ginger syrup. Sift together the flour and salt into the mixture, add the stem ginger and chocolate chips and stir until thoroughly combined. Shape the mixture into a log, wrap in clingfilm and chill in the refrigerator for 30–60 minutes.

Preheat the oven to 190°C/375°F/Gas Mark 5. Line 2 large baking sheets with baking paper.

Unwrap the log, cut it into 5-mm/¼-inch slices with a sharp serrated knife and place them on the baking sheets, spaced well apart. Bake in the preheated oven for 12–15 minutes, or until golden brown.

Leave to cool on the baking sheets for 5–10 minutes, then transfer the cookies to wire racks to cool completely.

427 Sticky citrus cookies

Replace the chocolate chips with chopped mixed peel.

428 Treacle & spice drizzles

200 g/7 oz butter, softened
2 tbsp black treacle
140 g/5 oz caster sugar
1 egg yolk, lightly beaten
280 g/10 oz plain flour
1 tsp ground cinnamon
½ tsp grated nutmeg
½ tsp ground cloves

2 tbsp chopped walnuts
pinch of salt

ICING
115 g/4 oz icing sugar
1 tbsp hot water
few drops of yellow food colouring
few drops of pink food colouring

Place the butter, treacle and sugar in a large bowl and beat together until fluffy, then beat in the egg yolk.

Sift together the flour, cinnamon, nutmeg, cloves and salt into the mixture, add the walnuts and stir until thoroughly combined. Halve the dough, shape into balls, wrap in clingfilm and chill for 30–60 minutes.

Preheat the oven to 190°C/375°F/Gas Mark 5. Line 2 baking sheets with baking paper. Unwrap the dough and roll out between 2 sheets of baking paper to about 5 mm/¼ inch thick. Cut out rounds with a 6-cm/2½-inch fluted cutter and place them on the baking sheets.

Bake in the preheated oven for 10–15 minutes, or until firm. Leave to cool on the baking sheets for 5–10 minutes, then transfer the cookies to wire racks to cool completely.

To make the icing, sift the icing sugar into a bowl, then gradually stir in the hot water until the icing has the consistency of thick cream. Spoon half the icing into another bowl and stir a few drops of yellow food colouring into one bowl and a few drops of pink food colouring into the other. Leave the cookies on the racks and, using teaspoons, drizzle the yellow icing over them in one direction and the pink icing over them at right angles. Leave to set.

429 Syrup drizzles

Replace the treacle with golden syrup and decorate the cookies with the icing leaving out the food colouring.

430 Cinnamon & orange crisps

225 g/8 oz butter, softened
200 g/7 oz caster sugar
finely grated rind of 1 orange
1 egg yolk, lightly beaten

4 tsp orange juice
280 g/10 oz plain flour
pinch of salt
2 tsp ground cinnamon

Place the butter, 140 g/5 oz of the sugar and the orange rind in a large bowl and beat together until light and fluffy, then beat in the egg yolk and 2 teaspoons of the orange juice. Sift together the flour and salt into the mixture and stir until thoroughly combined. Shape the dough into a ball, wrap in clingfilm and chill in the refrigerator for 30–60 minutes.

Unwrap the dough and roll out between 2 sheets of baking paper into a 30-cm/12-inch square. Brush with the remaining orange juice and sprinkle with cinnamon. Lightly roll with the rolling pin. Roll up the dough like a Swiss roll. Wrap in clingfilm and chill for 30 minutes.

Preheat the oven to 190°C/375°F/Gas Mark 5. Line 2 large baking sheets with baking paper.

Unwrap the dough and cut into thin slices, then place on the baking sheets, spaced well apart. Bake in the preheated oven for 10–12 minutes. Leave to cool for 5–10 minutes, then transfer to wire racks to cool completely.

431 With white chocolate coating

Place 150 g/5½ oz white chocolate in a heatproof bowl, set the bowl over a saucepan of gently simmering water and heat until melted. Dip the cooled cookies to coat half of each one and leave to set on a wire rack.

Classic saffron cookies

100 g/3½ oz currants
125 ml/4 fl oz sweet white wine
225 g/8 oz butter, softened
140 g/5 oz caster sugar

1 egg yolk, lightly beaten
280 g/10 oz plain flour
½ tsp powdered saffron
pinch of salt

Place the currants in a bowl, pour in the wine and leave to soak for 1 hour. Drain the currants and reserve any remaining wine.

Preheat the oven to 190°C/375°F/Gas Mark 5. Line 2 large baking sheets with baking paper. Place the butter and sugar in a large bowl and beat together until light and fluffy, then beat in the egg yolk and 2 teaspoons of the reserved wine. Sift together the flour, saffron and salt into the mixture and stir until thoroughly combined.

Scoop up tablespoons of the dough and place them on the baking sheets, spaced well apart. Flatten gently and smooth the tops with the back of the spoon.

Bake in the preheated oven for 10–15 minutes, or until light golden brown. Leave to cool on the baking sheets for 5–10 minutes, then transfer the cookies to wire racks to cool completely.

433 With sweet wine frosting

Omit the currants from the dough and drizzle the cookies with icing made from sifting 100 g/3½ oz icing sugar into a bowl and mixing with 1 tablespoon of sweet white wine until smooth. Leave to set.

434 Mint cookies with white chocolate ganache

225 g/8 oz butter, softened
140 g/5 oz caster sugar
1 egg yolk, lightly beaten
2 tsp vanilla extract
280 g/10 oz plain flour
pinch of salt

100 g/3½ oz chocolate mint sticks, finely chopped
icing sugar, for dusting

WHITE CHOCOLATE GANACHE
2 tbsp double cream
100 g/3½ oz white chocolate, broken into pieces

Place the butter and sugar in a large bowl and beat together until light and fluffy, then beat in the egg yolk and vanilla extract. Sift together the flour and salt into the mixture, add the chocolate sticks and stir until combined. Halve the dough, shape into balls, wrap and chill for 30–60 minutes.

Preheat the oven to 190°C/375°F/Gas Mark 5. Line 2 large baking sheets with baking paper. Unwrap the dough and roll out between 2 sheets of baking paper. Cut out cookies with a 6-cm/2½-inch fluted round cutter and place them on the baking sheets, spaced well apart. Bake in the preheated oven for 10–15 minutes, or until light golden brown.

Leave the cookies to cool on the baking sheets for 5–10 minutes, then transfer to wire racks to cool completely.

Pour the cream into a saucepan, add the chocolate and melt over a low heat, stirring occasionally, until smooth. Leave to cool, then chill in the refrigerator until the mixture has a spreadable consistency. Spread the ganache over half the cookies and top with the remaining cookies, then dust with sifted icing sugar.

435 With mint ganache

Replace the white chocolate in the ganache with chopped plain mint chocolate.

436 *Flower gems*

225 g/8 oz butter, softened
140 g/5 oz caster sugar
1 egg yolk, lightly beaten
1 tsp lemon juice
280 g/10 oz plain flour
pinch of salt
2 tbsp jasmine tea leaves

TO DECORATE
1 tbsp lemon juice
1 tbsp water
200 g/7 oz icing sugar
orange, pink, blue and yellow
    food colouring
orange, pink, blue and yellow
    sugar flowers

Place the butter and sugar in a large bowl and beat together until light and fluffy, then beat in the egg yolk and lemon juice. Sift together the flour and salt into the mixture, add the tea leaves and stir until thoroughly combined. Halve the dough, shape it into balls, wrap in clingfilm and chill for 30–60 minutes.

Preheat the oven to 190°C/375°F/Gas Mark 5. Line 2 large baking sheets with baking paper. Roll out the dough between 2 sheets of baking paper to about 3 mm/⅛ inch thick. Cut out flowers with a 5-cm/2-inch flower cutter and place them on the baking sheets, spaced well apart.

Bake in the preheated oven for 10–12 minutes, or until golden brown. Leave to cool on the baking sheets for 5–10 minutes, then transfer the cookies to wire racks to cool completely.

To decorate, mix the lemon juice and water together in a bowl, then gradually stir in enough icing sugar until it is the consistency of thick cream. Divide the icing among 4 separate bowls and add a drop of different food colouring to each.

Leave the cookies on the racks. Spread orange icing on one quarter of the cookies, pink on another quarter and so on. When the icing is beginning to set, add a matching flower to the centre of each. Leave to cool.

437 *Petal gems*

Roll out the dough as before but cut out the dough with a 2.5-cm/1-inch round cutter and press 6 discs together for each cookie as petals to form a flower, then use the sugar flowers as the centres. Makes about 20.

438 *Lavender cookies*

225 g/8 oz butter, softened
175 g/6 oz caster sugar
1 large egg, lightly beaten

250 g/9 oz plain flour
2 tsp baking powder
1 tbsp dried lavender, chopped

Preheat the oven to 190°C/375°F/Gas Mark 5. Line 2–3 large baking sheets with baking paper. Place the butter and sugar in a bowl and beat together until light and fluffy, then beat in the egg. Sift together the flour and baking powder into the mixture, add the lavender and stir well.

Place tablespoons of the mixture on the baking sheets, spaced well apart. Bake in the preheated oven for 15 minutes, or until golden brown. Leave to cool on the baking sheets for 5–10 minutes, then transfer the cookies to wire racks to cool completely.

439 *Rosemary cookies*

Replace the lavender with 1½ teaspoons of chopped dried rosemary.

440 Rose flower cookies

225 g/8 oz butter, softened
225 g/8 oz caster sugar
1 large egg, lightly beaten
1 tbsp rose water
280 g/10 oz plain flour
1 tsp baking powder
pinch of salt

ICING
1 egg white
250 g/9 oz icing sugar
2 tsp plain flour
2 tsp rose water
few drops of pink food colouring

Place the butter and sugar in a large bowl and beat together until light and fluffy, then beat in the egg and rose water. Sift together the flour, baking powder and salt into the mixture and stir until combined. Shape the dough into a log, wrap in clingfilm and chill in the refrigerator for 1–2 hours.

Preheat the oven to 190°C/375°F/Gas Mark 5. Line 2–3 baking sheets with baking paper.

Unwrap the dough, cut into thin slices with a sharp serrated knife and place on the baking sheets, spaced well apart.

Bake in the preheated oven for 10–12 minutes, or until light golden brown. Leave to cool on the baking sheets for 10 minutes, then transfer the cookies to wire racks to cool completely.

To make the icing, use a fork to lightly beat the egg white in a bowl. Sift in half the icing sugar and stir well, then sift in the remaining icing sugar and flour and mix in enough rose water to make a smooth, easy-to-spread icing. Stir in a few drops of pink food colouring.

Leave the cookies on the racks. Gently spread the icing over them and leave to set.

441 Violet flower cookies

Omit the rose water and pink food colouring. Tint the icing with a little lavender or violet food colouring, then spread the icing on the cookies and scatter over 85 g/3 oz chopped crystallized violets.

442 Zebra cookies

55 g/2 oz plain chocolate, broken into pieces
140 g/5 oz plain flour
1 tsp baking powder
1 egg
140 g/5 oz caster sugar

50 ml/2 fl oz sunflower oil, plus extra for greasing
½ tsp vanilla extract
2 tbsp icing sugar
1 small packet milk chocolate buttons
1 small packet white chocolate buttons

Place the chocolate in a heatproof bowl, set the bowl over a saucepan of gently simmering water and heat until melted. Leave to cool. Sift the flour and baking powder together. Meanwhile, place the egg, sugar, oil and vanilla extract in a large bowl and whisk together. Whisk in the cooled, melted chocolate until well blended, then gradually stir in the sifted flour. Cover the bowl and chill for at least 3 hours.

Preheat the oven to 190°C/375°F/Gas Mark 5. Grease 1–2 large baking sheets with the oil.

Using your hands, shape tablespoonfuls of the mixture into log shapes, each measuring about 5 cm/2 inches. Roll the logs generously in the icing sugar, then place on the baking sheets, spaced well apart. Bake in the preheated oven for 15 minutes, or until firm. As soon as the biscuits are done, place 3 chocolate buttons down the centre of each, alternating the colours. Transfer to a wire rack and leave to cool.

443 With zebra icing

Sift 115 g/4 oz icing sugar into a bowl, add 1 tablespoon of water and mix until smooth. Reserve one quarter and tint with black food colouring. Use the white icing to ice the cookies then add stripes with the black icing and leave to set.

444 Rum & raisin cookies with orange filling

100 g/3½ oz raisins
150 ml/5 fl oz rum
225 g/8 oz butter, softened
140 g/5 oz caster sugar
1 egg yolk, lightly beaten
280 g/10 oz plain flour
pinch of salt

ORANGE FILLING
175 g/6 oz icing sugar
85 g/3 oz butter, softened
2 tsp finely grated orange rind
1 tsp rum
few drops of yellow food colouring
(optional)

Place the raisins in a bowl, pour in the rum and leave to soak for 15 minutes, then drain, reserving the remaining rum.

Preheat the oven to 190°C/375°F/Gas Mark 5. Line 2 large baking sheets with baking paper.

Place the butter and sugar in a large bowl and beat together until light and fluffy, then beat in the egg yolk and 2 teaspoons of the reserved rum. Sift together the flour and salt into the mixture, add the raisins and stir until thoroughly combined.

Scoop up tablespoons of the dough and place them on the baking sheets, spaced well apart. Flatten gently and smooth the tops with the back of a spoon.

Bake in the preheated oven for 10–15 minutes, or until light golden brown. Leave to cool on the baking sheets for 5–10 minutes, then transfer the cookies to wire racks to cool completely.

To make the orange filling, sift the icing sugar into a bowl, add the butter, orange rind, rum and food colouring, if using, and beat well until smooth. Spread the filling over half the cookies and top with the remaining cookies.

445 With plain chocolate filling

Replace the orange filling with a chocolate filling made by heating 125 ml/4 fl oz double cream to boiling point and pouring over 125 g/4½ oz chopped plain chocolate, then mixing until smooth. Cool and chill until thick, then use to sandwich the biscuits together.

446 Gingernuts

350 g/12 oz self-raising flour
pinch of salt
200 g/7 oz caster sugar
1 tbsp ground ginger
1 tsp bicarbonate of soda

125 g/4½ oz butter, plus extra
for greasing
75 g/2¾ oz golden syrup
1 egg, lightly beaten
1 tsp grated orange rind

Preheat the oven to 160°C/325°F/Gas Mark 3. Lightly grease several large baking sheets.

Sift together the flour, salt, sugar, ginger and bicarbonate of soda into a large bowl. Heat the butter and golden syrup together in a saucepan over a very low heat until the butter has melted. Leave to cool slightly, then pour it onto the dry ingredients. Add the egg and orange rind and mix thoroughly to form a dough. Using your hands, carefully shape the dough into 30 even-sized balls.

Place the balls on the baking sheets, spaced well apart, then flatten them slightly with your fingers.

Bake in the preheated oven for 15–20 minutes, then carefully transfer the biscuits to a wire rack to cool.

447 Extra ginger gingernuts

Drain 3 balls of stem ginger in syrup, chop finely and add to the dough before baking.

225 g/8 oz butter, softened
140 g/5 oz caster sugar
1 egg yolk, lightly beaten
2 tsp vanilla extract
280 g/10 oz plain flour

pinch of salt
1 tsp ground ginger
1 tbsp finely grated orange rind
1 tbsp cocoa powder
1 egg white, lightly beaten

Place the butter and sugar in a large bowl and beat together until light and fluffy, then beat in the egg yolk and vanilla. Sift together the flour and salt into the mixture and stir until combined.

Divide the dough in half. Add the ginger and orange rind to one half and mix well. Shape the dough into a log 15 cm/6 inches long. Flatten the sides and top to square off the log to 5 cm/2 inches high. Wrap in clingfilm and chill for 30–60 minutes.

Sift the cocoa into the other half of the dough and mix well.

Shape into a flattened log exactly the same size as the first one, wrap in clingfilm and chill in the refrigerator for 30–60 minutes.

Unwrap the dough and cut each log lengthways into 3 slices. Cut each slice lengthways into 3 strips. Brush the strips with egg white and stack them in threes, alternating the colours, so they are the same shape as the original logs. Wrap in clingfilm and chill for 30–60 minutes.

Preheat the oven to 190°C/375°F/Gas Mark 5. Line 2 large baking sheets with baking paper.

Unwrap the logs and cut into slices with a sharp serrated knife, then place the cookies on the baking sheets, spaced well apart. Bake in the preheated oven for 12–15 minutes, or until firm. Leave to cool for 5–10 minutes, then transfer the cookies to wire racks to cool completely.

449 *Battenberg cookies*

Omit the orange rind and ginger. Use pink food colouring to tint one half of the dough and add cocoa to the other. Shape each dough portion into 2 logs and after chilling, cut each into 2 strips. Brush with egg white and stack a pink log on top of a chocolate one. Repeat and press the 4 pieces together into a rectangle. Wrap in clingfilm and chill. Cut into slices, then bake as before.

450 *Crunchy peanut biscuits*

125 g/4½ oz butter, softened, plus extra
    for greasing
150 g/5½ oz chunky peanut butter
225 g/8 oz granulated sugar
1 egg, lightly beaten

150 g/5½ oz plain flour
½ tsp baking powder
pinch of salt
75 g/2¾ oz unsalted natural peanuts,
    chopped

Lightly grease 2 large baking sheets. Place the butter and peanut butter in a large bowl and beat together. Gradually add the sugar and beat together well. Add the egg, a little at a time, until it is combined. Sift the flour, baking powder and salt into the peanut butter mixture. Add the peanuts and bring all of the ingredients together to form a soft dough. Wrap the dough in clingfilm and chill in the refrigerator for 30 minutes.

Preheat the oven to 190°C/375°F/Gas Mark 5. Form the dough into 20 balls and place them on the baking sheets, about 5 cm/2 inches apart. Flatten them slightly with your hand.

Bake in the preheated oven for 15 minutes, or until golden brown. Leave to cool on wire racks.

451 'I love you' vanilla hearts

225 g/8 oz plain flour, plus extra for dusting

150 g/5½ oz butter, cut into small pieces, plus extra for greasing

125 g/4½ oz caster sugar, plus extra for dusting

1 tsp vanilla extract

Preheat the oven to 180°C/350°F/Gas Mark 4. Grease a large baking sheet. Sift the flour into a large bowl, add the butter and rub it in with your fingertips until the mixture resembles fine breadcrumbs. Stir in the sugar and vanilla extract and mix together to form a firm dough.

Roll out the dough on a lightly floured work surface until it is 1 cm/½ inch thick. Cut out 12 hearts with a heart-shaped biscuit cutter measuring about 5 cm/2 inches across and arrange the hearts on the baking sheet.

Bake in the preheated oven for 15–20 minutes, or until just coloured. Transfer to a wire rack and leave to cool completely. Dust with a little caster sugar just before serving.

452 With vanilla topping

Beat 100 g/3½ oz unsalted butter with the seeds from a vanilla pod, sift in 150 g/5½ oz icing sugar and beat until smooth. Spread over the hearts.

453 Sugared hearts

225 g/8 oz butter, softened
280 g/10 oz caster sugar
1 egg yolk, lightly beaten
2 tsp vanilla extract
250 g/9 oz plain flour

25 g/1 oz cocoa powder
pinch of salt
3–4 food colouring pastes
100 g/3½ oz plain chocolate, broken into pieces

Place the butter and half the sugar in a large bowl and beat together until light and fluffy, then beat in the egg yolk and vanilla extract. Sift together the flour, cocoa and salt into the mixture and stir until combined. Halve the dough, shape into balls, wrap in clingfilm and chill for 30–60 minutes.

Preheat the oven to 190°C/375°F/Gas Mark 5. Line 2 large baking sheets with baking paper. Unwrap the dough and roll out between 2 sheets of baking paper. Cut out cookies with a heart-shaped cutter and place them on the baking sheets, spaced well apart. Bake in the preheated oven for 10–15 minutes, or until firm. Leave to cool on the baking sheets for 5–10 minutes, then transfer to wire racks to cool completely.

Meanwhile, divide the remaining sugar among 4 small plastic bags or bowls. Add a little food colouring paste to each and rub in until well mixed. Wear a plastic glove if mixing in bowls to prevent your hands from getting stained. Place the chocolate in a heatproof bowl, set the bowl over a saucepan of gently simmering water and heat until melted. Leave to cool slightly.

Leave the cookies on the racks. Spread the melted chocolate over them and sprinkle with the coloured sugar. Leave to set.

454 White sugar hearts

Replace the plain chocolate with white chocolate and sprinkle with desiccated coconut instead of the coloured sugar.

455 Traditional Easter cookies

225 g/8 oz butter, softened
140 g/5 oz caster sugar, plus extra for sprinkling
1 egg yolk, lightly beaten
280 g/10 oz plain flour
1 tsp mixed spice
pinch of salt
1 tbsp mixed peel
55 g/2 oz currants
1 egg white, lightly beaten

Place the butter and sugar in a large bowl and beat together until light and fluffy, then beat in the egg yolk. Sift together the flour, mixed spice and salt into the mixture, add the mixed peel and currants and stir until thoroughly combined. Halve the dough, shape into balls, wrap in clingfilm and chill in the refrigerator for 30–60 minutes.

Preheat the oven to 190°C/375°F/Gas Mark 5. Line 2 large baking sheets with baking paper.

Unwrap the dough and roll out between 2 sheets of baking paper. Cut out cookies with a 6-cm/2½-inch fluted round cutter and place them on the baking sheets, spaced well apart. Bake in the preheated oven for 7 minutes, then brush with the egg white and sprinkle with the sugar. Bake for a further 5–8 minutes, or until light golden brown. Leave to cool on the baking sheets for 5–10 minutes, then transfer to wire racks to cool completely.

456 Easter bunny cookies

225 g/8 oz butter, softened
140 g/5 oz caster sugar, plus extra for sprinkling
1 egg yolk, lightly beaten
2 tsp vanilla extract
250 g/9 oz plain flour
25 g/1 oz cocoa powder
pinch of salt
2 tbsp finely chopped stem ginger
1 egg white, lightly beaten
15 white mini marshmallows

ICING
140 g/5 oz icing sugar
few drops of pink food colouring

Place the butter and sugar in a large bowl and beat together until light and fluffy, then beat in the egg yolk and vanilla. Sift together the flour, cocoa and salt into the mixture, add the ginger and stir until combined. Halve the dough, shape into balls, wrap in clingfilm and chill for 30–60 minutes.

Preheat the oven to 190°C/ 375°F/Gas Mark 5. Line 2 large baking sheets with baking paper.

Unwrap the dough and roll out between 2 sheets of baking paper. Cut out 15 rounds with a 5-cm/ 2-inch plain cutter (bodies), 15 rounds with a 3-cm/1¼-inch plain cutter (heads), 30 rounds with a 2-cm/¾-inch plain cutter (ears) and 15 rounds with a 1-cm/½-inch plain cutter (tails). Make up the bunnies on the baking sheets, spaced well apart.

Bake in the preheated oven for 7 minutes, then brush the bunnies with egg white and sprinkle with caster sugar. Bake for a further 5–8 minutes, then remove from the oven and put a mini marshmallow in the centre of each tail. Return to the oven for 1 minute. Leave to cool for 5–10 minutes, then transfer to wire racks to cool completely.

Sift the icing sugar into a bowl and stir in enough water until it is the consistency of thick cream. Add a few drops of food colouring. Pipe a collar where the heads and bodies join and add initials if desired. Leave to set.

457 Easter egg cookies

Use half the dough to make Easter bunnies and use the remaining dough to cut out Easter egg shapes. Use coloured writing icing, dragées and mini marshmallows to decorate.

458 Easter nest cookies

225 g/8 oz butter, softened, plus extra
for greasing
140 g/5 oz caster sugar
1 egg yolk, lightly beaten
2 tsp lemon juice
280 g/10 oz plain flour
pinch of salt
1 tbsp chopped mixed peel
55 g/2 oz glacé cherries, finely
chopped

TO DECORATE
200 g/7 oz icing sugar
few drops of yellow food colouring
mini sugar-coated Easter eggs
yellow sugar sprinkles

Place the butter and sugar in a large bowl and beat together until light and fluffy, then beat in the egg yolk and lemon juice. Sift together the flour and salt into the mixture, add the mixed peel and glacé cherries and stir until combined. Halve the dough, shape into balls, wrap in clingfilm and chill for 30–60 minutes.

Preheat the oven to 190°C/375°F/Gas Mark 5. Generously grease several bun tins with butter.

Unwrap the dough and roll out between 2 sheets of baking paper. Cut out cookies with a 7–8-cm/2¾–3¼-inch sun-shaped cutter and place them in the prepared tins.

Bake in the preheated oven for 10–15 minutes, or until light golden brown. Leave to cool in the tins.

Sift the icing sugar into a bowl, add the food colouring and stir in just enough water to until it is the consistency of thick cream. Place the cookies on wire racks and gently spread the icing on them. When it is just beginning to set, gently press 3–4 eggs into it and sprinkle the sugar sprinkles around them. Leave to set.

459 Chocolate nests

Add 2 teaspoons of cocoa powder to the dough to make chocolate nests and replace the sugar-coated eggs with a mixture of chocolate-covered peanuts and yogurt-coated raisins.

---

460 Halloween spider's web cookies

225 g/8 oz butter, softened
140 g/5 oz caster sugar
1 egg yolk, lightly beaten
1 tsp peppermint extract
250 g/9 oz plain flour
25 g/1 oz cocoa powder
pinch of salt

ICING
175 g/6 oz icing sugar
few drops of vanilla extract
1–1½ tbsp hot water
few drops of black food colouring

between 2 sheets of baking paper. Cut out cookies with a 6-cm/2½-inch plain round cutter and place them on the baking sheets, spaced well apart. Bake in a preheated oven for 10–15 minutes, or until light golden brown. Leave to cool for 5–10 minutes, then transfer to wire racks to cool completely.

Sift the icing sugar into a bowl, add the vanilla and stir in the hot water until it is smooth and has the consistency of thick cream. Leave the cookies on the racks and spread the white icing over them, reserving 2 tablespoons. Add a few drops of black food colouring to the remaining icing and spoon it into a piping bag fitted with a fine nozzle. Starting from the middle of the cookie, pipe a series of concentric circles. Carefully draw a cocktail stick through the icing from the middle to the outside edge to divide the cookie first into quarters and then into eighths. Leave to set.

Place the butter and sugar in a large bowl, and beat together until light and fluffy, then beat in the egg yolk and peppermint extract. Sift together the flour, cocoa powder and salt into the mixture and stir until thoroughly combined. Halve the dough, shape into balls, wrap in clingfilm and chill for 30–60 minutes.

Preheat the oven to 190°C/375°F/Gas Mark 5. Line 2 large baking sheets with baking paper. Unwrap the dough and roll out

461 Halloween spook cookies

Use half the dough to make spiderwebs and cut the remaining dough out with novelty cookie cutters to make bat, pumpkin and cauldron shapes. Decorate with orange, green and black writing icing.

462 *Christmas angels*

225 g/8 oz butter, softened
140 g/5 oz caster sugar
1 egg yolk, lightly beaten
2 tsp passion fruit pulp
280 g/10 oz plain flour
pinch of salt
55 g/2 oz desiccated coconut

TO DECORATE
175 g/6 oz icing sugar
1–1½ tbsp passion fruit pulp
edible silver glitter

Place the butter and sugar in a large bowl and beat together until light and fluffy then beat in the egg yolk and passion fruit pulp. Sift together the flour and salt into the mixture, add the coconut and stir until thoroughly combined. Halve the dough, shape into balls, wrap in clingfilm and chill for 30–60 minutes.

Preheat the oven to 190°C/375°F/Gas Mark 5. Line 2 baking sheets with baking paper.

Unwrap the dough and roll out between 2 sheets of baking paper. Cut out cookies with a 7-cm/2¾-inch angel-shaped cutter and place them on the baking sheets, spaced well apart.

Bake in the preheated oven for 10–15 minutes, or until light golden brown. Leave to cool for 5–10 minutes, then transfer to wire racks to cool completely.

Sift the icing sugar into a bowl and stir in the passion fruit pulp until it is the consistency of thick cream. Leave the cookies on the racks and spread the icing over them. Sprinkle with the edible glitter and leave to set.

463 *Angel ornaments*

Before baking, make a hole with a metal skewer or straw in the top of each cookie. Check the holes are big enough when the cookies come out of the oven and re-pierce if necessary. Cool and decorate as before. Using thin white ribbon, string chains of the angels together to hang on the Christmas tree.

464 *Christmas bells*

225 g/8 oz butter, softened
140 g/5 oz caster sugar
finely grated rind of 1 lemon
1 egg yolk, lightly beaten
280 g/10 oz plain flour
½ tsp ground cinnamon
pinch of salt
100 g/3½ oz plain chocolate chips

TO DECORATE
2 tbsp lightly beaten egg white
2 tbsp lemon juice
225 g/8 oz icing sugar
30 silver dragées
food colouring pens

Place the butter, sugar and lemon rind in a large bowl and beat together until light and fluffy, then beat in the egg yolk. Sift together the flour, cinnamon and salt into the mixture, add the chocolate chips and stir until thoroughly combined. Halve the dough, shape into balls, wrap in clingfilm and chill in the refrigerator for 30–60 minutes.

Preheat the oven to 190°C/375°F/Gas Mark 5. Line 2 large baking sheets with baking paper. Unwrap the dough and roll out between 2 sheets of baking paper. Cut out cookies with a 5-cm/2-inch bell-shaped cutter and place them on the baking sheets, spaced well apart.

Bake in a preheated oven for 10–15 minutes, or until light golden brown. Leave the cookies to cool for 5–10 minutes, then transfer to wire racks to cool completely.

Mix the egg white and lemon juice together in a bowl, then gradually beat in the icing sugar until smooth. Leave the cookies on the racks and spread the icing over them. Place a silver dragée on the clapper shape at the bottom of the cookie and leave to set completely. When the icing is dry, use the food colouring pens to draw patterns on the cookies.

465 *Coloured bells*

Divide the icing into 3 portions. Leave one white, colour one portion with red food colouring and the third with green and use to decorate the bells. Leave to set, then tie 3 cookies together in a stack, one of each colour, using ribbon.

225 g/8 oz butter, softened
140 g/5 oz caster sugar
1 egg yolk, lightly beaten
2 tsp vanilla extract
280 g/10 oz plain flour
pinch of salt

1 egg white, lightly beaten
2 tbsp hundreds and thousands
400 g/14 oz fruit-flavoured boiled sweets
in different colours
25 lengths of ribbon, to hang

Place the butter and sugar into a bowl and beat together until light and fluffy, then beat in the egg yolk and vanilla extract. Sift together the flour and salt into the mixture and stir until combined. Halve the dough, shape into balls, wrap in clingfilm and chill for 30–60 minutes.

Preheat the oven to 190°C/375°F/Gas Mark 5. Line 2 large baking sheets with baking paper. Unwrap the dough and roll out between 2 sheets of baking paper. Cut out cookies with Christmas-themed cutters and place them on the baking sheets, spaced well apart.

Using the end of a large plain piping nozzle, cut out rounds from each shape and remove them. Make a small hole in the top of each cookie with a skewer so that they can be threaded with ribbon. Brush with egg white and sprinkle with hundreds and thousands. Bake in the preheated oven for 7 minutes. Meanwhile, lightly crush the sweets by tapping them with a rolling pin. Unwrap and sort into separate bowls by colour. Remove the cookies from the oven and fill the holes with the crushed sweets. Return to the oven and bake for a further 5–8 minutes, or until they are light golden brown and the sweets have melted and filled the holes. Leave to cool on the baking sheets and then transfer to wire racks. Thread thin ribbon through the holes in the top and hang.

75 g/6 oz plain flour, plus extra
for dusting
1 tsp ground cinnamon
1 tsp ground ginger
90 g/3¼ oz butter, cut into cubes
85 g/3 oz soft light brown sugar
finely grated rind of 1 orange
1 egg, lightly beaten

TO DECORATE
200 g/7 oz icing sugar
3–4 tsp cold water
edible silver cake sparkles
silver dragées

Preheat the oven to 180°C/350°F/Gas Mark 4. Line several large baking sheets with baking paper.

Sift the flour, cinnamon and ginger into a large bowl. Add the butter and rub it in with your fingertips until the mixture resembles fine breadcrumbs. Stir the sugar and orange rind into the mixture, add the egg and mix together to form a soft dough.

Roll the mixture out thinly to about 5 mm/¼ inch thick on a lightly floured work surface. Cut out shapes with a 6.5-cm/2½-inch snowflake- or star-shaped cutters and place on the baking sheets.

Bake in the preheated oven for 10–15 minutes, or until golden brown. Leave to cool on the baking sheets for 2–3 minutes, then transfer the cookies to a wire rack and leave to cool completely.

To make the icing, sift the icing sugar into a large bowl and add enough cold water to make a smooth, thick icing. Spread a little on each cookie and then sprinkle with sparkles and dragées.

468 *Easter animal cookies*

Use a rabbit-shaped cutter instead of a snowflake and add a raisin for the eyes. Alternatively, use a chick-shaped cutter and add a few drops of yellow food colouring to the icing.

Double heart cookies

1 sachet instant latte
1½ tsp hot water
225 g/8 oz butter, softened
140 g/5 oz caster sugar
1 egg yolk, lightly beaten

250 g/9 oz plain flour
1 tsp vanilla extract
3 tbsp cocoa powder
pinch of salt

Place the instant latte into a small bowl and stir in the hot, but not boiling, water to make a paste.

Place the butter and sugar in a large bowl and beat together until light and fluffy, then beat in the egg yolk. Divide the mixture in half. Beat the latte paste into one half. Sift 140 g/5 oz of the flour with the salt into the mixture and stir until combined. Shape the dough into a ball, wrap in clingfilm and chill in the refrigerator for 30–60 minutes. Beat the vanilla extract into the other bowl, then sift together the remaining flour, the cocoa powder and salt into the mixture. Stir until thoroughly combined. Shape the dough into a ball, wrap in clingfilm and chill for 30–60 minutes.

Preheat the oven to 190°C/ 375°F/Gas Mark 5. Line 2 large baking sheets with baking paper.

Unwrap both flavours of dough and roll out each between 2 sheets of baking paper. Cut out cookies with a 7-cm/2¾-inch heart-shaped cutter and place them on the baking sheets, spaced well apart. Using a 4–5-cm/ 1½–2-inch heart-shaped cutter, cut out the centres of each larger heart and remove from the baking sheets. Place a small chocolate-flavoured heart in the centre of each large coffee-flavoured heart and vice versa.

Bake in the preheated oven for 10–15 minutes. Leave to cool for 5–10 minutes, then transfer to wire racks to cool completely.

470 Pink hearts

Divide the dough into 3 portions and add pink food colouring to one portion, then make the cookies as before, contrasting the 3 different coloured doughs.

Chocolate-dipped Viennese fingers

100 g/3½ oz butter, plus extra for greasing
25 g/1 oz golden caster sugar

½ tsp vanilla extract
100 g/3½ oz self-raising flour
100 g/3½ oz plain chocolate

Preheat the oven to 160°C/325°F/Gas Mark 3. Grease 2 large baking sheets. Place the butter, sugar and vanilla extract in a large bowl and beat together until light and fluffy. Stir in the flour, mixing evenly to make a fairly stiff dough.

Place the mixture in a piping bag fitted with a large star nozzle and pipe about 16 fingers, each 6 cm/2½ inches long, onto the baking sheets. Bake in the preheated oven for 10–15 minutes, or until pale golden. Leave to cool on the baking sheets for 2–3 minutes, then transfer to a wire rack to cool completely.

Place the chocolate in a small heatproof bowl, set over a saucepan of gently simmering water and heat until melted. Remove from the heat. Dip the ends of each biscuit into the chocolate to coat, then place on a sheet of baking paper and leave to set.

472 Viennese pinks

Omit the chocolate and dip each end of the fingers into pink icing made by beating 115 g/4 oz sifted icing sugar with 1 tablespoon of water and a drop of pink food colouring. Before the icing is dry, dip the tips into pink sparkles, then leave to set.

473 Alphabet cookies

225 g/8 oz butter, softened
140 g/5 oz caster sugar
1 egg yolk, lightly beaten
2 tsp grenadine
280 g/10 oz plain flour

pinch of salt
5–6 tbsp unsalted dried pomegranate
    seeds or roasted melon seeds

Place the butter and sugar in a large bowl and beat together until light and fluffy, then beat in the egg yolk and grenadine. Sift together the flour and salt into the mixture and stir until combined. Halve the dough, shape into balls, wrap in clingfilm and chill for 30–60 minutes.

Preheat the oven to 190°C/375°F/Gas Mark 5. Line 2 large baking sheets with baking paper.

Unwrap the dough and roll out between 2 sheets of baking paper to about 3 mm/⅛ inch thick. Sprinkle half the seeds over each piece of dough and lightly roll the rolling pin over them. Cut out letters with alphabet cutters and place them on the baking sheets, spaced well apart.

Bake in the preheated oven for 10–12 minutes, or until golden brown. Leave to cool on the baking sheets for 5–10 minutes, then transfer the cookies to wire racks to cool completely.

474 Tutti frutti cookies

Replace the seeds with 25 g/1 oz each of chopped candied fruit, glacé cherries and angelica and add to the cookie dough.

475 Iced stars

225 g/8 oz butter, softened
140 g/5 oz caster sugar
1 egg yolk, lightly beaten
½ tsp vanilla extract
280 g/10 oz plain flour
pinch of salt

TO DECORATE
200 g/7 oz icing sugar
1–2 tbsp warm water
food colourings
silver and gold dragées
hundreds and thousands
desiccated coconut
sugar sprinkles
sugar stars, hearts and flowers

Place the butter and sugar in a large bowl and beat together until light and fluffy, then beat in the egg yolk and vanilla extract. Sift together the flour and salt into the mixture and stir until thoroughly combined. Halve the dough, shape into balls, wrap in clingfilm and chill for 30–60 minutes.

Preheat the oven to 190°C/ 375°F/Gas Mark 5. Line 2 large baking sheets with baking paper.

Unwrap the dough and roll out between 2 sheets of baking paper to about 3 mm/⅛ inch thick. Cut out cookies with a star-shaped cutter and place them on the baking sheets, spaced well apart. Bake in the preheated oven for 10–15 minutes, or until light golden brown. Leave to cool on the baking sheets for 5–10 minutes, then transfer to wire racks to cool completely.

To decorate, sift the icing sugar into a bowl and stir in enough warm water until it is the consistency of thick cream. Divide the icing among 3–4 bowls and add a few drops of your chosen food colourings to each. Leave the cookies on the racks and spread the different coloured icings over them to the edges. Arrange silver and gold dragées on top and/or sprinkle with hundreds and thousands and sugar shapes. If you like, colour desiccated coconut with food colouring in a contrasting colour. Leave the cookies to set.

476 Marzipan stars

Omit the icing and thinly roll 150 g/5½ oz white marzipan out on a work surface dusted with icing sugar. Cut out 30 stars with the star-shaped cutter and use a little beaten egg white to secure the marzipan to the cookies, then use a kitchen blow torch to toast the edges of the marzipan.

477 Name cookies

225 g/8 oz butter, softened
140 g/5 oz caster sugar
1 egg yolk, lightly beaten
2 tsp orange juice or orange liqueur
finely grated rind of 1 orange
280 g/10 oz plain flour
pinch of salt

TO DECORATE
1 egg white
225 g/8 oz icing sugar
few drops each of 2 food colourings
green balls or crystallized flowers

Place the butter and sugar in a large bowl and beat together until light and fluffy, then beat in the egg yolk, orange juice and grated rind. Sift together the flour and salt into the mixture and stir until combined. Halve the dough, shape into balls, wrap in clingfilm and chill in the refrigerator for 30–60 minutes.

Preheat the oven to 190°C/375°F/Gas Mark 5. Line 2 large baking sheets with baking paper. Unwrap the dough and roll out to 3 mm/ ⅛ inch thick. Depending on the occasion and age group, cut out appropriate shapes with cookie cutters and place them on the baking sheets, spaced well apart. Bake in the preheated oven for 10–15 minutes, or until light golden brown.

Leave to cool on the baking sheets for 5–10 minutes, then transfer the cookies to wire racks to cool completely.

Leave the cookies on the racks. Put the egg white and icing sugar into a bowl and beat until smooth, adding a little water if necessary. Transfer half the icing to another bowl and colour each bowl with a different colour. Put both icings in piping bags with fine nozzles and use to decorate the cookies and write initials. Finish with green balls or flowers and leave to set.

478 Number crunchers

225 g/8 oz butter, softened
140 g/5 oz caster sugar
1 egg yolk, lightly beaten
2 tsp vanilla extract
280 g/10 oz plain flour

1 tsp ground ginger
¼ tsp ground cinnamon
¼ tsp ground cloves
pinch of salt
4–5 tbsp chopped macadamia nuts

Place the butter and sugar in a large bowl and beat together until light and fluffy, then beat in the egg yolk and vanilla extract. Sift together the flour, ginger, cinnamon, cloves and salt into the mixture and stir until thoroughly combined. Halve the dough, shape into balls, wrap in clingfilm and chill in the refrigerator for 30–60 minutes.

Preheat the oven to 190°C/375°F/Gas Mark 5. Line 2 large baking sheets with baking paper. Unwrap the dough and roll out between 2 sheets of baking paper to 3 mm/⅛ inch thick. Sprinkle half the nuts over each piece of dough and roll the rolling pin over them. Cut out numbers with number-shaped cutters and place them on the baking sheets, spaced well apart. Bake in the preheated oven for 10–12 minutes, or until golden brown. Leave to cool for 5–10 minutes, then transfer to wire racks to cool completely.

479 Peanut number crunchers

Omit the spices and macadamia nuts. Chop 115 g/4 oz salted peanuts and sprinkle over the rolled dough.

480 S'mores

24 waffle biscuits
24 squares milk or plain chocolate
12 marshmallows

Prepare a barbecue or preheat the oven to 180°C/350°F/Gas Mark 4. If baking in the oven, line a baking sheet with baking paper.

Place 12 waffle biscuits on the baking sheet, then place 2 squares of chocolate on each, and top with a marshmallow. Bake in the preheated oven for 4–6 minutes, or until the chocolate is melting and the marshmallow soft and spreading. Remove from the oven and top each with a second waffle biscuit, then serve immediately.

Alternatively, carefully place the loaded biscuits onto the barbecue. When the chocolate and marshmallow are starting to melt, lift off and top with the second biscuit. Press down and serve immediately.

481 S'mores with banana

8 marshmallows
8 chocolate cookies
1 banana, thinly sliced
4 squares plain chocolate

Place 2 marshmallows at a time onto the end of a skewer and toast over a hot barbecue for a few minutes until they start to soften.

Place the marshmallows onto one of the cookies, top with a few slices of banana, then a square of chocolate then sandwich together with the remaining cookies.

Squeeze together well and repeat with the remaining cookies and marshmallows.

2 sachets instant malted food drink
1 tbsp hot water
225 g/8 oz butter, softened
140 g/5 oz caster sugar
1 egg yolk, lightly beaten
280 g/10 oz plain flour

pinch of salt
egg yolk and food colouring, to decorate

Place the malted drink in a bowl and stir in the hot, but not boiling water to make a paste.

Place the butter and sugar in a large bowl and beat together until light and fluffy, then beat in the egg yolk and malted drink paste. Sift together the flour and salt into the mixture and stir until thoroughly combined. Halve the dough, shape into balls, wrap in clingfilm and chill in the refrigerator for 30–60 minutes.

Preheat the oven to 190°C/375°F/Gas Mark 5. Line 2 large baking sheets with baking paper. Unwrap the dough and roll out between 2 sheets of baking paper. Cut out cookies with a butterfly-shaped cutter and place them on the baking sheets.

Whisk an egg yolk and put a little of it in an egg cup. Add a few drops of food colouring and mix well. Using a fine paintbrush, paint a pattern on the butterflies' wings. Mix other colours with the beaten egg yolk in egg cups and add to the pattern.

Bake in the preheated oven for 10–15 minutes, or until firm. Leave to cool on the baking sheets for 5–10 minutes, then transfer the cookies to wire racks to cool completely.

225 g/8 oz butter, softened
140 g/5 oz caster sugar
1 egg yolk, lightly beaten
2 tsp vanilla extract
280 g/10 oz plain flour, plus extra for dusting
pinch of salt
100 g/3½ oz desiccated coconut

TO DECORATE
1½ tbsp lightly beaten egg white
1½ tbsp lemon juice
175 g/6 oz icing sugar
red, yellow and green glacé cherries
red and green gummy bears or jelly babies

Place the butter and sugar in a large bowl and beat together until light and fluffy, then beat in the egg yolk and vanilla extract. Sift together the flour and salt into the mixture, add the coconut and stir until thoroughly combined. Halve the dough, roll each piece into a ball, wrap in clingfilm and chill for 30–60 minutes.

Preheat the oven to 190°C/375°F/Gas Mark 5. Line 2 large baking sheets with baking paper.

Roll out each piece of dough between 2 sheets of baking paper to a rectangle about 5 mm/¼ inch thick. Using a sharp knife, cut the dough into bars about 10 x 2-cm/4 x ¾-inches in size and place them on the baking sheets, spaced well apart. Bake in the preheated oven for 10–12 minutes, or until golden brown. Leave to cool on the baking sheets for 5–10 minutes, then transfer the cookies to wire racks to cool completely.

To make the icing, mix the egg white and lemon juice together in a bowl, then gradually beat in the icing sugar until smooth. Leave the cookies on the racks and spoon the icing over them. Decorate some with a vertical row of red, yellow and green glacé cherries for traffic lights. For pedestrian lights, put a red jelly baby or gummy bear at the top of a cookie and a green one at the bottom. Leave to set.

484 *With jelly bean topping*

Instead of the icing, place 150g/5½ oz plain chocolate in a heatproof bowl, set the bowl over a saucepan of gently simmering water and heat until melted. Spread the chocolate over the bars and press 3 jelly beans onto each.

485 Stained glass window cookies

MAKES ABOUT 25

350 g/12 oz plain flour, plus extra
for dusting
pinch of salt
1 tsp bicarbonate of soda
100 g/3½ oz unsalted butter
175 g/6 oz caster sugar

1 large egg
1 tsp vanilla extract
4 tbsp golden syrup
50 mixed coloured boiled fruit sweets
(about 250 g/9 oz), chopped
25 lengths of ribbon, to hang

Sift the flour, salt and bicarbonate of soda into a large bowl, add the butter and rub it in until the mixture resembles breadcrumbs. Stir in the sugar. Place the egg, vanilla extract and golden syrup in a separate bowl and whisk together. Pour the egg into the flour mixture and mix to form a smooth dough. Wrap in clingfilm and chill in the refrigerator for 30 minutes.

Preheat the oven to 180°C/350°F/Gas Mark 4. Line 2 large baking sheets with baking paper. Roll the dough out on a floured work surface to 5 mm/¼ inch thick. Use a variety of floured cookie cutter shapes to cut out the biscuits.

Transfer them to the baking sheets and cut out shapes from the centre of the biscuits. Fill the holes with the sweets. Using a skewer, make a hole at the top of each biscuit.

Bake in the preheated oven for 10–12 minutes, or until the sweets are melted. Make sure the holes are still there, and re-pierce if necessary. Leave to cool on the baking sheets until the centres have hardened. When cold, thread thin ribbon through the holes to hang up the biscuits.

486 Mint window cookies

Cut all the cookies out with a round cookie cutter and use chopped, clear mint boiled sweets to fill the cavities. Hang using lengths of white ribbon.

487 Chocolate dominoes

MAKES ABOUT 28

225 g/8 oz butter, softened
140 g/5 oz caster sugar
1 egg yolk, lightly beaten
2 tsp vanilla extract
250 g/9 oz plain flour
25 g/1 oz cocoa powder
pinch of salt
25 g/1 oz desiccated coconut
50 g/1¾ oz white chocolate chips

Place the butter and sugar in a large bowl and beat together until light and fluffy, then beat in the egg yolk and vanilla extract. Sift together the flour, cocoa and salt into the mixture, add the coconut and stir until combined. Halve the dough, shape into balls, wrap in clingfilm and chill in the refrigerator for 30–60 minutes.

Preheat the oven to 190°C/375°F/Gas Mark 5. Line 2 large baking sheets with baking paper.

Unwrap the dough and roll out between 2 sheets of baking paper. Cut out biscuits with a 9-cm/3½-inch plain square cutter, then cut them in half to make rectangles. Place them on the baking sheets and, using a knife, make a line across the centre of each without cutting through. Arrange the chocolate chips on top of the biscuits to look like dominoes, pressing them in gently.

Bake in the preheated oven for 10–15 minutes, or until golden brown. Leave to cool for 5–10 minutes, then transfer to wire racks to cool completely.

488 With black icing

Sift 115 g/4 oz icing sugar into a bowl and beat in 1 tablespoon of water until smooth. Add a few drops of black food colouring and mix until black. Use to ice the cookies, leave to set, then add the white dots with white writing icing.

145

Nut lovers' cookie brittle

½ tsp groundnut oil, for greasing
225 g/8 oz unsalted butter, softened
200 g/7 oz granulated sugar
1 tsp vanilla extract
280 g/10 oz plain flour

pinch of salt
175 g/6 oz milk chocolate chips
150 g/5½ oz pecan nuts, chopped
150 g/5½ oz almonds, toasted
   and chopped

Preheat the oven to 190°C/375°F/Gas Mark 5. Grease a 38 x 25-cm/15 x 10-inch Swiss roll tin with the oil. Place the butter and sugar in a large bowl and beat together until light and fluffy, then stir in the vanilla extract. Sift together the flour and salt into the mixture and beat until combined. Mix in 90 g/3¼ oz of the chocolate chips and the nuts and press the mixture into the tin, making sure the dough fills the tin and is evenly spread. Bake in the preheated oven for 20–25 minutes, or until golden. Leave to cool in the tin.

Place the remaining chocolate chips in a heatproof bowl, set the bowl over a saucepan of gently simmering water and heat until melted. Drizzle the chocolate over the cookie brittle and leave to set, then break the brittle into irregular pieces.

490 *Lemon almond brittle*

Omit the chocolate and nuts, and add the finely grated rind of 2 lemons to the mixture before pressing into the tin. Top with 150 g/5½ oz flaked almonds and bake as before. Cool and break into pieces.

491 *Dark & white chocolate cookies*

200 g/7 oz butter, softened, plus extra
   for greasing
200 g/7 oz caster sugar
½ tsp vanilla extract
1 large egg

225 g/8 oz plain flour
pinch of salt
1 tsp bicarbonate of soda
115 g/4 oz white chocolate chips
115 g/4 oz plain chocolate chips

Preheat the oven to 180°C/350°F/Gas Mark 4. Grease 2 large baking sheets. Place the butter, sugar and vanilla extract in a large bowl and beat together. Gradually beat in the egg until the mixture is light and fluffy. Sift the flour, salt and bicarbonate of soda over the mixture and fold in. Fold in the chocolate chips.

Drop heaped teaspoonfuls of the mixture onto the baking sheets, spaced well apart. Bake in the preheated oven for 10–12 minutes, or until crisp outside but still soft inside.

Leave to cool on the baking sheets for 2 minutes, then transfer the cookies to wire racks to cool completely.

492 *Dark chocolate & hazelnut cookies*

Replace the white chocolate chips with chopped toasted hazelnuts.

493 Ice cream cookie sandwiches

225 g/8 oz butter, softened
140 g/5 oz caster sugar
1 egg yolk, lightly beaten
2 tbsp finely chopped stem ginger, plus
   2 tsp syrup from the jar
250 g/9 oz plain flour
25 g/1 oz cocoa powder
½ tsp ground cinnamon
pinch of salt
450 ml/15 fl oz vanilla, chocolate
   or coffee ice cream

Place the butter and sugar in a large bowl and beat together until light and fluffy, then beat in the egg yolk, ginger and ginger syrup. Sift together the flour, cocoa powder, cinnamon and salt into the mixture and stir until combined. Halve the dough, shape into balls, wrap in clingfilm and chill for 30–60 minutes.

Preheat the oven to 190°C/375°F/Gas Mark 5. Line 2 large baking sheets with baking paper. Unwrap the dough and roll out between 2 sheets of baking paper. Cut out cookies with a 6-cm/2½-inch fluted round cutter and place them on the baking sheets, spaced well apart.

Bake in the preheated oven for 10–15 minutes, or until light golden brown. Leave to cool for 5–10 minutes, then transfer to wire racks to cool completely.

Remove the ice cream from the freezer about 15 minutes before serving, to allow it to soften. Put a generous scoop of ice cream on half the cookies and top with the remaining cookies. Press together gently so that the filling spreads to the edges. If not serving immediately, wrap the cookies individually in foil and store in the freezer.

494 Chocolate mint sandwiches

Replace the stem ginger in the cookie dough with 1 teaspoon of peppermint extract, then fill the cookies with chocolate chip ice cream.

495 Coffee cream & walnut cookies

225 g/8 oz butter, softened
140 g/5 oz caster sugar
1 egg yolk, lightly beaten
2 tsp vanilla extract
225 g/8 oz plain flour
pinch of salt
55 g/2 oz ground walnuts
55 g/2 oz walnuts, finely chopped
icing sugar, for dusting (optional)

COFFEE CREAM
85 g/3 oz butter, softened
140 g/5 oz icing sugar
1½ tsp strong black coffee

Preheat the oven to 190°C/375°F/Gas Mark 5. Line 2 baking sheets with baking paper. Unwrap the dough and roll out between 2 sheets of baking paper. Cut out cookies with a 6-cm/2½-inch fluted round cutter and place them on the baking sheets, spaced well apart.

Bake in the preheated oven for 10–15 minutes, or until light golden brown. Leave to cool on the baking sheets for 5–10 minutes, then transfer the cookies to wire racks to cool completely.

To make the coffee cream, place the butter and icing sugar in a bowl and beat together until smooth and thoroughly combined, then beat in the coffee.

Sandwich the cookies together in pairs with the coffee cream, then press together gently so that the cream oozes out of the sides. Smooth the sides with a dampened finger. Spread out the chopped walnuts in a shallow dish and roll the cookies in them to coat the sides of the coffee cream filling. Dust the tops with sifted icing sugar, if liked.

Place the butter and sugar in a large bowl and beat together until light and fluffy, then beat in the egg yolk and vanilla extract. Sift together the flour and salt into the mixture, add the ground walnuts and stir until combined. Halve the dough, shape into balls, wrap in clingfilm and chill in the refrigerator for 30–60 minutes.

496 Chocolate cream & walnut cookies

Replace the coffee with 1 teaspoon of cocoa powder.

497 The gooiest chocolate cookies

- 115 g/4 oz unsalted butter, softened
- 250 g/9 oz light soft brown sugar
- 1 large egg, lightly beaten
- 2 tsp vanilla extract
- 275 g/9½ oz plain flour
- 15 g/½ oz cocoa powder
- 1 tsp bicarbonate of soda
- 1 tsp salt
- 200 g/7 oz plain chocolate, chopped
- 150 g/5½ oz milk chocolate, chopped

Preheat the oven to 180°C/350°F/Gas Mark 4. Line 2 large baking sheets with non-stick baking paper. Place the butter and sugar in a large bowl and beat together until light and fluffy. Place the egg and vanilla extract in a separate bowl and whisk together, then gradually add to the butter mixture and beat until smooth. Mix in the flour, cocoa powder, bicarbonate of soda and salt until well combined. Add 100 g/3½ oz each of the plain and milk chocolates, then mix well.

Spoon 6 heaped tablespoons of the mixture onto each baking sheet, spacing them well apart. Divide the remaining chocolate among the cookies and press in lightly.

Bake in the preheated oven for 15–17 minutes. Leave to cool on the baking sheets for 5 minutes, then transfer to a wire rack to cool.

498 With extra chocolate

Place 150 g/5½ oz milk chocolate in a heatproof bowl, set the bowl over a saucepan of gently simmering water and heat until melted. Leave to cool for a few minutes then spread over the cold cookies and leave to set.

499 Peanut butter cookies

Makes About 26

- 115 g/4 oz butter, softened, plus extra for greasing
- 115 g/4 oz crunchy peanut butter
- 115 g/4 oz golden caster sugar
- 115 g/4 oz light muscovado sugar
- 1 egg, lightly beaten
- ½ tsp vanilla extract
- 85 g/3 oz plain flour
- ½ tsp bicarbonate of soda
- ½ tsp baking powder
- pinch of salt
- 115 g/4 oz rolled oats

Preheat the oven to 180°C/350°F/Gas Mark 4. Grease 3 large baking sheets. Place the butter and peanut butter in a bowl and beat together, then beat in the sugars. Gradually beat in the egg and vanilla extract. Sift the flour, bicarbonate of soda, baking powder and salt into the mixture, add the oats and stir until just combined.

Place spoonfuls of the mixture on the baking sheets, spaced well apart, and flatten slightly with a fork. Bake in the preheated oven for 12 minutes, or until lightly browned. Leave to cool on the baking sheets for 2 minutes, then transfer to wire racks to cool completely.

500 With banana filling

Spread a cookie with smooth peanut butter and top with thin slices of banana tossed in lemon juice, then top with a second cookie and sandwich together. Makes about 13.

148

501 Carrot cake cookies

115 g/4 oz butter, softened
85 g/3 oz caster sugar
75 g/2¾ oz soft light brown sugar
1 large egg
½ tsp vanilla extract
150 g/5½ oz plain flour

½ tsp bicarbonate of soda
½ tsp ground cinnamon
25 g/1 oz desiccated coconut
85 g/3 oz carrots, finely grated
25 g/1 oz walnut halves, chopped

Preheat the oven to 190°C/375°F/Gas Mark 5. Line several large baking sheets with baking paper.

Place the butter and sugars in a large bowl and whisk together until pale and creamy. Whisk the egg and vanilla extract into the mixture until smooth. Sift in the flour, bicarbonate of soda and cinnamon, then beat together until well mixed. Add the grated carrot, chopped walnuts and coconut to the mixture and mix well together.

Drop heaped teaspoonfuls of the mixture onto the baking sheets, spaced well apart. Bake in the preheated oven for 8–10 minutes, or until lightly golden brown around the edges.

Leave to cool on the baking sheets for 2–3 minutes, then transfer to a wire rack to cool completely.

502 Frosted carrot cake cookies

When the cookies are cold, top with a cream cheese frosting. Put 40 g/ 1½ oz soft cream cheese, 25 g/1 oz butter and ½ teaspoon of vanilla extract in a large bowl and beat together until smooth. Sift in 200 g/7 oz icing sugar and beat together until combined, then spread on top of the cookies.

503 Banana & chocolate cookies

125 g/4½ oz butter
125 g/4½ oz caster sugar
1 large egg, lightly beaten
1 ripe banana, mashed
175 g/6 oz self-raising flour

1 tsp mixed spice
2 tbsp milk
100 g/3½ oz chocolate, cut into chunks
55 g/2 oz raisins

Preheat the oven to 190°C/375°F/Gas Mark 5. Line 2 large baking sheets with baking paper. Place the butter and sugar in a large bowl and beat together until light and fluffy. Gradually add the egg, beating well after each addition. Mash the banana and add it to the mixture, beating well until smooth.

Sift together the flour and mixed spice into the mixture and fold in with a spatula. Add the milk to give a soft consistency, then fold in the chocolate and raisins. Drop dessertspoons of the mixture onto the baking sheets, spaced well apart. Bake in the centre of the preheated oven for 15–20 minutes, or until lightly golden. Leave to cool slightly, then transfer to a wire rack to cool completely.

504 Chocolate sprinkle cookies

225 g/8 oz butter, softened
140 g/5 oz caster sugar
1 egg yolk, lightly beaten
2 tsp vanilla extract
225 g/8 oz plain flour, plus extra
for dusting

55 g/2 oz cocoa powder
pinch of salt
200 g/7 oz white chocolate, broken
into pieces
85 g/3 oz chocolate vermicelli

Place the butter and sugar in a large bowl and mix well with a wooden spoon, then beat in the egg yolk and vanilla extract.

Sift together the flour, cocoa and salt into the mixture and stir until thoroughly combined. Halve the dough, roll each piece into a ball, wrap in clingfilm and chill in the refrigerator for 30–60 minutes.

Preheat the oven to 190°C/ 375°F/Gas Mark 5. Line 2 large baking sheets with baking paper.

Unwrap the dough and roll out between 2 pieces of baking paper to about 5 mm/¼ inch thick. Cut out 30 cookies with a 6–7-cm/2½–2¾-inch fluted round cutter and place them on the baking sheets, spaced well apart. Bake in the preheated oven for 10–12 minutes. Leave to cool on the baking sheets for 5–10 minutes, then transfer the cookies to wire racks to cool completely.

Place the white chocolate in a heatproof bowl, set the bowl over a saucepan of gently simmering water and heat until melted. Immediately remove from the heat and spread the melted chocolate over the cookies. Leave to cool slightly then sprinkle with the chocolate vermicelli. Leave to cool and set before serving.

505 Marbled cookies

Omit the chocolate vermicelli and use 100 g/3½ oz melted plain chocolate to swirl into the white chocolate topping to create a marbled effect.

506 Shortbread

115 g/4 oz butter, cut into small pieces,
plus extra for greasing
175 g/6 oz plain flour, plus extra
for dusting

pinch of salt
55 g/2 oz caster sugar, plus extra
for sprinkling

Preheat the oven to 150°C/300°F/Gas Mark 2. Grease a loose-bottomed 20-cm/8-inch round fluted tart tin with butter.

Place the flour, salt and sugar in a large bowl and mix together. Add the butter and rub it into the dry ingredients. Continue to work the mixture until it forms a soft dough. Make sure you do not overwork the shortbread or it will be tough.

Lightly press the dough into the tart tin. If you don't have a fluted tin, roll out the dough on a lightly floured board, place on a baking sheet and pinch the edges to form a scalloped pattern.

Using a knife, mark the dough into 8 pieces and prick all over with a fork. Bake in the preheated oven for 45–50 minutes, or until the shortbread is firm and just coloured. Leave to cool for a few minutes in the tin, then sprinkle with sugar. Cut into portions and transfer to a wire rack to cool.

507 Lemon & vanilla shortbread

Split a vanilla pod in half lengthways, carefully scrape out the seeds and add to the flour along with the finely grated rind of 1 lemon.

175 g/6 oz butter, softened
50 g/1¾ oz icing sugar, plus extra
for dusting
1 small egg yolk

2½ tsp brandy
375 g/13 oz plain white flour
¼ tsp baking powder

Preheat the oven to 180°C/350°F/Gas Mark 4. Line 2–3 large baking sheets with baking paper.

Place the butter and icing sugar in a large bowl and beat together until light and fluffy. Add the egg yolk and brandy and beat until the mixture is smooth. Sift the flour and baking powder into the mixture and beat until combined then, using your hands, knead the mixture until smooth.

Roll small pieces of the dough into smooth balls, then place them on the baking sheets, spaced well apart, and flatten slightly with your hands. Bake in the preheated oven for 15 minutes, or until firm to the touch and pale golden brown. Meanwhile, sift a layer of icing sugar into a large roasting tin.

Leave the shortbread to cool for 2–3 minutes on the baking sheets, then place in the roasting tin in a single layer. Sift more icing sugar generously over the top and leave to cool completely.

509 *Greek almond shortbread*

Use only 2 teaspoons of brandy and add ½ teaspoon of almond extract. Replace 125 g/4½ oz of the flour with ground almonds.

510 *Greek pistachio shortbread*

Add 50 g/1¾ oz finely chopped pistachio nuts to the mixture after adding the flour and baking powder.

511 *Greek lemon shortbread*

Add the finely grated rind of 1 lemon to the mixture with the egg yolk and replace the brandy with 2½ teaspoons of lemon juice.

512 *Pistachio biscotti*

225 g/8 oz butter, softened
140 g/5 oz caster sugar
finely grated rind of 1 lemon
1 egg yolk, lightly beaten
2 tsp brandy

280 g/10 oz plain flour
85 g/3 oz pistachio nuts
pinch of salt
icing sugar, for dusting

Place the butter, sugar and lemon rind in a large bowl and beat together until light and fluffy, then beat in the egg yolk and brandy. Sift together the flour, pistachio nuts and salt into the mixture and stir until thoroughly combined. Shape the mixture into a log, flatten slightly, wrap in clingfilm and chill in the refrigerator for 30–60 minutes.

Preheat the oven to 190°C/375°F/Gas Mark 5. Line 2 large baking sheets with baking paper. Unwrap the log, cut it slightly on the diagonal into 5-mm/¼-inch slices with a sharp serrated knife and place them on the baking sheets.

Bake in the oven for 10 minutes, or until golden brown. Leave to cool for 5–10 minutes, then transfer to wire racks to cool completely. Dust with sifted icing sugar.

513 *Hazelnut biscotti*

Replace the pistachio nuts with hazelnuts and replace the lemon rind with the finely grated rind of 1 orange.

514 *Zesty lemon biscotti*

butter, for greasing
280 g/10 oz plain flour, plus extra
    for dusting
1 tsp baking powder

150 g/5½ oz caster sugar
85 g/3 oz blanched almonds
2 large eggs, lightly beaten
finely grated rind and juice of 1 lemon

Preheat the oven to 180°C/350°F/Gas Mark 4. Grease a large baking sheet. Sift the flour and baking powder into a large bowl. Add the sugar, almonds, beaten eggs, lemon rind and juice to the flour and mix together to form a soft dough. Turn the dough onto a lightly floured work surface and, with floured hands, knead for 2–3 minutes, or until smooth.

Divide the dough in half and shape each portion into a log shape measuring about 4 cm/1½ inches in diameter. Place the logs on the baking sheet and flatten until each is about 2.5 cm/1 inch thick.

Bake in the preheated oven for 25 minutes, or until lightly golden brown. Remove from the oven. Reduce the oven temperature to 150°C/300°F/Gas Mark 2. Leave to cool for 15 minutes.

Using a serrated knife, cut the baked dough into 1-cm/½-inch thick slices and place cut-side down on ungreased baking sheets. Bake for a further 10 minutes. Turn and bake for 10–15 minutes, or until golden brown and crisp. Transfer to a wire rack and leave to cool and harden.

515 *Zesty orange & walnut biscotti*

Replace the grated lemon rind and juice with orange. Replace the almonds with chopped walnut halves.

516 *Almond biscotti*

250 g/9 oz plain flour, plus extra
for dusting
1 tsp baking powder
pinch of salt
150 g/5½ oz caster sugar
2 eggs, lightly beaten
finely grated rind of 1 orange
100 g/3½ oz whole blanched almonds,
lightly toasted

Preheat the oven to 180°C/350°F/
Gas Mark 4. Lightly dust a large
baking sheet with flour. Sift the
flour, baking powder and salt into
a bowl. Add the sugar, eggs and
orange rind and mix to form a
dough. Knead in the almonds.

Roll the dough into a ball,
cut in half, roll out each portion
into a log about 4 cm/1½ inches
in diameter and place the logs
on the baking sheet. Bake in the
preheated oven for 10 minutes.
Leave to cool for 5 minutes.

Using a serrated knife, cut the
baked dough into 1-cm/½-inch
thick diagonal slices. Arrange the
slices on ungreased baking sheets
and return to the oven for
15 minutes, or until slightly
golden. Transfer to a wire rack to
cool and harden.

517 *Vanilla & almond biscotti*

*Omit the grated orange rind and add 2 teaspoons of vanilla extract to the
mixture with the beaten eggs. Sprinkle 2 tablespoons of chopped blanched
almonds on top of the logs before baking and press lightly into the dough.*

518 *Rosewater biscotti*

*Omit the orange rind and add 2 teaspoons of rosewater to the mixture with
the beaten eggs. Before baking, mix 1 egg white with 1 teaspoon of water.
Brush over the dough and sprinkle 1 tablespoon of caster sugar over each log.*

butter, for greasing
150 g/5½ oz blanched almonds
150 g/5½ oz plain chocolate, broken
into pieces
250 g/9 oz plain flour, plus extra
for dusting
1 tsp baking powder
150 g/5½ oz caster sugar
2 large eggs, lightly beaten
1 tsp vanilla extract

Preheat the oven to 160°C/325°F/ Gas Mark 3. Grease a large baking sheet. Spread the almonds on another baking sheet and bake in the preheated oven for 5–10 minutes, or until lightly toasted. Leave to cool.

Place the chocolate in a heatproof bowl, set the bowl over a saucepan of gently simmering water and heat until melted. Remove from the heat and stir until smooth, then leave to cool.

Sift the flour and baking powder into a large bowl. Add the sugar, cooled almonds, chocolate, eggs and vanilla extract and mix together to form a soft dough.

Turn the dough onto a lightly floured work surface and, with floured hands, knead for 2–3 minutes, or until smooth. Divide the dough in half and shape each portion into a log shape measuring about 5 cm/2 inches in diameter. Place the logs on the baking sheet and flatten until each is 2.5 cm/1 inch thick.

Bake in the preheated oven for 20–30 minutes, or until firm to the touch. Leave to cool for 15 minutes. Reduce the oven temperature to 150°C/300°F/ Gas Mark 2. Using a serrated knife, cut the baked dough into 1-cm/½-inch thick slices and place, cut-side down, on ungreased baking sheets.

Bake in the oven for 10 minutes. Turn and bake for a further 10–15 minutes, or until crisp. Transfer to a wire rack to cool and harden.

520 *Double chocolate biscotti*

Replace the almonds with 100 g/3½ oz white chocolate chips, adding them with the sugar.

521 *Chocolate & orange biscotti*

Omit the almonds and vanilla extract and add the finely grated rind of 1 orange and 100 g/3½ oz chopped candied orange peel with the sugar.

522 Marbled biscotti

100 g/3½ oz plain chocolate, broken into pieces
85 g/3 oz butter, softened
140 g/5 oz caster sugar
2 large eggs, lightly beaten
½ tsp vanilla extract

finely grated rind of 1 orange
280 g/10 oz plain flour, plus extra for dusting
1½ tsp baking powder
75 g/2¾ oz blanched almonds, chopped

Preheat the oven to 190°C/375°F/Gas Mark 5.

Place the chocolate in a heatproof bowl, set the bowl over a saucepan of gently simmering water and heat until melted. Remove from the heat and stir until smooth, then leave to cool.

Place the butter and sugar in a large bowl and whisk together until pale and creamy. Whisk in the eggs, vanilla extract and orange rind. Sift the flour and baking powder into the mixture.

Add the chopped almonds and mix together to form a soft dough. Divide the dough in half and put each half into a bowl. Add the melted chocolate to one half, then mix together. Add the grated orange rind to the other half, then mix together.

Turn the dough halves onto a lightly floured work surface and, with floured hands, knead each separately for 2–3 minutes, or until smooth. Divide each piece of dough in half and roll each portion into a sausage shape measuring about 30 cm/12 inches long.

Place a roll of each colour, side by side, on a baking sheet and twist the rolls around each other. Flatten to a thickness of about 2.5 cm/1 inch. Repeat with the remaining dough rolls. Bake in the preheated oven for 25 minutes,

or until lightly browned. Remove from the oven and leave to cool for 15 minutes. Reduce the oven temperature to 170°C/325°F/Gas Mark 3.

Using a serrated knife, cut the dough into 1-cm/½-inch thick slices and place, cut-side down, on ungreased baking sheets. Bake in the oven for 10 minutes. Turn and bake for a further 10–15 minutes, or until golden brown and crisp. Transfer to a wire rack to cool and harden.

523 Walnut & rosemary biscotti

55 g/2 oz butter, softened, plus extra for greasing
75 g/2¾ oz caster sugar
2 large eggs, lightly beaten
225 g/8 oz plain flour, plus extra for dusting

1¼ tsp baking powder
85 g/3 oz walnut halves, roughly chopped
1¼ tsp dried rosemary

Preheat the oven to 190°C/375°F/Gas Mark 5. Grease a large baking sheet.

Place the butter and sugar in a large bowl and whisk together until pale and creamy. Whisk in the eggs. Sift in the flour and baking powder. Add the chopped walnuts and dried rosemary and mix together to form a soft dough.

Turn the dough onto a lightly floured work surface and with floured hands, knead for

2–3 minutes, or until smooth. Divide the dough in half and shape each portion into a log shape measuring about 4 cm/1½ inches in diameter. Place the logs on the baking sheet and flatten to a thickness of 2.5 cm/1 inch. Bake in the preheated oven for 20–25 minutes, or until lightly browned. Remove from the oven and leave to cool for 15 minutes. Reduce the oven temperature to 160°C/325°F/Gas Mark 3.

Using a serrated knife, cut the baked dough into 1-cm/½-inch thick slices and place, cut-side down, on ungreased baking sheets. Bake in the oven for 10 minutes. Turn and bake for a further 10–15 minutes, or until golden brown and crisp. Transfer to a wire rack to cool and harden.

524 Pine kernel & lemon biscotti

Replace the walnuts with pine kernels. Replace the rosemary with the finely grated rind of 1 large lemon.

525 · Apricot biscotti

butter, for greasing
150 g/5½ oz ready-to-eat dried apricots
275 g/9½ oz plain flour, plus extra for
    dusting
1 tsp baking powder

150 g/5½ oz caster sugar
2 large eggs, lightly beaten
¼ tsp almond extract
finely grated rind of 1 lemon

Preheat the oven to 190°C/375°F/Gas Mark 5. Grease a large baking sheet. Using scissors, snip the apricots into small pieces.

Sift the flour and baking powder into a large bowl. Add the snipped apricots and sugar and mix together. Add the eggs, almond extract and lemon rind and mix together to form a soft dough.

Turn the dough onto a lightly floured work surface and, with floured hands, knead for 2–3 minutes, or until smooth. Divide the dough in half and shape each portion into a log shape measuring about 4 cm/1½ inches in diameter. Place the logs on the baking sheet and flatten until each is about 2.5 cm/1 inch thick.

Bake in the preheated oven for 20–30 minutes, or until lightly browned. Remove from the oven and leave to cool for 15 minutes. Reduce the oven temperature to 160°C/325°F/Gas Mark 3. Using a serrated knife, cut the baked dough into 1-cm/½-inch thick slices and place, cut-side down, on ungreased baking sheets. Bake in the preheated oven for 10 minutes. Turn and bake for a further 10 minutes, or until crisp. Transfer to a wire rack to cool and harden.

526 Sultana or raisin biscotti

Replace the apricots with sultanas or raisins and replace the almond extract with vanilla extract.

527 Saffron-flecked biscotti

butter, for greasing
100 g/3½ oz blanched almonds
280 g/10 oz plain flour, plus extra
    for dusting

½ tsp bicarbonate of soda
150 g/5½ oz caster sugar
2 large pinches of saffron strands
2 large eggs, lightly beaten

Preheat the oven to 190°C/375°F/Gas Mark 5. Grease a large baking sheet. Spread the almonds on a baking sheet and bake in the preheated oven for 5–10 minutes, or until lightly toasted. Leave to cool.

Sift the flour and bicarbonate of soda into a large bowl. Add the sugar, cooled almonds and saffron and stir together. Add the eggs and mix together to form a soft dough.

Turn the dough onto a lightly floured work surface and, with floured hands, knead for 2–3 minutes, or until smooth. Divide the dough in half and shape each portion into a log shape measuring about 4 cm/1½ inches in diameter. Place the logs on the baking sheet and flatten slightly until each is about 2.5 cm/1 inch thick.

Bake in the preheated oven for 15 minutes, or until lightly golden brown. Remove from the oven and leave to cool for 15–20 minutes. Reduce the oven temperature to 160°C/325°F/Gas Mark 3. Using a serrated knife, cut the baked dough into 1-cm/½-inch thick slices and place, cut-side down, on ungreased baking sheets. Bake in the oven for 5 minutes. Turn and bake for a further 5–10 minutes, or until lightly golden brown and crisp. Transfer to a wire rack to cool and harden.

Mocha biscotti

*50 g/1¾ oz butter, softened, plus extra
for greasing
100 g/3½ oz caster sugar
2 large eggs, lightly beaten
4 tsp chicory and coffee essence*

*300 g/10½ oz plain flour, plus extra
for dusting
1 tsp baking powder
15 g/½ oz cocoa powder
35 g/1¼ oz chopped blanched almonds*

Preheat the oven to 190°C/375°F/Gas Mark 5. Grease a large baking sheet. Place the butter and sugar in a large bowl and whisk together until pale and creamy. Whisk the eggs and chicory and coffee essence into the mixture. Sift in the flour, baking powder and cocoa. Add the almonds and mix together to form a soft dough.

Turn the dough onto a lightly floured work surface and, with floured hands, knead for 2–3 minutes, or until smooth. Divide the dough in half and shape each portion into a log shape measuring about 4 cm/1½ inches in diameter. Place the logs on the baking sheet and flatten until each is about 2.5 cm/1 inch thick.

Bake in the preheated oven for 20–25 minutes, or until firm to the touch. Remove from the oven and leave to cool for 15 minutes. Reduce the oven temperature to 160°C/325°F/Gas Mark 3. Using a serrated knife, cut the baked dough into 1-cm/½-inch thick slices and place, cut-side down, on ungreased baking sheets. Bake for a further 10 minutes. Turn and bake for another 10–15 minutes, or until crisp. Transfer to a wire rack to cool and harden.

Honey & sesame biscotti

*40 g/1½ oz butter, softened, plus extra
for greasing
50 g/1¾ oz caster sugar
2 large eggs, lightly beaten
85 g/3 oz clear honey*

*300 g/10½ oz plain flour, plus extra
for dusting
1 tsp baking powder
5 tbsp sesame seeds*

Preheat the oven to 190°C/375°F/Gas Mark 5. Grease a large baking sheet. Place the butter and sugar in a large bowl and whisk together until pale and creamy. Whisk the eggs and honey into the mixture. Sift in the flour and baking powder. Add 3 tablespoons of the sesame seeds and mix together to form a soft dough.

Turn the dough onto a lightly floured work surface and, with floured hands, knead for 2–3 minutes, or until smooth. Divide the dough in half and shape each portion into a log shape measuring about 4 cm/1½ inches in diameter.

Sprinkle the remaining sesame seeds on a sheet of baking paper and roll the logs in the seeds. Place the logs on the baking sheet and flatten to a thickness of about 2.5 cm/1 inch. Sprinkle any remaining sesame seeds on top of the logs and press into the dough.

Bake in the preheated oven for 15–20 minutes, or until lightly golden brown. Remove from the oven and leave to cool for 15 minutes. Reduce the oven temperature to 160°C/325°F/Gas Mark 3. Using a serrated knife, cut the baked dough into 1-cm/½-inch thick slices and place, cut-side down, on ungreased baking sheets. Bake the cookies in the oven for 10 minutes. Turn and bake for a further 5–10 minutes, or until crisp. Transfer to a wire rack and leave to cool and harden.

530 Spicy nut biscotti

50 g/1¾ oz butter, softened, plus extra
   for greasing
50 g/1¾ oz caster sugar
50 g/1¾ oz soft light brown sugar
2 large eggs, lightly beaten
275 g/9¾ oz plain flour, plus extra
   for dusting

1¼ tsp baking powder
¼ tsp ground cinnamon
¼ tsp grated nutmeg
¼ tsp ground ginger
100 g/3½ oz blanched almonds, chopped

Preheat the oven to 190°C/375°F/Gas Mark 5. Grease a large baking sheet. Place the butter and sugars in a large bowl and whisk together until pale and creamy. Whisk the eggs into the mixture. Sift in the flour, baking powder, cinnamon, nutmeg and ginger. Add the chopped almonds, reserving 2 tablespoons, and mix together to form a soft dough.

Turn the dough onto a lightly floured work surface and, with floured hands, knead for 2–3 minutes, or until smooth. Divide the dough in half and shape each portion into a log shape measuring about 4 cm/1½ inches in diameter.

Place the logs on the baking sheet and flatten until each is about 2.5 cm/1 inch thick.

Sprinkle the reserved almonds on top of the logs and press into the dough.

Bake in the preheated oven for 20–25 minutes, or until lightly golden brown. Remove from the oven and leave to cool for 15 minutes. Reduce the oven temperature to 160°C/325°F/Gas Mark 3. Using a serrated knife, cut the baked dough into 1-cm/½-inch thick slices and place, cut-side down, on ungreased baking sheets. Bake for a further 10 minutes. Turn and bake for another 10–15 minutes, or until lightly golden brown and crisp. Transfer to a wire rack to cool and harden.

531 Cherry & almond biscotti

50 g/1¾ oz butter, softened, plus extra
   for greasing
100 g/3½ oz caster sugar
1 large egg, lightly beaten
200 g/7 oz plain flour, plus extra
   for dusting
1¼ tsp baking powder
100 g/3½ oz glacé cherries, cut in half
35 g/1¼ oz blanched almonds,
   roughly chopped

Preheat the oven to 190°C/375°F/Gas Mark 5. Grease a large baking sheet. Place the butter and sugar in a large bowl and whisk together until pale and creamy. Whisk in the egg. Sift the flour and baking powder into the mixture. Add the cherries and chopped almonds and mix together to form a soft dough. Turn the dough onto a lightly floured work surface and,

with floured hands, knead for 2–3 minutes, or until smooth. Divide the dough in half and shape each portion into a log shape measuring about 4 cm/1½ inches in diameter. Place the logs on the baking sheet and flatten until each is about 2.5 cm/1 inch thick.

Bake in the preheated oven for 20–25 minutes, or until lightly golden brown. Remove from the oven and leave to cool for 15 minutes. Reduce the oven temperature to 160°C/325°F/Gas Mark 3. Using a serrated knife, cut the baked dough into 1-cm/½-inch thick slices and place, cut-side

down, on ungreased baking sheets. Bake for a further 10 minutes. Turn and bake for another 10–15 minutes until crisp. Transfer to a wire rack to cool and harden.

532 Mixed berry biscotti

Replace the cherries with 75 g/2¾ oz dried cranberries and 25 g/1 oz dried blueberries.

533 Mixed cherry biscotti

Use multi-coloured glacé cherries that include red, green and yellow ones.

534 Traditional oatcakes

225 g/8 oz oatmeal, plus extra
for dusting
½ tsp bicarbonate of soda

½ tsp salt
15 g/½ oz unsalted butter, melted
150 ml/5 fl oz warm water

Preheat the oven to 180°C/350°F/Gas Mark 4. Place the oatmeal and bicarbonate of soda into a large bowl and stir in the salt, making a well in the middle. Pour the melted butter and warm water into the oatmeal mixture and mix together to form a soft dough.

Roll the dough out on a work surface lightly dusted with oatmeal. Cut out oatcakes with a cookie cutter. Re-roll any trimmings and cut out more oatcakes. Place the oatcakes on 2 large non-stick baking sheets.

Bake in the preheated oven for 20 minutes, turning them 3 times while cooking. Leave on a wire rack to cool completely.

535 Cranberry oatcakes

Add 50 g/1¾ oz chopped dried cranberries to the mixture and knead in before rolling out the dough.

536 Gingerbread people

115 g/4 oz butter, plus extra
for greasing
450 g/1 lb plain flour, plus extra
for dusting
2 tsp ground ginger
1 tsp ground mixed spice
2 tsp bicarbonate of soda
100 g/3½ oz golden syrup
115 g/4 oz light muscovado sugar
1 egg, lightly beaten

TO DECORATE
currants
glacé cherries
85 g/3 oz icing sugar
3–4 tsp water

Preheat the oven to 160°C/325°F/Gas Mark 3. Grease 3 large baking sheets. Sift the flour, ginger, mixed spice and bicarbonate of soda into a large bowl. Place the butter, golden syrup and muscovado sugar in a saucepan over a low heat and stir until melted. Pour onto the dry ingredients and add the egg. Mix together to form a dough. The dough will be sticky to start with, but will become firmer as it cools.

Roll out the dough on a floured work surface to about 3 mm/⅛ inch thick and cut out gingerbread people shapes. Place on the baking sheets. Re-knead and re-roll the trimmings and cut out more shapes. Decorate with currants for eyes and pieces of glacé cherry for mouths.

Bake in the preheated oven for 15–20 minutes, or until firm and lightly browned. Leave to cool on the baking sheets for a few minutes, then transfer the cookies to wire racks to cool completely.

Place the icing sugar and water in a small bowl and mix together until it is thick. Place the icing in a small piping bag fitted with a plain nozzle and use to pipe buttons and bows onto the cookies.

537 Gingerbread ark

Use animal cookie cutters to make gingerbread animals. Make a Noah's Ark gift box with 2 gingerbread people and several animals.

538 Cheese sables

150 g/5½ oz plain flour, plus extra
for dusting
150 g/5½ oz mature Cheddar cheese,
grated

150 g/5½ oz butter, diced, plus extra
for greasing
1 egg yolk
sesame seeds, for sprinkling

Place the flour and cheese in a bowl and mix together. Add the butter
and rub it in with your fingertips until combined. Stir in the egg yolk
and mix to form a dough. Wrap the dough in clingfilm and chill in the
refrigerator for about 30 minutes.

Preheat the oven to 200°C/400°F/Gas Mark 6. Lightly grease several
large baking sheets. Roll out the dough thinly on a lightly floured work
surface. Cut out 6-cm/2½-inch rounds with a biscuit cutter. Re-roll
the trimmings to make about 35 rounds and place them on the baking
sheets. Sprinkle the sesame seeds over the top of them.

Bake in the preheated oven for 10 minutes, or until the sables are
light golden brown. Transfer the cookies to a wire rack to cool slightly
before serving.

539 Gruyère sables

Replace the Cheddar cheese with finely grated Gruyère cheese.

540 Cheese straws

115 g/4 oz plain flour, plus extra
for dusting
pinch of salt
1 tsp curry powder

55 g/2 oz butter, plus extra for greasing
55 g/2 oz grated Cheddar cheese
1 egg, lightly beaten
poppy and cumin seeds, for sprinkling

Sift the flour, salt and curry powder into a bowl. Add the butter and rub
it in with your fingertips until the mixture resembles breadcrumbs. Add
the cheese and half the egg and mix to form a dough. Wrap in clingfilm
and chill in the refrigerator for 30 minutes.

Preheat the oven to 200°C/400°F/Gas Mark 6. Grease several large
baking sheets. Roll out the dough on a floured work surface to 5 mm/
¼ inch thick, then cut into 7.5 x 1-cm/3 x ½-inch strips. Pinch the
strips lightly along the sides and place on the baking sheets.

Brush the strips with the remaining egg and sprinkle half with
poppy seeds and half with cumin seeds. Bake in the preheated oven for
10–15 minutes, or until golden. Transfer to wire racks to cool.

541 Celery & cheese straws

Replace the curry powder with 1½ teaspoons of celery salt.

542 Breadsticks

350 g/12 oz strong white flour, plus
extra for dusting
1½ tsp salt
1½ tsp easy-blend dried yeast

200 ml/7 fl oz lukewarm water
3 tbsp olive oil, plus extra for greasing
sesame seeds, for coating

Sift together the flour and salt into a warmed bowl. Stir in the yeast and make a well in the middle. Add the water and oil to the well and mix to form a soft dough. Turn out the dough onto a floured work surface and knead for 5–10 minutes, or until smooth and elastic. Place the dough in a greased bowl, cover with a damp tea towel and leave to rise in a warm place for 1 hour, or until doubled in size.

Preheat the oven to 200°C/400°F/Gas Mark 6. Lightly grease 2 large baking sheets. Turn out the dough and knead lightly, then roll out into a 23 x 20-cm/9 x 8-inch rectangle. Cut the dough into 3 x 20-cm/8-inch long strips, then cut each strip across into 10 pieces. Roll and stretch each piece into a 30-cm/12-inch long stick and brush with oil.

Spread out the sesame seeds on a large plate. Roll each breadstick in the sesame seeds, then put on the baking sheets, spaced well apart. Brush with oil, cover with a damp tea towel and leave in a warm place for 15 minutes.

Bake in the preheated oven for 10 minutes. Turn over and bake for a further 5–10 minutes, or until golden. Transfer to a wire rack to cool.

543 With mixed seed coating

Crush 1 tablespoon each of cumin and coriander seeds. Mix with 1 tablespoon each of poppy seeds and sesame seeds and use to coat the breadsticks.

544 Savoury oat crackers

100 g/3½ oz unsalted butter, plus extra
for greasing
90 g/3¼ oz rolled oats
25 g/1 oz wholemeal flour
½ tsp coarse sea salt

1 tsp dried thyme
40 g/1½ oz walnut halves, finely chopped
1 egg, lightly beaten
40 g/1½ oz sesame seeds

Preheat the oven to 180°C/350°F/Gas Mark 4. Grease 2 large baking sheets. Place the oats and flour in a large bowl. Add the butter and rub it in with your fingertips. Stir in the salt, thyme and walnuts, then add the egg and mix to form a soft dough. Spread out the sesame seeds on a large plate.

Roll walnut-sized pieces of dough into balls, then roll in the sesame seeds to coat and put on the baking sheets, spaced well apart. Roll the rolling pin over them to flatten as much as possible.

Bake in the preheated oven for 12–15 minutes, or until firm and pale golden. Leave to cool on the baking trays for 3–4 minutes, then transfer to a wire rack to cool completely.

545 Spiced oat crackers

Add ½ teaspoon of ground cumin and ½ teaspoon of crushed coriander seeds to the dough and replace half the sesame seeds with 15 g/½ oz poppy seeds.

Blissful Brownies
and Bars

225 g/8 oz butter, diced, plus extra for greasing
150 g/5½ oz plain chocolate, chopped
225 g/8 oz self-raising flour
125 g/4½ oz dark muscovado sugar
4 eggs, lightly beaten

60 g/2¼ oz blanched hazelnuts, chopped
60 g/2¼ oz sultanas
100 g/3½ oz plain chocolate chips
115 g/4 oz white chocolate, melted, to decorate

Preheat the oven to 180°C/350°F/Gas Mark 4. Grease and line a shallow 28 x 18-cm/11 x 7-inch rectangular baking tin. Place the butter and chocolate in a saucepan and stir over a low heat until melted. Remove the pan from the heat.

Sift the flour into a large bowl, add the sugar and mix well. Stir the eggs into the chocolate mixture, then beat into the flour mixture. Add the nuts, sultanas and chocolate chips and mix well. Spoon evenly into the cake tin and smooth the surface.

Bake in the preheated oven for 30 minutes, or until firm and a skewer inserted into the centre comes out clean. Leave to cool for 15 minutes, then turn out onto a wire rack to cool completely.

To decorate, drizzle the melted white chocolate in fine lines over the cake, then cut into squares. Leave to set before serving.

547 *Sugar-coated chocolates brownies*

Use light muscovado sugar instead of the dark muscovado. Replace the sultanas with 150 g/5½ oz sugar-coated chocolates.

548 *Chocolate & date brownies*

Replace the hazelnuts, sultanas and chocolate chips with 175 g/6 oz chopped dried dates. Decorate with milk chocolate instead of white chocolate.

549 *Chocolate chilli brownies*

Add ¼ teaspoon of chilli flakes to the melted butter and chocolate.

225 g/8 oz butter, softened, plus extra
  for greasing
225 g/8 oz self-raising flour
1 tsp baking powder
1 tsp cocoa powder, plus extra for dusting
225 g/8 oz caster sugar
4 eggs, lightly beaten
3 tbsp instant coffee granules, dissolved
  in 2 tbsp hot water, cooled

WHITE CHOCOLATE FROSTING
115 g/4 oz white chocolate, broken
  into pieces
55 g/2 oz butter, softened
3 tbsp milk
175 g/6 oz icing sugar

Preheat the oven to 180°C/350°F/ Gas Mark 4. Grease and line the base of a shallow 28 x 18-cm/ 11 x 7-inch rectangular baking tin. Sift the flour, baking powder and cocoa into a bowl and add the butter, sugar, eggs and coffee. Beat well until smooth, then spoon into the tin and smooth the top.

Bake in the preheated oven for 35–40 minutes, or until risen and firm. Leave to cool in the tin for 10 minutes, then turn out onto a wire rack and peel off the lining paper. Leave to cool completely.

To make the frosting, place the chocolate, butter and milk in a saucepan and stir over a low heat until the chocolate has melted. Remove the pan from the heat and sift in the icing sugar. Beat until smooth, then spread over the cake. Dust the top with sifted cocoa and cut into squares.

551 *Coffee iced brownies*

Replace the white chocolate icing with coffee icing. Melt 55 g/2 oz butter in a small saucepan with 3 tablespoons of milk, then add 4 teaspoons of instant coffee granules and stir until dissolved. Sift 225 g/8 oz icing sugar into a bowl and beat in the coffee mixture to form a smooth icing. Allow to cool slightly until thickened. Spread over the brownies and leave to set before cutting into squares.

115 g/4 oz butter, plus extra for greasing
115 g/4 oz plain chocolate, broken
  into pieces
½ tsp coarsely ground black peppercorns
4 eggs, lightly beaten
250 g/9 oz caster sugar
½ tsp vanilla extract
3 tbsp Kahlúa liqueur
2 tbsp vodka

150 g/5½ oz plain flour
¼ tsp baking powder
55 g/2 oz chopped walnuts, plus extra
  to decorate
cocoa powder, for dusting

KAHLÚA CREAM TOPPING
2 tbsp Kahlúa liqueur
200 g/7 oz crème fraîche

Preheat the oven to 180°C/350°F/Gas Mark 4. Grease and line the base of a shallow 30 x 20-cm/12 x 8-inch rectangular baking tin. Place the chocolate, butter and peppercorns in a small saucepan and heat gently until the chocolate and butter are melted. Leave to cool slightly.

Place the eggs, sugar and vanilla extract in a large bowl and beat together, then stir in the chocolate mixture, Kahlúa and vodka. Sift together the flour and baking powder and stir into the chocolate mixture. Stir in the walnuts and pour into the tin. Bake in the preheated oven for 20–25 minutes, or until just firm to the touch. Leave to cool for a few minutes, then cut into bars or squares and lift carefully from the tin onto serving plates.

To make the topping, stir the Kahlúa into the crème fraîche and spoon a generous dollop on each serving of brownie. Sprinkle with a little cocoa, decorate with walnuts and serve immediately.

115 g/4 oz butter, plus extra for greasing
85 g/3 oz plain flour
½ tsp baking powder
55 g/2 oz cocoa powder
2 eggs, lightly beaten
175 g/6 oz caster sugar
1 tsp vanilla extract
½ tsp almond extract

140 g/5 oz pitted dark cherries, quartered
chocolate curls and whole fresh cherries,
to decorate

CHERRY CREAM
150 ml/5 fl oz double cream
1 tbsp kirsch liqueur

Preheat the oven to 180°C/350°F/Gas Mark 4. Grease a shallow 28 x 18-cm/11 x 7-inch rectangular baking tin. Sift together the flour and baking powder. Place the butter in a large saucepan over a medium heat and stir until melted. Remove from the heat and add the cocoa, stirring until smooth. Beat in the eggs, sugar, vanilla extract and almond extract. Fold in the flour mixture and cherries and pour into the tin.

Bake in the preheated oven for 25–30 minutes, or until just firm to the touch. Cool slightly, then cut into squares and remove from the tin.

To make the cherry cream, place the cream and kirsch in a bowl and whip together. Spoon a little onto each brownie, then decorate with chocolate curls and serve with fresh cherries.

554 *Chocolate & raspberry brownies*

Replace the cherries with raspberries. To serve, whip the cream with 1 tablespoon of framboise and serve with extra raspberries.

555 *Chocolate blueberry brownies*

Replace the cherries with blueberries and serve with cassis-flavoured cream and extra blueberries.

556 Double chocolate brownies

115 g/4 oz butter, plus extra
for greasing
115 g/4 oz plain chocolate, broken
into pieces
300 g/10½ oz caster sugar
pinch of salt
1 tsp vanilla extract
2 large eggs
140 g/5 oz plain flour
2 tbsp cocoa powder
100 g/3½ oz white chocolate chips

FUDGE SAUCE
55 g/2 oz butter
225 g/8 oz caster sugar
150 ml/5 fl oz milk
250 ml/9 fl oz double cream
225 g/8 oz golden syrup
200 g/7 oz plain chocolate, broken
into pieces

Preheat the oven to 180°C/350°F/ Gas Mark 4. Grease and line the base of a 18-cm/7-inch square cake tin. Place the butter and chocolate in a saucepan and stir over a low heat until melted. Remove from the heat, then stir until smooth and leave to cool slightly. Stir in the sugar, salt and vanilla extract. Add the eggs, one at a time, and stir until blended.

Sift the flour and cocoa into the mixture and beat until smooth. Stir in the chocolate chips, then pour into the tin.

Bake in the preheated oven for 35–40 minutes, until a cocktail stick inserted into the centre comes out almost clean. Cool slightly.

Place the butter, sugar, milk, cream and golden syrup in a small saucepan and heat gently until the sugar has dissolved. Bring to the boil and stir for 10 minutes, or until the mixture is caramel-coloured. Remove from the heat and add the chocolate. Stir until smooth. Cut the brownies into squares and serve with the sauce.

557 Chocolate & butterscotch brownies

Replace the white chocolate chips with butterscotch chips.

558 Cranberry soured cream brownies

115 g/4 oz butter, plus extra for greasing
140 g/5 oz self-raising flour, plus extra
for dusting
4 tbsp cocoa powder
200 g/7 oz light muscovado sugar
2 eggs, lightly beaten
115 g/4 oz fresh cranberries

TOPPING
150 ml/5 fl oz soured cream
1 tbsp caster sugar
1 tbsp self-raising flour
1 egg yolk
½ tsp vanilla extract

Preheat the oven to 180°C/350°F/Gas Mark 4. Grease and lightly flour a shallow 30 x 20-cm/12 x 8-inch rectangular baking tin. Place the butter, cocoa and sugar in a saucepan and stir over a low heat until just melted. Leave to cool slightly. Quickly stir in the flour and eggs and beat hard until thoroughly mixed to a smooth batter. Stir in the cranberries, then spread the mixture into the tin.

To make the topping, place all the ingredients in a bowl and beat together until smooth, then spoon over the chocolate mixture, swirling evenly with a palette knife. Bake in the preheated oven for 35–40 minutes, or until risen and firm. Allow to cool in the tin, then cut into squares.

BROWNIE BASE
115 g/4 oz butter, plus extra for greasing
115 g/4 oz plain flour, plus extra for
dusting
115 g/4 oz plain chocolate
200 g/7 oz caster sugar
2 eggs, lightly beaten
50 ml/2 fl oz milk
strawberries dipped in melted chocolate,
to serve

TOPPING
500 g/1 lb 2 oz soft cream cheese
125 g/4½ oz caster sugar
3 eggs
1 tsp vanilla extract
115 g/4 oz natural yogurt
melted chocolate, for drizzling

Preheat the oven to 180°C/350°F/Gas Mark 4. Lightly grease and flour a 23-cm/9-inch round cake tin. Place the butter and chocolate in a saucepan and stir over a low heat until melted and smooth. Remove from the heat and beat in the sugar. Add the eggs and milk, beating well. Stir in the flour, mixing until just blended. Spoon into the tin, spreading evenly.

Bake in the preheated oven for 25 minutes. Remove from the oven and reduce the oven temperature to 160°C/325°F/Gas Mark 3.

To make the topping, place the cheese, sugar, eggs and vanilla extract in a bowl and beat together until well blended. Stir in the yogurt, then pour over the brownie base. Bake for a further 45–55 minutes, or until the centre is almost set.

Run a knife around the edge of the cheesecake to loosen it from the tin. Leave to cool before removing from the tin.

Chill in the refrigerator for 4 hours or overnight before cutting into slices. Drizzle the top with the melted chocolate and serve with chocolate-dipped strawberries.

560 *Chocolate peach cheesecake*

For the topping, replace the vanilla extract with the finely grated rind of 1 orange and use a peach-flavoured yogurt.

561 *White chocolate brownie cheesecake*

For the topping, omit the yogurt and fold in 125 g/4½ oz melted white chocolate and 100 ml/3½ fl oz double cream after the vanilla extract is added.

225 g/8 oz butter, softened, plus extra
for greasing
150 g/5½ oz plain chocolate, broken
into pieces
280 g/10 oz plain flour
100 g/3½ oz caster sugar
4 eggs, lightly beaten
75 g/2¾ oz chopped pistachio nuts
100 g/3½ oz white chocolate,
coarsely chopped
icing sugar, for dusting (optional)

Preheat the oven to 180°C/350°F/
Gas Mark 4. Lightly grease and line
a 23-cm/9-inch square baking tin.

Place the butter and plain
chocolate in a saucepan and stir
over a low heat until melted.
Leave to cool slightly.

Sift the flour into a separate
bowl and stir in the sugar.

Stir the eggs into the melted
chocolate mixture, then pour
this mixture into the flour and
sugar mixture, beating well. Stir
in the pistachio nuts and white
chocolate, then pour the mixture
into the tin, spreading it evenly
into the corners.

Bake in the preheated oven
for 30–35 minutes, or until firm
to the touch. Leave to cool in the
tin for 20 minutes, then turn out
onto a wire rack and leave to cool
completely. Cut into 12 bars and
dust with sifted icing sugar, if
using.

563 *Peanut butter chip brownies*

Replace the pistachio nuts with peanuts and the white chocolate with peanut
butter chips.

564 *Minted chocolate chip brownies*

Replace the chocolate chips and pistachio nuts with 175 g/6 oz mint
chocolate, roughly chopped.

565 Low-fat banana cardamom brownies

butter, for greasing
115 g/4 oz plain flour
3 tbsp cocoa powder
2 tbsp dried milk powder
¼ tsp baking powder
¼ tsp salt

2 ripe bananas
150 g/5½ oz light muscovado sugar
2 egg whites
150 g/5½ oz low-fat natural yogurt
seeds from 2 cardamom pods, crushed
shredded coconut, toasted, to decorate

Preheat the oven to 180°C/350°F/Gas Mark 4. Grease a shallow 23-cm/9-inch square baking tin. Sift the flour, cocoa, milk powder, baking powder and salt into a large bowl and make a well in the centre.

Mash the bananas in a separate bowl, add the sugar, egg whites, yogurt and cardamom seeds and beat together until combined. Stir into the dry ingredients, mixing evenly, then spoon the mixture into the tin.

Bake in the preheated oven for 25–30 minutes, or until just firm. Leave to cool in the tin, then cut into squares and decorate with toasted shredded coconut.

566 Spiced banana brownies

Make the brownies with whole milk yogurt or soured cream and add 40 g/1½ oz chopped walnuts or pecan nuts. Replace the cardamom pods with ¼ teaspoon of freshly grated nutmeg, if liked.

567 Maple-glazed pistachio brownies

175 g/6 oz butter, plus extra for greasing
115 g/4 oz plain chocolate
250 g/9 oz caster sugar
4 eggs, lightly beaten
1 tsp vanilla extract
200 g/7 oz plain flour

85 g/3 oz pistachio nuts, shelled, skinned
   and chopped

GLAZE
115 g/4 oz plain chocolate
115 g/4 oz crème fraîche
2 tbsp maple syrup

Preheat the oven to 190°C/375°F/Gas Mark 5. Lightly grease a shallow 30 x 20-cm/12 x 8-inch rectangular baking tin. Place the chocolate and butter in a small saucepan over a very low heat and stir until melted. Remove the pan from the heat.

Place the sugar, eggs and vanilla extract in a large bowl and whisk together until pale and creamy. Beat in the melted chocolate mixture. Fold in the flour evenly, then stir in 55 g/2 oz of the pistachio nuts. Spoon into the tin and smooth the top. Bake in the preheated oven for 25–30 minutes, or until firm and golden brown. Leave to cool in the tin.

To make the glaze, place the chocolate in a heatproof bowl, set the bowl over a saucepan of gently simmering water and heat until melted. Stir in the crème fraîche and maple syrup and beat until smooth and glossy. Spread the glaze over the brownies evenly, then sprinkle with the remaining pistachio nuts. Leave to set, then cut into squares to serve.

568 Maple-glazed pecan brownies

Replace the pistachio nuts with pecan nuts and make the glaze with milk or plain chocolate.

569 *Mocha brownies*

55 g/2 oz butter, plus extra for greasing
115 g/4 oz plain chocolate, broken into
  pieces
175 g/6 oz dark muscovado sugar
2 eggs
1 tbsp instant coffee granules, dissolved
  in 1 tbsp hot water, cooled
85 g/3 oz plain flour

½ tsp baking powder
55 g/2 oz pecan nuts, roughly chopped

TOPPING
100 g/3½ oz icing sugar
1–2 tbsp water
chopped pecan nuts

Preheat the oven to 180°C/350°F/Gas Mark 4. Grease and line the base of a 20-cm/8-inch square baking tin. Place the butter and chocolate in a saucepan and stir over a low heat until melted. Leave to cool.

Place the sugar and eggs in a large bowl and beat together until light and fluffy. Fold in the chocolate mixture and cooled coffee and mix thoroughly. Sift in the flour and baking powder and lightly fold into the mixture. Carefully fold in the pecan nuts and pour the mixture into the tin. Bake in the preheated oven for 25–30 minutes, or until firm and a skewer inserted into the centre comes out clean.

Leave to cool in the tin for a few minutes, then run a knife around the edge of the cake to loosen it. Turn the cake out onto a wire rack, peel off the lining paper and leave to cool. When cold, cut into squares.

Place the icing sugar and water in a bowl and mix together until smooth, then trickle around each brownie. Sprinkle the brownie and icing with the pecan nuts.

570 *Mochachino brownies with white mocha sauce*

115 g/4 oz butter, plus extra for greasing
115 g/4 oz plain chocolate
2 tbsp strong black coffee
250 g/9 oz caster sugar
½ tsp ground cinnamon
3 eggs, lightly beaten
85 g/3 oz plain flour
55 g/2 oz milk chocolate chips

55 g/2 oz toasted walnuts, skinned and
  chopped, plus extra to decorate

WHITE MOCHA SAUCE
100 ml/3½ fl oz double cream
85 g/3 oz white chocolate, broken
  into pieces
1 tbsp strong black coffee

Preheat the oven to 180°C/350°F/ Gas Mark 4. Grease and line a 23-cm/9-inch square baking tin.

Place the butter, chocolate and coffee in a saucepan and stir over a low heat until melted. Leave to cool slightly, then whisk in the sugar, cinnamon and eggs. Beat in the flour, chocolate chips and walnuts. Pour into the tin.

Bake in the preheated oven for 30–35 minutes, until just firm but still moist inside. Cool in the tin then cut into squares or bars.

To make the sauce, place all the ingredients in a small pan and stir over a low heat until smooth.

Place the brownies on serving plates and spoon the warm sauce on top. Decorate with chopped walnuts and serve.

571 *With rich brandy sauce*

For the sauce, replace the white chocolate with plain chocolate. Heat the double cream and chocolate in a small saucepan over a low heat and stir until smooth. Remove from the heat and stir in 1 tablespoon of brandy instead of the coffee.

225 g/8 oz butter, plus extra
for greasing
70 g/2½ oz plain chocolate, broken
into pieces
125 g/4½ oz plain flour
¾ tsp bicarbonate of soda
¼ tsp baking powder
55 g/2 oz pecan nuts
100 g/3½ oz demerara sugar, plus
extra for dusting
½ tsp almond extract
1 egg
1 tsp milk

Preheat the oven to 180°C/350°F/
Gas Mark 4. Grease and line a
shallow 28 x 18-cm/11 x 7-inch
rectangular baking tin.

Place the chocolate in a
heatproof bowl, set the bowl over
a saucepan of gently simmering
water and heat until melted.
Meanwhile, sift together the flour,
bicarbonate of soda and baking
powder in a large bowl.

Finely chop the pecan nuts
and set aside. Place the butter and
sugar in a separate bowl and beat
together until light and fluffy, then
mix in the almond extract and
egg. Remove the chocolate from
the heat and stir into the butter
mixture. Add the flour mixture,
milk and chopped nuts to the
bowl and stir until well combined.
Spoon the mixture into the tin and
smooth the top.

Bake in the preheated oven for
30 minutes, or until firm to the
touch and still a little soft in the
centre. Leave to cool completely.
Sprinkle with demerara sugar and
cut into 20 squares before serving.

573 Walnut brownies

Replace the pecan nuts with walnuts.

574 Apricot brownies

Replace the pecan nuts with chopped dried apricots.

115 g/4 oz butter, plus extra
for greasing
175 g/6 oz light muscovado sugar
2 eggs, lightly beaten
200 g/7 oz plain flour
1 tsp baking powder
½ tsp bicarbonate of soda
1½ tsp ground mixed spice
2 eating apples, peeled and coarsely
grated
85 g/3 oz hazelnuts, chopped

TOFFEE APPLE TOPPING
85 g/3 oz light muscovado sugar
55 g/2 oz butter
1 dessert apple, cored and thinly
sliced

Preheat the oven to 180°C/350°F/ Gas Mark 4. Grease a shallow 23-cm/9-inch square baking tin. To make the topping, place the sugar and butter in a small saucepan and heat gently, stirring, until melted. Pour into the tin and arrange the apple slices over the mixture.

To make the brownies, place the butter and sugar in a large bowl and beat together until light and fluffy, then gradually beat in the eggs. Sift together the flour, baking powder, bicarbonate of soda and mixed spice, and fold into the mixture. Stir in the apples and nuts, then pour into the tin.

Bake in the preheated oven for 35–40 minutes, or until firm and golden. Leave to cool in the tin for 10 minutes, then cut into squares.

576 *Upside-down pineapple brownies*

For the topping, replace the apple with 4 canned pineapple slices. Replace the apples in the brownie mixture with 6 chopped, canned pineapple slices.

577 *Upside-down toffee pear brownies*

For the topping, replace the apple with 1 peeled, cored and sliced pear. Replace the apples in the brownie mixture with pears.

578 Ginger chocolate chip brownies

4 pieces stem ginger in syrup
225 g/8 oz plain flour
1½ tsp ground ginger
1 tsp ground cinnamon
¼ tsp ground cloves

¼ tsp grated nutmeg
115 g/4 oz soft light brown sugar
115 g/4 oz butter
115 g/4 oz golden syrup
100 g/3½ oz plain chocolate chips

Preheat the oven to 150°C/300°F/Gas Mark 2. Finely chop the stem ginger. Sift the flour, ground ginger, cinnamon, cloves and nutmeg into a large bowl, then stir in the chopped stem ginger and sugar.

Place the butter and the golden syrup in a saucepan and heat gently until melted. Bring to the boil, then pour the mixture into the flour, stirring constantly. Beat until the mixture is cool enough to handle. Add the chocolate chips and press the mixture evenly into a shallow 30 x 20-cm/12 x 8-inch rectangular baking tin.

Bake in the preheated oven for 30 minutes, or until golden brown. Cut into fingers and leave to cool in the tin.

579 Chocolate chip & cherry brownies

Replace the stem ginger with 40 g/1½ oz chopped glacé cherries. Sift the flour and spices into a bowl, omitting the ground ginger.

580 Carrot streusel brownies

115 g/4 oz butter, softened, plus extra
    for greasing
350 g/10½ oz light muscovado sugar
2 eggs, lightly beaten
1 tsp vanilla extract
175 g/6 oz plain flour
½ tsp bicarbonate of soda
½ tsp baking powder
85 g/3 oz sultanas

125 g/4½ oz carrots, finely grated
55 g/2 oz walnuts, chopped

STREUSEL TOPPING
40 g/1½ oz finely chopped walnuts
40 g/1½ oz dark muscovado sugar
15 g/½ oz plain flour
½ tsp ground cinnamon
15 g/½ oz butter, melted

Preheat the oven to 180°C/350°F/Gas Mark 4. Grease a shallow 30 x 20-cm/12 x 8-inch rectangular baking tin. Place the sugar and butter in a large bowl and beat together until light and fluffy, then beat in the eggs and vanilla extract. Sift the flour, bicarbonate of soda and baking powder into the mixture and fold in evenly. Stir in the sultanas, carrots and walnuts, then spread the mixture into the tin.

Place all the ingredients for the topping in a bowl and mix together to make a crumbly mixture, then sprinkle evenly over the cake mixture.

Bake in the preheated oven for 45–55 minutes, or until golden brown and firm to the touch. Cool in the tin, then cut into bars.

581 Hazelnut streusel brownies

Replace the sultanas and walnuts with raisins and chopped toasted hazelnuts, and the cinnamon with ground nutmeg.

175 g/6 oz butter,
plus extra for greasing
200 g/7 oz plain chocolate, broken
into pieces
200 g/7 oz granulated sugar
4 eggs, lightly beaten
2 tsp vanilla extract
1 tbsp stem ginger syrup
100 g/3½ oz plain flour
55 g/2 oz stem ginger in syrup,
chopped
25 g/1 oz chopped crystallized
ginger, to decorate

PORT CREAM
200 ml/7 fl oz ruby port
200 ml/7 fl oz double cream
1 tbsp icing sugar
1 tsp vanilla extract

Preheat the oven to 180°C/350°F/ Gas Mark 4. Grease a shallow 20-cm/8-inch round baking tin. Place the chocolate and butter in a saucepan and heat gently, stirring, until melted. Remove from the heat and stir in the sugar.

Beat the eggs, vanilla extract and ginger syrup into the chocolate mixture, stir in the flour and ginger and pour into the tin. Bake in the preheated oven for 30–35 minutes, or until just firm to the touch.

Meanwhile, to make the port cream, place the port in a pan and simmer over a medium–high heat until reduced to about 4 tablespoons. Leave to cool. Place the cream in a bowl and whip until beginning to thicken, then beat in the sugar, reduced port and vanilla extract, continuing to whip until soft peaks form.

Remove the brownies from the oven, cool for 2–3 minutes in the tin, then cut into 8 wedges. Place on serving plates and add a spoonful of port cream. Top with crystallized ginger and serve.

583 *Walnut & cherry brownies*

Replace the ginger syrup with maple syrup, omit the stem ginger and add 55 g/2 oz chopped walnuts. Decorate with 25 g/1 oz chopped glacé cherries.

584 *With brandy cream*

For a brandy cream, whip the cream until it starts to thicken, then beat in 2 tablespoons of icing sugar and 3 tablespoons of brandy. Whip to soft peaks.

585 White chocolate brownies

115 g/4 oz butter, plus extra for greasing
225 g/8 oz white chocolate
75 g/2¾ oz walnut pieces

2 eggs
115 g/4 oz soft light brown sugar
115 g/4 oz self-raising flour

Preheat the oven to 180°C/350°F/Gas Mark 4. Lightly grease an 18-cm/7-inch square baking tin. Coarsely chop 175 g/6 oz of the chocolate and all the walnuts. Place the remaining chocolate and the butter in a heatproof bowl, set the bowl over a saucepan of gently simmering water and heat until melted. Stir together, then cool slightly.

Place the eggs and sugar in a large bowl and whisk together, then beat in the cooled chocolate mixture until combined. Fold in the flour, chopped chocolate and walnuts, spoon the mixture into the tin and smooth the surface.

Bake in the preheated oven for about 30 minutes, or until just set and still a little soft in the centre. Cool in the tin, then cut into squares.

586 Milk chocolate & pistachio brownies

Replace the white chocolate with milk chocolate and the walnuts with chopped pistachio nuts.

587 Soured cream brownies

55 g/2 oz butter, plus extra for greasing
115 g/4 oz plain chocolate, broken
    into pieces
175 g/6 oz soft brown sugar
2 eggs
2 tbsp strong coffee, cooled
85 g/3 oz plain flour
½ tsp baking powder
pinch of salt

55 g/2 oz walnuts, chopped
mini chocolate balls, to decorate

FROSTING
115 g/4 oz plain chocolate, broken
    into pieces
150 ml/5 fl oz soured cream

Preheat the oven to 180°C/350°F/Gas Mark 4. Grease and line a 20-cm/8-inch square baking tin. Place the butter and chocolate in a saucepan and stir over a low heat until melted. Leave to cool.

Place the sugar and eggs in a large bowl and whisk together until pale and thick. Fold in the chocolate and coffee and mix well. Sift the flour, baking powder and salt into the mixture and fold in. Fold in the walnuts and pour into the tin. Bake in the preheated oven for 20–25 minutes, or until set. Leave to cool in the tin.

To make the frosting, melt the chocolate in a heatproof bowl set over a pan of simmering water. Stir in the soured cream and beat well. Spoon the topping over the brownies and leave to set. Cut into bars, remove from the tin and decorate with mini chocolate balls.

588 Yogurt-topped brownies

For the brownies, replace the plain chocolate with milk chocolate and the coffee with milk. For the frosting, replace the plain chocolate with milk chocolate and soured cream with whole milk natural yogurt. Add the yogurt after the melted chocolate has been taken off the heat.

175 g/6 oz butter, plus extra
for greasing
3 tbsp cocoa powder
200 g/7 oz caster sugar
2 eggs, lightly beaten
125 g/4½ oz plain flour

CHEESECAKE MIX
250 g/9 oz ricotta cheese
40 g/1½ oz caster sugar
1 egg

Preheat the oven to 180°C/350°F/
Gas Mark 4. Grease a 28 x 18-cm/
11 x 7-inch rectangular baking tin.
Place the butter in a saucepan and
heat gently until melted. Remove
from the heat and stir in the cocoa
and sugar. Beat in the eggs, add
the flour and stir to mix evenly.
Pour into the tin.

For the cheesecake mix, place
the ricotta, sugar and egg in a
bowl and beat together, then
drop teaspoonfuls of the mixture
over the chocolate mixture. Use a
palette knife to swirl the mixtures
together lightly.

Bake in the preheated oven for
40–45 minutes, or until just firm
to the touch. Leave to cool in the
tin, then cut into rectangles.

590 *Marbled creamy brownies*

*Add 40 g/1½ oz chopped walnuts to the brownie mix. Replace the ricotta
with cream cheese, and fold 40 g/1½ oz chocolate chips into the cheese mix.*

591 *Marbled chocolate orange brownies*

*Finely grate the rind of 1 orange and juice the orange. Add half the rind and
juice to the brownie mix with the eggs, and add the rest to the ricotta mix.*

592 Super mocha brownies

100 g/3½ oz butter, plus extra
    for greasing
150 g/5½ oz plain chocolate
1 tsp strong instant coffee
1 tsp vanilla extract

100 g/3½ oz ground almonds
175 g/6 oz caster sugar
4 eggs, separated
icing sugar, for dusting (optional)

Preheat the oven to 180°C/350°F/Gas Mark 4. Grease and line the base of a 20-cm/8-inch square baking tin. Place the butter and chocolate in a saucepan and stir over a low heat until melted. Leave to cool slightly, then stir in the coffee and vanilla. Add the almonds and sugar and mix until combined.

Place the egg yolks in a separate bowl and beat together lightly, then stir into the chocolate mixture.

Whisk the egg whites in a separate large bowl until stiff peaks form. Gently fold a large spoonful of the egg whites into the chocolate mixture, then fold in the remainder until completely incorporated and spoon the mixture into the tin.

Bake in the preheated oven for 35–40 minutes, or until risen and firm on top but still slightly gooey in the centre. Leave to cool in the tin, then turn out, remove the lining paper and cut into squares. Dust with sifted icing sugar before serving, if using.

593 Mocha & macadamia nut brownies

Replace the ground almonds with plain flour. Fold 40 g/1½ oz coarsely chopped macadamia nuts into the chocolate mixture before adding the egg whites.

594 Rocky road brownies

225 g/8 oz butter, melted, plus extra
    for greasing
100 g/3½ oz plain flour, plus extra
    for dusting
140 g/5 oz caster sugar
3 tbsp cocoa powder
½ tsp baking powder
2 eggs, lightly beaten
1 tsp vanilla extract
70 g/2½ oz glacé cherries, quartered
70 g/2½ oz blanched almonds,
    chopped
100 g/3½ oz marshmallows, chopped

FUDGE FROSTING
200 g/7 oz icing sugar
2 tbsp cocoa powder
3 tbsp evaporated milk
½ tsp vanilla extract

Preheat the oven to 160°C/325°F/Gas Mark 3. Grease and lightly flour a shallow 23-cm/9-inch square baking tin. Sift together the flour, sugar, cocoa and baking powder into a large bowl and make a well in the centre. Stir in the melted butter, eggs and vanilla extract and beat well. Stir in the cherries and almonds and pour into the tin.

Bake in the preheated oven for 35–40 minutes, or until just firm on top. Leave to cool in the tin.

To make the frosting, place all the ingredients in a large bowl and beat well until smooth. Spread the cooled brownies with the frosting, and sprinkle with marshmallows. Leave to set, then cut into squares.

Chocolate fudge brownies

85 g/3 oz butter, plus extra for greasing
200 g/7 oz low-fat soft cheese
½ tsp vanilla extract
225 g/8 oz caster sugar
2 eggs
3 tbsp cocoa powder
100 g/3½ oz self-raising flour
50 g/1¾ oz pecan nuts, chopped
pecan nut halves, to decorate (optional)

FUDGE ICING
55 g/2 oz butter
1 tbsp milk
75 g/2¾ oz icing sugar
2 tbsp cocoa powder

Preheat the oven to 180°C/350°F/Gas Mark 4. Lightly grease and line a shallow 20-cm/8-inch square cake tin.

Place the cheese, vanilla extract and 5 teaspoons of the sugar in a large bowl and beat together until smooth.

Place the eggs and remaining sugar in a separate bowl and beat together until light and fluffy. Place

the butter and cocoa in a small saucepan and heat gently, stirring until the butter melts and the mixture combines, then stir it into the egg mixture.

Fold in the flour and nuts, pour half of the batter into the tin and smooth the top. Carefully spread the cheese mixture over, then cover it with the remaining batter. Bake in the preheated oven

for 40–45 minutes. Leave to cool in the tin.

To make the icing, melt the butter with the milk in a pan. Stir in the icing sugar and cocoa. Spread the icing over the brownies and decorate with pecan nuts, if using. Leave to set, then cut into squares or rectangles.

596 *Nutty walnut fudge brownies*

Replace the pecan nuts in the brownies with 85 g/3 oz chopped walnuts and decorate with walnut halves.

597 *Blonde brownie hearts with raspberry sauce*

115 g/4 oz butter, plus extra for greasing
140 g/5 oz plain flour, plus extra for dusting
115 g/4 oz white chocolate
2 eggs, lightly beaten
150 g/5½ oz caster sugar
seeds from 1 vanilla pod
8 small squares plain chocolate

RASPBERRY SAUCE
250 g/9 oz raspberries, fresh or frozen (thawed)
2 tbsp amaretto
1 tbsp icing sugar

Preheat the oven to 180°C/350°F/Gas Mark 4. Grease and lightly flour 8 individual heart-shaped baking tins, each 150 ml/5 fl oz capacity. Place the white chocolate and butter in a saucepan and stir over a low heat until just melted. Remove from the heat.

Place the eggs, sugar and vanilla seeds in a bowl and whisk

together until smooth and thick. Fold in the flour, then stir in the chocolate mixture. Pour the mixture into the tins, adding a square of chocolate to the centre of each, without pressing down. Bake in the preheated oven for 20–25 minutes, or until just firm. Leave in the tins for 5 minutes.

To make the raspberry sauce, place half the raspberries, the amaretto and icing sugar in a food processor and process until

smooth. Transfer the mixture to a sieve placed on top of a bowl and rub through to remove the pips.

Run a knife around the edge of each heart to loosen from the tin and turn out onto serving plates. Spoon the raspberry sauce around, decorate with the remaining raspberries and serve.

598 *With strawberry sauce*

For a strawberry sauce, blend 185 g/6½ oz hulled strawberries, 2 tablespoons of orange flavoured liqueur and 1 tablespoon of icing sugar until smooth, then push through a sieve. Serve the brownies with extra strawberries.

599 Walnut & cinnamon blondies

115 g/4 oz butter, plus extra for greasing
225 g/8 oz soft light brown sugar
1 egg
1 egg yolk

140 g/5 oz self-raising flour
1 tsp ground cinnamon
85 g/3 oz coarsely chopped walnuts

Preheat the oven to 180°C/350°F/Gas Mark 4. Grease and line the base of a shallow 18-cm/7-inch square baking tin. Place the butter and sugar in a saucepan over a low heat and stir until the sugar has dissolved. Cook, stirring, for a further 1 minute. The mixture will bubble slightly, but do not let it boil. Leave to cool for 10 minutes.

Stir the egg and egg yolk into the mixture. Sift in the flour and cinnamon, add the nuts and stir until just blended, then pour the mixture into the tin and smooth the top.

Bake in the preheated oven for 20–25 minutes, or until springy in the centre and a skewer inserted into the middle of the cake comes out clean. Leave to cool in the tin for a few minutes, then run a knife around the edge of the cake to loosen it. Turn the cake out onto a wire rack and peel off the paper. Leave to cool completely, then cut into squares.

600 Apple & cinnamon blondies

Replace the walnuts with 1 dessert apple, peeled, cored and finely diced.

601 Butterfudge blondies

125 g/4½ oz butter, softened, plus extra
for greasing
200 g/7 oz soft light brown sugar
2 large eggs, lightly beaten
1 tsp vanilla extract
250 g/9 oz plain flour

1 tsp baking powder
125 g/4½ oz soft butter fudge, chopped
into small pieces
75 g/2¾ oz macadamia nuts, roughly
chopped
icing sugar, for dusting

Preheat the oven to 180°C/350°F/Gas Mark 4. Grease and line a shallow 20-cm/8-inch square baking tin.

Place the butter and sugar in a large bowl and whisk together until pale and creamy. Gradually whisk in the eggs and vanilla extract. Sift the flour and baking powder into the mixture and beat together until well mixed. Add the fudge pieces and chopped nuts and stir together until combined. Pour the mixture into the tin and smooth the surface.

Bake in the preheated oven for 40–45 minutes, or until risen and golden brown. Leave to cool in the tin, then dust with sifted icing sugar to decorate and cut into squares.

125 g/4½ oz butter, softened, plus extra
   for greasing
150 g/5½ oz full-fat cream cheese
100 g/3½ oz plain chocolate chips
200 g/7 oz soft light brown sugar

2 large eggs, lightly beaten
½ tsp vanilla extract
250 g/9 oz plain flour
1 tsp baking powder

Preheat the oven to 180°C/350°F/Gas Mark 4. Grease and line a shallow 20-cm/8-inch square baking tin. Place the cream cheese and chocolate chips in a large bowl and beat together until creamy.

Place the butter and sugar in a separate large bowl and whisk together until pale and creamy. Gradually whisk in the eggs and vanilla extract. Sift the flour and baking powder into the mixture and beat together until mixed. Place half of the mixture into the tin and smooth the surface.

Place half the cream cheese mixture in spoonfuls, spaced well apart, on top of the mixture in the tin. Flatten the spoonfuls slightly. Repeat the layers and then draw a knife through the mixture in a spiral. Bake in the oven for 40–45 minutes, or until risen and golden brown. Leave to cool in the tin, then cut into squares.

125 g/4½ oz butter, softened, plus extra
   for greasing
200 g/7 oz soft light brown sugar
2 large eggs, lightly beaten
250 g/9 oz plain flour

1 tsp baking powder
1 tsp ground ginger
4 pieces stem ginger, finely chopped
100 g/3½ oz plain chocolate chips
icing sugar, for dusting

Preheat the oven to 180°C/350°F/Gas Mark 4. Grease and line a shallow 20-cm/8-inch square baking tin.

Place the butter and sugar in a large bowl and whisk together until pale and creamy. Gradually whisk in the eggs. Sift the flour, baking powder and ground ginger into the mixture and beat together until mixed. Add the stem ginger and chocolate chips and stir together until well mixed. Spoon the mixture into the tin and smooth the surface.

Bake in the preheated oven for 40–45 minutes, or until risen and golden brown. Leave to cool in the tin, then dust with sifted icing sugar to decorate and cut into squares.

Cherry & coconut blondies

125 g/4½ oz butter, softened, plus extra
    for greasing
200 g/7 oz soft light brown sugar
2 large eggs, lightly beaten
1 tsp vanilla extract

250 g/9 oz plain flour
1 tsp baking powder
100 g/3½ oz glacé cherries, cut into
    quarters
85 g/3 oz desiccated coconut

Preheat the oven to 180°C/350°F/Gas Mark 4. Grease and line a
20-cm/8-inch square baking tin. Place the butter and sugar in a large
bowl and whisk together until pale and creamy. Gradually whisk in
the eggs and vanilla extract. Sift the flour and baking powder into the
mixture and beat together until well mixed. Add the chopped cherries
and 60 g/2¼ oz of the coconut and stir together until combined. Pour
the mixture into the tin and smooth the surface. Sprinkle the remaining
coconut over the top.

Bake in the preheated oven for 40–45 minutes, or until risen and
golden brown. Leave to cool in the tin, then cut into squares.

Strawberry & almond blondies

125 g/4½ oz butter, softened, plus extra
    for greasing
200 g/7 oz soft light brown sugar
2 large eggs, lightly beaten
½ tsp almond extract

250 g/9 oz plain flour
1 tsp baking powder
50 g/1¾ oz blanched almonds, chopped
100 g/3½ oz fresh small strawberries
25 g/1 oz flaked almonds

Preheat the oven to 180°C/350°F/Gas Mark 4. Grease and line a shallow
20-cm/8-inch square baking tin. Place the butter and sugar in a large
bowl and whisk together until pale and creamy. Gradually whisk the
eggs and almond extract into the mixture. Sift in the flour and baking
powder and beat together until mixed. Add the chopped almonds and
stir together until combined. Add the strawberries to the mixture and
fold in, then spoon the mixture into the tin and smooth the surface.
Scatter the flaked almonds over the top.

Bake in the preheated oven for 40–45 minutes, or until risen and
golden brown. Leave to cool in the tin, then cut into squares.

85 g/3 oz butter, plus extra for greasing
350 g/12 oz white chocolate
1 tsp vanilla extract
3 eggs, lightly beaten
140 g/5 oz light muscovado sugar
115 g/4 oz self-raising flour

85 g/3 oz macadamia nuts, roughly chopped
100 g/3½ oz ready-to-eat dried apricots, roughly chopped

Preheat the oven to 190°C/375°F/Gas Mark 5. Grease and line a shallow 28 x 18-cm/11 x 7-inch rectangular baking tin.

Chop half the chocolate into small chunks. Place the remaining chocolate and the butter in a small saucepan and stir over a very low heat until melted. Remove from the heat and stir in the vanilla extract.

Place the eggs and sugar in a large bowl and whisk together until pale and creamy. Beat in the melted chocolate mixture. Fold in the flour, then stir in the macadamia nuts, apricots and chopped chocolate. Spoon into the tin and smooth the top.

Bake in the preheated oven for 25–30 minutes, or until firm and golden brown. Leave to cool in the tin, then cut into triangles.

607 *Prune blondies*

Replace the apricots with ready-to-eat pitted prunes, roughly chopped, and the macadamia nuts with chopped hazelnuts.

608 *Date blondies*

Replace the apricots with ready-to-eat pitted dates, roughly chopped, and the macadamia nuts with chopped walnuts.

609 *Fig blondies*

Replace the apricots with chopped dried figs and the macadamia nuts with chopped almonds.

Apple & walnut blondies

125 g/4½ oz butter, softened, plus extra
    for greasing
200 g/7 oz soft light brown sugar
2 large eggs, lightly beaten
1 tsp vanilla extract
250 g/9 oz plain flour

1 tsp baking powder
1 small cooking apple, peeled, cored
    and finely chopped.
100 g/3½ oz walnut halves, roughly
    chopped
icing sugar, for dusting

Preheat the oven to 180°C/350°F/Gas Mark 4. Grease and line a shallow
20-cm/8-inch square baking tin. Place the butter and sugar in a large
bowl and whisk together until pale and creamy. Gradually whisk in
the eggs and vanilla extract. Sift the flour and baking powder into the
mixture and beat together until well mixed. Add the chopped apple and
walnuts to the mixture and stir together until well mixed. Spoon the
mixture into the tin and smooth the surface.

Bake in the preheated oven for 40–45 minutes, or until risen and
golden brown. Leave to cool in the tin, then dust with sifted icing sugar
to decorate and cut into squares.

---

611 *Bursting cranberry blondies*

125 g/4½ oz butter, softened, plus extra
    for greasing
200 g/7 oz soft light brown sugar
2 large eggs, lightly beaten
1 tsp vanilla extract

250 g/9 oz plain flour
1 tsp baking powder
100 g/3½ oz dried or frozen cranberries
icing sugar, for dusting

Preheat the oven to 180°C/350°F/
Gas Mark 4. Grease and line a
shallow 20-cm/8-inch square
baking tin.

Place the butter and sugar in
a large bowl and whisk together
until pale and creamy. Gradually
whisk the eggs and vanilla into the
mixture.

Sift in the flour and baking
powder and beat together until well
mixed. Add the cranberries and stir
together until combined. Spoon
the mixture into the tin and smooth

the surface. Bake in the preheated
oven for 40–45 minutes, or until
risen and golden brown.

Leave the blondies to cool in
the tin, then dust them with sifted

icing sugar to decorate and cut
into squares before serving.

612 *Bursting berry blondies*

*Use dried cranberries and reduce the quantity to 50 g/1¾ oz, then add
50 g/1¾ oz dried blueberries to the mixture.*

613 *Cranberry & chocolate blondies*

*Use dried cranberries and reduce the quantity to 75 g/2¾ oz, then add
75 g/2¾ oz white chocolate chips to the mixture.*

Nutty flapjacks

115 g/4 oz butter, plus extra for greasing
200 g/7 oz rolled oats
115 g/4 oz chopped hazelnuts

55 g/2 oz plain flour
2 tbsp golden syrup
85 g/3 oz light muscovado sugar

Preheat the oven to 180°C/350°F/ Gas Mark 4. Grease a 23-cm/ 9-inch square cake tin. Place the oats, hazelnuts and flour in a large bowl and stir together.

Place the butter, golden syrup and sugar in a saucepan over a low heat and stir until melted. Pour onto the dry ingredients and mix well. Spoon the mixture into the tin and smooth the top.

Bake in the preheated oven for 20–25 minutes, or until golden and firm to the touch. Cut into 16 pieces and leave to cool in the tin until cold.

615 Chocolate-dipped nutty flapjacks

Melt 185 g/6½ oz plain or milk chocolate, broken into squares, in a heatproof bowl set over a saucepan of gently simmering water. Line a baking sheet with baking paper. Dip the flapjacks in the chocolate until half covered and place on the lined baking sheet. Leave to set before serving.

616 Hazelnut chocolate flapjacks

115 g/4 oz butter, plus extra for greasing
200 g/7 oz rolled oats
55 g/2 oz hazelnuts, lightly toasted and
    chopped
55 g/2 oz plain flour

85 g/3 oz light muscovado sugar
2 tbsp golden syrup
55 g/2 oz plain chocolate chips

Preheat the oven to 180°C/350°F/Gas Mark 4. Grease a shallow 23-cm/9-inch square baking tin. Place the oats, hazelnuts and flour in a large bowl and mix together.

Place the butter, sugar and golden syrup in a large saucepan and heat gently until the sugar has dissolved. Pour in the dry ingredients and mix well. Stir in the chocolate chips, then spoon the mixture into the tin.

Bake in the preheated oven for 20–25 minutes, or until golden brown and firm to the touch. Mark into 12 triangles and leave to cool completely in the tin.

sunflower oil, for greasing
175 g/6 oz butter or margarine
85 g/3 oz demerara sugar
55 g/2 oz clear honey
140 g/5 oz dried apricots, chopped
2 tsp sesame seeds
225 g/8 oz rolled oats

Preheat the oven to 180°C/350°F/Gas Mark 4. Very lightly grease a shallow 26 x 17-cm/10½ x 6½-inch rectangular baking tin. Place the butter, sugar and honey in a small saucepan over a low heat and heat until the ingredients have melted together. Stir in the apricots, sesame seeds and oats. Spoon the mixture into the tin and lightly smooth the top.

Bake in the preheated oven for 20–25 minutes, or until golden brown. Cut into 10 bars and leave to cool completely in the tin.

618 *Date flapjacks*

Replace the apricots with chopped pitted dates and omit the sesame seeds.

619 *Cranberry flapjacks*

Replace the apricots with chopped dried cranberries and the sesame seeds with sunflower seeds.

620 *Figgy flapjacks*

Replace the apricots with chopped dried figs and the sesame seeds with 25g/1oz chopped almonds or walnuts.

Fruity flapjacks

sunflower oil, for greasing
140 g/5 oz rolled oats
115 g/4 oz demerara sugar

85 g/3 oz raisins
115 g/4 oz butter, melted

Preheat the oven to 190°C/375°F/Gas Mark 5. Lightly grease a shallow 28 x 18-cm/11 x 7-inch rectangular baking tin. Place the oats, sugar, raisins and butter in a large bowl and stir well to combine. Spoon the oat mixture into the tin and press down firmly with the back of the spoon.

Bake in the preheated oven for 15–20 minutes, or until golden brown. Mark into 14 bars. Leave to cool in the tin for 10 minutes, then transfer the bars to a wire rack to cool completely.

Chocolate chip flapjacks

115 g/4 oz butter, plus extra for greasing
60 g/2¼ oz caster sugar
1 tbsp golden syrup

350 g/12 oz rolled oats
85 g/3 oz plain chocolate chips
85 g/3 oz sultanas

Preheat the oven to 180°C/350°F/Gas Mark 4. Lightly grease a shallow 20-cm/8-inch square cake tin. Place the butter, sugar and golden syrup in a saucepan and cook over a low heat, stirring constantly, until the butter and sugar melt and the mixture is well combined.

Remove the saucepan from the heat and stir in the rolled oats until they are well coated. Add the chocolate chips and sultanas and mix well to combine. Spoon into the tin and press down well.

Bake in the preheated oven for 30 minutes. Leave to cool slightly, then mark into squares. When almost cold, cut into bars and transfer to a wire rack to cool completely.

Panforte di siena

butter, for greasing
100 g/3½ oz blanched almonds
100 g/3½ oz blanched hazelnuts
50 g/1¾ oz dried ready-to-eat figs
50 g/1¾ oz walnut halves
100 g/3½ oz chopped mixed candied peel
50 g/1¾ oz plain flour
50 g/1¾ oz cocoa powder

⅛ tsp ground white pepper
¼ tsp ground mace
¼ tsp ground cloves
¼ tsp ground coriander
1 tsp ground cinnamon
100 g/3½ oz caster sugar
100 g/3½ oz clear honey
icing sugar, to dredge

Preheat the oven to 160°C/325°F/ Gas Mark 3. Grease a 20-cm/ 8-inch loose-bottomed cake tin and line the base with rice paper. Spread the almonds and hazelnuts on a baking tray and bake in the preheated oven for 5–10 minutes, until lightly toasted. Leave to cool.

Using scissors, snip the figs into small pieces and put in a large bowl. Roughly chop all the nuts, then add to the figs with the candied peel.

Sift the flour, cocoa, pepper, mace, cloves, coriander and cinnamon into the fruit and nuts and stir together until well mixed.

Put the sugar and honey into a saucepan and heat gently until the sugar has dissolved. Bring to the boil and boil, without stirring, until a little of the mixture, when dropped into a cup of cold water,

forms a ball between your fingers. If you have a sugar thermometer, it should reach 116°C/241°F (soft ball stage). Immediately remove the pan from the heat and quickly stir in the dry ingredients until mixed together. Spoon the mixture into the tin, press down with the back of a wet spoon and smooth the surface.

Bake in the preheated oven for 30–40 minutes, or until firm. Leave to cool in the tin. When cold, dredge with sifted icing sugar and cut into wedges to serve.

Torrone molle

175 g/6 oz butter, plus extra for greasing
175 g/6 oz butter biscuits
200 g/7 oz plain chocolate, broken into pieces
50 g/1¾ oz blanched almonds, chopped
50 g/1¾ oz blanched hazelnuts, chopped

50 g/1¾ oz walnut halves, chopped
175 g/6 oz caster sugar
3 tbsp water
1 large egg, lightly beaten
2 tbsp brandy

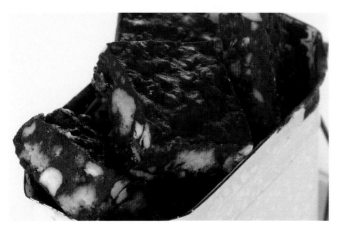

Grease and line a shallow 23-cm/9-inch square tin. Place the biscuits in a strong polythene bag and, using a wooden rolling pin, roughly crush into small pieces.

Place the butter and chocolate in a saucepan and stir over a low heat until melted. Remove from the heat and stir until smooth. Add the chopped nuts and stir well together.

Place the sugar in a separate saucepan, add the water and heat gently, stirring all the time, until the sugar dissolves. Bring to the boil and boil until the mixture starts to turn pale golden brown. Immediately pour the syrup into the chocolate mixture and mix together until combined.

Add the egg and brandy to the mixture and mix together, then add the crushed biscuits and stir until the ingredients are well mixed and coated in chocolate. Spoon the mixture into the tin, press down with the back of a wet spoon and smooth the surface. Leave to cool, then chill in the refrigerator for at least 2 hours, or until set.

When the mixture has set, remove from the tin and, using a hot, sharp knife, cut into 16 slices to serve.

100 g/3½ oz butter, plus extra for greasing	TOPPING
200 g/7 oz digestive biscuits	90 g/3¼ oz butter
50 g/1¾ oz caster sugar	300 g/10½ oz icing sugar
4 tbsp cocoa powder	2 tbsp milk
1 large egg	200 g/7 oz plain chocolate, broken
70 g/2½ oz macadamia nuts, chopped	into pieces
90 g/3¼ oz desiccated coconut	

Grease and line a shallow 23-cm/9-inch square tin. Place the biscuits in a strong polythene bag and, using a rolling pin, crush the biscuits into small pieces, then place in a large bowl.

Place the butter, sugar, cocoa and egg in a large heatproof bowl, set the bowl over a saucepan of gently simmering water and heat, whisking until the mixture thickens slightly. Remove from the heat.

Add the nuts and coconut to the biscuits and stir together. Add the chocolate custard and mix together, then spoon into the tin and press down with the back of a spoon. Chill in the refrigerator for 1 hour.

To make the topping, place 75 g/2¾ oz of the butter in a large bowl and beat until creamy. Sift in the icing sugar. Add the milk and beat together until smooth. Spread the mixture over the base of the tin.

Place the chocolate and the remaining butter in a heatproof bowl, set the bowl over a saucepan of gently simmering water and heat gently until the chocolate has melted. Remove from the heat and stir until smooth. Leave to cool for 5 minutes, then pour into the tin and spread to coat the top. Leave to set for about 1 hour.

When the chocolate has set, chill in the refrigerator for at least 3 hours. Before serving, remove from the tin and, using a hot, sharp knife, cut into 16 slices.

25 g/1 oz butter, plus extra for greasing	70 g/2½ oz cornmeal
175 g/6 oz plain chocolate, broken into pieces	finely grated rind of 1 lemon
	2 tsp amaretto
350 g/12 oz self-raising flour, plus extra for dusting	1 egg, lightly beaten
	115 g/4 oz pistachio nuts, roughly chopped
1½ tsp baking powder	
85 g/3 oz caster sugar	2 tbsp icing sugar, for dusting

Preheat the oven to 160°C/325°F/Gas Mark 3. Grease a baking sheet. Place the butter and chocolate in a saucepan and stir over a low heat until melted and smooth. Leave to cool slightly.

Sift the flour and baking powder into a large bowl and mix in the sugar, cornmeal, lemon rind, amaretto, egg and pistachio nuts. Stir in the chocolate mixture and mix to form a soft dough.

Lightly dust your hands with flour, divide the dough in half and shape each piece into a 28-cm/11-inch long cylinder. Transfer the cylinders to the baking sheet and flatten with the palm of your hand, to about 2 cm/¾ inch thick.

Bake in the preheated oven for about 20 minutes, or until firm to the touch. Leave to cool and don't turn the oven off. When cool, place the baked dough on a chopping board cut into thin diagonal slices. Return them to the baking sheet and bake for a further 10 minutes, or until crisp. Transfer the bars to a wire rack to cool, then dust lightly with sifted icing sugar.

627 Treasure chest gold bars

85 g/3 oz butter, plus extra
for greasing
115 g/4 oz plain chocolate, broken
into pieces
55 g/2 oz caster sugar
3 large eggs, separated
55 g/2 oz self-raising flour
25 g/1 oz ground almonds

TO DECORATE
15 g/½ oz butter
4 tbsp milk
3 tbsp cocoa powder
225 g/8 oz icing sugar
½ quantity buttercream icing
(page 10)
chocolate coins
gold sugar-coated almonds
gold dragées

Preheat the oven to 180°C/350°F/ Gas Mark 4. Lightly grease and line a 18-cm/7-inch square cake tin. Place the chocolate in a heatproof bowl, set the bowl over a saucepan of gently simmering water and heat until melted. Leave to cool.

Place the butter and sugar in a large bowl and beat together until light and fluffy, then beat in the melted chocolate. Beat in the egg yolks, 1 at a time.

Place the egg whites in a separate bowl and whisk until stiff peaks form, then fold half the egg whites into the chocolate mixture. Fold in the flour and ground almonds before folding in the remaining egg white, until just combined. Pour into the tin.

Bake in the preheated oven for 25 minutes, or until springy to the touch. Leave to cool in the tin for 5 minutes, then transfer to a wire rack to cool completely. Cut the cake into 10 bars, then return the bars to the wire rack and place over a tray.

To decorate, melt the butter in the milk over a low heat, then stir in the cocoa and beat until smooth. Whisk in the icing sugar until smooth. Leave to cool slightly, then spread the icing over the chocolate bars and leave to set.

Pipe a line of buttercream down the centre of the bars and decorate with chocolate coins, sugar almonds and gold dragées. Remember to remove the foil from the coins before eating!

628 Chocolate peppermint bars

55 g/2 oz butter, plus extra
for greasing
55 g/2 oz caster sugar
115 g/4 oz plain flour
175 g/6 oz icing sugar
1–2 tbsp warm water
½ tsp peppermint extract
2 tsp green food colouring (optional)
175 g/6 oz plain chocolate, broken
into pieces

Preheat the oven to 180°C/350°F/ Gas Mark 4. Grease and line a shallow 30 x 20-cm/12 x 8-inch baking tin. Place the butter and sugar in a large bowl and beat together until light and fluffy. Stir in the flour until the mixture binds together.

Knead the mixture to form a smooth dough, then press into the tin and prick the surface all over with a fork. Bake in the preheated oven for 10–15 minutes, or until lightly browned and just firm to the touch. Leave to cool in the tin.

Sift the icing sugar into a bowl. Gradually add the water, then add the peppermint extract and food colouring, if using. Spread the icing over the base, then leave to set.

Place the chocolate in a heatproof bowl, set the bowl over a saucepan of gently simmering water and heat until melted. Spread the chocolate over the icing, then leave to set. Cut into slices to serve.

125 g/4½ oz butter, plus extra
  for greasing
225 g/8 oz golden caster sugar
2 eggs, lightly beaten
finely grated rind of 1 orange
3 tbsp orange juice
150 ml/5 fl oz soured cream
140 g/5 oz self-raising flour

85 g/3 oz desiccated coconut
toasted shredded coconut, to decorate

FROSTING
1 egg white
200 g/7 oz icing sugar
85 g/3 oz desiccated coconut
about 1 tbsp orange juice

Preheat the oven to 180°C/350°F/Gas Mark 4. Grease a 23-cm/9-inch square cake tin and line the base with baking paper. Place the butter and sugar in a large bowl and beat together until light and fluffy, then gradually beat in the eggs. Stir in the orange rind, orange juice and soured cream. Fold in the flour and desiccated coconut evenly, then spoon the mixture into the cake tin and smooth the surface.

Bake in the preheated oven for 35–40 minutes, or until risen and firm to the touch. Leave to cool in the tin for 10 minutes, then turn out and finish cooling on a wire rack.

To make the frosting, place the egg white in a bowl and beat lightly, just enough to break it up. Stir in the icing sugar and desiccated coconut and add enough orange juice to mix to a thick paste. Spread over the top of the cake, sprinkle with toasted shredded coconut, then leave to set before slicing into bars.

630 *Coconut & cherry bars*

Omit the orange rind and replace the orange juice with milk. Add 40 g/ 1½ oz quartered glacé cherries to the cake mixture with the coconut.

631 *Coconut & lime bars*

Replace the orange juice and rind with lime juice and rind.

632 Rocky road bars

175 g/6 oz milk or plain chocolate
55 g/2 oz butter
100 g/3½ oz shortcake biscuits, broken
  into pieces

85 g/3 oz mini marshmallows
85 g/3 oz walnuts or peanuts

Break the chocolate into squares and place in a heatproof bowl, then set the bowl over a saucepan of gently simmering water and heat until melted. Add the butter and stir until melted and combined. Leave to cool slightly. Stir the broken biscuits, marshmallows and nuts into the chocolate mixture.

Line an 18-cm/7-inch cake tin with baking paper and pour in the chocolate mixture, pressing down with the back of a spoon. Chill in the refrigerator for at least 2 hours, or until firm. Carefully turn out of the tin and cut into 8 pieces.

633 Nutty granola squares

115 g/4 oz butter, plus extra for greasing
4 tbsp clear honey
25 g/1 oz caster sugar
250 g/9 oz rolled oats
25 g/1 oz dried cranberries

25 g/1 oz pitted dried dates, chopped
25 g/1 oz hazelnuts, chopped
70 g/2½ oz flaked almonds

Preheat the oven to 375°F/190°C/Gas Mark 5. Grease a 20-cm/8-inch square baking tin. Place the butter, honey and sugar in a saucepan and stir together over a low heat until the butter is melted. Add the remaining ingredients and mix thoroughly. Spoon the mixture into the tin and press down well.

Bake in the preheated oven for 20–30 minutes, or until golden brown. Leave to cool in the tin. When cold, cut into 16 squares to serve.

75 g/2¾ oz butter or margarine, plus
   extra for greasing
60 g/2¼ oz soft light brown sugar
140 g/5 oz plain flour
40 g/1½ oz rolled oats

CARAMEL FILLING
175 g/6 oz butter
115 g/4 oz soft light brown sugar
225 ml/8 fl oz condensed milk

TOPPING
100 g/3½ oz plain chocolate, broken
   into pieces
25 g/1 oz white chocolate, broken into
   pieces (optional)

Preheat the oven to 180°C/350°F/Gas Mark 4 and grease a shallow 20-cm/8-inch square cake tin. Place the butter and sugar in a bowl and beat together until light and fluffy. Beat in the flour and the oats, then use your fingertips to bring the mixture together, if necessary, and press the mixture into the base of the tin.

Bake in the preheated oven for 25 minutes, or until just golden and firm. Leave to cool in the tin.

To make the caramel filling, place all the ingredients in a saucepan and heat gently, stirring until the sugar has dissolved. Bring slowly to the boil over a very low heat and boil very gently for 3–4 minutes, stirring constantly, until thickened. Pour the caramel filling over the oat layer in the tin and leave to set.

Place the plain chocolate in a heatproof bowl, set the bowl over a pan of simmering water and heat until melted, then spread the chocolate over the caramel. If using the white chocolate, melt it in a heatproof bowl set over a pan of gently simmering water, then pipe lines of white chocolate over the plain chocolate. Using a cocktail stick, feather the white chocolate into the plain chocolate. Leave to set, then cut into squares to serve.

115 g/4 oz butter, plus extra for greasing
115 g/4 oz macadamia nuts
280 g/10 oz plain flour
175 g/6 oz soft light brown sugar

TOPPING
115 g/4 oz butter
100 g/3½ oz soft light brown sugar
200 g/7 oz milk chocolate chips

Preheat the oven to 180°C/350°F/Gas Mark 4. Grease a shallow 30 x 20-cm/12 x 8-inch rectangular baking tin. Coarsely chop the macadamia nuts. To make the base, place the flour, sugar and butter in a large bowl and rub together until the mixture resembles fine breadcrumbs. Press the mixture into the base of the tin and sprinkle over the macadamia nuts.

To make the topping, place the butter and sugar in a saucepan and, stirring constantly, slowly bring the mixture to the boil. Boil for 1 minute, stirring constantly, then carefully pour the mixture over the macadamia nuts.

Bake in the preheated oven for about 20 minutes, or until the caramel topping is bubbling. Remove from the oven and immediately sprinkle the chocolate chips evenly on top. Leave to cool for 2–3 minutes, or until the chocolate chips start to melt then, using the blade of a knife, swirl the chocolate over the top. Leave to cool in the tin, then cut into squares to serve.

636 Chocolate peanut butter squares

225 g/8 oz butter, plus extra for greasing
300 g/10½ oz milk chocolate
350 g/12 oz plain flour
1 tsp baking powder
350 g/12 oz soft light brown sugar

175 g/6 oz rolled oats
70 g/2½ oz chopped mixed nuts
1 egg, lightly beaten
400 g/14 oz condensed milk
70 g/2½ oz crunchy peanut butter

Preheat the oven to 180°C/350°F/Gas Mark 4. Grease a shallow 30 x 20-cm/12 x 8-inch rectangular baking tin. Finely chop the chocolate. Sift the flour and baking powder into a large bowl, add the butter and rub it in until the mixture resembles breadcrumbs. Stir in the sugar, oats and chopped nuts. Place a quarter of the mixture into a bowl and stir in the chopped chocolate. Set aside.

Stir the egg into the remaining mixture, then press into the base of the tin. Bake the base in the preheated oven for 15 minutes.

Meanwhile, place the condensed milk and peanut butter in a bowl and mix together. Pour the mixture over the base and spread evenly, then sprinkle the reserved chocolate mixture on top and press down lightly. Return to the oven and bake for a further 20 minutes, or until golden brown. Leave to cool in the tin, then cut into squares.

637 Coconut paradise slices

MAKES 16

100 g/3½ oz butter, plus extra for
  greasing
200 g/7 oz plain chocolate, broken into
  pieces
200 g/7 oz caster sugar

2 large eggs, lightly beaten
200 g/7 oz desiccated coconut
100 g/3½ oz sultanas
100 g/3½ oz glacé cherries

Grease and line a 23-cm/9-inch square baking tin. Place the chocolate in a heatproof bowl, set the bowl over a saucepan of gently simmering water and heat until melted. Remove from the heat and stir until smooth. Pour into the tin and leave to set for about 1 hour.

Preheat the oven to 180°C/350°F/Gas Mark 4. Place the butter and sugar in a large bowl and whisk together until pale and creamy. Gradually whisk in the eggs, then add the coconut, sultanas and glacé cherries and stir together until combined. Spoon the mixture into the tin on top of the chocolate and spread out evenly.

Bake in the preheated oven for 30–35 minutes, or until golden brown. Leave to cool in the tin, then turn out and cut into 16 slices to serve.

638 *Sticky pecan pie slices*

115 g/4 oz butter, plus extra for greasing
175 g/6 oz plain flour
130 g/4¾ oz soft light brown sugar
2 large eggs
50 g/1¾ oz pecan nuts, chopped into small pieces
175 g/6 oz golden syrup
½ tsp vanilla extract

Preheat the oven to 190°C/375°F/Gas Mark 5. Grease and line a shallow 23-cm/9-inch square baking tin. Grease the paper. Place 25 g/1 oz of the butter in a saucepan and heat gently until melted. Leave to cool slightly.

Place the flour and remaining butter, cut into cubes, in a large bowl and rub the butter in with your fingertips until the mixture resembles fine breadcrumbs. Stir in 40 g/1½ oz of the sugar, then spoon the mixture into the tin and press down firmly with the back of a spoon. Bake in the preheated oven for 20 minutes.

Meanwhile, place the eggs in a large bowl and beat lightly. Add the remaining sugar, the pecan nuts, melted butter, golden syrup and vanilla extract and stir together until combined. Pour the mixture over the base of the tin and bake in the oven for a further 15–20 minutes, or until firm to the touch and golden brown. Remove from the tin and leave to cool. When cold, cut into 10 slices to serve.

639 *Chocolate pecan pie slices*

Add 40 g/1½ oz plain chocolate chips to the mixture with the pecan nuts.

640 *Almond slices*

115 g/4 oz butter, plus extra for greasing
60 g/2¼ oz ground almonds
140 g/5 oz dried milk powder
200 g/7 oz granulated sugar
½ tsp saffron threads
3 eggs, lightly beaten
1 tbsp flaked almonds

Preheat the oven to 160°C/325°F/Gas Mark 3. Grease a shallow 20-cm/8-inch square baking tin. Place the ground almonds, dried milk powder, sugar and saffron in a large bowl and stir to mix well.

Place the butter in a small saucepan and melt over a low heat. Pour the melted butter over the dry ingredients and mix until thoroughly combined. Add the eggs to the mixture and stir to blend well.

Spread the mixture evenly in the tin and sprinkle with the flaked almonds. Bake in the preheated oven for 45 minutes, or until a skewer inserted into the centre comes out clean.

Cut into triangles or slices and serve hot or cold.

641 *Hazelnut slices*

Replace the ground almonds with ground toasted hazelnuts. Sprinkle the top with finely chopped toasted hazelnuts.

225 g/8 oz plain flour
1 tsp baking powder
100 g/3½ oz caster sugar
85 g/3 oz soft light brown sugar
225 g/8 oz butter

150 g/5½ oz rolled oats
225 g/8 oz strawberry jam
100 g/3½ oz plain chocolate chips
25 g/1 oz flaked almonds

Preheat the oven to 190°C/375°F/Gas Mark 5. Line a 30 x 20-cm/
12 x 8-inch rectangular baking tin. Sift the flour and baking powder
into a large bowl, add the sugars and mix well. Add the butter and rub
it in with your fingertips until the mixture resembles breadcrumbs. Stir
in the oats, then press three quarters of the mixture into the base of the
tin. Bake in the preheated oven for 10 minutes.

Spread the jam over the cooked base and sprinkle over the chocolate
chips. Place the remaining flour mixture and the almonds in a bowl and
mix together, then sprinkle evenly over the chocolate chips and press
down gently. Bake for a further 20–25 minutes, or until golden brown.
Leave to cool in the tin, then cut into slices to serve.

643 *Apricot & chocolate slices*

Replace the strawberry jam with apricot jam.

644 *Raspberry oat slices*

Add 1 teaspoon of almond extract with the butter. Replace the strawberry
jam with raspberry jam. Omit the chocolate chips and increase the flaked
almonds to 50 g/1¾ oz.

Chocolate cheesecake slices

85 g/3 oz butter, plus extra for greasing
200 g/7 oz chocolate digestive biscuits
400 g/14 oz full-fat cream cheese
125 g/4½ oz caster sugar
175 ml/6 fl oz soured cream

3 large eggs
½ tsp vanilla extract
50 g/1¾ oz plain flour
75 g/2¾ oz plain chocolate, broken
    into pieces

Preheat the oven to 160°C/325°F/Gas Mark 3. Grease and line a shallow 23-cm/9-inch square baking tin. Place the biscuits in a strong polythene bag and, using a rolling pin, crush into small pieces. Place the butter in a saucepan and heat gently until melted. Remove from the heat, add the crushed biscuits and mix together. Spoon the mixture into the tin, press down firmly with the back of a spoon and leave to chill in the refrigerator.

Meanwhile, place the cream cheese, sugar, soured cream, eggs and vanilla extract in a large bowl and whisk together until smooth. Add the flour and whisk together. Pour the mixture over the biscuits in the tin.

Bake in the preheated oven for about 40 minutes, or until set but not browned. Cool in the tin, then chill for at least 3 hours.

When ready to decorate, remove the cheesecake from the tin. Place the chocolate in a heatproof bowl, set the bowl over a saucepan of gently simmering water and heat until melted. Remove from the heat and stir until smooth. Using a teaspoon, drizzle the chocolate over the top of the cheesecake, backwards and forwards in a zig-zag design. Leave to set for 1 hour. Before serving, use a hot, sharp knife to cut into 16 bars.

Chocolate marshmallow fingers

350 g/12 oz digestive biscuits
125 g/4½ oz plain chocolate, broken
    into pieces
225 g/8 oz butter
25 g/1 oz caster sugar

2 tbsp cocoa powder
2 tbsp clear honey
55 g/2 oz mini marshmallows
100 g/3½ oz white chocolate chips

Place the digestive biscuits in a polythene bag and, using a rolling pin, crush into small pieces. Place the chocolate, butter, sugar, cocoa and honey in a saucepan and heat gently until melted. Remove from the heat and leave to cool slightly.

Stir the crushed biscuits into the chocolate mixture until well mixed. Add the marshmallows and mix well, then stir in the chocolate chips. Spoon the mixture into a 20-cm/8-inch square baking tin and lightly smooth the top. Chill in the refrigerator for 2–3 hours, or until set. Cut into fingers before serving.

175 g/6 oz plain chocolate, broken into squares

55 g/2 oz butter

2 tbsp golden syrup

115 g/4 oz digestive biscuits, broken into small pieces

175 g/6 oz mixed dried fruit

55 g/2 oz glacé cherries

Line an 18-cm/7-inch cake tin with baking paper and pour in the chocolate mixture, pressing down well with the back of a spoon. Chill for 2 hours, or until firm. Cut into 14 fingers to serve.

Place the chocolate in a heatproof bowl, set the bowl over a saucepan of gently simmering water and heat until melted. Add the butter and golden syrup and stir until combined. Remove from the heat. Stir the biscuits into the chocolate along with the mixed fruit and cherries.

648 *Chocolate fruit & nut bar*

Melt the chocolate, butter and syrup as before. Stir in the biscuits and add 115 g/4 oz sultanas and 115 g/4 oz chopped pecan nuts. Chill until set.

Chocolate caramel shortbread

115 g/4 oz butter, plus extra for greasing
175 g/6 oz plain flour
55 g/2 oz caster sugar

FILLING AND TOPPING
175 g/6 oz butter
115 g/4 oz caster sugar
3 tbsp golden syrup
400 g/14 oz canned condensed milk
200 g/7 oz plain chocolate, broken
    into pieces

Preheat the oven to 180°C/350°F/Gas Mark 4. Grease and line the base of a shallow 23-cm/9-inch square cake tin. Place the butter, flour and sugar in a food processor and process until it begins to bind together. Press the mixture into the tin and smooth the top. Bake in the preheated oven for 20–25 minutes, or until golden brown.

Meanwhile, to make the filling, place the butter, sugar, golden syrup and condensed milk in a saucepan and heat gently until the sugar has dissolved. Bring to the boil, then reduce the heat and simmer for 6–8 minutes, stirring, until the mixture becomes very thick. Pour over the shortbread base and chill in the refrigerator until firm.

To make the topping, place the chocolate in a heatproof bowl set over a pan of simmering water and heat until melted. Cool, then spread over the caramel. Chill until set, then cut into 12 pieces to serve.

No-cook chocolate & raisin biscuit cakes

100 g/3½ oz butter
25 g/1 oz cocoa powder
200 g/7 oz digestive biscuits, crushed
85 g/3 oz raisins or dried cranberries

1 egg, lightly beaten
125 g/4 oz milk chocolate, broken
    into squares

Line a 24-cm/9½-inch square baking tin with foil or baking paper. Place the butter in a saucepan and heat gently until melted. Stir in the cocoa powder, then remove from the heat and add the biscuits and dried fruit and stir well.

Add the egg and mix again until thoroughly mixed, then tip the mixture into the baking tin and press down with the back of a spoon.

Place the chocolate in a heatproof bowl, set the bowl over a pan of gently simmering water and heat until melted. Spread the chocolate evenly over the top of the cake and leave in a cool place to set. Cut into squares to serve.

Note: this recipe contains raw egg.

Moreish Muffins

651 Blueberry muffins

6 tbsp sunflower oil or 85 g/3 oz butter, melted and cooled, plus extra for greasing
280 g/10 oz plain flour
1 tbsp baking powder
pinch of salt
115 g/4 oz soft light brown sugar
150 g/5½ oz frozen blueberries
2 eggs
250 ml/9 fl oz milk
1 tsp vanilla extract
finely grated rind of 1 lemon

Preheat the oven to 200°C/400°F/Gas Mark 6. Grease a 12-hole muffin tin. Sift together the flour, baking powder and salt into a large bowl. Stir in the sugar and blueberries.

Place the eggs in a large jug or bowl and beat lightly, then beat in the milk, oil, vanilla extract and lemon rind. Make a well in the centre of the dry ingredients and pour in the beaten liquid ingredients. Stir until just combined; do not overmix. Spoon the mixture into the muffin tin.

Bake in the preheated oven for 20 minutes, or until well risen, golden brown and firm to the touch. Leave to cool in the tin for 5 minutes then serve warm or transfer to a wire rack to cool completely.

652 With white chocolate topping

Rub 40 g/1½ oz butter into 50 g/1¾ oz plain flour until the mixture resembles breadcrumbs, then stir in 2 tablespoons of caster sugar, 2 tablespoons of dried blueberries and 50 g/1¾ oz grated white chocolate and scatter over the muffins before baking.

653 Blackberry & apple muffins

6 tbsp sunflower oil or 85 g/3 oz butter, melted and cooled, plus extra for greasing
280 g/10 oz plain flour
1 tbsp baking powder
pinch of salt
115 g/4 oz soft light brown sugar
250 g/9 oz eating apples
2 eggs
250 ml/9 fl oz buttermilk
1 tsp vanilla extract
150 g/5½ oz frozen blackberries
40 g/1½ oz demerara sugar

Preheat the oven to 200°C/400°F/Gas Mark 6. Grease a 12-hole muffin tin. Sift together the flour, baking powder and salt into a large bowl. Stir in the brown sugar. Peel, core and finely chop the apple. Add to the flour mixture and stir together.

Place the eggs in a large jug or bowl and beat lightly, then beat in the buttermilk, oil and vanilla extract. Make a well in the centre of the dry ingredients, pour in the beaten liquid ingredients and add the blackberries. Stir gently until just combined; do not overmix. Spoon the mixture into the muffin tin. Sprinkle the demerara sugar over the tops of the muffins.

Bake in the preheated oven for 20 minutes until well risen, golden brown and firm to the touch. Leave to cool in the tin for 5 minutes, then serve warm or transfer to a wire rack to cool completely.

654 Blackcurrant muffins

Omit the apple and replace the blackberries with 200 g/7 oz fresh blackcurrants.

655 Apple streusel muffins

280 g/10 oz plain flour
1 tbsp baking powder
½ tsp ground cinnamon
pinch of salt
115 g/4 oz soft light brown sugar
250 g/9 oz cooking apple
2 eggs
250 ml/9 fl oz milk

6 tbsp sunflower oil or 85 g/3 oz butter,
   melted and cooled

STREUSEL TOPPING
50 g/1¾ oz plain flour
¼ tsp ground cinnamon
35 g/1¼ oz butter, cut into small pieces
25 g/1 oz soft light brown sugar

Preheat the oven to 200°C/400°F/Gas Mark 6. Line a 12-hole muffin tin with 12 paper cases.

To make the streusel topping, place the flour and cinnamon in a bowl. Add the butter and rub it in with your fingertips until the mixture resembles fine breadcrumbs. Stir in the sugar and set aside.

To make the muffins, sift together the flour, baking powder, cinnamon and salt into a large bowl. Stir in the sugar. Peel, core and finely chop the apple. Add to the flour mixture and stir together. Place the eggs in a large jug or bowl and beat lightly, then beat in the milk and oil.

Make a well in the centre of the dry ingredients and pour in the beaten liquid ingredients. Stir gently until just combined; do not overmix. Spoon the mixture into the paper cases. Scatter the streusel topping over each muffin.

Bake in the preheated oven for 20 minutes, or until well risen, golden brown and firm to the touch. Leave to cool in the tin for 5 minutes, then serve warm or transfer to a wire rack to cool completely.

656 With apple brandy butter

Beat 1 tablespoon of apple brandy and 2 tablespoons of finely chopped dried apple into 85 g/3 oz softened butter and serve with the muffins.

657 Apricot & banana muffins

6 tbsp sunflower oil or 85 g/3 oz butter,
   melted and cooled, plus extra
   for greasing
280 g/10 oz plain flour
1 tbsp baking powder
pinch of salt

115 g/4 oz caster sugar
55 g/2 oz dried apricots, finely chopped
2 bananas
about 150 ml/5 fl oz milk
2 eggs

Preheat the oven to 200°C/400°F/Gas Mark 6. Grease a 12-hole muffin tin. Sift together the flour, baking powder and salt into a large bowl. Stir in the sugar and apricots.

Mash the bananas and place in a jug, then add enough milk to make up the purée to 250 ml/9 fl oz.

Place the eggs in a large jug or bowl and beat lightly, then beat in the banana and milk mixture and the oil. Make a well in the centre of the dry ingredients and pour in the beaten liquid ingredients. Stir until just combined; do not overmix. Spoon the mixture into the muffin tin.

Bake in the preheated oven for 20 minutes, or until well risen, golden brown and firm to the touch. Leave to cool in the tin for 5 minutes, then serve warm or transfer to a wire rack to cool completely.

658 Double banana muffins

Omit the apricots and add 125 g/4½ oz chopped soft dried banana.

659 Apple & cinnamon muffins

200 g/7 oz wholemeal flour
75 g/2¾ oz fine oatmeal
2 tsp baking powder
125 g/4½ oz soft light brown sugar
2 large eggs

225 ml/8 fl oz semi-skimmed milk
100 ml/3½ fl oz groundnut oil
1 tsp vanilla extract
1 tsp ground cinnamon
1 large cooking apple

Preheat the oven to 180°C/350°F/Gas Mark 4. Line a 12-hole muffin tin with paper cases.

Sift the flour, oatmeal and baking powder together into a large bowl, then add the larger particles left in the sieve. Stir in the sugar. Place the eggs, milk and oil in a separate bowl and beat together until well combined. Add to the dry ingredients, along with the vanilla extract and cinnamon, and stir until just combined; do not overmix.

Peel, core and grate the apple and stir into the mixture, then spoon the mixture into the paper cases.

Bake in the preheated oven for 20–25 minutes, or until risen and golden brown. Leave to cool in the tin for a few minutes before serving warm or transfer to a wire rack to cool completely.

660 Buttermilk berry muffins

6 tbsp sunflower oil or 85 g/3 oz butter, melted and cooled, plus extra for greasing
150 g/5½ oz frozen mixed berries, such as blueberries, raspberries, blackberries, strawberries
280 g/10 oz plain flour
1 tbsp baking powder
pinch of salt
115 g/4 oz caster sugar
2 eggs
250 ml/9 fl oz buttermilk
1 tsp vanilla extract
icing sugar, for dusting

Preheat the oven to 200°C/400°F/Gas Mark 6. Grease a 12-hole muffin tin. Cut any large berries, such as strawberries, into small pieces. Sift together the flour, baking powder and salt into a large bowl. Stir in the sugar.

Place the eggs in a large jug or bowl and beat lightly, then beat in the buttermilk, oil and vanilla extract. Make a well in the centre of the dry ingredients, pour in the beaten liquid ingredients and add the berries. Stir until combined; do not overmix. Spoon the mixture into the muffin tin.

Bake in the preheated oven for 20 minutes, or until well risen, golden brown and firm to the touch. Leave to cool in the tin for 5 minutes, then serve warm or transfer to a wire rack to cool completely. Dust with sifted icing sugar before serving.

661 Buttermilk cranberry muffins

Replace the frozen berries with 150 g/5½ oz frozen cranberries mixed with ½ teaspoon of finely grated orange rind.

6 tbsp sunflower oil or 85 g/3 oz butter, melted and cooled, plus extra for greasing
2 oranges
about 125 ml/4 fl oz milk
225 g/8 oz plain flour
55 g/2 oz cocoa powder
1 tbsp baking powder
pinch of salt
115 g/4 oz soft light brown sugar

150 g/5½ oz plain chocolate chips
2 eggs
strips of orange zest, to decorate

ICING
55 g/2 oz plain chocolate, broken into pieces
25 g/1 oz butter
2 tbsp water
175 g/6 oz icing sugar

Preheat the oven to 200°C/400°F/ Gas Mark 6. Grease a 12-hole muffin tin. Finely grate the rind from the oranges and squeeze the juice. Add enough milk to make up the juice to 250 ml/9 fl oz, then add the orange rind. Sift together the flour, cocoa, baking powder and salt into a large bowl. Stir in the brown sugar and chocolate chips. Place the eggs in a large jug or bowl and beat lightly, then beat in the milk and orange mixture and the oil. Make a well in the centre of the dry ingredients and pour in the beaten liquid ingredients. Stir gently until just combined; do not overmix. Spoon the mixture into the muffin tin.

Bake in the preheated oven for 20 minutes, or until well risen and firm to the touch. Leave to cool in the tin for 5 minutes, then transfer to a wire rack to cool completely.

To make the icing, place the chocolate in a heatproof bowl, add the butter and water, then set the bowl over a saucepan of gently simmering water and heat, stirring, until melted. Remove from the heat, sift in the icing sugar and beat until smooth, then spread the icing on top of the muffins and decorate with strips of orange zest.

663 *With white chocolate icing*

Replace the plain chocolate with 55 g/2 oz white chocolate and top the muffins with crushed chocolate orange pieces.

---

664 *Brandied peach muffins*   MAKES 12

400 g/14 oz canned peaches in natural juice
280 g/10 oz plain flour
1 tbsp baking powder
pinch of salt
115 g/4 oz caster sugar
2 eggs

175 ml/6 fl oz buttermilk
6 tbsp sunflower oil or 85 g/3 oz butter, melted and cooled
3 tbsp brandy
finely grated rind of 1 orange

Preheat the oven to 200°C/400°F/Gas Mark 6. Line a 12-hole muffin tin with 12 paper cases. Drain and finely chop the peaches. Sift together the flour, baking powder and salt into a large bowl. Stir in the sugar.

Place the eggs in a large jug or bowl and beat lightly, then beat in the buttermilk, oil, brandy and orange rind. Make a well in the centre of the dry ingredients, pour in the beaten liquid ingredients and add the chopped peaches. Stir gently until just combined; do not overmix. Spoon the mixture into the paper cases.

Bake in the preheated oven for 20 minutes, or until well risen, golden brown and firm to the touch. Leave to cool in the tin for 5 minutes, then serve warm or transfer to a wire rack to cool completely.

665 *Pear and liqueur muffins*

Replace the peaches with 400 g/14 oz canned pears, drained and chopped, and use Poire William liqueur to replace the brandy.

666 *Brandy & apricot muffins*

100 g/3½ oz dried apricots, coarsely
   chopped
3 tbsp brandy
280 g/10 oz plain flour
1 tbsp baking powder
pinch of salt
115 g/4 oz caster sugar

2 eggs
175 ml/6 fl oz buttermilk
6 tbsp sunflower oil or 85 g/3 oz butter,
   melted and cooled

Put the chopped apricots in a bowl, add the brandy and leave to soak
for 1 hour. Preheat the oven to 200°C/400°F/Gas Mark 6. Line a 12-hole
muffin tin with 12 paper cases. Put the apricots and brandy in a food
processor and process to form a rough purée. Sift together the flour,
baking powder and salt into a large bowl. Stir in the sugar.

Place the eggs in a large jug or bowl and beat lightly, then beat in the
apricot purée, buttermilk and oil. Make a well in the centre of the dry
ingredients and pour in the beaten liquid ingredients. Stir gently until
just combined; do not overmix, then spoon the mixture into the paper
cases. Bake in the preheated oven for 20 minutes, or until well risen,
golden brown and firm to the touch. Leave to cool in the tin for
5 minutes, then serve warm or transfer to a wire rack to cool completely.

667 *With apricot brandy icing*

*Sift 100 g/3½ oz icing sugar into a bowl and mix to a smooth icing with
1 tablespoon of apricot brandy. Drizzle over the muffins and leave to set.*

668 *Caribbean rum & raisin muffins*

200 g/7 oz raisins
3 tbsp rum
6 tbsp sunflower oil or 85 g/3 oz butter,
   melted and cooled, plus extra
   for greasing
280 g/10 oz plain flour

1 tbsp baking powder
pinch of salt
115 g/4 oz soft dark brown sugar
2 eggs
200 ml/7 fl oz milk

Put the raisins in a bowl, add the rum and leave to soak for 1 hour.
Preheat the oven to 200°C/400°F/Gas Mark 6. Grease a 12-hole muffin
tin. Sift together the flour, baking powder and salt into a large bowl. Stir
in the sugar.

Place the eggs in a large jug or bowl and beat lightly, then beat in the
milk and oil. Make a well in the centre of the dry ingredients, pour in
the beaten liquid ingredients and add the raisins. Stir gently until just
combined; do not overmix. Spoon the mixture into the muffin tin.

Bake in the preheated oven for 20 minutes, or until well risen, golden
brown and firm to the touch. Leave to cool in the tin for 5 minutes, then
serve warm or transfer to a wire rack to cool completely.

669 *With coconut icing*

*Sift 100 g/3½ oz icing sugar into a bowl and mix to a smooth icing with
1–2 tablespoons of coconut cream. Spread over the cooled muffins.*

670 *Cherry & coconut muffins*

280 g/10 oz plain flour
1 tbsp baking powder
pinch of salt
115 g/4 oz caster sugar
40 g/1½ oz desiccated coconut
125 g/4½ oz glacé cherries, cut into small pieces

2 eggs
250 ml/9 fl oz coconut milk
6 tbsp sunflower oil or 85 g/3 oz butter, melted and cooled
1 tsp vanilla extract
12 whole fresh cherries on their stalks

Preheat the oven to 200°C/400°F/Gas Mark 6. Line a 12-hole muffin tin with 12 paper cases. Sift together the flour, baking powder and salt into a large bowl. Stir in the sugar, coconut and chopped glacé cherries.

Place the eggs in a large jug or bowl and beat lightly, then beat in the coconut milk, oil and vanilla extract. Make a well in the centre of the dry ingredients and pour in the beaten liquid ingredients. Stir gently until just combined; do not overmix. Spoon the mixture into the paper cases. Top each muffin with a whole fresh cherry.

Bake in the preheated oven for 20 minutes, or until well risen, golden brown and firm to the touch. Leave to cool in the tin for 5 minutes, then serve warm or transfer to a wire rack to cool completely.

671 *With coconut topping*

Omit the whole cherry on each muffin. Place 85 g/3 oz dried coconut, 3 tablespoons of soft brown sugar and 85 g/3 oz glacé cherries in a food processor and pulse to chop, then sprinkle over the muffins before baking.

672 *Citrus fruit muffins*

280 g/10 oz plain flour
1 tbsp baking powder
½ tsp bicarbonate of soda
pinch of salt
115 g/4 oz caster sugar
2 eggs
250 ml/9 fl oz natural yogurt
6 tbsp sunflower oil or 85 g/3 oz butter, melted and cooled
finely grated rind of 1 lemon
finely grated rind of 1 lime
finely grated rind of 1 orange
strips of citrus zest, to decorate

FROSTING
25 g/1 oz butter
100 g/3½ oz soft cream cheese
100 g/3½ oz icing sugar
1 tsp fresh lemon, lime or orange juice

Preheat the oven to 200°C/400°F/ Gas Mark 6. Line a 12-hole muffin tin with 12 paper cases. Sift together the flour, baking powder, bicarbonate of soda and salt into a large bowl. Stir in the sugar. Place the eggs in a large jug or bowl and beat lightly, then beat in the yogurt, oil and all the citrus rinds. Make a well in the centre of the dry ingredients and pour in the beaten liquid ingredients. Stir gently until just combined; do not overmix. Spoon the mixture into the paper cases.

Bake in the preheated oven for 20 minutes, or until well risen and golden brown. Leave to cool in the tin for 5 minutes, then transfer to a wire rack to cool completely.

To make the frosting, place the butter and cream cheese in a large bowl and, using an electric hand whisk, beat together until smooth. Sift the icing sugar into the mixture then beat together until mixed. Gradually beat in the citrus juice, adding enough to form a spreading consistency.

When the muffins are cold, spread the frosting on top of each then decorate them with strips of citrus zest.

673 *Kiwi fruit muffins*

Omit the citrus zest and rind and replace with 3 peeled, chopped kiwi fruit.

Cranberry & almond muffins

6 tbsp sunflower oil or 85 g/3 oz butter, melted and cooled, plus extra for greasing
225 g/8 oz plain flour
1 tbsp baking powder
pinch of salt
115 g/4 oz caster sugar
55 g/2 oz ground almonds
2 eggs
250 ml/9 fl oz buttermilk
½ tsp almond extract
150 g/5½ oz fresh or frozen cranberries
40 g/1½ oz demerara sugar
40 g/1½ oz flaked almonds

Preheat the oven to 200°C/400°F/Gas Mark 6. Grease a 12-hole muffin tin. Sift together the flour, baking powder and salt into a large bowl. Stir in the caster sugar and ground almonds.

Place the eggs in a large jug or bowl and beat lightly, then beat in the buttermilk, oil and almond extract. Make a well in the centre of the dry ingredients, pour in the beaten liquid ingredients and add the cranberries. Stir gently until just combined; do not overmix. Spoon the mixture into the muffin tin. Sprinkle the demerara sugar and flaked almonds over the tops of the muffins.

Bake in the preheated oven for 20 minutes, or until well risen, golden brown and firm to the touch. Leave to cool in the tin for 5 minutes, then serve warm or transfer to a wire rack to cool completely.

675 *With almond crunch topping*

Chop the flaked almonds and mix with the demerara sugar and 4 crushed amaretti biscuits, then sprinkle the mixture over the top of the muffins before baking.

---

676 *Fresh flower muffins*

280 g/10 oz plain flour
1 tbsp baking powder
pinch of salt
115 g/4 oz caster sugar
2 eggs
250 ml/9 fl oz buttermilk
6 tbsp sunflower oil or 85 g/3 oz butter, melted and cooled
finely grated rind of 1 lemon

TOPPING
85 g/3 oz butter, softened
175 g/6 oz icing sugar
12 edible flower heads, such as lavender, nasturtiums, violets, primroses or roses, to decorate

Preheat the oven to 200°C/400°F/ Gas Mark 6. Line a 12-hole muffin tin with 12 paper cases. Carefully wash the flower heads and leave to dry on kitchen paper.

Sift together the flour, baking powder and salt into a large bowl. Stir in the sugar. Place the eggs in a large jug or bowl and beat lightly, then beat in the buttermilk, oil and lemon rind. Make a well in the centre of the dry ingredients and pour in the beaten liquid ingredients. Stir gently until just combined; do not overmix. Spoon the mixture into the paper cases.

Bake in the preheated oven for 20 minutes, or until well risen, golden brown and firm to the touch. Leave to cool in the tin for 5 minutes, then transfer to a wire rack to cool completely.

To make the icing, place the butter in a large bowl and beat until fluffy. Sift in the icing sugar and beat together until smooth, then place in a piping bag fitted with a large star nozzle and pipe circles on top of each muffin. Just before serving, place a flower head on top to decorate.

677 *Sugar rose petal muffins*

Brush 12 fresh rose petals with beaten egg white and dredge in caster sugar, then place on baking paper to dry out and use to decorate the muffins.

678 Fresh orange muffins

6 tbsp sunflower oil, plus extra
 for greasing
5 oranges
140 g/5 oz wholemeal flour
140 g/5 oz plain flour

1 tbsp baking powder
115 g/4 oz caster sugar
2 eggs
250 ml/9 fl oz fresh orange juice

Preheat the oven to 200°C/400°F/Gas Mark 6. Grease a 12-hole muffin tin. Grate the rind from 2 of the oranges and set aside. Remove the peel from all of the oranges, discarding the white pith. Cut the flesh into segments, reserving 6 segments. Cut the reserved segments in half and set aside. Cut the remaining segments into small pieces.

Sift together both types of flour and the baking powder into a large bowl, adding any bran left in the sieve. Stir in the sugar.

Place the eggs in a large jug or bowl and beat lightly, then beat in the orange juice, oil and reserved orange rind.

Make a well in the centre of the dry ingredients, pour in the beaten liquid ingredients and add the chopped oranges. Stir until combined; do not overmix. Spoon the mixture into the muffin tin.

Place the halved orange segments on the top.

Bake in the preheated oven for 20 minutes, or until well risen, golden brown and firm to the touch. Cool for 5 minutes, then serve warm or transfer to a wire rack to cool completely.

679 Fresh peach muffins

Stone and peel 5 fresh peaches and proceed as for the oranges. Replace the orange juice with peach nectar.

680 Fresh strawberry & cream muffins

6 tbsp sunflower oil or 85 g/3 oz butter,
 melted and cooled, plus extra
 for greasing
150 g/5½ oz strawberries
280 g/10 oz plain flour
1 tbsp baking powder
pinch of salt
115 g/4 oz caster sugar

2 eggs
250 ml/9 fl oz single cream
1 tsp vanilla extract

TOPPING
125 ml/4 fl oz double cream
12 whole small strawberries, to decorate

Preheat the oven to 200°C/400°F/Gas Mark 6. Grease a 12-hole muffin tin. Chop the strawberries into small pieces. Sift together the flour, baking powder and salt into a large bowl. Stir in the sugar and chopped strawberries.

Place the eggs in a large jug or bowl and lightly beat, then beat in the single cream, oil and vanilla extract. Make a well in the centre of the dry ingredients and pour in the beaten liquid ingredients.

Stir gently until just combined; do not overmix. Spoon the mixture into the muffin tin.

Bake in the preheated oven for 20 minutes until well risen, golden brown and firm to the touch. Leave to cool in the tin for 5 minutes, then transfer to a wire rack to cool completely.

Place the double cream in a bowl and whip until stiff. When the muffins are cold, pipe or spread the cream on top of each muffin, then top with a small strawberry.

681 With sweet wine & strawberry topping

Hull and slice the strawberries, pour over 2 tablespoons of sweet white wine and leave to macerate for 10 minutes before spooning a few strawberry slices onto each muffin.

682 *Chocolate cream muffins*

225 g/8 oz plain flour
55 g/2 oz cocoa powder
1 tbsp baking powder
pinch of salt
115 g/4 oz soft light brown sugar
150 g/5½ oz white chocolate chips

2 eggs
250 ml/9 fl oz double cream
6 tbsp sunflower oil or 85 g/3 oz butter,
    melted and cooled

Preheat the oven to 200°C/400°F/Gas Mark 6. Line a 12-hole muffin tin with 12 paper cases. Sift together the flour, cocoa, baking powder and salt into a large bowl. Stir in the sugar and white chocolate chips.

Place the eggs in a large jug or bowl and beat lightly, then beat in the cream and oil. Make a well in the centre of the dry ingredients and pour in the beaten liquid ingredients. Stir gently until just combined; do not overmix. Spoon the mixture into the paper cases.

Bake in the preheated oven for 20 minutes, or until well risen and firm to the touch. Leave to cool in the tin for 5 minutes, then serve warm or transfer to a wire rack to cool completely.

683 *Chocolate fudge muffins*

Add 55 g/2 oz chopped chocolate fudge to the muffin mix and bake as before.

684 *Frosted cream cheese muffins*

215 g/7½ oz soft cream cheese
50 g/1¾ oz icing sugar
280 g/10 oz plain flour
1 tbsp baking powder
pinch of salt
115 g/4 oz soft dark brown sugar
2 eggs

200 ml/7 fl oz soured cream
6 tbsp sunflower oil or 85 g/3 oz butter,
    melted and cooled
finely grated rind of 1 lemon
2 tsp fresh lemon juice

Preheat the oven to 200°C/400°F/Gas Mark 6. Line a 12-hole muffin tin with 12 paper cases. Put 100 g/3½ oz of the cream cheese in a bowl. Sift in 15 g/½ oz of the icing sugar and beat together.

Sift together the flour, baking powder and salt into a large bowl. Stir in the brown sugar.

Place the eggs in a large jug or bowl and beat lightly, then beat in the soured cream, oil and lemon rind. Make a well in the centre of the dry ingredients and pour in the beaten liquid ingredients. Stir gently until just combined; do not overmix. Spoon half of the mixture into the paper cases. Add a spoonful of the cream cheese mixture to the centre of each then spoon in the remaining mixture.

Bake in the preheated oven for 20 minutes, or until well risen, golden brown and firm to the touch. Leave to cool in the tin for 5 minutes, then transfer to a wire rack to cool completely.

To make the frosting, place the remaining cream cheese in a bowl and sift in the remaining icing sugar. Add the lemon juice and beat well together. Spread the icing on top of the muffins and chill in the refrigerator until ready to serve.

685 Coffee & cream muffins

6 tbsp sunflower oil or 85 g/3 oz butter,
  melted and cooled, plus extra
  for greasing
2 tbsp instant coffee granules
2 tbsp boiling water
280 g/10 oz plain flour
1 tbsp baking powder
pinch of salt
115 g/4 oz soft dark brown sugar

2 eggs
200 ml/7 fl oz double cream

TOPPING
300 ml/10 fl oz whipping cream
cocoa powder, for dusting
12 chocolate-covered coffee beans,
  to decorate

Preheat the oven to 200°C/400°F/ Gas Mark 6. Grease a 12-hole muffin tin. Put the coffee granules and boiling water in a cup and stir until dissolved. Leave to cool.

Meanwhile, sift together the flour, baking powder and salt into a large bowl. Stir in the sugar. Place the eggs in a large jug or bowl and beat lightly, then beat in the double cream, oil and dissolved coffee. Make a well in the centre of the dry ingredients and pour in the beaten liquid ingredients.

Stir gently until just combined; do not overmix. Spoon the mixture into the muffin tin.

Bake in the preheated oven for 20 minutes, or until well risen, golden brown and firm to the touch. Leave to cool in the tin for 5 minutes, then transfer to a wire rack to cool completely.

Just before serving, whisk the whipping cream until it holds its shape. Spoon a dollop of the cream on top of each muffin, dust lightly with cocoa powder and top with a chocolate-covered coffee bean.

686 With mocha cream topping

Mix ½ teaspoon of cocoa powder, ½ teaspoon of espresso coffee powder and 1 tablespoon of coffee liqueur together in a bowl until smooth, then whisk into the whipping cream before topping the muffins.

687 Decadent chocolate dessert muffins

6 tbsp sunflower oil or 85 g/3 oz butter,
  melted and cooled, plus extra
  for greasing
225 g/8 oz plain flour
55 g/2 oz cocoa powder
1 tbsp baking powder
pinch of salt
115 g/4 oz soft light brown sugar
2 eggs

250 ml/9 fl oz single cream
85 g/3 oz plain chocolate, broken
  into pieces

SAUCE
200 g/7 oz plain chocolate
25 g/1 oz butter
50 ml/2 fl oz single cream

Preheat the oven to 200°C/400°F/ Gas Mark 6. Grease a 12-hole muffin tin. Sift together the flour, cocoa, baking powder and salt into a large bowl. Stir in the sugar.

Place the eggs in a large jug or bowl and beat lightly, then beat in the cream and oil. Make a well in the centre of the dry ingredients and pour in the beaten liquid ingredients. Stir gently until just combined; do not overmix. Spoon half of the mixture into the muffin tin, then place a piece of chocolate into the centre of each. Spoon in the remaining mixture.

Bake in the preheated oven for 20 minutes, or until well risen and firm to the touch.

Meanwhile, to make the sauce, place the chocolate and butter in a heatproof bowl set over a saucepan of gently simmering water. Stir until blended then stir in the cream and mix together. Remove from the heat and stir until smooth.

Leave the muffins in the tin for 5 minutes, then remove and place on serving plates. Serve warm with the chocolate sauce poured over the top of each muffin.

688 With Kirsch cherry topping

Place 12 pitted black cherries in a small bowl. Pour over 2 tablespoons of Kirsch, stir and leave for 15 minutes. Top each muffin with a cherry before pouring over the sauce.

2 tbsp instant coffee granules
2 tbsp boiling water
280 g/10 oz plain flour
1 tbsp baking powder
pinch of salt
115 g/4 oz soft light brown sugar
2 eggs

100 ml/3½ fl oz milk
6 tbsp sunflower oil or 85 g/3 oz butter, melted and cooled
6 tbsp coffee liqueur
40 g/1½ oz demerara sugar

Preheat the oven to 200°C/400°F/Gas Mark 6. Line a 12-hole muffin tin with 12 paper cases. Put the coffee granules and boiling water in a cup and stir until dissolved. Leave to cool.

Meanwhile, sift together the flour, baking powder and salt into a large bowl. Stir in the brown sugar. Place the eggs in a large jug or bowl and beat lightly, then beat in the milk, oil, dissolved coffee and liqueur. Make a well in the centre of the dry ingredients and pour in the beaten liquid ingredients. Stir gently until just combined; do not overmix. Spoon the mixture into the paper cases. Sprinkle the demerara sugar over the tops of the muffins.

Bake in the preheated oven for 20 minutes, or until well risen, golden brown and firm to the touch. Leave to cool in the tin for 5 minutes, then serve warm or transfer to a wire rack to cool completely.

690 *With espresso icing*

Sift 100 g/3½ oz icing sugar into a bowl, mix 1 teaspoon of espresso coffee powder with 1 tablespoon of boiling water and add to the icing sugar, then mix to a smooth icing and spoon over the muffins.

691 *Mocha muffins*

225 g/8 oz plain flour
1 tbsp baking powder
2 tbsp cocoa powder
pinch of salt
115 g/4 oz butter, melted
150 g/5½ oz demerara sugar
1 large egg, lightly beaten
125 ml/4 fl oz milk
1 tsp almond extract
2 tbsp strong coffee

1 tbsp instant coffee powder
55 g/2 oz plain chocolate chips
25 g/1 oz raisins

COCOA TOPPING
3 tbsp demerara sugar
1 tbsp cocoa powder
1 tsp allspice

Preheat the oven to 190°C/375°F/Gas Mark 5. Line a 12-hole muffin tin with 12 muffin paper cases. Sift the flour, baking powder, cocoa and salt into a large bowl.

Place the butter and demerara sugar in a separate bowl and beat together until light and fluffy, then stir in the beaten egg. Pour in the milk, almond extract and coffee, then add the coffee powder, chocolate chips and raisins and gently mix together.

Add the raisin mixture to the flour mixture and stir together until just combined. Do not overmix. Spoon the mixture into the paper cases.

To make the topping, place the demerara sugar in a bowl, add the cocoa and allspice and mix together well, then sprinkle the topping over the muffins.

Bake in the preheated oven for 20 minutes, or until well risen and golden brown. Leave to cool in the tin for 5 minutes, then serve warm or transfer to a wire rack to cool completely.

692 *With molten chocolate filling*

Omit the raisins from the mix; you will need 100 g/3½ oz plain chocolate chips to make the centres. Spoon half the mixture into each muffin paper and add a few chocolate chips to the middle, then top with the remaining mix and bake as before.

693 *Spiced chocolate muffins*

MAKES 12

100 g/3½ oz butter, softened
150 g/5½ oz caster sugar
115 g/4 oz soft light brown sugar
2 large eggs
150 ml/5 fl oz soured cream
5 tbsp milk

250 g/9 oz plain flour
1 tsp bicarbonate of soda
2 tbsp cocoa powder
1 tsp allspice
200 g/7 oz plain chocolate chips

Preheat the oven to 190°C/375°F/Gas Mark 5. Line a 12-hole muffin tin with 12 paper cases. Place the butter, caster sugar and brown sugar in a large bowl and beat together, then beat in the eggs, soured cream and milk until thoroughly mixed.

Sift the flour, bicarbonate of soda, cocoa and allspice into a separate bowl and stir into the mixture. Add the chocolate chips and mix well. Spoon the mixture into the paper cases.

Bake in the preheated oven for 25–30 minutes. Leave to cool in the tin for 10 minutes, then transfer to a wire rack to cool completely.

694 *Rhubarb, ginger & raisin muffins*

MAKES 12

250 g/9 oz rhubarb
125 g/4½ oz butter, melted and cooled
100 ml/3½ fl oz milk
2 eggs, lightly beaten
200 g/7 oz plain flour

2 tsp baking powder
125 g/4 oz caster sugar
3 tbsp raisins
3 pieces stem ginger, chopped

Preheat the oven to 190°C/375°F/Gas Mark 5. Line a 12-hole muffin tin with 12 paper cases. Chop the rhubarb into lengths of about 1 cm/ ½ inch. Pour the melted butter and milk into a large bowl and beat in the eggs. Sift the flour and baking powder together and lightly fold into the wet mixture with the sugar. Gently stir in the rhubarb, raisins and stem ginger. Spoon the mixture into the paper cases.

Bake in the preheated oven for 15–20 minutes, or until the muffins are risen and golden and spring back when gently touched in the centre with the tip of a forefinger. Leave to cool in the tin for 5 minutes, then serve warm.

695 *With Greek yogurt icing*

Stir 1 tablespoon of ginger syrup into 150 g/5½ oz Greek yogurt and spread over the warm muffins.

213

696 Dark chocolate & ginger muffins

6 tbsp sunflower oil or 85 g/3 oz butter, melted and cooled, plus extra for greasing
225 g/8 oz plain flour
55 g/2 oz cocoa powder
1 tbsp baking powder
1 tbsp ground ginger
pinch of salt

115 g/4 oz soft dark brown sugar
3 pieces stem ginger in syrup, finely chopped, plus 2 tbsp syrup from the jar
2 eggs
220 ml/7½ fl oz milk

Preheat the oven to 200°C/400°F/Gas Mark 6. Grease a 12-hole muffin tin. Sift together the flour, cocoa, baking powder, ground ginger and salt into a large bowl. Stir in the sugar and finely chopped stem ginger.

Place the eggs in a large jug or bowl and beat lightly, then beat in the milk, oil and ginger syrup. Make a well in the centre of the dry ingredients and pour in the beaten liquid ingredients. Stir gently until just combined; do not overmix. Spoon the mixture into the muffin tin.

Bake in the preheated oven for 20 minutes, or until well risen and firm to the touch. Leave to cool in the tin for 5 minutes, then serve warm or transfer to a wire rack to cool completely.

697 With ginger buttermilk icing

Beat 100 g/3½ oz cream cheese with 3 tablespoons of buttermilk, 100 g/3½ oz icing sugar and ½ teaspoon of ground ginger, then spread the icing over the cooled muffins and drizzle over a little ginger syrup.

698 Ginger wheatgerm muffins

6 tbsp sunflower oil, plus extra for greasing
140 g/5 oz plain flour
1 tbsp baking powder
4 tsp ground ginger
115 g/4 oz soft dark brown sugar

140 g/5 oz wheatgerm
3 pieces stem ginger in syrup, finely chopped
2 eggs
250 ml/9 fl oz skimmed milk

Preheat the oven to 200°C/400°F/Gas Mark 6. Grease a 12-hole muffin tin. Sift together the flour, baking powder and ground ginger into a large bowl. Stir in the sugar, wheatgerm and stem ginger.

Place the eggs in a large jug or bowl and beat lightly, then beat in the milk and oil. Make a well in the centre of the dry ingredients and pour in the beaten liquid ingredients. Stir gently until just combined; do not overmix. Spoon the mixture into the muffin tin.

Bake in the preheated oven for 20 minutes, or until well risen, golden brown and firm to the touch. Leave to cool in the tin for 5 minutes then serve warm or transfer to a wire rack to cool completely.

699 With ginger crunch topping

Crush 200 g/7 oz ginger thin biscuits and mix with 2 tablespoons of soft brown sugar, then spoon over the muffins before baking.

225 g/8 oz plain flour
1 tsp bicarbonate of soda
¼ tsp salt
1 tsp allspice
115 g/4 oz caster sugar
3 large egg whites

3 tbsp low-fat margarine
150 ml/5 fl oz thick low-fat natural
    yogurt or blueberry-flavoured yogurt
1 tsp vanilla extract
85 g/3 oz fresh blueberries

Preheat the oven to 190°C/375°F/Gas Mark 5. Line a 12-hole muffin tin with 12 paper cases. Sift the flour, bicarbonate of soda, salt and half the allspice into a large bowl. Add 6 tablespoons of the sugar and mix well.

Place the egg whites in a separate bowl and whisk together. Add the margarine, yogurt and vanilla extract and mix well, then stir in the blueberries until thoroughly mixed. Add the fruit mixture to the dry ingredients, then gently stir until just combined; do not overmix. Spoon the mixture into the paper cases. Mix the remaining sugar with the remaining allspice, then sprinkle the mixture over the muffins.

Bake in the preheated oven for 25 minutes, or until well risen, golden brown and firm to the touch. Leave to cool in the tin for 5 minutes, then serve warm or transfer to a wire rack to cool completely.

701 *Low-fat cherry muffins*

Replace the blueberries with fresh pitted cherries, cut in half and use low-fat cherry yogurt.

280 g/10 oz plain flour
1 tbsp baking powder
½ tsp bicarbonate of soda
115 g/4 oz caster sugar
2 egg whites

250 ml/9 fl oz low-fat natural yogurt
3 tbsp sunflower oil
1 tsp vanilla extract

Preheat the oven to 200°C/400°F/Gas Mark 6. Line a 12-hole muffin tin with 12 paper cases. Sift together the flour, baking powder and bicarbonate of soda into a large bowl. Stir in the sugar.

Place the egg whites in a large jug or bowl and beat lightly, then beat in the yogurt, oil and vanilla extract. Make a well in the centre of the dry ingredients and pour in the beaten liquid ingredients. Stir gently until just combined; do not overmix. Spoon the mixture into the paper cases.

Bake in the preheated oven for 20 minutes, or until well risen, golden brown and firm to the touch. Leave to cool in the tin for 5 minutes, then serve warm.

703 High fibre muffins

140 g/5 oz high fibre bran cereal
250 ml/9 fl oz skimmed milk
140 g/5 oz plain flour
1 tbsp baking powder
1 tsp ground cinnamon
½ tsp freshly grated nutmeg

115 g/4 oz caster sugar
100 g/3½ oz raisins
2 eggs
6 tbsp sunflower oil

Preheat the oven to 200°C/400°F/Gas Mark 6. Line a 12-hole muffin tin with 12 paper cases. Put the cereal and milk in a bowl and leave to soak for about 5 minutes, or until the cereal has softened.

Meanwhile, sift together the flour, baking powder, cinnamon and nutmeg into a large bowl. Stir in the sugar and raisins.

Place the eggs in a large jug or bowl and beat lightly, then beat in the oil. Make a well in the centre of the dry ingredients and pour in the beaten liquid ingredients and the cereal mixture. Stir gently until just combined; do not overmix. Spoon the mixture into the paper cases.

Bake in the preheated oven for 20 minutes, or until well risen, golden brown and firm to the touch. Leave to cool in the tin for 5 minutes, then serve warm or transfer to a wire rack to cool completely.

704 High fibre seed muffins

Add 3 tablespoons of chopped mixed seeds, such as pumpkin, sunflower and hemp seeds with the raisins.

705 Sunflower seed muffins

140 g/5 oz plain flour
1 tbsp baking powder
115 g/4 oz soft light brown sugar
140 g/5 oz porridge oats
100 g/3½ oz sultanas
125 g/4½ oz sunflower seeds

2 eggs
250 ml/9 fl oz skimmed milk
6 tbsp sunflower oil
1 tsp vanilla extract

Preheat the oven to 200°C/400°F/Gas Mark 6. Line a 12-hole muffin tin with 12 paper cases. Sift together the flour and baking powder into a large bowl. Stir in the sugar, oats, sultanas and 100 g/3½ oz of the sunflower seeds.

Place the eggs in a large jug or bowl and beat lightly, then beat in the milk, oil and vanilla extract. Make a well in the centre of the dry ingredients and pour in the beaten liquid ingredients. Stir gently until just combined; do not overmix. Spoon the mixture into the paper cases. Sprinkle the remaining sunflower seeds over the tops of the muffins.

Bake in the preheated oven for 20 minutes, or until well risen, golden brown and firm to the touch. Leave to cool in the tin for 5 minutes, then serve warm or transfer to a wire rack to cool completely.

706 With cheese topping

Beat 150 g/5½ oz cream cheese, 30 g/1 oz finely grated Cheddar cheese and ½ teaspoon of Tabasco sauce together and spread over the cooled muffins.

707 Muesli muffins

140 g/5 oz plain flour
1 tbsp baking powder
280 g/10 oz unsweetened muesli
115 g/4 oz soft light brown sugar

2 eggs
250 ml/9 fl oz buttermilk
6 tbsp sunflower oil

Preheat the oven to 200°C/400°F/Gas Mark 6. Line a 12-hole muffin tin with 12 paper cases. Sift together the flour and baking powder into a large bowl. Stir in the muesli and sugar.

Place the eggs in a large jug or bowl and beat lightly, then beat in the buttermilk and oil. Make a well in the centre of the dry ingredients and pour in the beaten liquid ingredients. Stir gently until just combined; do not overmix. Spoon the mixture into the paper cases.

Bake in the preheated oven for 20 minutes, or until well risen, golden brown and firm to the touch. Leave to cool in the tin for 5 minutes, then serve warm or transfer to a wire rack to cool completely.

708 Apple & muesli muffins

Add 50 g/1¾ oz chopped dried apple to the muffin mix and add a dried apple ring to the top of each muffin before baking.

709 Wheatgerm, banana & pumpkin seed muffins

6 tbsp sunflower oil, plus extra for
    greasing
140 g/5 oz plain flour
1 tbsp baking powder
115 g/4 oz caster sugar
140 g/5 oz wheatgerm

85 g/3 oz pumpkin seeds
2 bananas
about 150 ml/5 fl oz skimmed milk
2 eggs

Preheat the oven to 200°C/400°F/Gas Mark 6. Grease a 12-hole muffin tin. Sift together the flour and baking powder into a large bowl. Stir in the sugar, wheatgerm and 50 g/1¾ oz of the pumpkin seeds. Mash the bananas and place in a jug, then add enough milk to make up the purée to 250 ml/9 fl oz.

Place the eggs in a large jug or bowl and beat lightly, then beat in the banana and milk mixture and the oil. Make a well in the centre of the dry ingredients and pour in the beaten liquid ingredients. Stir gently until just combined; do not overmix. Spoon the mixture into the muffin tin. Sprinkle the remaining pumpkin seeds over the top.

Bake in the preheated oven for 20 minutes, or until well risen, golden brown and firm to the touch. Leave to cool in the tin for 5 minutes, then serve warm or transfer to a wire rack to cool completely.

710 With crunchy topping

Chop 2 tablespoons of pumpkin seeds and 85 g/3 oz banana chips and mix with 2 tablespoons of soft brown sugar. Scatter over the muffins before baking.

Wholemeal banana muffins

50 g/1¾ oz raisins
3 tbsp fresh orange juice
140 g/5 oz plain flour
140 g/5 oz wholemeal flour
1 tbsp baking powder
115 g/4 oz caster sugar
2 bananas
about 100 ml/3½ fl oz skimmed milk
2 eggs
6 tbsp sunflower oil
finely grated rind of 1 orange

Put the raisins in a bowl, add the orange juice and leave to soak for 1 hour. Preheat the oven to 200°C/400°F/Gas Mark 6. Line a 12-hole muffin tin with 12 paper cases.

Sift together both types of flour and the baking powder into a large bowl, adding any bran left in the sieve. Stir in the sugar.

Mash the bananas and place in a jug, then add enough milk to make up the purée to 200 ml/7 fl oz. Place the eggs in a large jug or bowl and beat lightly, then beat in the banana and milk mixture, oil, soaked raisins and orange rind. Make a well in the centre of the dry ingredients and pour in the beaten liquid ingredients. Stir gently until just combined; do not overmix. Spoon the mixture into the paper cases.

Bake in the preheated oven for 20 minutes, or until well risen, golden brown and firm to the touch. Leave to cool in the tin for 5 minutes, then serve warm or transfer to a wire rack to cool completely.

712 *With banana topping*

Mash 1 ripe banana with ½ teaspoon of lemon juice. Beat 150 g/5½ oz cream cheese with 2 tablespoons of icing sugar and mix in the banana, then spread over the muffins.

713 *Yogurt & spice muffins*

140 g/5 oz wholemeal flour
140 g/5 oz plain flour
1 tbsp baking powder
½ tsp bicarbonate of soda
4 tsp mixed spice
115 g/4 oz caster sugar
100 g/3½ oz mixed dried fruit
2 eggs
250 ml/9 fl oz low-fat natural yogurt
6 tbsp sunflower oil

Preheat the oven to 200°C/400°F/Gas Mark 6. Line a 12-hole muffin tin with 12 paper cases. Sift together both types of flour, the baking powder, bicarbonate of soda and mixed spice into a large bowl, adding any bran left in the sieve. Stir in the sugar and dried fruit.

Place the eggs in a large jug or bowl and beat lightly, then beat in the yogurt and oil. Make a well in the centre of the dry ingredients and pour in the beaten liquid ingredients. Stir gently until just combined; do not overmix. Spoon the mixture into the paper cases.

Bake in the preheated oven for 20 minutes, or until well risen, golden brown and firm to the touch. Leave to cool in the tin for 5 minutes, then serve warm or transfer to a wire rack to cool completely.

714 *Vanilla & spice muffins*

Omit the dried fruit and use vanilla yogurt and the seeds from a vanilla pod.

715 *Three grain muffins*

MAKES 12

6 tbsp sunflower oil, plus extra for
    greasing
75 g/2¾ oz wholemeal flour
75 g/2¾ oz plain flour
1 tbsp baking powder
115 g/4 oz soft dark brown sugar

60 g/2¼ oz medium polenta
70 g/2½ oz porridge oats
2 eggs
250 ml/9 fl oz buttermilk
1 tsp vanilla extract

Preheat the oven to 200°C/400°F/Gas Mark 6. Grease a 12-hole muffin tin. Sift together the flours and the baking powder into a large bowl, adding any bran left in the sieve. Stir in the sugar, polenta and oats.

Place the eggs in a large jug or bowl and beat lightly, then beat in the buttermilk, oil and vanilla extract. Make a well in the centre of the dry ingredients and pour in the beaten liquid ingredients. Stir gently until just combined; do not overmix. Spoon the mixture into the muffin tin.

Bake in the preheated oven for 20 minutes, or until well risen, golden brown and firm to the touch. Leave to cool in the tin for 5 minutes, then serve warm or transfer to a wire rack to cool completely.

716 *With goat's cheese topping*

Chop 3 tablespoons of soft herbs, such as chervil, dill, chive and parsley, and stir into 200 g/7 oz soft goat's cheese, such as Chavroux. Spread over the muffins to serve.

717 *Sweetcorn polenta muffins*

MAKES 12

6 tbsp sunflower oil or 85 g/3 oz butter,
    melted and cooled, plus extra
    for greasing
175 g/6 oz plain flour
1 tbsp baking powder
pinch of salt

freshly ground black pepper
115 g/4 oz medium polenta
2 eggs
250 ml/9 fl oz milk
175 g/6 oz frozen sweetcorn kernels

Preheat the oven to 200°C/400°F/Gas Mark 6. Grease a 12-hole muffin tin. Sift together the flour, baking powder, salt and pepper to taste into a large bowl. Stir in the polenta.

Place the eggs in a large jug or bowl and beat lightly, then beat in the milk and oil. Make a well in the centre of the dry ingredients, pour in the beaten liquid ingredients and add the sweetcorn. Stir gently until just combined; do not overmix. Spoon the mixture into the muffin tin.

Bake in the preheated oven for 20 minutes, or until well risen, golden brown and firm to the touch. Leave to cool in the tin for 5 minutes, then serve warm or transfer to a wire rack to cool completely.

718 Oat & cranberry muffins

6 tbsp sunflower oil, plus extra for
   greasing
140 g/5 oz plain flour
1 tbsp baking powder
115 g/4 oz soft dark brown sugar
140 g/5 oz porridge oats

85 g/3 oz dried cranberries
2 eggs
250 ml/9 fl oz buttermilk
1 tsp vanilla extract

Preheat the oven to 200°C/400°F/Gas Mark 6. Grease a 12-hole muffin tin. Sift together the flour and baking powder into a large bowl. Stir in the sugar, oats and cranberries.

Place the eggs in a large jug or bowl and beat lightly, then beat in the buttermilk, oil and vanilla extract. Make a well in the centre of the dry ingredients and pour in the beaten liquid ingredients. Stir gently until just combined; do not overmix. Spoon the mixture into the muffin tin.

Bake in the preheated oven for 20 minutes, or until well risen, golden brown and firm to the touch. Leave to cool in the tin for 5 minutes, then serve warm or transfer to a wire rack to cool completely.

719 Fresh cranberry oat-topped muffins

Omit the dried cranberries and replace with 125 g/4½ oz fresh cranberries. Scatter 3 tablespoons of porridge oats over the muffins before baking.

720 Raisin bran muffins

6 tbsp sunflower oil, plus extra for
   greasing
140 g/5 oz plain flour
1 tbsp baking powder
140 g/5 oz wheat bran
115 g/4 oz caster sugar

150 g/5½ oz raisins
2 eggs
250 ml/9 fl oz skimmed milk
1 tsp vanilla extract

Preheat the oven to 200°C/400°F/Gas Mark 6. Grease a 12-hole muffin tin. Sift together the flour and baking powder into a large bowl. Stir in the bran, sugar and raisins.

Place the eggs in a large jug or bowl and beat lightly, then beat in the milk, oil and vanilla extract. Make a well in the centre of the dry ingredients and pour in the beaten liquid ingredients. Stir gently until just combined; do not overmix. Spoon the mixture into the muffin tin.

Bake in the preheated oven for 20 minutes, or until well risen, golden brown and firm to the touch. Leave to cool in the tin for 5 minutes, then serve warm or transfer to a wire rack to cool completely.

721 Sultana bran muffins

Omit the raisins and replace with 2 tablespoons of finely chopped sultanas.

140 g/5 oz plain flour
1 tbsp baking powder
115 g/4 oz soft light brown sugar
140 g/5 oz porridge oats
150 g/5½ oz pitted prunes, chopped

2 eggs
250 ml/9 fl oz buttermilk
6 tbsp sunflower oil
1 tsp vanilla extract

Preheat the oven to 200°C/400°F/Gas Mark 6. Line a 12-hole muffin tin with 12 paper cases. Sift together the flour and baking powder into a large bowl. Stir in the sugar, oats and prunes.

Place the eggs in a large jug or bowl and beat lightly, then beat in the buttermilk, oil and vanilla extract. Make a well in the centre of the dry ingredients and pour in the beaten liquid ingredients. Stir gently until just combined; do not overmix. Spoon the mixture into the paper cases.

Bake in the preheated oven for 20 minutes, or until well risen, golden brown and firm to the touch. Leave to cool in the tin for 5 minutes, then serve warm or transfer to a wire rack to cool completely.

723 *Apricot & sunflower seed muffins*

Omit the prunes and replace with 150 g/5½ oz chopped soft dried apricots and scatter over 3 tablespoons of sunflower seeds before baking the muffins.

724 *Granola muffins* MAKES 12

6 tbsp sunflower oil, plus extra for
  greasing
140 g/5 oz wholemeal flour
140 g/5 oz plain flour
1 tbsp baking powder
85 g/3 oz soft light brown sugar
2 eggs
250 ml/9 fl oz skimmed milk

GRANOLA
75 g/2¾ oz porridge oats
25 g/1 oz blanched almonds, chopped
25 g/1 oz sunflower seeds
25 g/1 oz raisins
25 g/1 oz soft light brown sugar

Preheat the oven to 200°C/400°F/Gas Mark 6. Grease a 12-hole muffin tin. Sift together both flours and the baking powder into a large bowl, adding any bran left in the sieve. Stir in the sugar and granola.

Place the eggs in a large jug or bowl and beat lightly, then beat in the milk and oil. Make a well in the centre of the dry ingredients and pour in the beaten liquid ingredients. Stir gently until just combined; do not overmix. Spoon the mixture into the muffin tin.

Bake in the preheated oven for 20 minutes, or until well risen, golden brown and firm to the touch. Leave to cool in the tin for 5 minutes, then serve warm or transfer to a wire rack to cool completely.

To make the granola, place the oats in a large, dry frying pan and toast over a low heat for 1 minute. Add the almonds, sunflower seeds and raisins and toast for a further 6–8 minutes, or until browned. Add the sugar and stir for 1 minute until it melts. Remove from the heat and stir until mixed.

725 *Apricot & pecan muffins*

Omit the raisins from the granola and add 55 g/2 oz chopped dried apricots and replace the almonds with 30 g/1 oz chopped pecan nuts.

Malted chocolate muffins

6 tbsp sunflower oil or 85 g/3 oz
butter, melted and cooled, plus
extra for greasing
150 g/5½ oz malted chocolate balls
225 g/8 oz plain flour
55 g/2 oz cocoa powder
1 tbsp baking powder
pinch of salt
115 g/4 oz soft light brown sugar
2 eggs
250 ml/9 fl oz buttermilk

ICING
55 g/2 oz plain chocolate, broken
into pieces
115 g/4 oz butter, softened
225 g/8 oz icing sugar

Preheat the oven to 200°C/400°F/Gas Mark 6. Grease a 12-hole muffin tin. Roughly crush the chocolate balls, reserving 12 whole ones to decorate. Sift together the flour, cocoa, baking powder and salt into a large bowl. Stir in the brown sugar and the crushed chocolate balls.

Place the eggs in a large jug or bowl and beat lightly, then beat in the buttermilk and oil. Make a well in the centre of the dry ingredients and pour in the beaten liquid ingredients. Stir gently until just combined; do not overmix. Spoon the mixture into the muffin tin.

Bake in the preheated oven for 20 minutes, or until well risen and firm to the touch. Leave to cool in the tin for 5 minutes, then transfer to a wire rack to cool completely.

To make the icing, place the chocolate in a heatproof bowl, set the bowl over a saucepan of gently simmering water and heat until melted. Remove from the heat. Place the butter in a large bowl and beat until fluffy. Sift in the icing sugar and beat together until smooth and creamy. Add the melted chocolate and beat together. Spread the icing on top of the muffins and decorate each with one of the reserved chocolate balls.

Glazed honey muffins

6 tbsp sunflower oil, plus extra
for greasing
140 g/5 oz wholemeal flour
140 g/5 oz plain flour
1 tbsp baking powder
½ tsp bicarbonate of soda
½ tsp ground mixed spice
50 g/1¾ oz soft light brown sugar
100 g/3½ oz sultanas
2 eggs
200 ml/7 fl oz low-fat natural yogurt
8 tbsp clear honey

Preheat the oven to 200°C/400°F/Gas Mark 6. Grease a 12-hole muffin tin. Sift together both flours, the baking powder, bicarbonate of soda and mixed spice into a large bowl, adding any bran left in the sieve. Stir in the sugar and sultanas.

Place the eggs in a large jug or bowl and beat lightly, then beat in the yogurt, oil and 4 tablespoons of the honey. Make a well in the centre of the dry ingredients and pour in the beaten liquid ingredients. Stir until combined; do not overmix. Spoon the mixture into the muffin tin.

Bake in the preheated oven for 20 minutes, or until well risen, golden brown and firm to the touch. Leave to cool in the tin for 5 minutes, then drizzle 1 teaspoon of the remaining honey on top of each muffin. Serve warm or transfer to a wire rack to cool completely.

728 *With honey ricotta topping*

Beat 150 g/5½ oz ricotta with 2 tablespoons of clear honey and use to top the muffins, then scatter with chopped chocolate-covered honeycomb before serving.

729 Carrot cake muffins

6 tbsp sunflower oil, plus extra
for greasing
280 g/10 oz plain flour
1 tbsp baking powder
1 tsp ground mixed spice
pinch of salt
115 g/4 oz soft dark brown sugar
200 g/7 oz carrots, grated
50 g/1¾ oz walnuts or pecan nuts,
coarsely chopped
50 g/1¾ oz sultanas
2 eggs
175 ml/6 fl oz milk
finely grated rind and juice
of 1 orange
strips of orange zest, to decorate

ICING
75 g/2¾ oz soft cream cheese
40 g/1½ oz butter
35 g/1¼ oz icing sugar

Preheat the oven to 200°C/400°F/Gas Mark 6. Grease a 12-hole muffin tin. Sift together the flour, baking powder, mixed spice and salt into a large bowl. Stir in the brown sugar, carrots, walnuts and sultanas.

Place the eggs in a large jug or bowl and beat lightly, then beat in the milk, oil, orange rind and orange juice. Make a well in the centre of the dry ingredients and pour in the beaten liquid ingredients. Stir gently until just combined; do not overmix. Spoon the mixture into the muffin tin.

Bake in the preheated oven for 20 minutes, or until well risen, golden brown and firm to the touch. Leave to cool in the tin for 5 minutes, then transfer to a wire rack to cool completely.

To make the icing, place the cream cheese and butter in a bowl and sift in the icing sugar. Beat together until light and fluffy. When the muffins are cold, spread the icing on top of each, then decorate with strips of orange zest. Chill the muffins in the refrigerator until ready to serve.

730 With carrot decoration

Cut 6 ready-to-eat dried apricots in half and roll lengthways to form a carrot shape, place on each muffin and add green 'stalks' with pieces of angelica.

731 Gooey butterscotch cream muffins

150 g/5½ oz hard butterscotch sweets
280 g/10 oz plain flour
1 tbsp baking powder
pinch of salt
115 g/4 oz soft dark brown sugar

2 eggs
250 ml/9 fl oz double cream
6 tbsp sunflower oil or 85 g/3 oz butter,
melted and cooled

Preheat the oven to 200°C/400°F/Gas Mark 6. Line a 12-hole muffin tin with 12 paper cases. Place the butterscotch sweets in a strong polythene bag and hit with a meat mallet or the end of a wooden rolling pin until finely crushed.

Sift together the flour, baking powder and salt into a large bowl. Stir in the sugar and crushed sweets.

Place the eggs in a large jug or bowl and beat lightly, then beat in the cream and oil. Make a well in the centre of the dry ingredients and pour in the beaten liquid ingredients. Stir gently until just combined; do not overmix. Spoon the mixture into the paper cases.

Bake in the preheated oven for 20 minutes, or until well risen, golden brown and firm to the touch. Leave to cool in the tin for 5 minutes, then serve warm or transfer to a wire rack to cool completely.

732 With butterscotch topping

Whip 200 ml/7 fl oz double cream with ½ teaspoon of vanilla extract, spread over the muffins and scatter over 85 g/3 oz crushed butterscotch sweets.

733 Crunchy peanut butter muffins

280 g/10 oz plain flour
1 tbsp baking powder
pinch of salt
115 g/4 oz soft dark brown sugar
2 eggs
175 ml/6 fl oz milk

6 tbsp sunflower oil or 85 g/3 oz butter,
    melted and cooled
175 g/6 oz crunchy peanut butter

PEANUT TOPPING
50 g/1¾ oz unsalted roasted peanuts
40 g/1½ oz demerara sugar

Preheat the oven to 200°C/400°F/Gas Mark 6. Line a 12-hole muffin tin with 12 paper cases. To make the peanut topping, finely chop the peanuts, place in a bowl, add the demerara sugar, mix together and set aside.

Sift together the flour, baking powder and salt into a large bowl. Stir in the brown sugar.

Place the eggs in a large jug or bowl and beat lightly, then beat in the milk, oil and peanut butter. Make a well in the centre of the dry ingredients and pour in the beaten liquid ingredients. Stir gently until just combined; do not overmix. Spoon the mixture into the paper cases. Sprinkle the peanut topping over the muffins.

Bake in the preheated oven for 20 minutes, or until well risen, golden brown and firm to the touch. Leave to cool in the tin for 5 minutes, then serve warm or transfer to a wire rack to cool completely.

734 With peanut frosting

Omit the peanut topping and bake the muffins as before. Beat 25 g/1 oz crunchy peanut butter with 100 g/3½ oz cream cheese and 100 g/3½ oz icing sugar, then spread over the cooled muffins and sprinkle over 100 g/ 3½ oz chopped peanuts.

735 Double chocolate muffins

100 g/3½ oz butter, softened
125 g/4½ oz caster sugar
100 g/3½ oz dark muscovado sugar
2 eggs
150 ml/5 fl oz soured cream

5 tbsp milk
250 g/9 oz plain flour
1 tsp bicarbonate of soda
2 tbsp cocoa powder
190 g/6½ oz plain chocolate chips

Preheat the oven to 190°C/375°F/Gas Mark 5. Line a 12-hole muffin tin with 12 paper cases. Place the butter and both sugars into a large bowl and beat well. Beat in the eggs, soured cream and milk until mixed.

Sift the flour, bicarbonate of soda and cocoa into a separate bowl and stir into the mixture. Add the chocolate chips and mix well. Spoon the mixture into the paper cases.

Bake in the preheated oven for 25–30 minutes. Leave to cool in the tin for 10 minutes, then transfer to a wire rack to cool completely.

736 Hazelnut & coffee muffins

MAKES 12

*6 tbsp sunflower oil or 85 g/3 oz butter,
    melted and cooled, plus extra
    for greasing
2 tbsp instant coffee granules
2 tbsp boiling water
150 g/5½ oz hazelnuts
280 g/10 oz plain white flour*

*1 tbsp baking powder
pinch of salt
115 g/4 oz soft light brown sugar
2 eggs
200 ml/7 fl oz buttermilk*

Preheat the oven to 200°C/400°F/Gas Mark 6. Grease a 12-hole muffin tin. Put the coffee granules and boiling water in a cup and stir until dissolved. Leave to cool.

Meanwhile, finely chop 100 g/3½ oz of the hazelnuts and coarsely chop the remaining hazelnuts. Sift together the flour, baking powder and salt into a large bowl. Stir in the sugar and finely chopped hazelnuts.

Place the eggs in a large jug or bowl and beat lightly, then beat in the buttermilk, oil and dissolved coffee. Make a well in the centre of the dry ingredients and pour in the beaten liquid ingredients. Stir gently until just combined; do not overmix. Spoon the mixture into the muffin tin. Scatter the reserved chopped hazelnuts over the tops of the muffins.

Bake in the preheated oven for 20 minutes, or until well risen, golden brown and firm to the touch. Leave to cool in the tin for 5 minutes, then serve warm or transfer to a wire rack to cool completely.

737 With hazelnut cream topping

Whip 200 ml/7 fl oz double cream until thick. Stir in 1 tablespoon of hazelnut liqueur, whip again until stiff, then spoon over the cooled muffins.

738 Chocolate chip muffins

MAKES 12

*80 g/3 oz butter, plus extra for greasing
200 g/7 oz caster sugar
2 large eggs
150 ml/5 fl oz natural yogurt*

*5 tbsp milk
280 g/10 oz plain flour
1 tsp bicarbonate of soda
175 g/6 oz plain chocolate chips*

Preheat the oven to 200°C/400°F/Gas Mark 6. Grease a 12-hole muffin tin. Place the butter and sugar in a large bowl and beat together until light and fluffy, then beat in the eggs, yogurt and milk until thoroughly combined.

Sift the flour and bicarbonate of soda into the mixture and stir until just blended. Stir in the chocolate chips, then spoon the mixture into the muffin tin.

Bake in the preheated oven for 25 minutes, or until a fine skewer inserted into the centre of one of the muffins comes out clean. Leave to cool in the tin for 5 minutes, then transfer to a wire rack to cool completely.

739 White chocolate & raspberry muffins

Replace the plain chocolate chips with 125 g/4½ oz white chocolate chips and add 85 g/3 oz fresh raspberries.

225

740 Pecan brownie muffins

> 115 g/4 oz pecan nuts
> 100 g/3½ oz plain flour
> 175 g/6 oz caster sugar
> ¼ tsp salt
> 1 tbsp baking powder
>
> 225 g/8 oz butter
> 115 g/4 oz plain chocolate
> 4 eggs, lightly beaten
> 1 tsp vanilla extract

Preheat the oven to 200°C/400°F/Gas Mark 6. Line a 12-hole muffin tin with 12 paper cases. Reserve 12 pecan halves and roughly chop the rest.

Sift the flour, sugar, salt and baking powder into a large bowl and make a well in the centre. Melt the butter and chocolate in a small saucepan over a very low heat, stirring frequently. Add to the flour mixture and stir to mix evenly.

Add the eggs and vanilla extract and mix together just until the ingredients are evenly moistened. Stir in the chopped pecan nuts. Spoon the mixture into the paper cases and add a pecan half on top of each.

Bake in the preheated oven for 20–25 minutes, or until well risen and firm to the touch. Leave to cool in the tin for 5 minutes, then serve warm or transfer to a wire rack to cool completely.

741 With vanilla pecan topping

Omit the pecan nut from the top of each muffin and reserve. Beat 150 g/ 5½ oz butter with the seeds from a vanilla pod, add 90 g/3¼ oz soft brown sugar and beat until smooth, then spread over the muffins and top each with the pecan nut.

742 Jam doughnut muffins

> 6 tbsp sunflower oil or 85 g/3 oz butter,
>   melted and cooled, plus extra
>   for greasing
> 280 g/10 oz plain flour
> 1 tbsp baking powder
> pinch of salt
> 115 g/4 oz caster sugar
> 2 eggs
>
> 200 ml/7 fl oz milk
> 1 tsp vanilla extract
> 4 tbsp strawberry jam or raspberry jam
>
> TOPPING
> 150 g/5½ oz granulated sugar
> 115 g/4 oz butter, melted

Preheat the oven to 200°C/400°F/ Gas Mark 6. Grease a 12-hole muffin tin. Sift together the flour, baking powder and salt into a large bowl. Stir in the caster sugar.

Place the eggs in a large jug or bowl and beat lightly, then beat in the milk, oil and vanilla extract. Make a well in the centre of the dry ingredients and pour in the beaten liquid ingredients. Stir gently until just combined; do not overmix.

Spoon half of the mixture into the muffin tin. Add a teaspoon of jam to the centre of each, then spoon in the remaining mixture. Bake in the preheated oven for 20 minutes, or until they are well risen, golden brown and firm to the touch.

Leave the muffins in the tin to cool for 5 minutes.

To make the topping, spread the sugar in a wide, shallow bowl, then dip the tops of the muffins in the melted butter and roll in the sugar. Serve warm or transfer to a wire rack to cool.

743 Custard doughnut muffins

Omit the jam and replace with 4–5 tablespoons of ready-made custard.

744 Triple chocolate chip muffins

6 tbsp sunflower oil or 85 g/3 oz butter,
    melted and cooled, plus extra
    for greasing
280 g/10 oz plain flour
1 tbsp baking powder
pinch of salt
115 g/4 oz soft light brown sugar

50 g/1¾ oz plain chocolate chips
50 g/1¾ oz milk chocolate chips
50 g/1¾ oz white chocolate chips
2 eggs
250 ml/9 fl oz soured cream
1 tsp vanilla extract

Preheat the oven to 200°C/400°F/Gas Mark 6. Grease a 12-hole muffin tin. Sift together the flour, baking powder and salt into a large bowl. Stir in the sugar and chocolate chips.

Place the eggs in a large jug or bowl and beat lightly, then beat in the soured cream, oil and vanilla extract. Make a well in the centre of the dry ingredients and pour in the beaten liquid ingredients. Stir until combined; do not overmix. Spoon the mixture into the muffin tin.

Bake in the preheated oven for 20 minutes, or until well risen, golden brown and firm to the touch. Leave to cool in the tin for 5 minutes, then serve warm or transfer to a wire rack to cool completely.

745 Marzipan muffins

175 g/6 oz marzipan
280 g/10 oz plain flour
1 tbsp baking powder
pinch of salt
115 g/4 oz caster sugar
2 eggs

200 ml/7 fl oz milk
6 tbsp sunflower oil or 85 g/3 oz butter,
    melted and cooled
1 tsp almond extract
12 whole blanched almonds

Preheat the oven to 200°C/400°F/ Gas Mark 6. Line a 12-hole muffin tin with 12 paper cases. Cut the marzipan into 12 equal pieces.

Roll each piece into a ball, and then flatten with the palm of your hand, making sure that they are no larger than the paper cases.

Sift together the flour, baking powder and salt into a large bowl. Stir in the sugar. Place the eggs in a large jug or bowl and beat lightly, then beat in the milk, oil and almond extract.

Make a well in the centre of the dry ingredients and pour in the beaten liquid ingredients. Stir gently until just combined; do not overmix. Spoon half of the mixture into the paper cases.

Place a piece of marzipan in the centre of each, then spoon in the remaining mixture. Top each muffin with a whole blanched almond. Bake in the preheated oven for 20 minutes, or until well risen, golden brown and firm to the touch. Leave to cool in the tin for 5 minutes, then serve warm or transfer to a wire rack to cool completely.

746 Strawberry & amaretto muffins

Add 1 tablespoon of amaretto liqueur and 12 hulled chopped strawberries to the muffin mix and bake as before.

747 Maple pecan muffins

280 g/10 oz plain flour
1 tbsp baking powder
pinch of salt
115 g/4 oz caster sugar
100 g/3½ oz pecan nuts, coarsely chopped
2 eggs

175 ml/6 fl oz buttermilk
75 ml/2½ fl oz maple syrup, plus extra for glazing
6 tbsp sunflower oil or 85 g/3 oz butter, melted and cooled
12 pecan nut halves

Preheat the oven to 200°C/400°F/Gas Mark 6. Line a 12-hole muffin tin with 12 paper cases. Sift together the flour, baking powder and salt into a large bowl. Stir in the sugar and pecan nuts.

Place the eggs in a large jug or bowl and beat lightly, then beat in the buttermilk, maple syrup and oil. Make a well in the centre of the dry ingredients and pour in the beaten liquid ingredients. Stir gently until just combined; do not overmix. Spoon the mixture into the paper cases and top each muffin with a pecan half.

Bake in the preheated oven for 20 minutes, or until well risen, golden brown and firm to the touch. Leave to cool in the tin for 5 minutes, then brush the tops with the maple syrup to glaze. Serve warm or transfer to a wire rack to cool completely.

748 With maple crunch topping

Omit the pecan nuts from the top. Chop 150 g/5½ oz pecan nuts and mix with 3 tablespoons of soft brown sugar and 2 tablespoons of maple syrup, then spoon over the muffins before baking.

749 Lemon polenta muffins

6 tbsp sunflower oil, plus extra for greasing
4 lemons
about 3 tbsp low-fat natural yogurt
175 g/6 oz plain flour
1 tbsp baking powder

½ tsp bicarbonate of soda
280 g/10 oz medium polenta
115 g/4 oz caster sugar
2 eggs

Preheat the oven to 200°C/400°F/Gas Mark 6. Grease a 12-hole muffin tin. Finely grate the rind from the lemons and squeeze the juice. Add enough yogurt to make the juice up to 250 ml/9 fl oz, then stir in the lemon rind.

Sift the flour, baking powder and bicarbonate of soda into a large bowl. Stir in the polenta and sugar. Place the eggs in a large jug or bowl and beat lightly, then beat in the oil. Make a well in the centre of the dry ingredients and pour in the beaten liquid ingredients with the lemon and yogurt mixture. Stir gently until just combined; do not overmix. Spoon the mixture into the muffin tin.

Bake in the preheated oven for 20 minutes, or until well risen, golden brown and firm to the touch. Leave to cool in the tin for 5 minutes, then serve warm or transfer to a wire rack to cool completely.

750 With Limoncello icing

Beat 150 g/5½ oz mascarpone cheese, 50 g/1¾ oz icing sugar and 1 tablespoon of Limoncello liqueur together and spread over the cooled muffins. Scatter over chopped candied lemon peel.

2 oranges
about 100 ml/3½ fl oz milk
280 g/10 oz plain flour
1 tbsp baking powder
pinch of salt
115 g/4 oz caster sugar

6 cardamom pods, seeds removed and
    crushed
2 eggs
6 tbsp sunflower oil or 85 g/3 oz butter,
    melted and cooled

Preheat the oven to 200°C/400°F/Gas Mark 6. Line 2 x 24-hole mini muffin tins with 48 mini paper cases. Finely grate the rind from the oranges and squeeze the juice. Add enough milk to make the juice up to 250 ml/9 fl oz, then stir in the orange rind.

Sift together the flour, baking powder and salt into a large bowl. Stir in the sugar and crushed cardamom seeds. Place the eggs in a jug and beat lightly, then beat in the orange and milk mixture and the oil. Make a well in the centre of the dry ingredients and pour in the beaten liquid ingredients. Stir gently until just combined; do not overmix. Spoon the mixture into the paper cases. Bake in the preheated oven for 15 minutes. or until well risen, golden brown and firm to the touch. Leave to cool in the tins for 5 minutes, then serve warm or transfer to a wire rack to cool completely.

752 *With white chocolate icing*

Place 150 g/5½ oz white chocolate in a heatproof bowl, set the bowl over a saucepan of simmering water and heat until melted. Stir in ½ teaspoon of orange flower water and drizzle over the muffins.

753 *Mint chocolate chip muffins* MAKES 12

280 g/10 oz plain flour
1 tbsp baking powder
pinch of salt
115 g/4 oz caster sugar
150 g/5½ oz plain chocolate chips
2 eggs
250 ml/9 fl oz milk
6 tbsp sunflower oil or 85 g/3 oz
    butter, melted and cooled
1 tsp peppermint extract
1–2 drops of green food colouring
    (optional)
icing sugar, for dusting

chocolate chips. Place the eggs in a large jug or bowl and beat lightly, then beat in the milk, oil and peppermint extract. Add 1–2 drops of food colouring, if using.

Make a well in the centre of the dry ingredients and pour in the beaten liquid ingredients. Stir gently until just combined; do not overmix. Spoon the mixture into the paper cases.

Bake in the preheated oven for 20 minutes, or until well risen and firm to the touch. Leave to cool in the tin for 5 minutes, then serve warm or transfer to a wire rack to cool completely. Dust with sifted icing sugar before serving.

Preheat the oven to 200°C/400°F/Gas Mark 6. Line a 12-hole muffin tin with 12 paper cases.

Sift together the flour, baking powder and salt into a large bowl, then stir in the caster sugar and

754 *With chocolate ganache*

Heat 175 ml/6 fl oz double cream in a saucepan until simmering, then pour over 175 g/6 oz chopped plain chocolate and stir until smooth. Cool and chill until thick, then spread over the muffins.

755 Moist gingerbread muffins

> 6 tbsp sunflower oil or 85 g/3 oz butter, melted and cooled, plus extra for greasing
> 280 g/10 oz plain flour
> 1 tbsp baking powder
> 4 tsp ground ginger
> 1½ tsp ground cinnamon
> pinch of salt
> 115 g/4 oz soft light brown sugar
> 3 pieces stem ginger in syrup, finely chopped
> 2 eggs
> 175 ml/6 fl oz milk
> 4 tbsp golden syrup

Preheat the oven to 200°C/400°F/Gas Mark 6. Grease a 12-hole muffin tin. Sift together the flour, baking powder, ginger, cinnamon and salt into a large bowl. Stir in the sugar and stem ginger.

Place the eggs in a large jug or bowl and beat lightly, then beat in the milk, oil and golden syrup. Make a well in the centre of the dry ingredients and pour in the beaten liquid ingredients. Stir gently until just combined; do not overmix. Spoon the mixture into the muffin tin.

Bake in the preheated oven for 20 minutes, or until well risen, golden brown and firm to the touch. Leave to cool in the tin for 5 minutes, then serve warm or transfer to a wire rack to cool completely.

756 With lemon icing

Sift 150 g/5½ oz icing sugar into a bowl, add 1 tablespoon of lemon juice and mix until smooth, then spread over the muffins and leave to set.

757 Moist orange & almond muffins

> 2 oranges
> about 100 ml/3½ fl oz milk
> 225 g/8 oz plain flour
> 1 tbsp baking powder
> pinch of salt
> 115 g/4 oz caster sugar
> 55 g/2 oz ground almonds
> 2 eggs
> 6 tbsp sunflower oil or 85 g/3 oz butter, melted and cooled
> ½ tsp almond extract
> 40 g/1½ oz demerara sugar

Preheat the oven to 200°C/400°F/Gas Mark 6. Line a 12-hole muffin tin with 12 paper cases. Finely grate the rind from the oranges and squeeze the juice. Add enough milk to make the juice up to 250 ml/9 fl oz, then stir in the orange rind. Sift together the flour, baking powder and salt into a large bowl. Stir in the caster sugar and ground almonds.

Place the eggs in a bowl and beat lightly, then beat in the orange mixture, oil and almond extract. Make a well in the centre of the dry ingredients, pour in the liquid ingredients and mix. Spoon the mixture into the paper cases. Sprinkle the demerara sugar over the tops.

Bake in the preheated oven for 20 minutes, or until well risen, golden brown and firm to the touch. Leave to cool in the tin for 5 minutes, then serve warm or transfer to a wire rack to cool completely.

758 With flaked almond topping

Scatter 100 g/3½ oz flaked almonds over the muffins before they are baked.

Orange, walnut & rosemary muffins

280 g/10 oz plain flour
1 tbsp baking powder
½ tsp bicarbonate of soda
pinch of salt
115 g/4 oz caster sugar
70 g/2½ oz walnuts, coarsely chopped
2 eggs
250 ml/9 fl oz natural yogurt
6 tbsp sunflower oil or 85 g/3 oz
butter, melted and cooled
finely grated rind of 2 oranges
1 tbsp finely chopped fresh rosemary
leaves, plus extra sprigs to decorate

ICING
175 g/6 oz icing sugar
3–4 tsp fresh orange juice
finely grated rind of ½ orange

Preheat the oven to 200°C/400°F/Gas Mark 6. Line a 12-hole muffin tin with 12 paper cases. Sift together the flour, baking powder, bicarbonate of soda and salt into a large bowl. Stir in the caster sugar and walnuts.

Place the eggs in a large jug or bowl then beat in the yogurt, oil, orange rind and chopped rosemary leaves. Make a well in the centre of the dry ingredients and pour in the beaten liquid ingredients. Stir gently until just combined; do not overmix. Spoon the mixture into the paper cases.

Bake in the preheated oven for 20 minutes, or until well risen, golden brown and firm to the touch. Leave to cool in the tin for 5 minutes, then transfer to a wire rack to cool completely.

When the muffins are cold, make the icing. Sift the icing sugar into a bowl. Add the orange juice and orange rind and stir until the mixture is smooth and thick enough to coat the back of a wooden spoon.

Spoon the icing on top of each muffin. Decorate with a rosemary sprig and leave to set for about 30 minutes before serving.

Marbled chocolate muffins

6 tbsp sunflower oil or 85 g/3 oz butter,
melted and cooled, plus extra
for greasing
280 g/10 oz plain flour
1 tbsp baking powder
pinch of salt

115 g/4 oz caster sugar
2 eggs
250 ml/9 fl oz milk
1 tsp vanilla extract
2 tbsp cocoa powder

Preheat the oven to 200°C/400°F/Gas Mark 6. Grease a 12-hole muffin tin. Sift together the flour, baking powder and salt into a large bowl. Stir in the sugar.

Place the eggs in a large jug or bowl and beat lightly, then beat in the milk, oil and vanilla extract. Make a well in the centre of the dry ingredients and pour in the beaten liquid ingredients. Stir gently until just combined; do not overmix.

Divide the mixture between 2 bowls. Sift the cocoa powder into one bowl and mix together. Using teaspoons, spoon the mixtures into the muffin tin, alternating the chocolate mixture and the plain mixture.

Bake in the preheated oven for 20 minutes, or until well risen, golden brown and firm to the touch. Leave to cool in the tin for 5 minutes, then serve warm or transfer to a wire rack to cool completely.

761 ## Marbled coffee muffins

Replace the cocoa powder with espresso coffee powder.

762 Raspberry crumble muffins

6 tbsp sunflower oil or 85 g/3 oz butter,
    melted and cooled, plus extra
    for greasing
280 g/10 oz plain flour
1 tbsp baking powder
½ tsp bicarbonate of soda
pinch of salt
115 g/4 oz caster sugar
2 eggs

250 ml/9 fl oz natural yogurt
1 tsp vanilla extract
150 g/5½ oz frozen raspberries

CRUMBLE TOPPING
50 g/1¾ oz plain flour
35 g/1¼ oz butter, cut into pieces
25 g/1 oz caster sugar

Preheat the oven to 200°C/400°F/Gas Mark 6. Grease a 12-hole muffin tin.

To make the crumble topping, place the flour into a bowl. Add the butter and rub it in with your fingertips until the mixture resembles fine breadcrumbs. Stir in the sugar and set aside.

To make the muffins, sift together the flour, baking powder, bicarbonate of soda and salt into a large bowl. Stir in the sugar.

Place the eggs in a large jug or bowl and beat lightly, then beat in the yogurt, oil and vanilla extract. Make a well in the centre of the dry ingredients, pour in the beaten liquid ingredients and add the raspberries.

Stir gently until just combined; do not overmix. Spoon the mixture into the muffin tin. Scatter the crumble topping over each muffin and then press down lightly.

Bake in the preheated oven for 20 minutes, or until well risen, golden brown and firm to the touch. Leave to cool in the tin for 5 minutes, then serve warm or transfer to a wire rack to cool completely.

763 With almond crunch topping

Add 50 g/1¾ oz chopped toasted flaked almonds and 6 crushed amaretti biscuits to the crumble topping before scattering over the muffins.

764 Soured cream & pineapple muffins

6 tbsp sunflower oil or 85 g/3 oz
    butter, melted and cooled, plus
    extra for greasing
2 slices canned pineapple slices in
    natural juice, plus 2 tbsp juice
    from the can
280 g/10 oz plain flour
1 tbsp baking powder
pinch of salt
115 g/4 oz caster sugar
2 eggs
200 ml/7 fl oz soured cream
1 tsp vanilla extract

Preheat the oven to 200°C/400°F/Gas Mark 6. Grease a 12-hole muffin tin. Drain and finely chop the pineapple slices.

Sift together the flour, baking powder and salt into a large bowl. Stir in the sugar and chopped pineapple.

Place the eggs in a large jug or bowl and beat lightly, then beat in the soured cream, oil, pineapple juice and vanilla extract. Make a well in the centre of the dry ingredients and pour in the beaten liquid ingredients. Stir gently until just combined; do not overmix. Spoon the mixture into the muffin tin.

Bake in the preheated oven for 20 minutes, or until well risen, golden brown and firm to the touch. Leave to cool in the tin for 5 minutes, then serve warm or transfer to a wire rack to cool completely.

765 With pineapple frosting

Beat 100 g/3½ oz cream cheese with 2 tablespoons of icing sugar and 1 tablespoon of pineapple juice, then spread over the cooled muffins.

766 Spicy apple & oat muffins

6 tbsp sunflower oil, plus extra for
greasing
140 g/5 oz plain flour
1 tbsp baking powder
1 tsp ground mixed spice
115 g/4 oz soft light brown sugar

175 g/6 oz porridge oats
250 g/9 oz eating apples
2 eggs
125 ml/4 fl oz skimmed milk
125 ml/4 fl oz fresh apple juice

Preheat the oven to 200°C/400°F/Gas Mark 6. Grease a 12-hole muffin tin. Sift together the flour, baking powder and mixed spice into a large bowl. Stir in the sugar and 140 g/5 oz of the oats.

Finely chop the unpeeled apples, discarding the cores. Add to the flour mixture and stir together.

Place the eggs in a large jug or bowl and beat lightly, then beat in the milk, apple juice and oil. Make a well in the centre of the dry ingredients and pour in the beaten liquid ingredients. Stir gently until just combined; do not overmix. Spoon the mixture into the muffin tin and sprinkle the tops with the remaining oats.

Bake in the preheated oven for 20 minutes, or until well risen, golden brown and firm to the touch. Leave to cool in the tin for 5 minutes, then serve warm or transfer to a wire rack to cool completely.

767 Pear, oat & nutmeg muffins

Replace the apple and apple juice with 250 g/9 oz peeled, cored and chopped pear and pear juice, and add ½ teaspoon of ground nutmeg.

768 Spicy dried fruit muffins

6 tbsp sunflower oil or 85 g/3 oz butter,
melted and cooled
280 g/10 oz plain flour
1 tbsp baking powder
1 tbsp mixed spice
pinch of salt

115 g/4 oz caster sugar
175 g/6 oz mixed dried fruit
2 eggs
250 ml/9 fl oz milk

Preheat the oven to 200°C/400°F/Gas Mark 6. Line a 12-hole muffin tin with 12 paper cases. Sift together the flour, baking powder, mixed spice and salt into a large bowl. Stir in the sugar and dried fruit.

Place the eggs in a large jug or bowl and beat lightly, then beat in the milk and oil. Make a well in the centre of the dry ingredients and pour in the beaten liquid ingredients. Stir gently until just combined; do not overmix. Spoon the mixture into the paper cases.

Bake in the preheated oven for 20 minutes, or until well risen, golden brown and firm to the touch. Leave to cool in the tin for 5 minutes, then serve warm or transfer to a wire rack to cool completely.

769 With brandy cream

Whip 200 ml/7 fl oz double cream with 1 tablespoon of brandy and 1 tablespoon of caster sugar until stiff, then spoon onto the cooled muffins.

770 Chocolate muffins

225 g/8 oz plain flour
55 g/2 oz cocoa powder
1 tbsp baking powder
pinch of salt
115 g/4 oz soft light brown sugar
2 eggs

200 ml/7 fl oz soured cream
6 tbsp sunflower oil or 85 g/3 oz butter,
    melted and cooled
3 tbsp golden syrup

Preheat the oven to 200°C/400°F/Gas Mark 6. Line a 12-hole muffin tin with 12 paper cases. Sift together the flour, cocoa powder, baking powder and salt into a large bowl. Stir in the sugar.

Place the eggs in a large jug or bowl and beat lightly, then beat in the soured cream, oil and golden syrup. Make a well in the centre of the dry ingredients and pour in the beaten liquid ingredients. Stir gently until just combined; do not overmix. Spoon the mixture into the paper cases.

Bake in the preheated oven for 20 minutes, or until well risen and firm to the touch. Leave to cool in the tin for 5 minutes, then serve warm or transfer to a wire rack to cool completely.

771 With chocolate topping

Spread the cooled muffins with 200 g/7 oz chocolate hazelnut spread.

772 Sticky toffee muffins

6 tbsp sunflower oil or 85 g/3 oz butter,
    melted and cooled, plus extra
    for greasing
250 g/9 oz pitted dates
250 ml/9 fl oz water
280 g/10 oz plain flour
1 tbsp baking powder

pinch of salt
115 g/4 oz soft dark brown sugar
2 eggs
4 tbsp dulce de leche (from a jar),
    to serve

Preheat the oven to 200°C/400°F/Gas Mark 6. Grease a 12-hole muffin tin. Put the dates and water in a food processor and blend to form a rough purée. Sift together the flour, baking powder and salt into a large bowl. Stir in the sugar.

Place the eggs in a large jug or bowl and beat lightly, then beat in the date purée and oil. Make a well in the centre of the dry ingredients and pour in the beaten liquid ingredients. Stir gently until just combined; do not overmix. Spoon the mixture into the muffin tin.

Bake in the preheated oven for 20 minutes, or until well risen, golden brown and firm to the touch. Leave to cool in the tin for 5 minutes, then serve warm or transfer to a wire rack to cool completely. Spread a teaspoon of dulce de leche over the top of each muffin before serving.

Toasted almond & apricot muffins

100 g/3½ oz dried apricots, cut into small pieces
3 tbsp fresh orange juice
50 g/1¾ oz blanched almonds
280 g/10 oz plain flour
1 tbsp baking powder
pinch of salt
115 g/4 oz caster sugar

2 eggs
200 ml/7 fl oz buttermilk
6 tbsp sunflower oil or 85 g/3 oz butter, melted and cooled
¼ tsp almond extract
40 g/1½ oz flaked almonds

Place the apricots in a bowl, add the orange juice and leave to soak for 1 hour.

Preheat the oven to 200°C/400°F/Gas Mark 6. Line a 12-hole muffin tin with 12 paper cases. Preheat the grill and line a grill pan with foil. Spread out the almonds on the grill pan and toast until golden, turning frequently. Cool then chop coarsely.

Sift together the flour, baking powder and salt into a large bowl. Stir in the sugar and almonds.

Place the eggs in a large jug or bowl and beat lightly, then beat in the buttermilk, oil and almond extract. Make a well in the centre of the dry ingredients, pour in the beaten liquid ingredients and add the soaked apricots. Stir gently until just combined; do not overmix. Spoon the mixture into the paper cases. Scatter the flaked almonds on top of each muffin.

Bake in the preheated oven for 20 minutes, or until well risen, golden brown and firm to the touch. Leave to cool in the tin for 5 minutes, then serve warm or transfer to a wire rack to cool completely.

774 *With apricot centres*

Half fill each muffin case with mixture and spoon in a little apricot conserve in the middle, then cover with the remaining mix.

Tropical banana & passion fruit muffins

2 bananas
about 150 ml/5 fl oz milk
280 g/10 oz plain flour
1 tbsp baking powder
pinch of salt
115 g/4 oz soft light brown sugar
2 eggs

6 tbsp sunflower oil or 85 g/3 oz butter, melted and cooled
1 tsp vanilla extract
2 passion fruits
2 tbsp clear honey

Preheat the oven to 200°C/400°F/Gas Mark 6. Line a 12-hole muffin tin with 12 paper cases. Mash the bananas and put in a jug. Add enough milk to make the purée up to 250 ml/9 fl oz.

Sift together the flour, baking powder and salt into a large bowl. Stir in the sugar.

Place the eggs in a large jug or bowl and beat lightly, then beat in the banana and milk mixture, oil and vanilla extract. Make a well in the centre of the dry ingredients and pour in the beaten liquid ingredients. Stir gently until just combined; do not overmix. Spoon the mixture into the paper cases.

Bake in the preheated oven for 20 minutes, or until well risen, golden brown and firm to the touch. Leave to cool in the tin for 5 minutes, then transfer to a wire rack to cool completely.

Meanwhile, halve the passion fruits and spoon the pulp into a small saucepan. Add the honey and heat very gently until warmed through. Spoon on top of the muffins before serving.

776 Walnut & cinnamon muffins

280 g/10 oz plain flour
1 tbsp baking powder
1 tsp ground cinnamon
pinch of salt
115 g/4 oz soft light brown sugar
100 g/3½ oz walnuts, coarsely chopped

2 eggs
250 ml/9 fl oz milk
6 tbsp sunflower oil or 85 g/3 oz butter,
    melted and cooled
1 tsp vanilla extract

Preheat the oven to 200°C/400°F/Gas Mark 6. Line a 12-hole muffin tin with 12 paper cases. Sift together the flour, baking powder, cinnamon and salt into a large bowl. Stir in the sugar and walnuts.

Place the eggs in a large jug or bowl and beat lightly, then beat in the milk, oil and vanilla extract. Make a well in the centre of the dry ingredients and pour in the beaten liquid ingredients. Stir gently until just combined; do not overmix. Spoon the mixture into the paper cases.

Bake in the preheated oven for 20 minutes, or until well risen, golden brown and firm to the touch. Leave to cool in the tin for 5 minutes, then serve warm or transfer to a wire rack to cool completely.

777 Hazelnut & vanilla seed muffins

Replace the walnuts and cinnamon with 100 g/3½ oz chopped toasted hazelnuts and the seeds from a vanilla pod.

778 Lemon & poppy seed muffins

350 g/12 oz plain flour
1 tbsp baking powder
115 g/4 oz caster sugar
2 tbsp poppy seeds

55 g/2 oz butter
1 large egg, lightly beaten
225 ml/8 fl oz milk
finely grated rind and juice of 1 lemon

Preheat the oven to 190°C/375°F/Gas Mark 5. Line a 12-hole muffin tin with paper cases. Sift the flour and baking powder into a large bowl and stir in the sugar.

Heat a heavy-based frying pan over a medium-high heat and add the poppy seeds, then toast for about 30 seconds, shaking the pan to prevent them burning. Remove from the heat and add to the flour mixture.

Place the butter in a separate saucepan and heat over a low heat until melted. Transfer to a bowl and beat with the egg, milk, lemon rind and lemon juice. Pour into the dry mixture and stir well to form a soft, sticky dough. Add a little more milk if the mixture is too dry. Spoon the mixture into the paper cases.

Bake in the preheated oven for 25–30 minutes, or until risen, golden brown and firm to touch. Transfer to a wire rack to cool completely.

779 Cream & spice muffins

MAKES 12

6 tbsp sunflower oil or 85 g/3 oz
   butter, melted and cooled, plus extra
   for greasing
280 g/10 oz plain flour
1 tbsp baking powder
1 tsp ground cinnamon
½ tsp ground allspice

½ tsp freshly grated nutmeg
pinch of salt
115 g/4 oz soft light brown sugar
2 eggs
250 ml/9 fl oz double cream
icing sugar, for dusting

Preheat the oven to 200°C/400°F/Gas Mark 6. Grease a 12-hole muffin tin. Sift together the flour, baking powder, cinnamon, allspice, nutmeg and salt into a large bowl. Stir in the brown sugar.

Place the eggs in a large jug or bowl and beat lightly, then beat in the cream and oil. Make a well in the centre of the dry ingredients and pour in the beaten liquid ingredients. Stir gently until just combined; do not overmix. Spoon the mixture into the muffin tin.

Bake in the preheated oven for 20 minutes, or until well risen, golden brown and firm to the touch. Leave to cool in the tin for 5 minutes, then serve warm or transfer to a wire rack to cool completely. Dust with sifted icing sugar before serving.

780 With spice butter topping

Blend 150 g/5½ oz butter with 3 tablespoons of icing sugar and 1 teaspoon of ground mixed spice, then spread over the cooled muffins.

781 Triple chocolate muffins

MAKES 12

250 g/9 oz plain flour
25 g/1 oz cocoa powder
2 tsp baking powder
½ tsp bicarbonate of soda
100 g/3½ oz plain chocolate chips

100 g/3½ oz white chocolate chips
2 eggs, lightly beaten
300 ml/10 fl oz soured cream
85 g/3 oz light muscovado sugar
85 g/3 oz butter, melted

Preheat the oven to 200°C/400°F/Gas Mark 6. Line a 12-hole muffin tin with 12 paper cases. Sift the flour, cocoa, baking powder and bicarbonate of soda into a large bowl, then stir in the plain and white chocolate chips. Stir in the sugar.

Place the eggs, soured cream and butter in a separate bowl and mix well. Add the wet ingredients to the dry ingredients and stir gently until just combined; do not overmix. Spoon the mixture into the paper cases.

Bake in the preheated oven for 20 minutes, or until well risen and firm to the touch. Leave to cool in the tin for 5 minutes, then serve warm or transfer to a wire rack to cool completely.

782 Chocolate & cherry muffins

Replace the white chocolate chips with 85 g/3 oz chopped glacé cherries.

783 Easter muffins

MAKES 12

6 tbsp sunflower oil or 85 g/3 oz
    butter, melted and cooled, plus extra
    for greasing
225 g/8 oz plain flour
55 g/2 oz cocoa powder
1 tbsp baking powder
pinch of salt
115 g/4 oz soft light brown sugar

2 eggs
250 ml/9 fl oz buttermilk

TOPPING
1 quantity buttercream icing (page 10)
250 g/9 oz sugar-coated mini chocolate
    eggs, to decorate

Preheat the oven to 200°C/400°F/Gas Mark 6. Grease a 12-hole muffin tin. Sift together the flour, cocoa powder, baking powder and salt into a large bowl. Stir in the brown sugar.

Place the eggs in a large jug or bowl and beat lightly, then beat in the buttermilk and oil. Make a well in the centre of the dry ingredients and pour in the beaten liquid ingredients. Stir gently until just combined; do not overmix. Spoon the mixture into the muffin tin.

Bake in the preheated oven for 20 minutes, or until well risen and firm to the touch. Leave to cool in the tin for 5 minutes, then transfer to a wire rack to cool.

Place the icing in a piping bag fitted with a large star nozzle and pipe a circle around the top of each muffin to form a 'nest'. Place the eggs in the centre of each muffin to decorate.

784 Simnel muffins

Omit the icing. Roll out 100g/3½ oz marzipan and cut out 12 x 3-cm/ 1½-inch circles. Brush each muffin with a little apricot jam and press a marzipan circle onto the top of each muffin. Using 85 g/3 oz marzipan, roll out 12 balls and press one on top of each muffin, then use a kitchen blow torch to toast the tops.

785 Thanksgiving cranberry & orange muffins

MAKES 12

200 g/7 oz dried cranberries
3 tbsp fresh orange juice
6 tbsp sunflower oil or 85 g/3 oz butter,
    melted and cooled, plus extra
    for greasing
280 g/10 oz plain flour

1 tbsp baking powder
pinch of salt
115 g/4 oz caster sugar
2 eggs
200 ml/7 fl oz milk
finely grated rind of 1 orange

Put the cranberries in a bowl, add the orange juice and leave to soak for 1 hour. Preheat the oven to 200°C/400°F/Gas Mark 6. Grease a 12-hole muffin tin. Sift together the flour, baking powder and salt into a large bowl. Stir in the sugar.

Place the eggs in a large jug or bowl and beat lightly, then beat in the milk, oil and orange rind. Make a well in the centre of the dry ingredients, pour in the beaten liquid ingredients and add the cranberries and orange juice. Stir gently until just combined; do not overmix. Spoon the mixture into the muffin tin.

Bake in the preheated oven for 20 minutes, or until well risen, golden brown and firm to the touch. Leave to cool in the tin for 5 minutes, then serve warm or transfer to a wire rack to cool completely.

786 Cranberry, orange & pecan muffins

Add 85 g/3 oz chopped pecan nuts to the mixture for an extra crunch.

787 Halloween pumpkin muffins

280 g/10 oz plain flour
1 tbsp baking powder
1 tsp mixed spice
pinch of salt
115 g/4 oz soft dark brown sugar
2 eggs

200 ml/7 fl oz milk
6 tbsp sunflower oil or 85 g/3 oz butter, melted and cooled
425 g/15 oz canned pumpkin flesh
4 tbsp dulce de leche (from a jar)

Preheat the oven to 200°C/400°F/Gas Mark 6. Line a 12-hole muffin tin with 12 paper cases. Sift together the flour, baking powder, mixed spice and salt into a large bowl. Stir in the sugar.

Place the eggs in a large jug or bowl and beat lightly, then beat in the milk and oil. Make a well in the centre of the dry ingredients, pour in the beaten liquid ingredients and add the pumpkin flesh. Stir until combined; do not overmix. Spoon the mixture into the paper cases.

Bake in the preheated oven for 20 minutes, or until well risen, golden brown and firm to the touch. Leave to cool in the tin for 5 minutes, then serve warm or transfer to a wire rack to cool. Spread a teaspoon of dulce de leche over the top of each muffin before serving.

788 With maple butter icing

Omit the dulce de leche and make a butter icing by beating 175 g/6 oz butter with 3 tablespoons of maple syrup and 2 tablespoons of icing sugar. Spread over the cooled muffins.

789 Christmas snowflake muffins

280 g/10 oz plain flour
1 tbsp baking powder
1 tsp allspice
pinch of salt
115 g/4 oz soft dark brown sugar
2 eggs
100 ml/3½ fl oz milk
6 tbsp sunflower oil or 85 g/ 3 oz butter, melted and cooled
200 g/7 oz luxury mincemeat with cherries and nuts

TOPPING
450 g/1 lb ready-to-roll icing
icing sugar, for dusting
2½ tsp apricot jam
silver dragées, to decorate

Preheat the oven to 200°C/400°F/Gas Mark 6. Line a 12-hole muffin tin with 12 paper cases. Sift together the flour, baking powder, allspice and salt into a large bowl. Stir in the brown sugar.

Place the eggs in a large jug or bowl and beat lightly, then beat in the milk and oil. Make a well in the centre of the dry ingredients and pour in the liquid ingredients and mincemeat. Stir until combined; do not overmix. Spoon the mixture into the paper cases.

Bake in the preheated oven for 20 minutes, or until well risen, golden brown and firm to the touch. Leave to cool in the tin for 5 minutes, then transfer to a wire rack and leave to cool completely.

Knead the icing until pliable. Roll out the icing on a surface dusted with icing sugar to a thickness of 5 mm/¼ inch. Using a 7-cm/2¾-inch fluted cutter, cut out 12 'snowflakes'.

Heat the apricot jam until runny, then brush over the tops of the muffins. Place a snowflake on top of each one, then decorate with silver dragées.

790 Christmas holly muffins

Tint 50 g/1¾ oz royal icing with green food colouring and roll out, then cut out holly leaves and use to decorate the muffins. Add cranberries for the holly berries.

Rose-topped wedding muffins

MAKES 12

280 g/10 oz plain flour
1 tbsp baking powder
pinch of salt
115 g/4 oz caster sugar
2 eggs
250 ml/9 fl oz milk
6 tbsp sunflower oil or 85 g/3 oz butter, melted and cooled

1 tsp vanilla extract
12 ready-made sugar roses or fresh rose petals or buds, to decorate

ICING
175 g/6 oz icing sugar
3–4 tsp hot water

Preheat the oven to 200°C/400°F/Gas Mark 6. Increase the quantity of ingredients according to the number of wedding guests invited, double quantities each time to make 24 muffins. Line the appropriate number of muffin tins with paper cases.

Sift together the flour, baking powder and salt into a large bowl. Stir in the sugar. Place the eggs in a large jug or bowl and beat lightly, then beat in the milk, oil and vanilla extract. Make a well in the centre of the dry ingredients and pour in the beaten liquid ingredients. Stir gently until just combined; do not overmix. Spoon the mixture into the paper cases.

Bake in the preheated oven for 20 minutes, or until well risen, golden brown and firm to the touch. Leave to cool in the tin or tins for 5 minutes, then transfer to a wire rack to cool completely. Store in the freezer until required.

On the day of serving, if using fresh flowers, rinse and dry on kitchen paper. For the icing, sift the icing sugar into a bowl. Add the water and stir until the mixture is smooth and thick enough to coat the back of a wooden spoon. Spoon the icing on top of each muffin, then top with a rose petal, rose bud or sugar rose.

792 Berry-topped wedding muffins

Instead of the sugar roses, top with piles of jewel berries: mix red and white currants, pomegranate seeds and tiny wild strawberries and spoon onto the icing, then sift over a little icing sugar to finish.

793 Anniversary muffins

MAKES 12

6 tbsp sunflower oil or 85 g/3 oz butter, melted and cooled, plus extra for greasing
280 g/10 oz plain flour
1 tbsp baking powder
pinch of salt
115 g/4 oz caster sugar
2 eggs

250 ml/9 fl oz buttermilk
finely grated rind of 1 lemon

TOPPING
85 g/3 oz butter, softened
175 g/6 oz icing sugar
gold or silver dragées, to decorate

Preheat the oven to 200°C/400°F/Gas Mark 6. Grease a 12-hole muffin tin. Sift together the flour, baking powder and salt into a large bowl. Stir in the caster sugar.

Place the eggs in a large jug or bowl and beat lightly, then beat in the buttermilk, oil and lemon rind. Make a well in the centre of the dry ingredients and pour in the beaten liquid ingredients. Stir gently until just combined; do not overmix. Spoon the mixture into the muffin tin.

Bake in the preheated oven for 20 minutes, or until well risen, golden brown and firm to the touch. Leave to cool in the tin for 5 minutes, then transfer to a wire rack to cool completely.

To make the icing, place the butter in a large bowl and beat until fluffy. Sift in the icing sugar and beat together until smooth and creamy.

When the muffins are cold, put the icing in a piping bag fitted with a large star nozzle and pipe circles on top of each muffin to cover the top. Sprinkle with the gold or silver dragées to decorate.

794 Anniversary hearts

Tint 100 g/3½ oz royal icing with red food colouring and roll out thinly, then use a small heart-shaped cutter to cut out heart shapes and decorate the topping with 3 hearts set upright on each muffin.

795 Mother's day breakfast muffins

280 g/10 oz plain flour
1 tbsp baking powder
pinch of salt
115 g/4 oz caster sugar
2 eggs
250 ml/9 fl oz milk

6 tbsp sunflower oil or 85 g/3 oz butter,
    melted and cooled
1 tsp orange extract
icing sugar, for dusting
fresh strawberries, to serve

Preheat the oven to 200°C/400°F/Gas Mark 6. Line a 12-hole muffin tin with 12 paper cases. Sift together the flour, baking powder and salt into a large bowl. Stir in the caster sugar.

Place the eggs in a large jug or bowl and beat lightly, then beat in the milk, oil and orange extract. Make a well in the centre of the dry ingredients and pour in the beaten liquid ingredients. Stir gently until just combined; do not overmix. Spoon the mixture into the paper cases.

Bake in the preheated oven for 20 minutes, or until well risen, golden brown and firm to the touch. Leave to cool in the tin for 5 minutes. Meanwhile, arrange the strawberries in a bowl. Dust the muffins with sifted icing sugar and serve warm.

796 With chocolate honeycomb butter

Omit the strawberries and make honeycomb butter by beating 200 g/7 oz butter until soft, crushing 100 g/3½ oz chocolate-covered honeycomb and mixing into the butter, then serve with the muffins.

797 Valentine heart muffins

6 tbsp sunflower oil or 85 g/3 oz butter,
    melted and cooled, plus extra
    for greasing
225 g/8 oz plain flour
55 g/2 oz cocoa powder
1 tbsp baking powder
pinch of salt
115 g/4 oz soft light brown sugar
2 eggs
250 ml/9 fl oz buttermilk

MARZIPAN HEARTS
icing sugar, for dusting
70 g/2½ oz marzipan, coloured with
    a few drops of red food colouring

ICING
55 g/2 oz plain chocolate, broken
    into pieces
115 g/4 oz butter, softened
225 g/8 oz icing sugar

Preheat the oven to 200°C/400°F/Gas Mark 6. Grease a 12-hole heart-shaped muffin tin. Sift together the flour, cocoa powder, baking powder and salt into a large bowl. Stir in the brown sugar.

Place the eggs in a large jug or bowl and beat lightly, then beat in the buttermilk and oil. Make a well in the centre of the dry ingredients and pour in the beaten liquid ingredients. Stir until combined. Spoon the mixture into the muffin tin.

Bake in the preheated oven for 20 minutes, or until well risen and firm to the touch. Leave for 5 minutes, then transfter to a wire rack to cool completely.

Melt the chocolate. Beat the butter in a bowl until fluffy, sift in the icing sugar and beat until smooth. Add the chocolate and beat. Spread the icing on top of the muffins then decorate with a marzipan heart.

To make the marzipan hearts, dust a work surface with icing sugar, then roll out the marzipan to a thickness of 5 mm/¼ inch. Using a small heart-shaped cutter, cut out 12 hearts. Line a tray with baking paper, dust with icing sugar and place the hearts on it. Leave for 3–4 hours until dry.

798 White heart muffins

Omit the cocoa powder from the muffin mix and bake as before. Make the icing with white chocolate and cut the hearts from white marzipan.

799 Marshmallow muffins

6 tbsp sunflower oil or 85 g/3 oz butter, melted and cooled, plus extra for greasing
100 g/3½ oz mini white marshmallows
225 g/8 oz plain white flour
55 g/2 oz cocoa powder
1 tbsp baking powder
pinch of salt
115 g/4 oz soft light brown sugar
2 eggs
250 ml/9 fl oz milk

Preheat the oven to 200°C/400°F/Gas Mark 6. Grease a 12-hole muffin tin. Using scissors, cut the marshmallows in half. Sift together the flour, cocoa, baking powder and salt into a large bowl. Stir in the sugar and marshmallows.

Place the eggs in a large jug or bowl and beat lightly, then beat in the milk and oil. Make a well in the centre of the dry ingredients and pour in the beaten liquid ingredients. Stir gently until just combined; do not overmix. Spoon the mixture into the muffin tin.

Bake in the preheated oven for 20 minutes, or until well risen and firm to the touch. Leave to cool in the tin for 5 minutes, then serve warm or transfer to a wire rack to cool completely.

800 Chocolate chunk muffins

280 g/10 oz plain flour
1 tbsp baking powder
pinch of salt
115 g/4 oz caster sugar
175 g/6 oz chocolate chunks
2 eggs
250 ml/9 fl oz milk
6 tbsp sunflower oil or 85 g/3 oz butter, melted and cooled
1 tsp vanilla extract

Preheat the oven to 200°C/400°F/Gas Mark 6. Line a 12-hole muffin tin with 12 paper cases. Sift together the flour, baking powder and salt into a large bowl. Stir in the sugar and chocolate chunks.

Place the eggs in a large jug or bowl and beat lightly, then beat in the milk, oil and vanilla extract. Make a well in the centre of the dry ingredients and pour in the beaten liquid ingredients. Stir gently until just combined; do not overmix. Spoon the mixture into the paper cases.

Bake in the preheated oven for 20 minutes, or until well risen, golden brown and firm to the touch. Leave to cool in the tin for 5 minutes, then serve warm or transfer to a wire rack to cool completely.

801 Chocolate chunk & peanut muffins

Use 100 g/3½ oz chocolate chunks and 85 g/3 oz chopped salted peanuts.

802 Children's party muffins

280 g/10 oz plain flour
1 tbsp baking powder
½ tsp salt
115 g/4 oz caster sugar
2 eggs
250 ml/9 fl oz milk
6 tbsp sunflower oil or 85 g/3 oz butter,
   melted and cooled

1 tsp vanilla extract

TOPPING
175 g/6 oz icing sugar
3–4 tsp hot water
variety of small sweets, to decorate

Preheat the oven to 200°C/400°F/ Gas Mark 6. Line a 12-hole muffin tin with 12 paper cases. Sift together the flour, baking powder and salt into a large bowl. Stir in the caster sugar.

Place the eggs in a large jug or bowl and beat lightly, then beat in the milk, oil and vanilla extract. Make a well in the centre of the dry ingredients and pour in the beaten liquid ingredients. Stir until combined. Spoon the mixture into the paper cases.

Bake in the preheated oven for 20 minutes, or until well risen, golden brown and firm to the touch. Leave to cool in the tin for 5 minutes, then transfer to a wire rack to cool completely.

When the muffins are cold, make the icing. Sift the icing sugar into a bowl. Add the water and stir until the mixture is smooth and thick enough to coat the back of a wooden spoon. Spoon the icing on top of each muffin, then add the decoration of your choice. Leave to set for about 30 minutes before serving.

803 Signature muffins

Spread each muffin with the white icing and when set, write each child's name on a muffin with writing icing.

804 Birthday muffins

6 tbsp sunflower oil or 85 g/3 oz butter,
   melted and cooled, plus extra
   for greasing
280 g/10 oz plain flour
1 tbsp baking powder
pinch of salt
115 g/4 oz caster sugar
2 eggs

250 ml/9 fl oz milk
finely grated rind of 1 lemon
12 candles and candleholders, to decorate

ICING
85 g/3 oz butter, softened
175 g/6 oz icing sugar

Preheat the oven to 200°C/400°F/ Gas Mark 6. Grease a 12-hole muffin tin. Sift together the flour, baking powder and salt into a large bowl. Stir in the sugar.

Place the eggs in a large jug or bowl and beat lightly, then beat in the milk, oil and lemon rind. Make a well in the centre of the dry ingredients and pour in the beaten liquid ingredients. Stir gently until just combined; do not overmix. Spoon the mixture into the muffin tin.

Bake in the preheated oven for 20 minutes, or until well risen and golden brown. Leave to cool in the tin for 5 minutes then, transfer to a wire rack to cool completely.

To make the icing, place the butter in a large bowl and beat until fluffy. Sift in the icing sugar and beat together until smooth and creamy. When the muffins are cold, spread each one with a little of the icing, then place a candleholder and candle on top.

805 Multi-coloured muffins

Divide the butter icing into 4 portions and tint each one with a different food colouring. Spread over the muffins and match the candle colour to the icing colour.

6 tbsp sunflower oil or 85 g/3 oz butter, melted and cooled, plus extra for greasing
225 g/8 oz plain flour
55 g/2 oz cocoa powder
1 tbsp baking powder
pinch of salt
115 g/4 oz caster sugar
100 g/3½ oz white chocolate chips
50 g/1¾ oz white mini marshmallows, cut in half
2 eggs
250 ml/9 fl oz milk

Preheat the oven to 200°C/400°F/ Gas Mark 6. Grease a 12-hole muffin tin. Sift together the flour, cocoa powder, baking powder and salt into a large bowl. Stir in the sugar, chocolate chips and marshmallows.

Place the eggs in a large jug or bowl and beat lightly, then beat in the milk and oil. Make a well in the centre of the dry ingredients and pour in the beaten liquid ingredients. Stir gently until just combined; do not overmix. Spoon the mixture into the muffin tin.

Bake in the preheated oven for 20 minutes, or until risen and firm to the touch. Leave to cool in the tin for 5 minutes, then serve warm or transfer to a wire rack to cool completely.

807 *Extra rocky muffins*

Use 55 g/2 oz white chocolate chips and add 85 g/3 oz chopped Brazil nuts to the muffin mix for extra texture.

Brie & redcurrant muffins

6 tbsp sunflower oil or 85 g/3 oz butter,
  melted and cooled, plus extra
  for greasing
280 g/10 oz plain flour
1 tbsp baking powder
½ tsp bicarbonate of soda

pinch of salt
freshly ground black pepper
150 g/5½ oz Brie, finely cubed
2 eggs
250 ml/9 fl oz natural yogurt
4 tbsp redcurrant jelly

Preheat the oven to 200°C/400°F/Gas Mark 6. Grease a 12-hole muffin tin. Sift together the flour, baking powder, bicarbonate of soda, salt and pepper to taste into a large bowl. Stir in the Brie.

Place the eggs in a large jug or bowl and beat lightly, then beat in the yogurt and oil. Make a well in the centre of the dry ingredients and pour in the liquid ingredients. Stir until combined; do not overmix. Spoon half of the mixture into the muffin tin. Add a teaspoon of redcurrant jelly to the centre of each, then spoon in the remaining mixture.

Bake in the preheated oven for 20 minutes, or until well risen, golden brown and firm to the touch. Leave to cool in the tin for 5 minutes, then serve warm.

809 Fontina & pesto muffins

Replace the Brie with Fontina cheese and replace the redcurrant jelly with red pesto.

810 Caramelized onion muffins

7 tbsp sunflower oil
3 onions, finely chopped
1 tbsp red wine vinegar
2 tsp sugar
280 g/10 oz plain flour

1 tbsp baking powder
pinch of salt
freshly ground black pepper
2 eggs
250 ml/9 fl oz buttermilk

Preheat the oven to 200°C/400°F/Gas Mark 6. Line a 12-hole muffin tin with 12 paper cases. Heat 2 tablespoons of the oil in a frying pan. Add the onions and cook for 3 minutes, or until beginning to soften. Add the vinegar and sugar and cook, stirring occasionally, for a further 10 minutes, or until golden brown. Remove from the heat and leave to cool.

Meanwhile, sift together the flour, baking powder and salt and pepper to taste into a large bowl.

Place the eggs in a large jug or bowl and beat lightly, then beat in the buttermilk and the remaining oil. Make a well in the centre of the dry ingredients, pour in the beaten liquid ingredients and add the onion mixture, reserving 4 tablespoons for the topping. Stir gently until just combined;

do not overmix. Spoon the mixture into the paper cases. Sprinkle the reserved onion mixture on top of the muffins. Bake in the preheated oven for 20 minutes, or until well risen, golden brown and firm to the touch. Leave to cool in the tin for 5 minutes, then serve warm.

811 Caramelized red onion muffins

Replace the onion with red onions and use balsamic vinegar instead of wine vinegar.

812 Carrot & coriander muffins

6 tbsp sunflower oil or 85 g/3 oz butter,
  melted and cooled, plus extra
  for greasing
280 g/10 oz plain flour
1 tbsp baking powder
pinch of salt
freshly ground black pepper

200 g/7 oz carrots, grated
2 eggs
250 ml/9 fl oz buttermilk
3 tbsp chopped fresh coriander, plus
  extra sprigs to garnish

Preheat the oven to 200°C/400°F/Gas Mark 6. Grease a 12-hole muffin
tin. Sift together the flour, baking powder, salt and pepper to taste into
a large bowl. Stir in the grated carrots.

Place the eggs in a large jug or bowl and beat lightly, then beat in the
buttermilk, oil and chopped coriander. Make a well in the centre of the
dry ingredients and pour in the beaten liquid ingredients. Stir until just
combined; do not overmix. Spoon the mixture into the muffin tin.

Bake in the preheated oven for 20 minutes, or until well risen, golden
brown and firm to the touch. Leave to cool in the tin for 5 minutes, then
serve warm, garnished with sprigs of coriander.

813 Carrot, coriander & onion muffins

Add 2 finely chopped spring onions to the mixture along with the carrots.

814 Cheese & ham muffins

280 g/10 oz plain flour
1 tbsp baking powder
pinch of salt
100 g/3½ oz sliced ham, finely chopped
140 g/5 oz mature Cheddar cheese,
  coarsely grated

2 eggs
250 ml/9 fl oz milk
6 tbsp sunflower oil or 85 g/3 oz butter,
  melted and cooled
freshly ground black pepper

Preheat the oven to 200°C/400°F/Gas Mark 6. Line a 12-hole muffin
tin with 12 paper cases. Sift together the flour, baking powder, salt and
pepper to taste into a large bowl. Stir in the ham and 100 g/3½ oz of the
Cheddar cheese.

Place the eggs in a large jug or bowl and beat lightly, then beat in the
milk and oil. Make a well in the centre of the dry ingredients and pour
in the beaten liquid ingredients. Stir gently until just combined; do not
overmix. Spoon the mixture into the paper cases. Scatter the remaining
cheese over the tops of the muffins.

Bake in the preheated oven for 20 minutes, or until well risen, golden
brown and firm to the touch. Leave to cool in the tin for 5 minutes, then
serve warm.

815 Double cheese muffins

Cut 175 g/6 oz mozzarella cheese into cubes, omit the ham and add a cube
of mozzarella cheese to the middle of each muffin, then bake.

Chicken & sweetcorn muffins

7 tbsp sunflower oil, plus extra for
  greasing
1 onion, finely chopped
1 skinless chicken breast, about 175 g/
  6 oz, finely chopped
280 g/10 oz plain flour
1 tbsp baking powder

pinch of salt
freshly ground black pepper
2 eggs
250 ml/9 fl oz buttermilk
75 g/2¾ oz frozen sweetcorn kernels
ground paprika, to garnish

Preheat the oven to 200°C/400°F/Gas Mark 6. Grease a 12-hole muffin tin. Heat 1 tablespoon of the oil in a frying pan. Add the onion and cook for 2 minutes. Add the chicken and cook for about 5 minutes, stirring occasionally, until tender. Remove from the heat and leave to cool. Meanwhile, sift together the flour, baking powder, salt and pepper to taste into a large bowl.

Place the eggs in a large jug or bowl and beat lightly, then beat in the buttermilk and remaining oil. Make a well in the centre of the dry ingredients, pour in the beaten liquid ingredients and add the chicken mixture and sweetcorn. Stir gently until just combined; do not overmix. Spoon the mixture into the muffin tin.

Bake in the preheated oven for 20 minutes, or until well risen, golden brown and firm to the touch. Leave to cool in the tin for 5 minutes, sprinkle with paprika then serve warm.

817 Turkey & cranberry muffins

Replace the chicken breast with 175 g/6 oz turkey escalope and replace the sweetcorn with 85 g/3 oz frozen cranberries.

---

818 Courgette & sesame seed muffins

6 tbsp sunflower oil or 85 g/3 oz butter,
  melted and cooled, plus extra
  for greasing
300 g/10½ oz small, firm courgettes
280 g/10 oz plain flour
1 tbsp baking powder

pinch of salt
freshly ground black pepper
2 tbsp sesame seeds
½ tsp dried mixed herbs
2 eggs
250 ml/9 fl oz buttermilk

Preheat the oven to 200°C/400°F/Gas Mark 6. Grease a 12-hole muffin tin. Grate the courgettes, squeezing out any excess moisture.

Sift together the flour, baking powder, salt and pepper to taste into a large bowl. Stir in 4 teaspoons of the sesame seeds and the mixed herbs.

Place the eggs in a large jug or bowl and beat lightly, then beat in the buttermilk and oil. Make a well in the centre of the dry ingredients, pour in the beaten liquid ingredients and add the courgettes. Stir gently until just combined; do not overmix. Spoon the mixture into the muffin tin. Scatter the remaining 2 teaspoons of sesame seeds over the tops of the muffins.

Bake in the preheated oven for 20 minutes, or until well risen, golden brown and firm to the touch. Leave to cool in the tin for 5 minutes, then serve warm.

819 Courgette & feta cheese muffins

Add 150 g/5½ oz crumbled feta with the courgettes, then add a thin slice of courgette to the top of each muffin before scattering over the seeds.

820 Crispy bacon muffins

250 g/9 oz rindless, smoked streaky
  bacon
7 tbsp sunflower oil
1 onion, finely chopped
280 g/10 oz plain flour
1 tbsp baking powder

pinch of salt
freshly ground black pepper
2 eggs
250 ml/9 fl oz buttermilk

Preheat the oven to 200°C/400°F/ Gas Mark 6. Line a 12-hole muffin tin with 12 paper cases. Chop the bacon, reserving 3 rashers to garnish. Cut each of the reserved rashers into 4 pieces and set aside.

Heat 1 tablespoon of the oil in a frying pan. Add the onion and cook for 2 minutes.

Add the chopped bacon and cook for 5 minutes, stirring occasionally, until crispy. Leave to cool.

Meanwhile, sift together the flour, baking powder, salt and pepper to taste into a large bowl.

Place the eggs in a large jug or bowl and beat lightly, then beat in the buttermilk and remaining oil. Make a well in the centre of the dry ingredients, pour in the beaten liquid ingredients and add the bacon mixture. Stir gently until just combined; do not overmix. Spoon the mixture into

the paper cases. Place one of the reserved pieces of bacon on top of each muffin.

Bake in the preheated oven for 20 minutes, or until well risen, golden brown and firm to the touch. Leave to cool in the tin for 5 minutes, then serve warm.

821 Crispy bacon & spinach muffins

Melt 1 tablespoon of butter in a frying pan, add 85 g/3 oz fresh baby spinach leaves and stir for 1–2 minutes until wilted. Transfer to a sieve, press all the liquid out and chop, then add to the mixture before baking.

822 Crumble-topped cheese & chive muffins

6 tbsp sunflower oil or 85 g/3 oz butter,
  melted and cooled, plus extra
  for greasing
280 g/10 oz plain flour
1 tbsp baking powder
pinch of salt
freshly ground black pepper
150 g/5½ oz mature Cheddar cheese,
  coarsely grated

4 tbsp snipped fresh chives
2 eggs
250 ml/9 fl oz buttermilk

CRUMBLE TOPPING
50 g/1¾ oz plain flour
35 g/1¼ oz butter, cut into pieces
25 g/1 oz Cheddar cheese, finely grated
salt and freshly ground black pepper

Make a well in the centre of the dry ingredients and pour in the beaten liquid ingredients. Stir gently until just combined; do not overmix. Spoon the mixture into the muffin tin. Scatter the topping over the muffins.

Bake in the preheated oven for 20 minutes, or until well risen, golden brown and firm to the touch. Leave to cool in the tin for 5 minutes, then serve warm.

Preheat the oven to 200°C/400°F/ Gas Mark 6. Grease a 12-hole muffin tin.

To make the crumble topping, place the flour into a bowl. Add the butter and rub it in with your fingertips until the mixture resembles fine breadcrumbs. Stir in the Cheddar cheese and season

to taste with salt and pepper.

To make the muffins, sift together the flour, baking powder, salt and pepper to taste into a large bowl. Stir in the Cheddar cheese and chives.

Place the eggs in a large jug or bowl and beat lightly, then beat in the buttermilk and oil.

823 Parmesan & sage muffins

Replace the Cheddar cheese with 100 g/3½ oz finely grated Parmesan cheese and replace the chives with 2 tablespoons of finely shredded sage leaves.

Italian pesto muffins

280 g/10 oz plain flour
1 tbsp baking powder
pinch of salt
freshly ground black pepper
50 g/1¾ oz pine kernels
2 eggs

150 ml/5 fl oz buttermilk
6 tbsp sunflower oil or 85 g/3 oz butter,
    melted and cooled
6 tbsp pesto
10 g/¼ oz freshly grated Parmesan
    cheese

Preheat the oven to 200°C/400°F/Gas Mark 6. Line a 12-hole muffin tin with 12 paper cases. Sift together the flour, baking powder, salt and pepper to taste into a large bowl. Stir in the pine kernels.

Place the eggs in a large jug or bowl and beat lightly, then beat in the buttermilk, oil and pesto. Make a well in the centre of the dry ingredients and pour in the beaten liquid ingredients. Stir gently until just combined; do not overmix. Spoon the mixture into the paper cases. Scatter the Parmesan cheese over the tops of the muffins.

Bake in the preheated oven for 20 minutes, or until well risen, golden brown and firm to the touch. Leave to cool in the tin for 5 minutes, then serve warm.

825 *With ricotta cheese topping*

Beat 200 g/7 oz ricotta cheese with a pinch of salt and some freshly ground black pepper, pile into a serving bowl and drizzle over a little extra virgin olive oil, then use to spread on the warm muffins.

826 *Mini blue cheese & pear muffins*

6 tbsp sunflower oil or 85 g/3 oz
    butter, melted and cooled, plus
    extra for greasing
400 g/14 oz canned pear halves in
    natural juice, drained
280 g/10 oz plain flour
1 tbsp baking powder
pinch of salt
freshly ground black pepper
100 g/3½ oz blue cheese, such as
    Stilton or Danish Blue, finely
    crumbled
2 eggs
250 ml/9 fl oz milk
40 g/1½ oz walnut pieces

Preheat the oven to 200°C/400°F/Gas Mark 6. Oil 2 x 24-hole mini muffin tins. Chop the pears into small pieces. Sift together the flour, baking powder, salt and pepper to taste into a large bowl. Stir in the blue cheese and pears.

Place the eggs in a large jug or bowl and beat lightly, then beat in the milk and oil. Make a well in the centre of the dry ingredients and pour in the beaten liquid ingredients. Stir gently until just combined; do not overmix. Spoon the mixture into the muffin tins. Scatter the walnuts over the tops of the muffins.

Bake in the preheated oven for 15 minutes, or until well risen and golden brown. Leave to cool in the tins for 5 minutes, then serve warm.

827 *Mini blue cheese & onion muffins*

Replace the pears with 3 finely chopped spring onions.

828 Mini prawn & parsley muffins

6 tbsp sunflower oil or 85 g/3 oz butter,
  melted and cooled, plus extra
  for greasing
250 g/9 oz cooked peeled prawns
280 g/10 oz plain flour
1 tbsp baking powder

pinch of salt
freshly ground black pepper
2 eggs
250 ml/9 fl oz buttermilk
3 tbsp chopped fresh parsley

Preheat the oven to 200°C/400°F/Gas Mark 6. Grease 2 x 24-hole mini muffin tins. Chop the prawns into small pieces. Sift together the flour, baking powder, salt and pepper to taste into a large bowl. Stir in the chopped prawns.

Place the eggs in a large jug or bowl and beat lightly, then beat in the buttermilk, oil and parsley. Make a well in the centre of the dry ingredients and pour in the beaten liquid ingredients. Stir gently until just combined; do not overmix. Spoon the mixture into the muffin tin.

Bake in the preheated oven for 15 minutes, or until well risen, golden brown and firm to the touch. Leave to cool in the tin for 5 minutes, then serve warm.

829 Mini prawn & dill muffins

Stir 1 teaspoon of creamed horseradish into the buttermilk and replace the parsley with 2 tablespoons of finely chopped dill.

830 Parmesan & pine kernel muffins

280 g/10 oz plain flour
1 tbsp baking powder
pinch of salt
freshly ground black pepper
85 g/3 oz freshly grated Parmesan cheese
60 g/2¼ oz pine kernels
2 eggs

250 ml/9 fl oz buttermilk
6 tbsp sunflower oil or 85 g/3 oz butter,
  melted and cooled

TOPPING
10 g/¼ oz freshly grated Parmesan
  cheese
35 g/1¼ oz pine kernels

Preheat the oven to 200°C/400°F/Gas Mark 6. Line a 12-hole muffin tin with 12 paper cases. To make the topping, mix together the Parmesan cheese and pine kernels and set aside.

To make the muffins, sift together the flour, baking powder, salt and pepper to taste into a large bowl. Stir in the Parmesan and pine kernels.

Place the eggs in a large jug or bowl and beat lightly, then beat in the buttermilk and oil. Make a well in the centre of the dry ingredients and pour in the beaten liquid ingredients. Stir gently until just combined; do not overmix.

Spoon the mixture into the paper cases, then scatter the topping over the muffins.

Bake in the preheated oven for 20 minutes, or until well risen, golden brown and firm to the touch. Leave for 5 minutes then serve warm.

831 Pepperoni & sun-dried tomato muffins

MAKES 12

sunflower oil, for greasing
280 g/10 oz plain flour
1 tbsp baking powder
pinch of salt
freshly ground black pepper
1 tsp dried oregano
75 g/2¾ oz sun-dried tomatoes in oil,
drained (oil reserved) and finely
chopped
100 g/3½ oz pepperoni slices, finely
chopped
2 eggs
250 ml/9 fl oz buttermilk
1 garlic clove, crushed

Preheat the oven to 200°C/400°F/ Gas Mark 6. Grease a 12-hole muffin tin. Sift together the flour, baking powder, salt and pepper to taste into a large bowl. Stir in the oregano, tomatoes and pepperoni.

Place the eggs in a large jug or bowl and beat lightly, then beat in the buttermilk, 6 tablespoons of the reserved oil from the tomatoes and the garlic. Make a well in the centre of the dry ingredients and pour in the beaten liquid ingredients. Stir gently until just combined; do not overmix. Spoon the mixture into the muffin tin.

Bake in the preheated oven for 20 minutes, or until well risen, golden brown and firm to the touch. Leave to cool in the tin for 5 minutes, then serve warm.

832 Anchovy & caper muffins

Omit the pepperoni and add 3 chopped, drained anchovies and 2 teaspoons of chopped capers.

833 Shredded vegetable muffins

MAKES 12

6 tbsp sunflower oil, plus extra for
  greasing
125 g/4½ oz firm courgettes
125 g/4½ oz carrots
140 g/5 oz wholemeal flour
140 g/5 oz plain flour

1 tbsp baking powder
115 g/4 oz caster sugar
50 g/1¾ oz sultanas
2 eggs
250 ml/9 fl oz buttermilk

Preheat the oven to 200°C/400°F/Gas Mark 6. Grease a 12-hole muffin tin. Grate the courgettes and squeeze out any excess moisture. Place in a bowl and grate in the carrots.

Sift together both flours and the baking powder into a large bowl, adding any bran left in the sieve. Stir in the sugar and sultanas.

Place the eggs in a large jug or bowl and beat lightly, then beat in the buttermilk and oil. Make a well in the centre of the dry ingredients, pour in the beaten liquid ingredients and add the grated vegetables. Stir gently until just combined; do not overmix. Spoon the mixture into the muffin tin.

Bake in the preheated oven for 20 minutes, or until well risen, golden brown and firm to the touch. Leave to cool in the tin for 5 minutes, then serve warm or transfer to a wire rack to cool completely.

834 Shredded vegetable & cheese muffins

Omit the sultanas and sugar. Add 2 finely chopped spring onions and 3 tablespoons of finely grated Parmesan cheese.

835 Smoked salmon & dill muffins

> 6 tbsp sunflower oil or 85 g/3 oz butter, melted and cooled, plus extra for greasing
> 280 g/10 oz plain flour
> 1 tbsp baking powder
> pinch of salt
> freshly ground black pepper
>
> 2 eggs
> 250 ml/9 fl oz buttermilk
> 150 g/5½ oz smoked salmon, finely chopped, plus extra to garnish
> 2 tbsp chopped fresh dill, plus extra sprigs to garnish

Preheat the oven to 200°C/400°F/Gas Mark 6. Grease a 12-hole muffin tin. Sift together the flour, baking powder, salt and pepper to taste into a large bowl.

Place the eggs in a large jug or bowl and beat lightly, then beat in the buttermilk and oil. Make a well in the centre of the dry ingredients, pour in the beaten liquid ingredients and add the smoked salmon and chopped dill. Stir gently until just combined; do not overmix. Spoon the mixture into the muffin tin.

Bake in the preheated oven for 20 minutes, or until well risen, golden brown and firm to the touch. Leave to cool in the tin for 5 minutes, then serve warm. Serve garnished with smoked salmon and dill.

836 With lumpfish roe topping

Top each cooled muffin with a spoonful of crème fraîche, a strip of smoked salmon and ½ teaspoon of lumpfish roe. Finish with a dill sprig.

837 Soft cheese & garlic muffins

> 6 tbsp sunflower oil or 85 g/3 oz butter, melted and cooled, plus extra for greasing
> 280 g/10 oz plain flour
> 1 tbsp baking powder
> ½ tsp bicarbonate of soda
>
> pinch of salt
> freshly ground black pepper
> 2 eggs
> 150 ml/5 fl oz natural yogurt
> 150 g/5½ oz full-fat soft cheese, flavoured with garlic and herbs

Preheat the oven to 200°C/400°F/Gas Mark 6. Grease a 12-hole muffin tin. Sift together the flour, baking powder, bicarbonate of soda, salt and pepper to taste into a large bowl.

Place the eggs in a large jug or bowl and beat lightly, then beat in the yogurt, oil and soft cheese until smooth. Make a well in the centre of the dry ingredients and pour in the beaten liquid ingredients. Stir until just combined; do not overmix. Spoon the mixture into the muffin tin.

Bake in the preheated oven for 20 minutes, or until well risen, golden brown and firm to the touch. Leave to cool in the tin for 5 minutes, then serve warm.

838 Blue cheese & walnut muffins

Omit the full-fat soft cheese and use 150 g/5½ oz soft blue cheese, such as Gorgonzola, and add 2 tablespoons of chopped walnuts.

839 *Spicy chorizo muffins*

MAKES 12

280 g/10 oz plain flour
1 tbsp baking powder
pinch of salt
1 tsp ground paprika, plus extra to garnish
100 g/3½ oz chorizo sausage, outer casing removed, finely chopped
1 small red pepper, cored, deseeded and finely chopped
2 eggs
250 ml/9 fl oz buttermilk
6 tbsp sunflower oil or 85 g/3 oz butter, melted and cooled
1 garlic clove, crushed

Preheat the oven to 200°C/400°F/Gas Mark 6. Line a 12-hole muffin tin with 12 paper cases. Sift together the flour, baking powder, salt and paprika into a large bowl. Stir in the chorizo sausage and red pepper.

Place the eggs in a large jug or bowl and beat lightly, then beat in the buttermilk, oil and garlic. Make a well in the centre of the dry ingredients and pour in the beaten liquid ingredients. Stir gently until just combined; do not overmix. Spoon the mixture into the paper cases.

Bake in the preheated oven for 20 minutes, or until well risen, golden brown and firm to the touch. Leave to cool in the tin for 5 minutes, sprinkle with paprika, then serve warm.

840 *Spicy chorizo & green olive muffins*

Omit the red pepper and add 15 chopped, pitted green olives to the mix. Top each muffin with 1 whole pitted green olive before baking.

841 *Asparagus & soured cream muffins*

MAKES 12

7 tbsp sunflower oil, plus extra for greasing
225 g/8 oz fresh asparagus
280 g/10 oz plain white flour
1 tbsp baking powder
pinch of salt
freshly ground black pepper
2 eggs
250 ml/9 fl oz soured cream
40 g/1½ oz Cheddar cheese, finely grated

Preheat the oven to 200°C/400°F/Gas Mark 6. Grease a 12-hole muffin tin. Place 1 tablespoon of the oil in a roasting tin. Add the asparagus and turn in the oil. Roast in the oven for 10 minutes, or until tender. When cool enough to handle, coarsely chop the asparagus.

Sift together the flour, baking powder, salt and pepper to taste into a large bowl. Stir in the asparagus. Place the eggs in a large jug or bowl and beat lightly, then beat in the soured cream and remaining oil. Make a well in the centre of the dry ingredients and pour in the beaten liquid ingredients. Stir gently until just combined; do not overmix. Spoon the mixture into the muffin tin. Scatter the cheese over the tops.

Bake in the preheated oven for 20 minutes, or until well risen and firm to the touch. Leave to cool in the tin for 5 minutes, then serve warm.

842 *With asparagus tip topping*

Roll 12 asparagus tips in olive oil and place one on the centre of each muffin before baking.

253

843 Spinach & nutmeg muffins

8 tbsp sunflower oil, plus extra for
   greasing
250 g/9 oz frozen chopped spinach,
   thawed
1 onion, finely chopped
1 garlic clove, finely chopped
280 g/10 oz plain flour
1 tbsp baking powder

½ tsp freshly grated nutmeg
pinch of salt
freshly ground black pepper
2 eggs
250 ml/9 fl oz buttermilk
35 g/1¼ oz pine kernels

Preheat the oven to 200°C/400°F/Gas Mark 6. Grease a 12-hole muffin tin. Place the spinach in a sieve and drain well, squeezing out as much of the moisture as possible.

Heat 2 tablespoons of the oil in a frying pan. Add the onion and cook for about 3 minutes, or until beginning to soften. Add the garlic and cook for 1 minute. Add the spinach and cook for a further 2 minutes, stirring all the time. Remove from the heat and leave to cool.

Meanwhile, sift together the flour, baking powder, nutmeg, salt and pepper to taste into a large bowl.

Place the eggs in a large jug or bowl and beat lightly, then beat in the buttermilk and remaining oil. Make a well in the centre of the dry ingredients, pour in the beaten liquid ingredients and add the spinach mixture. Stir gently until just combined; do not overmix. Spoon the mixture into the muffin tin. Scatter the pine kernels over the tops.

Bake in the preheated oven for 20 minutes, or until well risen, golden brown and firm to the touch. Leave to cool in the tin for 5 minutes, then serve warm.

844 Spring onion & goat's cheese muffins

6 tbsp sunflower oil or 85 g/3 oz butter,
   melted and cooled, plus extra
   for greasing
280 g/10 oz plain flour
1 tbsp baking powder
pinch of salt

1 bunch spring onions, finely sliced
150 g/5½ oz goat's cheese, finely diced
2 eggs
250 ml/9 fl oz buttermilk
freshly ground black pepper

Preheat the oven to 200°C/400°F/Gas Mark 6. Grease a 12-hole muffin tin. Sift together the flour, baking powder, salt and pepper to taste into a large bowl. Stir in the spring onions and goat's cheese.

Place the eggs in a large jug or bowl and beat lightly, then beat in the buttermilk and oil. Make a well in the centre of the dry ingredients and pour in the beaten liquid ingredients. Stir gently until just combined; do not overmix. Spoon the mixture into the muffin tin.

Bake in the preheated oven for 20 minutes, or until well risen, golden brown and firm to the touch. Leave to cool in the tin for 5 minutes, then serve warm.

845 Goat's cheese & leek muffins

Omit the spring onions and sauté 1 finely chopped leek in 25 g/1 oz butter until soft. Cool and add to the muffin mix along with ½ teaspoon of English mustard powder and a pinch of cayenne pepper, then bake, as before.

846 Tomato & basil muffins

sunflower oil, for greasing
280 g/10 oz plain flour
1 tbsp baking powder
pinch of salt
freshly ground black pepper
100 g/3½ oz sun-dried tomatoes in oil,
    drained (oil reserved) and finely
    chopped

2 eggs
250 ml/9 fl oz buttermilk
4 tbsp chopped fresh basil leaves
1 garlic clove, crushed
10 g/¼ oz freshly grated Parmesan
    cheese

Preheat the oven to 200°C/400°F/Gas Mark 6. Grease a 12-hole muffin tin. Sift together the flour, baking powder, salt and pepper to taste into a large bowl. Stir in the sun-dried tomatoes.

Place the eggs in a large jug or bowl and beat lightly, then beat in the buttermilk, 6 tablespoons of the reserved oil from the tomatoes, the basil and garlic. Make a well in the centre of the dry ingredients and pour in the beaten liquid ingredients. Stir gently until just combined; do not overmix. Spoon the mixture into the muffin tin. Scatter the Parmesan cheese over the tops of the muffins.

Bake in the preheated oven for 20 minutes, or until well risen, golden brown and firm to the touch. Leave to cool in the tin for 5 minutes then serve warm.

847 Tomato, basil & black olive muffins

Use 5 tablespoons of oil, as before, plus 1 tablespoon of black olive tapenade.

848 Tuna & olive muffins

6 tbsp sunflower oil or 85 g/3 oz butter,
    melted and cooled, plus extra
    for greasing
90 g/3¼ oz pitted black olives
280 g/10 oz plain flour
1 tbsp baking powder
pinch of salt

freshly ground black pepper
2 eggs
250 ml/9 fl oz buttermilk
400 g/14 oz canned tuna in olive oil,
    drained and flaked

Preheat the oven to 200°C/400°F/Gas Mark 6. Grease a 12-hole muffin tin. Coarsely chop the olives, reserving 12 whole ones to garnish.

Sift together the flour, baking powder, salt and pepper to taste into a large bowl. Stir in the chopped olives. Place the eggs in a large jug or bowl and beat lightly, then beat in the buttermilk and oil. Make a well in the centre of the dry ingredients, pour in the beaten liquid ingredients and add the tuna. Stir gently until just combined; do not overmix. Spoon the mixture into the muffin tin. Top each muffin with one of the reserved olives.

Bake in the preheated oven for 20 minutes, or until well risen, golden brown and firm to the touch. Leave for 5 minutes, then serve warm.

849 Tuna, olive & caper muffins

For extra piquancy, add 2 teaspoons of chopped, drained capers to the mix.

Tempting Treats

CHOUX PASTRY
70 g/2½ oz butter, plus extra
for greasing
200 ml/7 fl oz water
100 g/3½ oz plain flour
3 eggs, lightly beaten

CREAM FILLING
300 ml/10 fl oz double cream
3 tbsp caster sugar
1 tsp vanilla extract

CHOCOLATE SAUCE
125 g/4½ oz plain chocolate, broken
into small pieces
35 g/1¼ oz butter
6 tbsp water
2 tbsp brandy

Preheat the oven to 200°C/400°F/Gas Mark 6. Grease a large baking sheet. Sift the flour. Place the butter and water into a pan and heat gently until the butter has melted. Bring to a boil, then remove from the heat and immediately add all the flour, beating well until the mixture leaves the sides of the saucepan and forms a ball. Leave to cool slightly. Beat in enough of the eggs to give the mixture a soft dropping consistency. Transfer the mixture to a piping bag fitted with a 1-cm/½-inch plain nozzle and pipe small balls onto the baking tray.

Bake in the preheated oven for 25 minutes. Remove from the oven and pierce each ball with a skewer to allow the steam to escape.

For the filling, place the cream, sugar and vanilla extract in a bowl and whip together. Cut the pastry balls almost in half and fill with the cream.

To make the sauce, place the chocolate, butter and water in a heatproof bowl, set the bowl over a saucepan of gently simmering water and heat until smooth. Stir in the brandy. Pile the profiteroles into individual serving dishes or into a pyramid on a raised cake stand. Pour over the sauce and serve.

851 *Chocolate & banana profiteroles*

Make the profiteroles and sauce. Just before serving, whip the cream, sugar and vanilla until just holding soft peaks. Mash 1 large ripe banana with a fork until smooth, then fold into the cream. Fill the profiteroles and serve immediately.

852 *With strawberry coulis*

Whiz 250 g/9 oz strawberries in a food processor, then push through a sieve to remove the pips. Stir in 25 g/1 oz icing sugar and 2 tablespoons of Framboise or peach schnapps. Serve with the profiteroles.

853 Flaky cream puffs

450 g/1 lb puff pastry, thawed if frozen
plain flour, for dusting
1 egg
1 tbsp water
4 tbsp caster sugar

250 ml/9 fl oz double cream or
whipping cream
1 tsp vanilla extract
85 g/3 oz raspberry or strawberry jam

Preheat the oven to 220°C/425°F/Gas Mark 7. Line a large baking sheet with baking paper. Roll the pastry out on a lightly floured work surface to a little larger than 25 cm/10 inches square. Using a sharp knife, trim the edges and cut out 4 x 13-cm/5-inch squares. Cut each square in half diagonally to produce 8 triangles and place on the lined baking sheet.

Beat the egg with the water and brush over the tops of the triangles, taking care not to let it run down the sides. Sprinkle the tops with half the sugar.

Bake in the preheated oven for 15 minutes, or until risen, crisp and golden. Transfer to a wire rack to cool completely.

Place the cream, remaining sugar and vanilla extract in a large bowl and whip until peaks form. Spoon into a piping bag fitted with a star nozzle. Split the puff pastry triangles in half horizontally and spread jam on the bottom halves. Pipe the cream on top of the jam and sandwich the 2 halves back together. Chill in the refrigerator until required.

854 Flaky apple cream puffs

While the pastry is cooking, peel, core and slice 4 eating apples. Place in a saucepan with 25 g/1 oz butter, 25 g/1 oz soft light brown sugar and ½ teaspoon of mixed spice and cook gently for 2–3 minutes, or until softened. Leave to cool. Whip the cream, omitting the sugar and vanilla. Spoon the apple into the pastry puffs and top with cream to sandwich the pastry back together.

855 Cinnamon knots

50 g/1¾ oz butter, plus extra for greasing
½ tsp ground cinnamon
1 tsp caster sugar

2 tbsp icing sugar
6 sheets filo pastry (total weight about
90 g/3¼ oz)

Preheat the oven to 180°C/350°F/Gas Mark 4. Grease a large baking sheet. Place the butter in a saucepan and heat gently until melted, then cool.

Place the cinnamon and sugars in a large bowl and stir together. Brush 1 sheet of filo pastry with melted butter. Cover the remaining sheets with a damp tea towel. Sprinkle a little of the cinnamon mixture over the pastry. Lay a second sheet of pastry on top and repeat until the pastry and cinnamon mix have been used, reserving a little of the cinnamon mix to decorate. Cut the pastry widthways into 2-cm/¾-inch strips and tie each strip into a knot. Place on the baking sheet.

Bake in the preheated oven for 15–20 minutes, or until golden brown. Leave to cool. Dust with the reserved cinnamon mixture.

CHOUX PASTRY
70 g/2½ oz butter, diced, plus extra
    for greasing
150 ml/5 fl oz water
100 g/3½ oz plain flour
2 eggs

PASTRY CREAM
2 eggs, lightly beaten
4 tbsp caster sugar
2 tbsp cornflour

300 ml/10 fl oz milk
¼ tsp vanilla extract

ICING
25 g/1 oz butter
1 tbsp milk
1 tbsp cocoa powder
55 g/2 oz icing sugar
50 g/1¾ oz white chocolate,
    broken into pieces

Preheat the oven to 200°C/400°F/Gas Mark 6. Grease a baking sheet. Sift the flour. Place the butter and water in a saucepan and heat gently until the butter has melted. Bring to a boil, then remove from the heat and immediately add all the flour, beating well until the mixture leaves the sides of the saucepan and forms a ball.

Leave to cool slightly, then gradually beat in the eggs to form a smooth, glossy mixture. Spoon into a large piping bag fitted with a 1-cm/½-inch plain nozzle. Sprinkle the baking sheet with a little water and pipe éclairs 7.5 cm/3 inches long, spaced well apart.

Bake in the preheated oven for 30–35 minutes, or until crisp and golden. Make a small slit in the side of each éclair, then transfer to a wire rack to cool. Meanwhile, to make the pastry cream, place the eggs and sugar in a large bowl and whisk together until thick and creamy. Fold in the cornflour. Heat the milk in a pan until almost boiling,

then pour onto the egg mixture, whisking. Transfer to the pan and cook gently, stirring until thick. Remove from the heat and stir in the vanilla extract. Cover and leave to cool.

To make the icing, melt the butter and milk in a separate saucepan. Remove from the heat and stir in the cocoa and icing sugar. Split the éclairs lengthways and pipe in the pastry cream. Spread the icing over the top of the éclairs. Place the white chocolate in a heatproof bowl, set the bowl over a saucepan of gently simmering water and heat until melted, then drizzle over the chocolate icing and leave to set.

857 *Double choc éclairs*

To make a chocolate pastry cream, add 85 g/3 oz finely chopped milk or plain chocolate to the hot milk and stir until the chocolate has melted to produce a chocolate milk.

858 *Coffee éclairs*

To make a coffee pastry cream, stir 2 tablespoons of instant coffee into the hot milk. To make coffee icing, melt the butter with the milk and 1 tablespoon of instant coffee.

859 Toffee chocolate puff tarts

375 g/13 oz ready-rolled puff pastry
140 g/5 oz plain chocolate, broken
into pieces
300 ml/10 fl oz double cream
50 g/1¾ oz caster sugar
4 egg yolks
4 tbsp ready-made toffee sauce
whipped cream, to serve
cocoa powder, for dusting

Line the bases of a 12-hole muffin tin with discs of baking paper. Cut out 12 x 5-cm/2-inch rounds from the edge of the pastry and cut the remainder into 12 strips. Roll the strips to half their thickness and line the sides of each hole with 1 strip. Place a disc of pastry in each base and press together to seal and make a tart case. Prick the bases

and chill in the refrigerator for 30 minutes.

Preheat the oven to 200°C/400°F/Gas Mark 6. While the pastry is chilling, place the chocolate in a heatproof bowl, set the bowl over a saucepan of gently simmering water and heat until melted. Leave to cool slightly, then stir in the cream.

Place the sugar and egg yolks in a bowl and beat together, then mix well with the melted chocolate. Place a teaspoonful of the toffee sauce into each tart case, then divide the chocolate mixture evenly between the tarts.

Bake in the preheated oven for 20–25 minutes, turning the tray

around halfway through cooking, until just set. Leave to cool in the tin, then remove carefully and serve with whipped cream, dusted with cocoa.

860 Cherry chocolate puff tarts

Replace the toffee sauce with black cherry jam.

861 Toffee nut chocolate puffs

Stir 55 g/2 oz chopped hazelnuts or pecan nuts into the melted chocolate, before stirring in the cream.

862 Crown loaf

25 g/1 oz butter, diced, plus extra
for greasing
225 g/8 oz strong white flour, plus
extra for dusting
½ tsp salt
7 g/¼ oz easy-blend dried yeast
125 ml/4 fl oz tepid milk
1 egg, lightly beaten

FILLING
55 g/2 oz butter, softened
50 g/1¾ oz soft light brown sugar
2 tbsp chopped hazelnuts
1 tbsp chopped stem ginger
50 g/1¾ oz chopped mixed peel
1 tbsp dark rum or brandy

ICING
115 g/4 oz icing sugar
1–2 tbsp lemon juice

Grease a large baking sheet. Sift the flour and salt into a bowl, then stir in the yeast. Add the butter and rub it in with your fingertips. Add the milk and egg and mix to form a dough. Place the dough in a greased bowl, cover and stand in a warm place for 40 minutes, until doubled in size. Punch down the dough lightly for 1 minute, then

roll out on a lightly floured work surface to a rectangle measuring 30 x 23 cm/12 x 9 inches.

For the filling, place the butter and sugar in a large bowl and beat together until light and fluffy. Stir in the hazelnuts, ginger, mixed peel and rum and spread the filling over the dough, leaving a 2.5-cm/1-inch border. Roll up the dough, starting from one of the long edges, into a sausage shape. Cut into slices at 5-cm/2-inch intervals and place, cut-side down, in a circle on the baking tray with the slices just

touching. Cover and stand in a warm place for 30 minutes.

Preheat the oven to 190°C/375°F/Gas Mark 5. Bake the loaf for 20–30 minutes, or until golden. Meanwhile, mix the icing sugar with enough lemon juice to form a thin icing.

Leave the loaf to cool slightly before drizzling with the icing. Leave to set before serving.

863 Cherry & almond crown

Replace the hazelnuts with chopped almonds and the stem ginger and mixed peel with 55 g/2 oz chopped glacé cherries.

175 g/6 oz butter, softened, plus extra
for greasing
500 g/1 lb 2 oz strong white flour, plus
extra for dusting
½ tsp salt
7 g/¼ oz easy-blend dried yeast

25 g/1 oz lard or white vegetable fat
1 egg, lightly beaten
225 ml/8 fl oz tepid water
100 g/3½ oz plain chocolate, broken
into 12 squares
beaten egg, for glazing

Grease a large baking sheet. Sift the flour and salt into a bowl and stir
in the yeast. Add the lard and rub it in with your fingertips. Add the
egg and enough of the water to form a soft dough. Knead for
10 minutes until the dough is smooth and elastic.

Roll the dough out on a lightly floured work surface to a 38 x 20-cm/
15 x 8-inch rectangle and mark it vertically into thirds. Divide the
butter into 3 portions and dot one portion over the first two thirds of
the rectangle, leaving a small border around the edge. Fold the rectangle
into 3 by first folding over the plain part of the dough, then folding over
the other side. Seal the edges of the dough by pressing with a rolling
pin. Give the dough a quarter turn and roll out as big as the original
rectangle. Fold again (without adding butter), then wrap in clingfilm
and chill for 30 minutes. Repeat this rolling, folding and turning twice
more until all of the butter has been used, chilling the dough each time.
Re-roll and fold twice more without butter. Chill for a final 30 minutes.

Roll the dough out on a lightly floured work surface to 45 x 30 cm/
18 x 12 inches and halve lengthways. Cut each half into 6 rectangles
and brush with beaten egg. Place a chocolate square at one end of each
rectangle and roll up to form a sausage. Press the ends together and
place, seam-side down, on the baking sheet. Cover and leave in a warm
place for 40 minutes.

Preheat the oven to 220°C/425°F/Gas Mark 7. Brush each pastry with
egg and bake in the preheated oven for 20–25 minutes, or until golden.
Cool on a wire rack. Serve warm or cold.

865 *Pain au chocolat et noisette*

*Place a rounded teaspoon of chocolate hazelnut spread instead of the
chocolate in each pastry.*

866 *Pain au apricot*

*Mix 85 g/3 oz chopped ready-to-eat dried apricots with 3 tablespoons of
ground almonds and 1 tablespoon of caster sugar and use to fill the pastries.*

500 g/1 lb 2 oz strong white flour,
plus extra for dusting
40 g/1½ oz caster sugar
1 tsp salt
2 tsp easy-blend dried yeast
300 ml/10 fl oz lukewarm milk
300 g/10½ oz butter, softened,
plus extra for greasing
1 egg, lightly beaten with 1 tbsp milk,
for glazing

Sift the dry ingredients into a large bowl, make a well in the centre and add the milk. Mix to form a soft dough, adding more milk if too dry, then knead on a lightly floured surface for 5–10 minutes, or until smooth and elastic. Place in a large, greased bowl, cover and leave in a warm place until doubled in size.

Meanwhile, place the butter between 2 sheets of baking paper and flatten with a rolling pin to form a rectangle about 5 mm/¼ inch thick. Leave to chill in the refrigerator.

Knead the dough for 1 minute. Remove the butter from the refrigerator and leave to soften slightly. Roll the dough out on a well-floured work surface to 46 x 15 cm/18 x 6 inches.

Place the butter in the centre, folding up the sides and squeezing the edges together gently. With the short end of the dough towards you, fold the top third down towards the centre, then fold the bottom third up. Give the dough a quarter turn, roll out as big as the original rectangle and fold again. If the butter feels soft, wrap the dough in clingfilm and chill for 30 minutes. Repeat the rolling process twice more. Cut the dough in half.

Roll out each half into a rectangle about 5 mm/¼ inch thick. To cut out the croissants,

use a cardboard triangular template, with a 18-cm/7-inch base and 20-cm/8-inch side.

Brush the triangles lightly with the glaze. Roll into croissant shapes, starting at the base and tucking the point underneath to prevent the croissants from unrolling while cooking. Brush again with the glaze. Place on a baking sheet and leave to double in size.

Preheat the oven to 200°C/ 400°F/Gas Mark 6. Bake the croissants in the preheated oven for 15–20 minutes, or until golden brown. Transfer to a wire rack to cool and serve warm.

868 *Ham & cheese croissants*

Make and roll out the croissants as before. Sprinkle the dough triangles with grated cheese and chopped ham before rolling into croissant shapes.

869 *Sun-dried tomato croissants*

Spread the dough triangles with sun-dried tomato paste before rolling up and shaping the croissants.

870 *Almond croissants*

Roll a walnut-sized piece of marzipan into a sausage shape a little shorter than the long side of each triangle of dough and roll up the croissants around the marzipan. After baking, dust with icing sugar to serve.

Apple danish

DANISH PASTRY DOUGH
280 g/10 oz strong white flour, plus extra for dusting
175 g/6 oz butter, well chilled, plus extra for greasing
¼ tsp salt
7 g/¼ oz easy-blend dried yeast
2 tbsp caster sugar
1 egg
1 tsp vanilla extract
6 tbsp lukewarm water
milk, for glazing

FILLING
2 cooking apples, peeled, cored and chopped
grated rind of 1 lemon
4 tbsp sugar

Place the flour in a bowl, add 25 g/1 oz of the butter and rub it in with your fingertips. Chill the remaining butter in the freezer until hard but not frozen. Dust with flour and grate coarsely into a bowl. Leave to chill in the refrigerator. Stir the salt, yeast and sugar into the flour mixture.

Place the egg, vanilla extract and water in a bowl and beat together, then add to the flour mixture and mix to form a dough. Knead for 10 minutes on a floured work surface, then chill for 10 minutes. Roll the dough out on a lightly floured work surface to 30 x 20cm/12 x 8 inches and mark it into thirds lengthways. Sprinkle the grated butter over the top two thirds, leaving a 1–2-cm/½–¾-inch border around the edge. Fold the bottom third of dough over the centre, then fold down the top third. Give the dough a quarter turn and roll out as big as the original rectangle. Fold the bottom third up and the top third down again. Wrap and chill for 30 minutes. Repeat this rolling, folding and turning 4 times, chilling each time. Chill the dough overnight.

Preheat the oven to 200°C/400°F/Gas Mark 6. Grease 2 baking sheets. Mix together the apples, lemon rind and 3 tablespoons of the sugar. Roll the dough out into a 40-cm/16-inch square and cut into 16 squares. Pile a little of the filling in the centre of each square. Brush the edges with milk and fold the corners together into the centre. Chill on the baking sheets for 15 minutes.

Brush the pastries with milk and sprinkle with the remaining sugar. Bake in the preheated oven for 10 minutes. Reduce the oven temperature to 180°C/350°F/Gas Mark 4 and bake for a further 10–15 minutes.

872 Apple & sultana danish

Replace the cooking apples with 2 dessert apples and add 85 g/3 oz sultanas.

873 Apricot danish

For the filling, drain and chop 400 g/14 oz canned apricots in natural juice. Toss with the lemon rind, sugar and ½ teaspoon of ground nutmeg.

874 Cherry & almond danish

For the filling, drain and chop 400 g/14 oz canned cherries. Toss with the lemon rind, sugar and 55 g/2 oz ground almonds and 2 tablespoons of the cherry juice from the can.

875 Pear & raisin danish

For the filling, replace the apples with 2 pears and add 85 g/3 oz raisins.

FILLING AND TOPPING
2 tsp powdered gelatine
2 tbsp water
350 g/12 oz strawberries
225 g/8 oz ricotta cheese
1 tbsp caster sugar
2 tsp crème de fraises de bois
icing sugar, for dusting

PETITS CHOUX
100 g/3½ oz plain flour
2 tbsp cocoa powder
pinch of salt
85 g/3 oz butter
225 ml/8 fl oz water
2 eggs, plus 1 egg white, lightly beaten

Sprinkle the gelatine over the water in a heatproof bowl and leave to soften for 2 minutes, then place the bowl over a saucepan of simmering water and stir until the gelatine dissolves. Remove from the heat.

Place 225 g/8 oz of the strawberries in a blender with the ricotta, sugar and liqueur and process until blended. Add the gelatine and process briefly. Transfer the mousse to a bowl, cover with clingfilm and chill in the refrigerator for 1–1½ hours, or until set.

Preheat the oven to 220°C/425°F/Gas Mark 7. Line a large baking sheet with baking paper.

To make the petits choux, sift together the flour, cocoa and salt. Place the butter and water in a saucepan and heat gently until the butter has melted. Bring to a boil, then remove from the heat and immediately add all the flour mixture, beating well until the mixture leaves the sides of the saucepan and forms a ball. Leave to cool slightly.

Gradually beat the eggs and egg white into the flour paste and continue beating until it is smooth and glossy, then drop 12 rounded tablespoonfuls of the mixture onto the baking sheet. Bake in the preheated oven for 20–25 minutes, or until puffed up and crisp.

Make a slit in the side of each petit chou, then return to the oven for a further 5 minutes. Transfer to a wire rack to cool.

Slice the remaining strawberries. Cut the petits choux in half and divide the mousse and strawberries between them. Replace the tops and dust with sifted icing sugar. Chill in the refrigerator until required, but eat within 1½ hours of making.

877 *Raspberry petits choux*

Replace the strawberries with raspberries and place whole raspberries into the filled pastries with the mousse.

878 *Apricot petits choux*

Drain 2 x 400 g/14 oz canned apricots in natural juice and use in place of the strawberries.

MOCHA MOUSSE
200 g/7 oz plain chocolate, broken
into pieces
1½ tsp cold, strong black coffee
1 egg yolk
1½ tsp Kahlùa or other coffee liqueur
2 egg whites
200 g/7 oz raspberries

SPONGE CAKE
20 g/¾ oz butter, for greasing
1 egg, plus 1 egg white
4 tbsp caster sugar
5 tbsp plain flour

To make the mocha mousse, place 55 g/2 oz of the chocolate in a heatproof bowl, set the bowl over a saucepan of gently simmering water and heat until melted. Add the coffee and stir over a low heat until smooth, then leave to cool slightly. Stir in the egg yolk and the coffee liqueur. Place the egg whites in a separate bowl and whisk until stiff peaks form. Fold into the chocolate mixture, cover with clingfilm and chill for 2 hours, or until set.

For the sponge cake, lightly grease a 20-cm/8-inch square cake tin and line the base with baking paper. Place the egg and extra white with the sugar in a heatproof bowl set over a saucepan of gently simmering water. Whisk for 5–10 minutes, or until pale and thick. Remove from the heat and continue whisking

for 10 minutes until cold and a trail is left when the whisk is dragged across the surface.

Preheat the oven to 180°C/350°F/Gas Mark 4. Sift the flour over the egg mixture and fold it in. Pour the mixture into the tin and spread evenly. Bake in the preheated oven for 20–25 minutes, or until firm to the touch. Cool on a wire rack, then invert the cake, leaving the paper in place.

To make the chocolate boxes, grease a 30 x 23-cm/12 x 9-inch Swiss roll tin and line with baking paper. Place the remaining chocolate in a heatproof bowl,

set the bowl over a pan of gently simmering water and heat until melted, but not too runny. Pour into the pan and spread evenly with a spatula. Leave to set in a cool place for about 30 minutes.

Turn out the set chocolate onto baking paper. Cut it into 36 rectangles, measuring about 7.5 x 2.5 cm/3 x 1 inches. Cut 12 of these rectangles in half to make 24 rectangles measuring about 4 x 2.5 cm/1½ x 1 inches.

Trim the edges off the sponge cake, then cut it into 12 slices, measuring about 7.5 x 3 cm/3 x 1¼-inches. Spread a little of

the mocha mousse along the sides of each sponge rectangle and press 2 long and 2 short chocolate rectangles onto the sides to make boxes. Divide the remaining mousse among the boxes and top with raspberries. Chill in the refrigerator until ready to serve.

880 *Strawberry chocolate boxes*

Make as before but omit the coffee and replace the coffee liqueur with cassis. Use fresh strawberries instead of raspberries.

881 *White chocolate & raspberry boxes*

To make the mousse, melt 85 g/3 oz white chocolate. Remove from the heat then stir in 2 egg yolks and 2 tablespoons of double cream. Whisk 2 egg whites until they form stiff peaks and fold into the chocolate mixture. Cover and leave to set. Complete as before using 150 g/5 oz plain chocolate.

PASTRY
125 g/4½ oz plain flour
2 tbsp icing sugar
70 g/2½ oz butter, at room
temperature, cut into small pieces
1 egg yolk
1–2 tbsp water

FILLING
1 vanilla pod, split
200 ml/7 fl oz milk
2 egg yolks
40 g/1½ oz caster sugar
1 tbsp plain flour
1 tbsp cornflour
125 ml/4 fl oz double cream,
lightly whipped
350 g/12 oz strawberries, hulled
4 tbsp redcurrant jelly, melted

To make the pastry, sift the flour and icing sugar into a bowl. Add the butter and egg yolk and mix with your fingertips, adding a little water, if necessary, to form a soft dough. Cover and chill in the refrigerator for 15 minutes.

Preheat the oven to 200°C/400°F/Gas Mark 6. Roll the pastry out on a lightly floured surface and use to line 4 x 9-cm/3½-inch tartlet tins. Prick the bases with a fork, line with baking paper and fill with baking beans. Bake blind in the preheated oven for 10 minutes. Remove the paper and beans and bake for a further 5 minutes, or until golden brown. Leave to cool.

To make the filling, place the vanilla pod in a saucepan with the milk and leave on a low heat to infuse, without boiling, for 10 minutes. Place the egg yolks, sugar, flour and cornflour in a large bowl and whisk together until smooth. Strain the milk into the bowl and whisk until smooth.

Pour the mixture back into the pan and stir over a medium heat until boiling, then cook, stirring constantly, for about 2 minutes, or until thickened and smooth. Remove from the heat and fold in the whipped cream. Spoon the mixture into the pastry cases.

When the filling has set slightly, top with strawberries, sliced if large, then spoon over a little redcurrant jelly to glaze.

883 *Kiwi tartlets*

Replace the strawberries with sliced kiwi and brush with apricot jam.

884 *Grape tartlets*

Replace the strawberries with red and green grapes and arrange in circles on top of the filling, then brush with warm apricot jam.

885 *Berry tartlets*

Replace the strawberries with raspberries or blueberries.

8 eating apples
1 tbsp lemon juice
115 g/4 oz sultanas
1 tsp ground cinnamon
½ tsp ground nutmeg
1 tbsp soft light brown sugar
6 sheets filo pastry thawed, if frozen

vegetable oil spray
icing sugar, to serve

SAUCE
1 tbsp cornflour
450 ml/16 fl oz dry cider

Preheat the oven to 190°C/375°F/Gas Mark 5. Line a baking sheet with baking paper. Peel and core the apples and chop them into 1-cm/½-inch dice. Toss the apples in a bowl with the lemon juice, sultanas, cinnamon, nutmeg and brown sugar.

Lay out a sheet of filo pastry, spray with vegetable oil and lay a second sheet on top. Repeat with a third sheet. Spread over half the apple mixture and roll up lengthways, tucking in the ends to enclose the filling. Repeat to make a second strudel, then slide onto the baking sheet and spray with oil. Bake in the preheated oven for 15–20 minutes.

To make the sauce, blend the cornflour in a saucepan with a little cider until smooth. Add the remaining cider and heat gently, stirring, until the mixture boils and thickens. Slice the strudel and serve warm or cold, dredged with icing sugar, and accompanied by the cider sauce.

887 *With toffee sauce*

For the sauce, place 100 ml/3½ fl oz double cream, 40 g/1½ oz butter, 55 g/2 oz dark brown sugar and 1 tablespoon of golden syrup in a saucepan and heat, stirring, until the sauce comes to the boil. Leave to cool slightly.

888 *With sabayon sauce*

For the sauce, whisk 3 egg yolks with 25 g/1 oz caster sugar in a heatproof bowl until thick, then set over a pan of simmering water. Add 50 ml/2 fl oz sweet white wine and whisk until thick. Serve warm with the strudel.

889 *Pear strudel with cider sauce*

Replace the apples with pears and the sultanas with raisins.

175 g/6 oz plain flour, plus extra
for dusting
40 g/1½ oz cocoa powder
55 g/2 oz caster sugar
pinch of salt
125 g/4½ oz butter
1 large egg yolk
200 g/7 oz blueberries
2 tbsp crème de cassis
10 g/¼ oz icing sugar, plus extra for
dusting

FILLING
140 g/5 oz plain chocolate, broken
into pieces
225 ml/8 fl oz double cream
150 ml/5 fl oz soured cream

To make the pastry, place the flour, cocoa, sugar and salt in a food processor and pulse to mix. Add the butter, pulse again, then add the egg yolk and a little cold water to form a dough. Alternatively, place the flour, cocoa, sugar and salt in a large bowl, add the butter and rub it in with your fingertips until the mixture resembles breadcrumbs. Add the egg and a little cold water to form a dough. Cover the pastry with clingfilm and chill in the refrigerator for 30 minutes.

Preheat the oven to 180°C/350°F/Gas Mark 4. Roll the pastry out on a floured work surface and use to line 10 x 10-cm/4-inch tart cases. Freeze for 30 minutes.

Bake in the preheated oven for 15–20 minutes. Leave to cool.

Place the blueberries, crème de cassis and sift the icing sugar into a saucepan and warm through so the berries become shiny, but do not burst. Remove from the heat and leave to cool.

For the filling, place the chocolate in a heatproof bowl, set the bowl over a saucepan of gently simmering water and heat until melted, then cool slightly. Place the cream in a large bowl and whip until stiff, then fold in the soured cream and chocolate.

Divide the chocolate filling evenly between the tart cases, smoothing the surface, and top with the blueberries. Dust with sifted icing sugar.

891 *Chocolate orange tarts*

Make the pastry cases and bake blind. Replace the soured cream with double cream and whip with the grated rind of 1 orange, then stir in 2 tablespoons of orange flavoured liqueur and add to the chocolate. Pour the filling into the pastry cases, then top with orange segments.

892 *Chocolate raspberry tarts*

Make the pastry cases and filling as before. Replace the blueberries with raspberries and substitute the crème de cassis with framboise.

893 Fresh black cherry tarts

225 g/8 oz plain flour, plus extra for dusting
115 g/4 oz butter, cut into cubes
2 tbsp icing sugar
1 tsp vanilla extract
1 egg yolk
2–3 tbsp cold water

FILLING
250 g/9 oz mascarpone
55 g/2 oz icing sugar
2 eggs
150 ml/5 fl oz double cream
250 g/9 oz black cherries
3 tbsp black cherry or blackcurrant jam
1 tbsp water

Place the flour in a large bowl. Add the butter to the flour and rub it in with your fingertips until the mixture resembles fine breadcrumbs. Add the icing sugar, vanilla extract, egg yolk and enough water to form a soft dough. Cover with clingfilm and chill for 15 minutes.

Roll the pastry out on a floured work surface and use to line 8 x 10-cm/4-inch shallow tartlet tins. Chill in the refrigerator for 30 minutes.

Preheat the oven to 200°C/400°F/Gas Mark 6. Prick the base of the cases, then line with baking paper and fill with baking beans. Bake in the preheated oven for 10 minutes, then remove the paper and beans and bake for a further 5–10 minutes, or until crisp and golden.

Transfer the tins to a wire rack to cool. Reduce the oven temperature to 180°C/350°F/Gas Mark 4.

To make the filling, place the mascarpone, icing sugar and eggs in a large bowl and whisk together until well combined, then stir in the double cream. Remove the

pastry cases from the tins and place on a baking sheet.

Fill each pastry case with the mascarpone mixture and bake in the oven for 10 minutes, or until the mixture begins to set. Leave to cool, then chill for 2 hours.

Stone the cherries and halve, then arrange on top of the tarts. Melt the jam with the water in a small saucepan, then drizzle over the fruit. Chill until required.

894 Fresh berry tartlets

Stir 2 tablespoons of framboise into the mascarpone mixture before filling the tartlet cases. Top the chilled cases with 250 g/9 oz fresh raspberries and use apricot jam or seedless raspberry jam to make the glaze.

895 Chocolate candied orange peels

2 thick-skinned oranges
150 g/5½ oz granulated sugar
150 ml/5 fl oz water

70 g/2½ oz caster sugar
60 g/2¼ oz plain chocolate, broken into pieces

Cut the oranges into quarters and remove the flesh. Cut each piece of orange peel into about 6 triangular shapes measuring about 1 cm/½ inch thick.

Place the peels into a large saucepan, just cover with cold water and bring to the boil. Drain, then cover with fresh water and bring to the boil again. Drain and repeat the process 3 more times. Finally, drain the orange peels.

Place the granulated sugar and water in the pan and heat gently, stirring all the time, until the sugar has dissolved. Add the orange peels, bring to the boil and boil gently, stirring occasionally, until the syrup has almost evaporated and the peel has softened. Leave to cool.

When the mixture is cold, drain the peels well. Spread the caster sugar on a large plate and, working in batches, turn the peel in the sugar until coated on both sides. Place the peel on a wire rack, in a single layer, over a tray or baking sheet.

Sprinkle any remaining sugar over the top of the peel and leave

to dry for at least 12 hours, or overnight.

When the peel is dry, line a baking sheet with baking paper. Place the chocolate in a heatproof bowl, set the bowl over a saucepan of gently simmering water and heat until melted. Remove from the heat and stir until smooth.

Dip the pieces of peel into the melted chocolate and then place on the baking sheet. Leave in a cool place for 2–3 hours, or until the chocolate is set.

896 *Rather rich chocolate tarts*

225 g/8 oz plain flour, plus extra for dusting
115 g/4 oz butter, cut into cubes
2 tbsp icing sugar
1 egg yolk
2–3 tbsp cold water

FILLING
250 g/9 oz plain chocolate, broken into pieces, plus extra to decorate
115 g/4 oz butter
50 g/1¾ oz icing sugar
300 ml/10 fl oz double cream

Place the flour in a large bowl. Add the butter and rub it in with your fingertips until the mixture resembles breadcrumbs. Add the icing sugar, egg yolk and enough water to form a soft dough. Cover and chill for 15 minutes.

Roll the pastry out on a lightly floured work surface and use to line 8 x 10-cm/4-inch shallow tartlet cases. Chill for 30 minutes.

Preheat the oven to 200°C/400°F/Gas Mark 6. Prick the base of the cases with a fork and line with a little crumpled foil. Bake in the preheated oven for 10 minutes, then remove the foil and bake for 5–10 minutes, until crisp. Transfer to a wire rack to cool. Reduce the oven temperature to 160°C/325°F/Gas Mark 3.

To make the filling, place the chocolate, butter and icing sugar in a heatproof bowl set over a saucepan of simmering water and heat until melted. Remove from the heat and stir in 200 ml/7 fl oz double cream. Remove the cases from the tins and place on a baking sheet. Fill each case with the chocolate. Bake for 5 minutes. Cool, then chill until required.

To serve, whip the remaining cream and pipe or spoon into the centre of each tart. Decorate with grated chocolate.

897 *Rich lemon tarts*

For a tangy lemon filling, preheat the oven to 180°C/350°F/Gas Mark 4. Place 4 eggs and 115 g/4 oz caster sugar into a bowl and whisk together. Add the grated rind of 2 lemons and 150 ml/5 fl oz lemon juice and whisk together, then finally whisk in 150 ml/5 fl oz double cream. Pour into the baked pastry cases and bake for 15–20 minutes, or until just set. Cool, then chill in the refrigerator. Serve on their own or with fresh raspberries.

898 *Dates & figs with an almond filling*

150 g/5½ oz ground almonds
150 g/5½ oz icing sugar
2 tsp rum or brandy
1 egg white, lightly beaten
24 pitted dates
24 ready-to-eat dried figs

Place the almonds and sugar in a bowl and stir until well combined. Add the rum and egg white and mix to a firm paste.

Cut the dates almost in half lengthways, then cut a cross into the centre of the figs. Divide the almond paste in half, then divide one half into 24 pieces and roll into small sausage shapes. Place in the centre of each date, then place the date into paper petit four cases.

Divide the remaining paste into 24 pieces and roll into balls, then use to fill the centre of each fig and place in petit four cases. Chill in the refrigerator until required.

899 *Marzipan-stuffed dates & figs*

Produce this delicious recipe in double-quick time by replacing the filling with ready-made marzipan.

271

25 g/1 oz butter, plus extra for greasing
250 g/9 oz plain chocolate, broken into
    pieces
4 tbsp evaporated milk

450 g/1 lb icing sugar
50 g/1¾ oz roughly chopped hazelnuts
50 g/1¾ oz sultanas

Lightly grease a 20-cm/8-inch square cake tin. Place the chocolate, butter and evaporated milk in a heatproof bowl, set the bowl over a saucepan of gently simmering water and stir until the chocolate and butter have melted and the mixture is well blended.

Remove from the heat, sift in the icing sugar a little at a time beating to incorporate. Stir the hazelnuts and sultanas into the mixture, then press the fudge into the tin and smooth the top. Chill in the refrigerator until firm.

Tip the fudge out onto a chopping board and cut into squares with a sharp knife. Chill in the refrigerator until required.

901 *Cranberry & pecan nut fudge*

Replace the sultanas with dried cranberries and the hazelnuts with pecan nuts.

902 *Mocha walnut fudge*

Add 1 tablespoon of instant coffee to the chocolate and evaporated milk and replace the sultanas and hazelnuts with 115 g/4 oz chopped walnuts.

903 Ginger chocolate fudge

115 g/4 oz butter, plus extra for greasing
6 pieces stem ginger
300 ml/10 fl oz milk

150 g/5½ oz plain chocolate, broken
into pieces
450 g/1 lb granulated sugar

Grease a shallow 18-cm/7-inch square tin or a shallow 20 x 15-cm/8 x 6-inch rectangular tin. Dry the syrup off the pieces of stem ginger on kitchen paper, then chop finely.

Pour the milk into a large saucepan and add the chocolate, butter and sugar. Heat gently, stirring all the time, until the chocolate and butter have melted and the sugar has completely dissolved.

Bring to the boil and boil for about 10–15 minutes, stirring occasionally, until a little of the mixture, when dropped into a small bowl of cold water, forms a soft ball when rolled between the fingers. The temperature on a sugar thermometer should reach 116°C/240°F (soft ball stage). Remove from the heat and stir in the chopped ginger. Leave to cool for 5 minutes.

Using a wooden spoon, beat the fudge until it begins to lose its shine and is thick and creamy. Immediately turn the mixture into the tin and leave to cool. When the mixture is cool, mark the surface into 2.5-cm/1-inch squares and leave until set. When set, cut the fudge into squares with a sharp knife.

904 Cherry chocolate fudge

Replace the stem ginger with 115 g/4 oz chopped glacé cherries.

905 Brown sugar fudge

100 g/3½ oz butter, cut into cubes, plus
extra for greasing
300 ml/10 fl oz full fat milk

800 g/1 lb 12 oz soft light brown sugar
1 tsp vanilla extract

Grease a shallow 18-cm/7-inch square tin. Place the milk, sugar and butter into a large saucepan and bring slowly to the boil, stirring constantly, until the butter has melted. Bring to the boil, then cover the pan with a lid and boil gently for 2 minutes. Uncover and continue to boil, stirring occasionally, until a little of the mixture, dropped into a small bowl of cold water, forms a soft ball when rolled between your fingers. The temperature on a sugar thermometer should reach 116°C/240°F (soft ball stage). Remove from the heat and stir in the vanilla extract. Leave to cool for 5 minutes.

Using a wooden spoon, beat the fudge until it begins to lose its shine and is thick and creamy. Immediately turn the mixture into the tin and leave to cool. When the mixture is cool, mark the surface into 2.5-cm/1-inch squares and leave until set. When set, cut the fudge into squares with a sharp knife.

906 | *Rich chocolate fudge*

MAKES 49 PIECES

85 g/3 oz butter, plus extra for greasing
450 g/1 lb granulated sugar
150 ml/5 fl oz evaporated milk
150 g/5½ oz plain chocolate, broken into pieces
2 tbsp cocoa powder

Grease and line an 18-cm/7-inch square cake tin. Place all the ingredients in a large saucepan and heat gently, stirring over a low heat until the sugar dissolves and the chocolate melts to form a smooth mixture.

Bring to the boil and boil for about 10–15 minutes, stirring occasionally, until a little of the mixture, when dropped into a small bowl of cold water, forms a soft ball when rolled between the fingers. The temperature on a sugar thermometer should reach 116°C/240°F (soft ball stage). Leave to cool for 5–10 minutes, then beat vigorously with a wooden spoon until the mixture thickens and begins to 'grain' (form small crystals). Pour into the tin and mark into squares.

Leave to cool and set before cutting into squares to serve.

907 *Vanilla fudge*

Heat 450 g/1 lb granulated sugar, 85 g/3 oz butter, 150 ml/5 fl oz evaporated milk and 150 ml/5 fl oz milk together in a saucepan until the sugar dissolves. Bring to the boil and boil as before. Add 1 teaspoon of vanilla extract to the mixture before beating with a wooden spoon. Stir the mixture occasionally because it burns very easily.

908 *Mocha fudge*

Add 4 tablespoons of instant coffee in place of the cocoa powder.

909 *Rum & raisin choc fudge*

Gently heat 2 tablespoons of rum until hot in a small saucepan, then add 115 g/4 oz raisins. Leave to cool while preparing the fudge, then add to the fudge when beating the mixture with a wooden spoon.

910 *Chocolate orange fudge*

Omit the cocoa powder and add the finely grated rind and juice of ½ orange.

274

Nutty chocolate clusters

175 g/6 oz white chocolate, broken
   into pieces
100 g/3½ oz digestive biscuits
100 g/3½ oz chopped macadamia nuts
   or Brazil nuts

25 g/1 oz stem ginger, chopped (optional)
175 g/6 oz plain chocolate, broken
   into pieces

Line a large baking sheet with a sheet of baking paper. Place the white chocolate in a large heatproof bowl, set the bowl over a saucepan of gently simmering water and heat until melted.

Break the digestive biscuits into small pieces. Stir the crumbs into the melted chocolate with the chopped nuts and stem ginger, if using, then place heaped teaspoons of the mixture on the baking sheet. Chill the mixture in the refrigerator until set, then remove from the baking paper.

Melt the plain chocolate and leave to cool slightly. Dip the clusters into the melted chocolate, allowing the excess to drip back into the bowl. Chill the clusters on the baking sheet until set.

912 *Cherry & walnut clusters*

Replace the macadamia nuts or Brazil nuts with walnuts and the ginger with chopped glacé cherries.

913 *Date & nut clusters*

Replace the stem ginger with 55 g/2 oz chopped dates and reduce the biscuits to 85 g/3 oz.

---

914 *Apricot & almond clusters*

115 g/4 oz plain chocolate, broken
   into pieces
2 tbsp clear honey
115 g/4 oz ready-to-eat dried
   apricots, chopped
55 g/2 oz blanched almonds, chopped

915 *Date & almond clusters*

Replace the apricots with ready-to-eat dried dates.

916 *Apricot & hazelnut clusters*

Replace the almonds with chopped toasted hazelnuts.

917 *Fig & almond clusters*

Replace the apricots with chopped dried figs.

Place the chocolate and honey in a heatproof bowl, set the bowl over a saucepan of gently simmering water and heat until melted and smooth.

Stir in the apricots and almonds, then drop teaspoonfuls of the mixture into paper sweet cases. Leave to set.

Nutty palmiers

butter, for greasing
175 g/6 oz ready-made puff pastry,
　thawed if frozen
plain flour, for dusting

40 g/1½ oz finely chopped roasted
　hazelnuts or pecan nuts
2 tbsp demerara sugar
1 egg white, lightly beaten

Preheat the oven to 200°C/400°F/ Gas Mark 6. Grease 2 large baking sheets. Roll out the pastry on a lightly floured work surface to form a 20 x 30-cm/8 x 12-inch rectangle. Trim the edges with sharp knife.

Place the nuts and sugar in a bowl and mix together. Brush the pastry with egg white and sprinkle with three quarters of the nuts and sugar. Fold the long sides of the pastry so that they reach halfway towards the centre. Fold again so that they just meet in the centre and roll gently with a rolling pin to flatten very slightly. Brush with a little more egg white and sprinkle the remaining sugar and nuts over the surface. Fold in half down the centre and gently flatten again with the rolling pin.

Using a sharp knife, cut the roll into about 20 thin slices and place cut side down on the baking sheets, spaced well apart.

Bake in the preheated oven for 10 minutes. Remove from the oven and turn the palmiers over. Return to the oven and bake for a further 5 minutes, or until golden and crisp. Transfer to a wire rack to cool completely.

919 *Chocolate palmiers*

Replace the sugar and nuts with 4 tablespoons of grated chocolate and 2 teaspoons of caster sugar. Chill in the refrigerator for 15 minutes before baking.

920 *Cheesy palmiers*

Replace the sugar and nuts with 85 g/3 oz grated Cheddar cheese and 2 finely chopped spring onions.

921 *Cinnamon palmiers*

Replace the sugar and nuts with a mixture of 4 tablespoons of caster sugar mixed with 1 teaspoon of ground cinnamon.

922 *Pesto & tomato palmiers*

Roll out the pastry and spread with 2 tablespoons of pesto. Finely chop 2 sun-dried tomatoes and sprinkle most of the tomato over the pastry. Fold as before, spreading the pastry with a little more pesto and the remaining tomato before the final fold.

923 *Sacristons*

Roll out the pastry, then brush the pastry with a little beaten egg white and sprinkle over 4 tablespoons of caster sugar and 50 g/2 oz chopped almonds. Lightly press the almonds into the pastry with a rolling pin. Cut into fingers measuring about 6 x 1 cm/2½ x ½ inch wide. Twist each finger and place on the baking sheets, spaced well apart. Bake in the preheated oven for 10–12 minutes, or until golden and crisp. Transfer to a wire rack to cool completely.

924 Chocolate mendiants

40 g/1½ oz ready-to-eat dried figs, dates
    or apricots or candied orange peel
40 g/1½ oz raisins, sultanas or
    cranberries
15 g/½ oz pistachio nuts or blanched
    hazelnuts

40 g/1½ oz blanched almonds
150 g/5½ oz plain chocolate, broken
    into pieces

Line several baking sheets with baking paper. If using figs, roughly snip into small pieces using scissors and place in a pile or in a small bowl. Place the remaining fruits and nuts in piles or in small bowls.

Place the chocolate in a heatproof bowl, set the bowl over a saucepan of gently simmering water and heat until melted. Remove from the heat and stir until smooth.

Place 4–5 heaped teaspoons of the chocolate on a baking sheet and spread into discs measuring about 5 cm/2 inches in diameter. Place equal amounts of the fruits and nuts on each disc, then repeat with the remaining chocolate, fruit and nuts. Leave in a cool place for 2–3 hours, or until set.

925 Almond macaroons

1 egg white
85 g/3 oz ground almonds
85 g/3 oz caster sugar, plus extra for
    rolling

½ tsp almond extract
6–7 blanched almonds, split in half

Preheat the oven to 180°C/350°F/Gas Mark 4. Line 2 large baking sheets with baking paper. Place the egg white in a bowl and beat with a fork until frothy, then stir in the ground almonds, sugar and almond extract, mixing to form a sticky dough.

Using lightly sugared hands, roll the dough into small balls and place on the baking sheets. Press an almond half into the centre of each.

Bake in the preheated oven for 15–20 minutes, or until pale golden. Transfer to a wire rack to cool completely.

926 Hazelnut macaroons

Grind 85 g/3 oz hazelnuts very finely in a food processor and use instead of the ground almonds. Decorate with halved hazelnuts.

927 Coconut macaroons

Replace the ground almonds with 85–115 g/3–4 oz desiccated coconut. Decorate with halved glacé cherries.

Walnut & honey triangles

50 g/1¾ oz butter
100 g/3½ oz full-fat cream cheese
1 tbsp clear honey
25 g/1 oz caster sugar
100 g/3½ oz walnut halves, finely chopped
finely grated rind of 1 lemon
6 sheets filo pastry (total weight about 90 g/3¼ oz)
icing sugar, to decorate

Preheat the oven to 180°C/350°F/Gas Mark 4. Grease a large baking sheet. Place the butter in a saucepan and heat gently until melted, then leave to cool slightly. Meanwhile, place the cream cheese, honey and sugar in a large bowl and beat together until combined. Add the chopped walnuts and lemon rind and stir together.

Brush 1 sheet of filo pastry with melted butter and cut into 3 equal strips. Cover the remaining sheets with a clean damp tea towel. Place 1 heaped teaspoon of the walnut mixture at the end of each strip. Fold over the end at a diagonal to form a triangle, then continue to fold up the pastry, maintaining the triangle shape.

Place on the baking sheet and brush with melted butter. Repeat with the remaining pastry and walnut mixture. Bake in the preheated oven for 10–15 minutes, or until golden brown. Leave to cool. To decorate, sift icing sugar lightly over the triangles and serve immediately.

Chocolate almond petits fours

40 g/1½ oz ground almonds
85 g/3 oz granulated sugar
5 tsp cocoa powder
1 egg white
8 blanched almonds, halved
55 g/2 oz plain chocolate, broken into pieces

Preheat the oven to 190°C/375°F/ Gas Mark 5. Line a large baking sheet with baking paper. Place the ground almonds, sugar and cocoa powder in a bowl and mix together well. Add the egg white and mix to form a firm mixture. Fill a piping bag, fitted with a small plain nozzle, with the mixture and pipe 5-cm/2-inch lengths, spaced well apart, onto the baking sheet. Place an almond half on top of each.

Bake in the preheated oven for 5 minutes, or until firm. Transfer to a wire rack to cool.

When the petits fours are cold, place the chocolate in a heatproof bowl, set the bowl over a saucepan of gently simmering water and heat until melted. Dip each end of the petits fours into the melted chocolate and leave to set.

Chocolate hazelnut petits fours

Grind 40 g/1½ oz hazelnuts in a food processor and use instead of the ground almonds. Place a halved hazelnut in the centre of each instead of the almond.

Coffee almond petits fours

Add 2 tablespoons of coffee powder instead of the cocoa powder. Dip the petits fours into the melted chocolate or leave them undipped.

50 g/1¾ oz butter, plus extra for
  greasing
6 sheets filo pastry (total weight about
  90 g/3¼ oz)
2 tbsp apricot jam

2 large egg whites
50 g/1¾ oz caster sugar
50 g/1¾ oz ground almonds
25 g/1 oz flaked almonds

Preheat the oven to 180°C/350°F/Gas mark 4. Grease a 12-hole muffin tin. Place the butter in a saucepan and heat gently until melted, then leave to cool slightly. Brush 1 sheet of filo pastry with melted butter. Cover the remaining sheets with a clean damp tea towel. Lay a second sheet of pastry on top, brush with butter and repeat with a third sheet.

Using an 8-cm/3¼-inch round cutter, cut the pastry into 6 rounds and place in the muffin tin. Repeat with the remaining pastry sheets and butter. Spoon the jam equally into the pastry tarts.

Place the egg whites in a large bowl and whisk until stiff. Add the sugar and ground almonds and, using a large metal spoon, fold in until combined. Spoon the mixture into the tarts and spread out to cover the jam. Sprinkle the flaked almonds over the top.

Bake in the preheated oven for 25 minutes, or until golden brown. Serve warm or transfer to a wire rack to cool.

933 *Tiny chocolate cupcakes with ganache icing*   MAKES 20

55 g/2 oz butter, softened
55 g/2 oz caster sugar
1 large egg, lightly beaten
55 g/2 oz self-raising flour
2 tbsp cocoa powder
1 tbsp milk
20 chocolate-coated coffee beans,
  to decorate

ICING
100 g/3½ oz plain chocolate, broken
  into pieces
100 ml/3½ fl oz double cream

Preheat the oven to 190°C/375°F/Gas Mark 5. Place 20 double-layer mini paper cases on 2 large baking sheets. Place the butter and sugar in a large bowl and beat together until light and fluffy, then gradually beat in the egg. Sift in the flour and cocoa and fold into the mixture. Stir in the milk.

Fill a piping bag fitted with a large plain nozzle with the mixture and pipe it into the paper cases, filling each one half full.

Bake in the preheated oven for 10–15 minutes, or until well risen and firm to the touch. Transfer to a wire rack to cool.

To make the icing, place the chocolate and cream in a saucepan and heat gently, stirring constantly, until the chocolate has melted. Pour into a large heatproof bowl and, using an electric hand whisk, beat the mixture for 10 minutes, or until thick, glossy and cool.

Fill a piping bag fitted with a large star nozzle with the icing and pipe a swirl on top of each cupcake. Alternatively, spoon the icing over the top of each cupcake. Chill in the refrigerator for 1 hour, then serve decorated with a chocolate-coated coffee bean.

934 *With milk chocolate ganache*

Replace the plain chocolate with milk chocolate and decorate with a white chocolate button or white chocolate curls made with a vegetable peeler.

935 *Tiny coffee & hazelnut cupcakes*

Replace the cocoa powder and milk with 2 tablespoons of instant coffee dissolved in 2 tablespoons of milk. Add 40 g/1½ oz chopped hazelnuts to the cake mixture and decorate with toasted hazelnuts instead of coffee beans.

936 Persian almond rolls

100 g/3½ oz butter, plus extra for
  greasing
225 g/8 oz blanched almonds, chopped
50 g/1¾ oz caster sugar
1 tsp ground cinnamon
12 sheets filo pastry (total weight about
  190 g/6½ oz)

SYRUP
75 g/2¾ oz granulated sugar
4 tbsp water
1½ tsp lemon juice

Preheat the oven to 180°C/350°F/Gas Mark 4. Grease a large baking
sheet. Place the butter in a saucepan and heat gently until melted, then
leave to cool slightly. Place the almonds, sugar and cinnamon in a bowl
and stir together.

Brush 1 sheet of filo pastry with melted butter. Lay a second sheet of
pastry on top and brush with butter. Cover the remaining sheets with
a damp tea towel. Spoon a little of the almond mixture along the long
edge of the pastry, leaving a 2-cm/¾-inch border at each end. Fold in
the sides and roll up. Place the rolls on the baking sheet and brush with
melted butter. Repeat with the remaining pastry and almond mixture.
Bake in the preheated oven for 15–20 minutes, or until golden brown.

Place the granulated sugar, water and lemon juice in a pan and heat
gently, stirring constantly until the sugar has dissolved. Bring to the boil
and boil for 5 minutes, then leave to cool. Pour the syrup over the top of
the rolls and leave to cool, then cut each roll into 5-cm/2-inch rolls.

937 Chocolate Easter egg nests

70 g/2½ oz butter
115 g/4 oz milk chocolate, broken into
  pieces
3 tbsp golden syrup
15 g/½ oz cocoa powder

100 g/3½ oz puffed rice cereal or flaked
  corn cereal, or shredded wheat cereal
  broken into strands
mini chocolate or marzipan Easter eggs,
  to decorate

Place 12 paper cases in a 12-hole muffin tin. Place the butter, chocolate,
golden syrup and cocoa powder in a saucepan and heat gently, stirring
constantly, until melted and combined. Remove from
the heat and carefully stir the cereal into the mixture, taking care not
to break it too much. Stir until well coated.

Spoon the chocolate mixture into the paper cake cases and make a
dip in the centre so that they form 'nests'. Chill in the refrigerator until
set. Remove from the paper cases, then arrange the eggs inside the nests.

938 *Baklava*

MAKES 25

225 g/8 oz walnut halves
225 g/8 oz shelled pistachio nuts
100 g/3½ oz blanched almonds
4 tbsp pine kernels, finely chopped
finely grated rind of 2 large oranges
6 tbsp sesame seeds
1 tbsp caster sugar
½ tsp ground cinnamon
½ tsp mixed spice

250 g/9 oz butter, melted, plus extra
   for greasing
24 sheets filo pastry, thawed, if frozen

SYRUP
450 g/1 lb caster sugar
450 ml/16 fl oz water
5 tbsp honey
3 cloves
2 large strips lemon zest

To make the filling, place the walnuts, pistachio nuts, almonds and pine kernels in a food processor and process gently, until finely chopped but not ground. Transfer the chopped nuts to a bowl and stir in the orange rind, sesame seeds, sugar, cinnamon and mixed spice.

Preheat the oven to 160°C/325°F/Gas Mark 3. Grease a square 25-cm/10-inch ovenproof dish, about 5 cm/2 inches deep. Cut the stacked filo sheets to size, using a ruler. Keep the sheets covered with a damp tea towel. Place a sheet of filo on the base of the dish and brush with melted butter. Top with 7 more sheets, brushing with butter between each layer.

Sprinkle with a generous 150 g/5½ oz of the filling. Top with 3 sheets of filo pastry, brushing each one with butter. Continue layering until you have used up all the filo and filling, ending with a top layer of 3 filo sheets. Brush with butter.

Cut the baklava into 5-cm/2-inch squares with a sharp knife and brush again with butter. Bake in the preheated oven for 1 hour.

Meanwhile, place all the ingredients for the syrup in a saucepan and slowly bring to the boil, stirring to dissolve the sugar. Reduce the heat and leave to simmer for 15 minutes, without stirring, until a thin syrup forms. Leave to cool.

Strain the cooled syrup over the top of the baklava, leave to cool in the dish and cut out the squares to serve.

939 *Filo Christmas crackers*

MAKES 12

50 g/1¾ oz ready-to-eat dried apricots
125 g/4½ oz mincemeat
50 g/1¾ oz blanched almonds, chopped
2 tbsp sherry

50 g/1¾ oz butter, plus extra for greasing
6 sheets filo pastry (total weight about
   90 g/3¼ oz)
icing sugar, for dusting

Cut the apricots finely with scissors and place in a large bowl. Add the mincemeat, almonds and sherry and leave to soak for 1–2 hours.

Preheat the oven to 180°C/350°F/Gas Mark 4. Grease a large baking sheet. Place the butter in a saucepan and heat gently until melted, then leave to cool slightly. Meanwhile, cut 1 sheet of pastry in half widthways and brush each half with melted butter. Cover the remaining sheets with a damp tea towel. Spoon a little of the mincemeat mixture along the long edge of the pastry sheets, leaving a 6-cm/2½-inch border at each end. Roll up, pinching the ends together to form a cracker shape. Place on the baking sheet and brush with melted butter. Repeat with the remaining pastry and filling. Bake in the preheated oven for 15–20 minutes, or until golden brown. Dust with sifted icing sugar to serve.

940 Galaktoboureko

140 g/5 oz butter
4 large eggs
125 g/4½ oz caster sugar
1 litre/1¾ pints milk
175 g/6 oz semolina

finely grated rind 1 lemon and 1½ tsp
    lemon juice
200 g/7 oz filo pastry
75 g/2¾ oz granulated sugar
4 tbsp water

Preheat the oven to 180°C/350°F/Gas Mark 4. Place 115 g/4 oz of the butter in a saucepan and heat gently until melted, then leave to cool slightly. Use a little of the melted butter to grease a shallow 25 x 18-cm/10 x 7-inch roasting tin.

Place the eggs and caster sugar in a large bowl and whisk together until pale and creamy. Heat the milk in a large pan until warm, then stir into the egg mixture. Return the mixture to the pan and add the semolina and lemon rind. Heat gently, stirring, until the mixture boils and thickens. Remove from the heat and stir in the remaining butter.

Line the roasting tin with a sheet of filo pastry and brush with melted butter. Cover the remaining sheets with a damp tea towel. Lay a second sheet of pastry on top, bringing it up the sides of the tin, and brush with butter. Continue until half of the pastry sheets have been used, bringing it up the sides of the tin each time. Spoon the milk mixture into the tin and spread out evenly. Cover with the remaining pastry sheets, brushing each sheet with butter and tucking down the edges. Cut the top layers of the pastry into 20 square shapes.

Bake in the preheated oven for 35–40 minutes, or until golden brown. Meanwhile, place the granulated sugar, water and lemon juice in a pan and heat, stirring until the sugar has dissolved. Bring to the boil, without stirring, and boil for 5 minutes.

Leave to cool, then pour the syrup over the top of the pastry. Cut along the lines to divide into pieces.

941 French beignets

85 g/3 oz butter, cut into pieces
200 ml/7 fl oz water
100 g/3½ oz strong white flour
2 eggs, lightly beaten
sunflower oil, for deep frying

RASPBERRY SAUCE
450 g/1 lb raspberries
75 g/2¾ oz caster sugar, plus extra
    for sprinkling
1 tbsp water

To make the sauce, place the raspberries, sugar and water in a small saucepan and heat gently until soft. Push through a sieve and reserve.

To make the beignets, place the butter and water in a pan and heat gently until the butter melts. Increase the heat and bring to a rapid boil. Remove from the heat, then add the flour and beat until the mixture forms a ball. Cool slightly, then gradually beat in the eggs until smooth and glossy.

Heat the oil in a suitable pan to 190°C/375°F. Drop rounded teaspoons of the mixture in batches into the oil and fry until the beignets rise to the top and are golden and crisp. Remove with a slotted spoon and drain on kitchen paper. Repeat until all the mixture has been used. Drizzle the sauce over the beignets and sprinkle with sugar.

942 With rum sauce

To make the rum sauce, grate the rind from ½ orange and squeeze the juice from 2 oranges. Mix 1 teaspoon of cornflour with a little orange juice, then add the remaining juice. Add 55 g/2 oz demerara sugar and heat until thick. Whisk in 25 g/1 oz butter, cut into cubes, stir in the orange rind and 4 tablespoons of rum and simmer for 1 minute, then serve with the beignets.

115 g/4 oz butter, softened
115 g/4 oz full-fat cream cheese
3 tbsp caster sugar
125 ml/4 fl oz soured cream
1 tsp vanilla extract
250 g/9 oz plain flour

FILLING
55 g/2 oz light muscovado sugar
1½ tsp ground cinnamon
85 g/3 oz raisins, chopped
85 g/3 oz walnuts, chopped
beaten egg, for glazing

Place the butter in a large bowl and beat until creamy, then beat in the cream cheese, sugar, soured cream and vanilla extract until well combined. Beat in the flour, then bring the mixture together with your fingertips to form a soft dough. Cover with clingfilm and chill in the refrigerator.

Preheat the oven to 180°C/350°F/Gas Mark 4. Line 2 large baking sheets with baking paper. To make the filling, place the sugar, cinnamon, raisins and walnuts in a bowl and mix together.

Divide the dough into 4 pieces and roll each piece into a 20-cm/ 8-inch round between 2 sheets of baking paper. (Keep the dough balls chilled until you roll them out.) Cut each round into 6 wedges and sprinkle evenly with one quarter of the filling. Starting at the wide end, roll towards the point, then curve into a crescent and place on the baking sheets. Repeat with the remaining dough, then brush the crescents with beaten egg.

Bake in the preheated oven for 15–20 minutes, or until golden brown. Transfer to a wire rack to cool.

944 *Apricot & pecan rugelach*

Spread each round of dough with 2–3 tablespoons of apricot jam and sprinkle with 1–2 tablespoons of finely chopped pecan nuts before cutting into wedges and shaping.

945 *Chocolate rugelach*

Sprinkle each round of dough with 3 tablespoons of chopped milk or plain chocolate before cutting into wedges and shaping.

946 *Raspberry & sultana rugelach*

Spread each round of dough with 2–3 tablespoons of raspberry jam and sprinkle with 1–2 tablespoons of chopped sultanas before cutting into wedges and shaping.

947 *Chocolate & hazelnut rugelach*

Spread each round of dough with 2–3 tablespoons of chocolate hazelnut spread and sprinkle with 1–2 tablespoons of finely chopped toasted hazelnuts before cutting into wedges and shaping.

948 *Marzipan rugelach*

Coarsely grate 115 g/4 oz marzipan and sprinkle one quarter over each round. Sprinkle a few poppy seeds over the marzipan, if liked, then cut into wedges and shape.

949 Tunisian almond cigars

85 g/3 oz butter
200 g/7 oz ground almonds
200 g/7 oz caster sugar
2 tbsp orange blossom water

1 egg white, lightly beaten
12 sheets filo pastry, about 28 x 38 cm/
11 x 15 inches
100 ml/3½ fl oz clear honey

Preheat the oven to 200°C/400°F/Gas Mark 6. Place the butter in a saucepan and heat gently until melted, then leave to cool slightly.

Place the almonds and sugar in a bowl and stir until well combined. Add the orange blossom water and egg white and mix to form a firm paste. Divide the mixture into 6 pieces and roll each piece into a long sausage about 28 cm/11 inches long. Place a sheet of filo pastry on the work surface and brush with melted butter. Place another sheet on top and brush with butter. Place a strip of almond paste on one end and roll up to enclose in layers of filo. Trim the ends and cut into 6 pieces, then place on a baking sheet. Repeat with the remaining pastry and paste.

Bake in the preheated oven for 25–30 minutes, or until crisp and golden. Warm the honey in a saucepan and pour over the cooked pastries, then leave to cool before serving.

950 Tunisian hazelnut cigars

Replace the ground almonds with finely ground hazelnuts.

951 Tunisian pistachio cigars

Replace the almonds with very finely chopped pistachio nuts.

952 Italian baked sweet ravioli

3 tbsp extra virgin olive oil, plus extra
    for greasing
200 g/7 oz plain flour, plus extra
    for dusting
85 g/3 oz caster sugar
3 egg yolks
3–4 tbsp water

FILLING
115 g/4 oz ricotta cheese
1½ tbsp caster sugar
grated rind of ½ lemon
1 tbsp lemon juice

GLAZE
1 egg white, lightly beaten
caster sugar

Preheat the oven to 180°C/350°F/Gas Mark 4. Lightly grease a large baking sheet. Place the flour and sugar in a large bowl and make a well in the centre. Add the egg yolks, oil and 3 tablespoons of water and mix to form a firm dough, adding a little extra water if required. Knead for a few minutes. Leave for 15 minutes.

Meanwhile, make the filling by combining all the ingredients in a small bowl. Divide the dough into 2 pieces and roll each piece out on a lightly floured work surface to a rectangle about 40 x 30 cm/16 x 12 inches. Cut into 5-cm/2-inch squares and place 1 teaspoon of filling on one square of dough. Moisten the edges of the dough with water, top with the second square and seal well with the tines of a fork. Place on the baking sheet and repeat with the remaining filling and dough.

Brush the tops of the ravioli with egg white and dust lightly with sugar. Bake in the preheated oven for 20–25 minutes, or until crisp and golden. Leave to cool slightly before serving.

953 Chocolate orange ravioli

For the filling, place 25 g/1 oz chocolate in a heatproof bowl, set the bowl over a saucepan of gently simmering water and heat until melted. Leave to cool, then beat into the ricotta with 1 tablespoon of orange-flavoured liqueur and the grated rind of ½ orange.

954 Bakewell slices

175 g/6 oz plain flour, plus extra
 for dusting
125 g/4½ oz butter
25 g/1 oz caster sugar
1 egg yolk
about 1 tbsp cold water

FILLING
115 g/4 oz butter
115 g/4 oz caster sugar
115 g/4 oz ground almonds
3 eggs, beaten
½ tsp almond extract
4 tbsp raspberry jam
2 tbsp flaked almonds

Sift the flour into a bowl, add the butter and rub it in with your fingertips until the mixture resembles fine breadcrumbs. Stir in the sugar, then mix the egg yolk with the water and stir in to form a firm dough, adding a little more water if necessary. Wrap in clingfilm and chill in the refrigerator for 15 minutes.

Preheat the oven to 200°C/400°F/Gas Mark 6. Roll the dough out on a floured work surface and use to line a 23-cm/9-inch square tart tin or shallow cake tin. Prick the base and chill for 15 minutes.

Place the butter and sugar in a large bowl and beat together until light and fluffy, then beat in the ground almonds, eggs and almond extract. Spread the jam over the pastry base and top with the almond mixture, spreading evenly. Sprinkle with the flaked almonds.

Bake in the preheated oven for 10 minutes, then reduce the oven temperature to 180°C/350°F/Gas Mark 4 and bake for 25–30 minutes, or until the filling is golden brown. Leave to cool, then cut into bars.

955 Apricot & almond slices

Add 55 g/2 oz chopped ready-to-eat dried apricots to the filling mixture and replace the raspberry jam with apricot jam.

956 Filo chocolate triangles

85 g/3 oz butter, melted, plus extra
 for greasing
150 g/5½ oz plain chocolate, coarsely
 chopped
115 g/4 oz chocolate cake crumbs

55g/2 oz toasted hazelnuts, chopped
25 g/1 oz light muscovado sugar
4 tbsp brandy or apple juice
5 large sheets filo pastry
icing sugar, for dusting

Preheat the oven to 200°C/400°F/Gas Mark 6. Lightly grease a large baking sheet. Place the butter in a saucepan and heat gently until melted, then leave to cool slightly. Place the chocolate, cake crumbs, hazelnuts, sugar and brandy in a large bowl and mix together.

Lay one sheet of filo pastry on the work surface and brush with melted butter. Cut in half widthways, then cut each half into 4 strips lengthways. Place a little of the chocolate mixture at one end of a strip of pastry. Fold over the end at a diagonal to form a triangle, then continue to fold up the pastry, maintaining the triangle shape. Place on the baking sheet and brush with butter. Repeat with the remaining strips of pastry, to make 8 triangles. Cut the remaining sheets of filo and make further triangles. Bake in the preheated oven for 8–10 minutes, or until golden. Leave to cool. Dust with icing sugar before serving.

957 Cherry & coconut triangles

For a fruity filling, drain and coarsely chop 425 g/15 oz canned black cherries and mix in a bowl with 55 g/2 oz desiccated coconut, 55 g/2 oz cake crumbs, 25 g/1 oz soft light brown sugar, ¼ teaspoon of ground cinnamon and 1 tablespoon of rum.

958 Rum & chocolate cups

55 g/2 oz plain chocolate, broken
    into pieces
12 toasted hazelnuts, to decorate

FILLING
115 g/4 oz plain chocolate, broken
    into pieces
1 tbsp dark rum
4 tbsp mascarpone cheese

To make the chocolate cups, place the chocolate in a heatproof bowl, set the bowl over a saucepan of gently simmering water and heat until just melted, but not too runny. Spoon about ½ teaspoon of melted chocolate into a foil sweet case and brush it over the base and up the sides. Coat 11 more foil cases in the same way and leave to set for 30 minutes. Chill in the refrigerator for 15 minutes. If necessary, reheat the chocolate in the heatproof bowl until melted, then coat the foil cases with a second, slightly thinner coating. Chill for a further 30 minutes.

Meanwhile, to make the filling, melt the chocolate as before, then leave to cool slightly. Stir in the rum and beat in the mascarpone cheese until fully incorporated and smooth, then leave to cool completely, stirring occasionally.

Spoon the filling into a piping bag fitted with a 1-cm/½-inch star nozzle and pipe the filling into the cups. Top each one with a toasted hazelnut.

959 Brandy & almond chocolate cups

Replace the rum with brandy and top the cups with a toasted almond.

960 Peppermint creams

300 g/10½ oz icing sugar, plus extra
    for dusting
1 egg white

peppermint extract, to taste
green food colouring (optional)

Line a large baking sheet with baking paper. Sift the icing sugar. Place the egg white in a large bowl and whisk with a fork until just frothy. Add half the icing sugar and beat in. Add a few drops of peppermint extract, then gradually add enough icing sugar to mix to a firm paste, ading a little more icing sugar, if necessary. Knead in extra peppermint extract to taste.

Divide the paste in half and colour one half pale green with a few drops of food colouring, if liked.

Sprinkle a little icing sugar on the work surface, then roll out the paste until it is about 5 mm/¼ inch thick. Cut out rounds or other shapes with a cutter and place on the baking paper. Leave to dry out in a cool, dry place for a few hours.

961 Bitter chocolate mint creams

Put 115 g/4 oz plain chocolate in a heatproof bowl, set the bowl over a saucepan of gently simmering water and heat until melted. Leave to cool slightly, then dip the peppermint creams into the chocolate to cover half of the mint. Replace on the baking paper and leave to set.

962 Chocolate creams

200 g/7 oz plain chocolate, broken
into pieces
2 tbsp single cream
225 g/8 oz icing sugar
drinking chocolate powder,
for dusting

Line a large baking sheet with baking paper. Place 55 g/2 oz of the chocolate in a large heatproof bowl, set the bowl over a saucepan of gently simmering water and heat until melted. Stir in the cream and remove the bowl from the heat.

Sift the icing sugar into the melted chocolate and, using a fork, mix together, then knead to form a firm, smooth and pliable mixture.

Lightly dust a work surface with drinking chocolate powder, and roll the mixture out until it is about 5-mm/¼-inch thick. Cut into rounds using a 2.5-cm/1-inch plain round cutter and place on the baking sheet. Leave to stand for about 12 hours, or overnight, until set and dry.

When the chocolate creams have set, line another baking sheet with baking paper. Melt the remaining chocolate as before and, using 2 forks, carefully dip each chocolate cream into the melted chocolate. Lift it out quickly, letting any excess chocolate drain back into the bowl, and place on the baking paper. Leave to set.

963 Coffee lovers' creams

350 g/12 oz icing sugar
2 tbsp condensed milk
2 tbsp strong black coffee
115 g/4 oz milk chocolate, broken
into pieces

Line a large baking sheet with baking paper. Sift the icing sugar. Place half the icing sugar, condensed milk and coffee in a large bowl and mix well, then knead in enough icing sugar to mix to a firm paste. Take small pieces of the paste and roll into a ball. Place on the baking paper and flatten with the tines of a fork. Leave to dry out in a cool, dry place for a few hours.

Place the chocolate in a heatproof bowl, set the bowl over a saucepan of gently simmering water and heat until melted. Leave to cool slightly, then dip the bottom of the creams into the chocolate. Allow the excess to run off and replace on the baking paper. Drizzle any remaining chocolate, backwards and forwards, over the tops of the creams and leave to set.

85 g/3 oz butter	FILLING
85 g/3 oz caster sugar	150 ml/5 fl oz double cream or whipping
3 tbsp golden syrup	cream
85 g/3 oz plain flour	1 tbsp brandy (optional)
1 tsp ground ginger	1 tbsp icing sugar
1 tbsp brandy	
finely grated rind of ½ lemon	

Preheat the oven to 160°C/325°F/Gas Mark 3. Line 3 large baking sheets with baking paper. Place the butter, sugar and golden syrup in a saucepan and heat gently, stirring occasionally, until melted. Leave to cool slightly, then sift the flour and ginger into the pan and beat until smooth. Stir in the brandy and lemon rind. Drop small spoonfuls of the mixture onto the baking sheets, leaving plenty of room for spreading.

Bake one baking sheet at a time in the preheated oven for 10–12 minutes, or until the snaps are golden brown. Remove the first baking sheet from the oven and leave to cool for about 30 seconds, then lift each round with a palette knife and wrap around the handle of a wooden spoon. If the brandy snaps start to become too firm to wrap, return them to the oven for about 30 seconds to soften again. When firm, remove from the handles and cool on a wire rack. Repeat with the remaining baking sheets.

For the filling, place the cream, brandy, if using, and icing sugar in a bowl and whip until thick. Just before serving, pipe the cream mixture into each end of the brandy snaps.

965 *With coffee cream*

Dissolve 2 tablespoons of instant coffee in 2 tablespoons of hot milk. Add to the cream with the icing sugar and brandy, if using, and whip until thick. Use to fill the brandy snaps.

966 *With vanilla mascarpone cream*

Place 500 g/1 lb 2 oz mascarpone with 1 tablespoon of caster sugar in a bowl. Split a vanilla pod lengthways and scoop out the seeds, add to the mascarpone and beat until combined. Use to fill the brandy snaps.

967 *Brandy snap cups*

Grease the outside of a teacup. Make and bake as before. After removing from the oven, leave to cool for 30 seconds, then lift each with a palette knife and place over the upturned teacup, gently shaping the edges into a cup shape. When firm, after a few seconds, remove from the cup and place on a wire rack. Serve filled with whipped cream and fruit or with spoonfuls of ice cream or other creamy desserts. Fill just before serving.

968 Rum truffles

175 g/6 oz plain chocolate, broken
into pieces
4 tbsp double cream
25 g/1 oz butter
2 tbsp icing sugar
3 tbsp rum
85 g/3 oz ground almonds
2–3 tbsp cocoa powder

Place the chocolate, cream and butter in a heatproof bowl, set the bowl over a saucepan of gently simmering water and heat until melted. Remove from the heat and stir in the icing sugar, the rum and the almonds.

Leave to cool until firm enough to roll into 24 balls. Sift the cocoa powder onto a plate and roll the truffles in it. Place in small paper cases and chill until they are required.

969 Almond truffles

For a non-alcoholic truffle, omit the rum and add 1 teaspoon of almond extract. Roll in a little grated chocolate or dip in white chocolate to complete.

970 Brandy truffles

Replace the ground almonds with very finely chopped hazelnuts and add 3 tablespoons of brandy instead of the rum.

971 Chocolate liqueurs

100 g/3½ oz plain chocolate, broken
into pieces
20 glacé cherries
20 hazelnuts or macadamia nuts
150 ml/5 fl oz double cream
2 tbsp icing sugar
4 tbsp liqueur
50 g/1¾ oz plain chocolate and
marbled chocolate caraque, to
decorate

Line a large baking sheet with baking paper. Place the plain chocolate in a heatproof bowl, set the bowl over a saucepan of gently simmering water and heat until melted. Spoon the chocolate into 40 small paper cases, spreading up the sides with a spoon or brush, then place upside down on the baking sheet and leave to set.

Carefully peel away the paper cases and place a cherry or nut in each cup.

To make the filling, place the double cream in a bowl and sift the icing sugar on top. Whip the cream until it is just holding its shape, then whip in the liqueur.

Place the cream in a piping bag fitted with a 1-cm/½-inch plain nozzle and pipe a little into each chocolate case. Leave to chill for 20 minutes.

To decorate, melt the chocolate as before, then spoon the melted chocolate over the cream to cover it. Add the caraque and leave to harden before serving.

972 Chocolate whisky cups

Replace the liqueur with whisky and add a little strong coffee to the cream.

973 White chocolate truffles

25 g/1 oz butter
5 tbsp double cream
1 tbsp orange liqueur (optional)

325 g/11½ oz white chocolate, broken
into pieces

Line a Swiss roll tin with baking paper. Place the butter and cream in a small saucepan. Bring slowly to the boil, stirring constantly, and boil for 1 minute, then remove from the heat. Add 225 g/8 oz of the chocolate to the cream and stir until melted, then beat in the liqueur, if using. Pour into the tin and chill in the refrigerator for about 2 hours until firm.

Break off pieces of the mixture and roll them into balls. Chill for a further 30 minutes before finishing the truffles.

To finish, place the remaining white chocolate in a heatproof bowl, set the bowl over a saucepan of gently simmering water and heat until melted. Dip the balls in the chocolate, letting the excess drip back into the bowl, and place on baking paper. Swirl the chocolate with the tines of a fork and leave to harden.

974 White & dark chocolate truffles

Replace the white chocolate for the coating with plain chocolate.

975 Milk chocolate truffles

Replace the white chocolate for the filling with milk chocolate and replace the orange liqueur with brandy or amaretto. Coat in white or milk chocolate.

976 Italian chocolate truffles

175 g/6 oz plain chocolate, broken into
pieces
2 tbsp amaretto or orange liqueur
40 g/1½ oz butter

4 tbsp icing sugar
50 g/1¾ oz ground almonds
50 g/1¾ oz grated plain chocolate

Place the chocolate and liqueur in a heatproof bowl, set the bowl over a saucepan of gently simmering water and heat until the chocolate has melted. Add the butter and stir until it has melted. Stir in the icing sugar and the ground almonds. Leave the mixture in a cool place until firm enough to roll into 24 balls.

Place the grated chocolate on a plate and roll the truffles in the chocolate to coat them. Place the truffles in 24 paper sweet cases and chill in the refrigerator until ready to serve.

977 Rocky road bites

125 g/4½ oz milk chocolate, broken
  into pieces
40 g/1½ oz mini multi-coloured
  marshmallows

25 g/1 oz chopped walnuts
25 g/1 oz ready-to-eat dried apricots,
  chopped

Line a large baking sheet with baking paper. Place the milk chocolate in a large heatproof bowl, set the bowl over a saucepan of gently simmering water and heat until melted. Stir in the marshmallows, walnuts and apricots and toss in the melted chocolate until well covered.

Place heaped teaspoonfuls of the mixture on the baking sheet, then chill in the refrigerator until set.

Once set, carefully remove the bites from the baking paper and place in small paper cases to serve, if liked.

978 Peanut & cherry bites

Replace the walnuts with roughly chopped peanuts and the apricots with quartered glacé cherries.

979 Chocolate ice cream bites

Line a baking sheet with clingfilm. Scoop out balls of ice cream with a melon baller and place them on the baking sheet. Alternatively, cut the ice cream into bite-sized cubes. Stick a cocktail stick in each piece and return to the freezer until very hard.

Place the chocolate and butter in a heatproof bowl, set the bowl over a saucepan of gently simmering water and heat until melted. Quickly dip the frozen ice cream balls or cubes into the warm chocolate and return to the freezer. Freeze until ready to serve.

600 g/1 lb 5 oz good-quality ice cream
200 g/7 oz plain chocolate, broken
  into pieces
25 g/1 oz butter

980 Peanut blossoms

85 g/3 oz butter, plus extra for greasing
85 g/3 oz caster sugar
115 g/4 oz peanut butter
1 egg
3 tbsp golden syrup
175 g/6 oz plain flour

FILLING
55 g/2 oz milk chocolate or plain
  chocolate, broken into pieces
25 g/1 oz butter
25 g/1 oz icing sugar

Place the butter and sugar in a large bowl and beat together until pale and fluffy. Add the peanut butter, egg and golden syrup, and beat until well combined. Sift the flour and work into the mixture to form a soft dough, then chill in the refrigerator for 30 minutes.

Preheat the oven to 180°C/350°F/Gas Mark 4. Grease a large baking sheet. Shape the dough into 2.5-cm/1-inch balls, place on the baking sheet, spaced well apart and flatten slightly with a palette knife. Press your finger into the centre of each ball to form a dip. Bake in the preheated oven for about 10 minutes or until golden brown. Leave to cool for a few minutes on the baking sheet, then transfer to a wire rack.

For the filling, place the chocolate and butter in a heatproof bowl, set the bowl over a saucepan of gently simmering water and heat until melted. Beat in the icing sugar. Spoon or pipe the filling into the centre of the cookies and leave to set.

981 Jammy blossoms

Replace the chocolate centre with a little jam of your choice and spoon into the dip of the biscuit before baking.

982 Brazil nut brittle

sunflower oil, for greasing
350 g/12 oz plain chocolate, broken
  into pieces
100 g/3½ oz shelled Brazil nuts, chopped

175 g/6 oz white chocolate, roughly
  chopped
175 g/6 oz fudge, roughly chopped

Brush the bottom of a square 20-cm/8-inch cake tin with oil to grease and line with baking paper. Place half the plain chocolate in a heatproof bowl, set the bowl over a saucepan of gently simmering water and heat until melted, then spread in the tin. Sprinkle with the chopped Brazil nuts, white chocolate and fudge.

Melt the remaining plain chocolate pieces and pour over the top. Let the brittle set, then break up into jagged pieces with the tip of a strong knife.

983 Macadamia nut brittle

Replace the Brazil nuts with macadamia nuts and replace the white chocolate with milk chocolate, if liked.

984 Honeycomb toffee

MAKES ABOUT 50 PIECES

butter, for greasing
500 g/1 lb 2 oz granulated sugar
300 ml/10 fl oz water

4 tbsp malt vinegar
½ tsp bicarbonate of soda

Grease a shallow 18-cm/7-inch square tin. Place the sugar, water and vinegar into a large saucepan and heat gently, stirring constantly, until the sugar has dissolved. Bring the mixture to the boil and boil, without stirring, until a little of the mixture, dropped into a cup of cold water, separates into hard threads. The temperature on a sugar thermometer should reach 138°C/280°F (soft crack stage).

Remove the pan from the heat, then immediately add the bicarbonate of soda and stir until mixed together. (The mixture will bubble and rise in the pan.) When the mixture stops bubbling, immediately pour it into the tin and leave to set.

When the toffee has set, turn out of the tin onto a board and break into pieces with the end of a rolling pin.

985 Almond stars

MAKES ABOUT 20

3 egg whites
200 g/7 oz caster sugar
½ tsp almond extract

200 g/7 oz ground almonds
10–12 glacé cherries, halved

Preheat the oven to 160°C/325°F/Gas Mark 3. Line 2 large baking sheets with baking paper. Place the egg whites in a large bowl and whisk until stiff peaks form. Gradually whisk in the sugar, then add the almond extract. Fold in the ground almonds until well combined.

Spoon the mixture into a piping bag fitted with a large star nozzle and pipe large stars onto the baking sheets, spaced well apart. Top each star with half a cherry.

Bake in the preheated oven for 25–30 minutes, or until lightly browned and crisp. Leave to cool on the baking sheet.

986 Coconut mounds

Replace the ground almonds with desiccated coconut. Chop the cherries and fold in with the coconut. Pile spoonfuls of the mixture onto the baking sheets and bake as before.

293

987 Chocolate meringues

4 egg whites
200 g/7 oz caster sugar
1 tsp cornflour
40 g/1½ oz plain chocolate, grated

FILLING
100 g/3½ oz plain chocolate, broken
    into pieces
150 ml/5 fl oz double cream
1 tbsp icing sugar
1 tbsp brandy (optional)

Preheat the oven to 140°C/275°F/Gas Mark 1. Line 2 large baking sheets with baking paper. Place the egg whites in a large bowl and whisk until soft peaks form, then gradually whisk in half the sugar. Continue whisking until the mixture is very stiff and glossy. Carefully fold in the remaining sugar, cornflour and grated chocolate. Spoon the mixture into a piping bag fitted with a large star or plain nozzle and pipe 16 large rosettes or mounds onto the baking sheets.

Bake in the preheated oven for about 1 hour, changing the position of the baking sheets after 30 minutes. Without opening the oven door, turn off the oven and leave the meringues to cool in the oven. Once cold, carefully peel off the baking paper.

To make the filling, place the chocolate in a heatproof bowl, set the bowl over a saucepan of gently simmering water and heat until melted. Carefully spread it over the bases of the meringues and stand them upside down on a wire rack until the chocolate has set. Place the cream, icing sugar and brandy, if using, in a bowl and whip until the cream holds its shape, then use to sandwich the chocolate-coated meringues together in pairs.

988 Ladies' kisses

175 g/6 oz butter
115 g/4 oz caster sugar
1 egg yolk
100 g/3½ oz ground almonds
175 g/6 oz plain flour
55 g/2 oz plain chocolate, broken
    into pieces

Place the butter and sugar in a large bowl and beat together until pale and fluffy. Beat in the egg yolk, then beat in the ground almonds and flour. Continue beating until thoroughly mixed. Shape the dough into a ball, wrap in clingfilm and chill in the refrigerator for 1½–2 hours.

Preheat the oven to 160°C/325°F/Gas Mark 3. Line 3 large baking sheets with baking paper.

Break off walnut-sized pieces of dough and roll them into balls between the palms of your hands, then place the dough balls on the baking sheets, spaced well apart. Bake in the preheated oven for 20–25 minutes, or until golden brown. Carefully transfer to wire racks to cool.

Place the chocolate in a heatproof bowl, set the bowl over a saucepan of gently simmering water and heat until melted. Spread the melted chocolate on the flat sides of the cookies and sandwich them together in pairs. Return to the wire racks to cool.

989 *Baby meringues*

4 egg whites
pinch of salt
125 g/4½ oz granulated sugar

125 g/4½ oz caster sugar
300 ml/10 fl oz double cream, lightly
  whipped, to serve

Preheat the oven to 120°C/250°F/Gas Mark ½. Line 3 large baking sheets with baking paper. Place the egg whites and salt in a large bowl and whisk until stiff. (You should be able to turn the bowl upside down without any movement from the whisked egg whites.) Whisk in the granulated sugar, a little at a time; the meringue should begin to look glossy at this stage. Sprinkle in the caster sugar, a little at a time, and continue whisking until all the sugar has been incorporated and the meringue forms thick peaks.

Transfer the meringue mixture to a piping bag fitted with a 2-cm/¾-inch star nozzle and carefully pipe about 26 small whirls of the mixture onto the baking sheets.

Bake in the preheated oven for 1½ hours, or until the meringues are pale golden and can be easily lifted off the paper. Without opening the oven door, turn off the oven and leave the meringues to cool in the oven.

Just before serving, sandwich the meringues together in pairs with the lightly whipped cream.

990 *Brown sugar meringues*

Replace the granulated and caster sugar with soft light brown sugar for a delicious, slightly chewy meringue.

991 *Nutty meringues*

Carefully fold in 55 g/2 oz finely chopped pistachio nuts or toasted hazelnuts after all the sugar has been added.

992 *Chewy date crunchies*

150 g/5 oz butter, plus extra for greasing
85 g/3 oz light muscovado sugar
85 g/3 oz clear honey

225 g/8 oz toasted oat cereal
85 g/3 oz rolled oats
115 g/4 oz chopped dates

Preheat the oven to 190°C/375°F/Gas Mark 5. Grease and line the base of a 20-cm/8-in square cake tin. Place the butter, sugar and honey in a saucepan and heat gently, stirring constantly, until the butter is melted and everything is well combined. Remove from the heat.

Lightly crush the oat cereals with a rolling pin to remove any large lumps and add to the pan, then stir in the dates. Spoon the mixture into the cake tin and press down lightly.

Bake in the preheated oven for 20 to 25 minutes. Leave to cool for a few minutes in the tin, then cut into 16 squares and finish cooling completely in the tin.

993 *Chewy apricot crunchies*

Replace the dates with chopped ready-to-eat dried apricots and add 25 g/1 oz lightly toasted flaked almonds for an extra nutty flavour.

75 g/2¾ oz butter
75 g/2¾ oz caster sugar
25 g/1 oz sultanas or raisins
25 g/1 oz glacé cherries, chopped
25 g/1 oz glacé ginger, chopped
25 g/1 oz sunflower seeds
100 g/3½ oz flaked almonds
2 tbsp double cream
175 g/6 oz plain or milk chocolate,
    broken into pieces

Preheat the oven to 180°C/350°F/Gas Mark 4. Line 2 large baking sheets with baking paper. Place the butter in a saucepan and heat gently until melted. Add the sugar, stir until dissolved, then bring the mixture to the boil. Remove from the heat and stir in the sultanas, glacé cherries, glacé ginger, sunflower seeds and almonds. Mix well, then beat in the cream. Place small teaspoons of mixture on the baking sheets, spaced well apart. You will need to do more than one batch.

Bake in the preheated oven for 10–12 minutes, or until light golden in colour. Remove from the oven and, while still hot, use a round biscuit cutter to pull in the edges to form perfect circles. Leave to cool and crisp before removing from the baking sheets.

Place the chocolate in a heatproof bowl, set the bowl over a saucepan of gently simmering water and heat until melted. Spread most of the chocolate onto a sheet of baking paper, and when the chocolate is nearly setting, place the biscuits flat-side down on the chocolate and leave to harden. Cut around the florentines and remove from the baking paper. Spread the remaining melted chocolate on the coated side of the florentines and use a fork to mark waves in the chocolate. Leave to set.

100 g/3½ oz plain butter biscuits
75 g/2¾ oz amaretti biscuits
200 g/7 oz plain chocolate
175 g/6 oz butter, cut into cubes, plus
    extra for greasing
3 tbsp amaretto, rum or brandy
1 large egg yolk
50 g/1¾ oz blanched almonds, chopped
icing sugar, for dusting

Place the butter biscuits and amaretti biscuits in a food processor and pulse until finely chopped. Transfer the biscuits to a large bowl.

Place the chocolate in a heatproof bowl, set the bowl over a saucepan of gently simmering water, add the butter and amaretto and heat gently until melted. Remove from the heat and stir together. Add the crushed biscuits, egg yolk and almonds to the chocolate mixture and mix well. Leave in a cool place for about 2 hours, or until cold.

Grease a large sheet of foil. Turn the chocolate mixture onto the foil and, using your hands and a palette knife, shape into a log shape about 30 cm/12 inches long with tapered ends to resemble an Italian salami. Wrap in the foil and chill in the freezer for at least 4 hours, or until firm.

Dust a sheet of baking paper generously with icing sugar. Remove the chocolate log from the foil and turn onto the baking paper. Roll the log in the icing sugar until it is evenly coated and looks like an Italian salami. Leave in a cool place for 1 hour, then cut into slices to serve.

996 Chocolate sparkles

300 g/10½ oz milk chocolate, broken
 into pieces
100 ml/3½ fl oz double cream
1 tsp vanilla extract
1 tbsp icing sugar
20 g/¾ oz butter

TO DECORATE
hundreds and thousands
silver or pink stars
grated or flaked white chocolate, or your
 favourite colourful decorations

Place the chocolate and cream in a heatproof bowl, set the bowl over a saucepan of gently simmering water and heat, stirring occasionally, until the chocolate is melted. Leave to cool slightly, then stir in the vanilla extract, icing sugar and butter until well combined. Chill the mixture in the refrigerator until firm.

Use a teaspoon to scoop up some of the mixture and roll into a ball shape. Repeat until the mixture is used up.

Dip the chocolate balls into your favourite coatings to decorate, turning them until they are evenly coated, and arrange the chocolates in small paper cases.

997 Alphabet apple pie

225 g/8 oz plain flour, plus extra for
 dusting
pinch of salt
2 tbsp icing sugar
120 g/4¼ oz cold butter (or half butter
 and half vegetable fat), cut into small
 pieces
1 egg, separated
1–2 tbsp cold water

FILLING
675 g/1 lb 8 oz eating apples, peeled,
 halved, cored and thinly sliced
2 tbsp orange juice
1 tsp ground cinnamon
3 tbsp caster sugar

Sift the flour, salt and icing sugar into a bowl. Add the butter and rub it in until the mixture resembles breadcrumbs. Mix in the egg yolk and water and form the dough into a ball. Cover and chill for 30 minutes.

Preheat the oven to 200°C/400°F/Gas Mark 6. Place the apple, orange juice, cinnamon and sugar in a bowl and mix together, then divide among 4 heatproof ramekin-style dishes. Wet the rim of each dish.

Roll the pastry out on a floured surface, cut 4 rounds and use to top each pie. Trim the edges and crimp with a fork. Brush with egg white and make a slit in the top. Cut out letters from the trimmings, place on a baking sheet and bake in the preheated oven for 30–35 minutes.

450 ml/16 fl oz double cream
6 tbsp caster sugar
1 vanilla pod
200 ml/7 fl oz crème fraîche
2 tsp powdered gelatine

3 tbsp water
50 g/1¾ oz plain chocolate, broken
   into pieces
marbled chocolate caraque, chopped,
   to decorate

Place the cream and sugar in a saucepan and add the vanilla pod. Heat gently, stirring until the sugar has dissolved, then bring to the boil. Reduce the heat and simmer for 2–3 minutes. Remove from the heat and take out the vanilla pod. Stir in the crème fraîche.

Sprinkle the gelatine over the water in a small heatproof bowl and leave until spongy, then set over a pan of hot water and stir until dissolved. Stir into the cream mixture and pour half of this mixture into another bowl.

Place the plain chocolate in a heatproof bowl, set the bowl over a pan of simmering water and heat until melted, then stir into one half of the cream mixture. Pour the chocolate mixture into 4 individual glasses and chill for 15–20 minutes, or until just set. While the chocolate mixture is chilling, keep the vanilla mixture at room temperature.

Spoon the vanilla mixture on top of the chocolate mixture and chill until the vanilla cream is set. Before serving, decorate with the caraque.

225 g/8 oz plain chocolate
4 eggs, separated
6 tbsp caster sugar
4 tbsp dark rum
4 tbsp double cream

TO DECORATE
whipped cream
marbled chocolate shapes

Place the chocolate in a heatproof bowl, set the bowl over a saucepan of gently simmering water and heat until melted. Leave to cool slightly.

Place the egg yolks and sugar in a large bowl and whisk until very pale and fluffy. Drizzle the melted chocolate into the mixture and fold in together with the rum and double cream.

Place the egg whites in a separate large bowl and whisk until soft peaks form, then fold the egg whites into the chocolate mixture in 2 batches. Divide the mixture among 6 individual dishes and chill in the refrigerator for at least 2 hours.

To serve, decorate with a little whipped cream and marbled chocolate shapes.

Note: this recipe contains raw eggs.

1000 *Cappuccino soufflé puddings*

butter, for greasing
25 g/1 oz caster sugar, plus extra
   for coating
6 tbsp whipping cream
2 tsp instant espresso coffee granules
2 tbsp Kahlúa

3 large eggs, separated, plus 1 extra
   white
150 g/5½ oz plain chocolate, broken
   into pieces
cocoa powder, for dusting

Preheat the oven to 190°C/375°F/Gas Mark 5. Grease the sides of 6 x 175-ml/6-fl oz ramekins, coat with the extra sugar and place on a baking sheet. Place the cream in a saucepan and warm gently. Stir in the coffee until dissolved, then add the Kahlúa. Divide the mixture among the ramekins.

Place the egg whites in a large bowl and whisk until soft peaks form, then gradually whisk in the sugar until they are stiff and glossy but not dry.

Place the chocolate in a heatproof bowl, set the bowl over a saucepan of gently simmering water and heat until melted. Add the egg yolks to the melted chocolate, then stir in a little of the whisked egg whites. Gradually fold in the egg whites and divide the mixture among the ramekins. Bake in the preheated oven for 15 minutes, or until just set. Dust with cocoa powder and serve immediately.

1001 *Rich chocolate mousses*

300 g/10½ oz plain chocolate, broken
   into pieces
5 tbsp caster sugar
20 g/¾ oz butter

1 tbsp brandy
4 eggs, separated
cocoa powder, for dusting

Place the chocolate in a heatproof bowl, set the bowl over a saucepan of gently simmering water, add the sugar and butter and melt together, stirring constantly, until smooth. Remove from the heat and stir in the brandy, then leave to cool slightly. Add the egg yolks and beat until smooth.

Place the egg whites in a separate bowl and whisk until stiff peaks form, then fold into the chocolate mixture. Place a stainless steel cooking ring on each of 4 small serving plates, then spoon the mixture into each ring and smooth the surfaces. Chill in the refrigerator for at least 4 hours, or until set.

Remove the mousses from the refrigerator and carefully remove the cooking rings. Dust with cocoa powder and serve immediately.

Note: this recipe contains raw eggs.

Index